RESPONSIBILITY, CHARACTER, AND THE EMOTIONS

For Miriam and Dmitri Schoeman, because of the richness they bring to my life, and for Herbert Fingarette, because of the direction he has brought to our understanding of responsibility and to me personally.

Responsibility, Character, and the Emotions

New Essays in Moral Psychology

Edited by

FERDINAND SCHOEMAN

Professor of Philosophy
University of South Carolina, Columbia

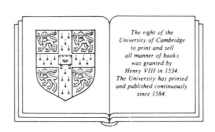

The right of the
University of Cambridge
to print and sell
all manner of books
was granted by
Henry VIII in 1534.
The University has printed
and published continuously
since 1584.

CAMBRIDGE UNIVERSITY PRESS

CAMBRIDGE

NEW YORK   NEW ROCHELLE   MELBOURNE   SYDNEY

Published by the Press Syndicate of the University of Cambridge
The Pitt Building, Trumpington Street, Cambridge CB2 1RP
32 East 57th Street, New York, NY 10022, USA
10 Stamford Road, Oakleigh, Melbourne 3166, Australia

First published 1987
Reprinted 1988

Printed in the United States of America

Library of Congress Cataloging-in-Publication Data
Responsibility, character, and the emotions : new essays in moral
psychology / edited by Ferdinand Schoeman.
p.   cm.
Includes index.
ISBN 0 521 32720 2.   ISBN 0 521 33951 0 (pbk.)
1. Responsibility.   2. Character.   3. Emotions – Moral and ethical
aspects.   I. Schoeman, Ferdinand David.
BJ1451.R47   1988
170–dc19   87–17768

British Library Cataloguing-in-Publication Data
Responsibility, character, and the emotions :
new essays in moral psychology.
1. Ethics
I. Schoeman, Ferdinand David
170   BJ1012
ISBN 0 521 32720 2 (hardcovers)
ISBN 0 521 33951 0 (paperback)

Contents

Contributors

RICHARD BURGH is professor of philosophy at Rider College. His research interests include philosophy of law, ethics, and medical ethics. His writings include the paper, "Do the Guilty Deserve Punishment?"

GERALD DWORKIN is chairman of the department of philosophy at the University of Illinois at Chicago. His research interests include the philosophy of law, moral theory, and applied ethics. He is an associate editor of the journal *Ethics*. His influential writings include "Acting Freely," "Autonomy and Behavior Control," and "Paternalism." He is editor of *Determinism, Free Will, and Moral Responsibility*.

JOHN MARTIN FISCHER is associate professor of philosophy at Yale University. His main interests are moral philosophy, metaphysics, and philosophy of religion. He is the editor of *Moral Responsibility*. His articles include "Freedom and Control" and "Responsibility and Failure."

HARRY FRANKFURT is chairman of the department of philosophy at Yale University. He is internationally known for his work in seventeenth-century philosophy, philosophy of mind, and moral philosophy. Among his important and influential works are *Demons, Dreamers and Madmen*, "Freedom of the Will and the Concept of a Person," "Alternate Possibilities and Moral Responsibility," and "The Importance of What We Care About."

LENN E. GOODMAN is professor of philosophy at the University of Hawaii in Honolulu. He has published seven books, including *Monotheism, Rambam*, and *The Case of Animals vs. Man*. His philosophical articles address issues of metaphysics, ethics, and biophilosophy as well as classical themes in the history of philosophy, especially those of the Jewish and Islamic thinkers who wrote in Arabic. His translation from the Arabic and philosophical commentary on Saadiah Gaon's *Book of Theodicy* (10th century Arabic translation and commentary on the Book of Job) will be published by Yale University Press next year.

PATRICIA GREENSPAN is associate professor of philosophy at the University of Maryland. Her book *Emotions and Reasons: An Inquiry into Emotional Justifications* is scheduled to be published by Routledge and Kegan Paul. Her influential papers include "Behavior Control and Freedom of Action" and "Conditional Oughts and Hypothetical Imperatives."

NILS JAREBORG is professor of criminal law and dean of faculty at Uppsala University, Sweden. He has authored fifteen books and numerous articles in criminal law and jurisprudence. He serves on several legislative committees. Current projects include work on the seriousness of crime, with Andrew von Hirsch.

HERBERT MORRIS is professor of philosophy and of law and dean of humanities at the University of California at Los Angeles. His interests include moral and legal philosophy and moral psychology. His influential papers include "Persons and Punishment," "Guilt and Suffering," "A Paternalistic Theory of Punishment," and "Punishment for Thoughts." He is editor of the volume *Freedom and Responsibility,* as well as of other collections.

MICHAEL S. MOORE holds a joint appointment in law at the University of California at Berkeley and at the University of Southern California, where he is the Robert Kingsley Professor of Law. He is the author of *Law and Psychiatry: Rethinking the Relationship* and has written papers on responsibility that have appeared in legal, philosophical, psychological, and psychiatric journals. He is currently working on a book on legal reasoning that will appear in the Clarendon Law Series of Oxford University Press.

JOHN SABINI is associate professor of psychology at the University of Pennsylvania. His interests are in understanding emotions and judgments of character. Along with Maury Silver, he is the author of *Moralities of Everyday Life,* and he is coeditor (with Michael Frese) of *Goal Directed Behavior.*

FERDINAND SCHOEMAN is professor of philosophy at the University of South Carolina. He is the editor of *Philosophical Dimensions of Privacy,* and is currently working on a book on privacy. His research interests include moral psychology and the limits of moral reasoning.

MAURY SILVER received his Ph.D. from the Graduate Center of C.U.N.Y. He is the author, along with John Sabini, of *Moralities of Everyday Life*. His professional interests include efforts at understanding how good people slide into evil, and how social control works beneath our notice (as with embarrassment and gossip). He is currently completing a project on humiliation and self-deception with the Social Psychology Group of the Institute of Psychology for CNR, Rome. His private interests include Chinese food and traveling to Italy.

ANDREW VON HIRSCH is professor at the School of Criminal Justice, Rutgers University, and *docent* (research fellow) in criminal law at Uppsala University, Sweden. He is the author of *Past or Future Crimes: Deservedness and Dangerousness in the Sentencing of Criminals*, and *Doing Justice: The Choice of Punishments*. He is coauthor of *The Sentencing Commission and Its Guidelines* and *The Question of Parole*. He has also written numerous articles on criminal sentencing philosophy and policy.

GARY WATSON is associate professor of philosophy at the University of California at Irvine. He has published on free will and topics in moral theory, including his influential paper "Free Agency." He is the editor of *Free Will*. His special interest is in the intersection of issues in philosophy of mind and the foundations of moral philosophy.

SUSAN WOLF is associate professor of philosophy at The Johns Hopkins University. She has published articles on ethics and the philosophy of mind and is currently working on a book entitled *Moral Freedom*. Her influential writings include "Moral Saints" and "Asymmetrical Freedom."

1

Introduction

FERDINAND SCHOEMAN

The essays that appear here are the result of an invitation from the editor to various distinguished authors soliciting original contributions on responsibility. Inevitably the contributions that emerge from such a request will be diverse in their approaches and themes. In spite of this, it can be said that the contributions gravitate toward one of two general themes: (1) responsibility for one's own character and (2) culpability and the role of the moral emotions. In this introduction I discuss these general topics and then relate the themes to the essays presented here.

We consider some, but not all, of our behavior to reflect something about ourselves as moral or rational agents. The fact that we can be related in different ways to behavior that has the same public profile causes us some difficulties. Take sleeping, for example: One can fall asleep despite one's best efforts at staying awake, even when one has every incentive to stay awake; or one can fall asleep as a result of a decision to get plenty of rest. In one case falling asleep is something that overcomes one; it is inevitable and has nothing to do with one's reasons. In the other case, falling asleep is something one does and is the result of rational deliberation. (I leave open the possibility that rational agency is itself the result of evolutionary design.) The way we describe or attribute behavior to people reflects our awareness of these differences in relationship to actions. These differences are important to us and are implicit in our practices of attributing behavior to people.[1]

It matters to us whether we are responsible because being responsible suggests our potential − that we are engaged as active and self-aware beings with perspectives on what we do and with a contributing and creative role to play in what we become.[2] To see ourselves as not

[1] See John Austin, "A plea for excuses," *Proceedings of the Aristotelian Society*, 1956−7.
[2] See Robert Nozick, *Philosophical Explanations* (Cambridge, MA: Harvard University Press, 1981), chapter IV, especially pp. 310ff.

responsible is to confront our limits – to regard our lives as passively reflecting personality factors beyond our capacity to effectively restructure, however good our reasons for doing so may be, and with at most an attenuated sense of self – leaving us in a diminished position in the great chain of being.

Reflections on responsibility often introduce a mistaken causal or psychological picture, perhaps because we suspect that if external and internal factors over which we have no control cause us to be what we are, then we are precluded from any kind of active contribution.[3] For instance, Aristotle characterizes behavior that is within our power or voluntary as behavior that is untraceable to starting points outside the agent. (Let's call this the *unmoved-mover principle*.) He illustrates what he means by finding the source of behavior outside the agent through a depiction of situations where behavior is not voluntary: Behavior is not voluntary if it results from constraint or is done in nonculpable ignorance.[4] In the case of actions performed under either of these circumstances, we think the behavior does not genuinely reflect the moral character of the agent.

It is not clear that the illustrations of nonvoluntary behavior really exemplify the unmoved-mover principle. Indeed, it is not clear that this principle has any rightful role to play in assessing human accountability. If we consider what else Aristotle says about conditions of accountability, we can show the misalignment between the unmoved-mover principle and the attribution practices Aristotle and we recognize.

Consider Aristotle's example of acting in ignorance. Acting on the basis of an understanding of one's environment may be *more* clearly traceable to causes external to the agent than acting in ignorance is. To the extent that knowledge and ignorance are treated as sources of behavior, Aristotle, in endorsing the unmoved-mover principle, has things reversed. Indeed, if most of a person's beliefs were purely internally caused and not appropriately connected with the world, we would immediately think the agent insane, not responsible.

Similarly, the values a person acts on are characteristically internal, even though they presumably have some external cause. The fact that one can offer a causal analysis of a person's values does not in itself

---

[3] Not everyone agrees that this picture is mistaken. See Peter Van Inwagen, *An Essay on Free Will* (Oxford: Oxford University Press, 1983). But see also Michael Slote, "Selective necessity and the free will problem," *Journal of Philosophy* 79 (1982), 5–24, and Richard Sorabji, *Necessity, Cause and Blame: Perspectives on Aristotle's Theory* (Ithaca, NY: Cornell University Press, 1983).
[4] Nicomachean Ethics III, 5.

undermine either the values' role as values or their authenticity in reflecting that individual's true character.[5] Still, if someone threatens me with a shot in the head unless I take a bite of putrid meat, I am not accountable for taking the snack. The source of the motive to eat the meat is partly external, but it is also partly internal – wanting to stay alive. Aristotle addresses this kind of problem by referring to what we would normally want to do. I would normally want to avoid eating putrid meat, but will choose to if my life depends on it. Although I have not necessarily lost control over what I will do if so threatened, I will have lost some personally valuable options – namely, one of not eating the meat *and* staying alive. This loss differentiates the type of case being considered from what we take to be the norm of action.

In addition to invoking the unmoved-mover principle, Aristotle works with what might be termed a *proper relationship principle*. According to this principle, an act is voluntary and an agent responsible if he or she has the right kind of relationship to the outcome. To see whether there is the right kind of relationship, we review the kinds of considerations social practice suggests as relevant. To take the two already mentioned, we can say that a person who acts out of ignorance, or a person who acts as a result of a threat that is not deserved, is not in the proper relationship to the outcome. We cannot draw the normal inferences about an individual's character when he or she acts as a result of a threat or acts in ignorance. A given bit of behavior performed under these circumstances reflects differently on the agent than that behavior would if the circumstances were normal.

Aristotle points out that we differentiate behavior that seems amenable to encouragement and behavior that does not seem so amenable. Roughly, the former is coextensive with the voluntary. However, Aristotle also acknowledges that people become fixed in their ways: Both the disciplined and the self-indulgent person may no longer be able to restructure their ways of thinking and acting, even though at an earlier stage in their lives they encountered real options.

The discussion continues in Aristotle: We differentiate between someone being ugly because of a birth defect and someone becoming ugly because of slovenly habits. Since slovenly habits are something we can rectify (or could at one time have rectified), it is fitting to blame an agent for being ugly for such causes. Here Aristotle stresses

---

[5] I say this realizing that there are ways to cause a person to value something that does undermine his or her relationship to the value. For a discussion of this, see my paper, "Responsibility and the problem of induced desires," *Philosophical Studies* 34 (1978), 293–301.

that what we can deliberate about and control is what we can be held responsible for, without regarding the ultimate source of movement. This criterion of the voluntary has nothing to do with the source of the behavior being internal or external. We can deliberate over and control things even if what we are is liable to a causal history.

Aristotle rounds off his discussion by considering the extent to which people can be said to control their own moral outlook – an aspect of selves that surely colors what people will think worthwhile trying to change. If one begins corrupted, there is no internally motivated escape: The misguided person chooses to avoid change, just as a normal person accepts the need for change. Aristotle's response to this fundamental challenge to common sense and legal practice seems to be to concede the point, but maintain its irrelevance. He allows that it is not choice that determines what we take to be the ultimate goods, but a "natural gift of vision" that permits every normal person to view things in their correct perspective. This suggests that something external to, as well as independent of, us – objective norms – either resonate within us or do not. If they do, we are normal and responsible, even if we choose bad things. If the correct perspective does not resonate within us, still *we* are the ones selecting what about our character is worthwhile changing, and our choices are attributable to us. Despite differentiating two orientations to transgressions – one thinking it legitimate, the other appreciating its illegitimacy – Aristotle treats them as equally voluntary, and once identified as voluntary, as equally attributable to the agent.

Aristotle has essentially abandoned the unmoved-mover principle in favor of a position that holds one accountable for behavior if the behavior stems from one's character in a voluntary way. (This is an interpretation of the proper relationship principle mentioned above.) Here the position is that even if one's fundamental outlook (including the changes in one's outlook one will think it important to strive for) is fixed by factors over which one cannot exercise control, this does not keep one's character itself from being within one's control, because obviously one *can* make (or at least at one time could have made) changes in one's personality, even though one in fact sees no reason to. Even if an agent's behavior is ultimately caused by external factors, there can be a personal contribution to the outcome – understood in terms of identification with the principles of action – sufficient to make the behavior attributable to the agent. Voluntariness marks the domain of the responsible.

For Aristotle, even though it would be unreasonable to expect of someone, in light of his background, that he find something attractive about certain important values, he is still morally responsible.[6] Although most writing on responsibility by philosophers would suggest that this view should be rejected, because having a fair opportunity to conform one's conduct to the expected standard is treated as a necessary condition of responsibility,[7] two of the papers in this volume – Greenspan's and Morris's – argue that there is a dimension of the ordinary conception of responsibility that *is* correctly captured by this objective standard.

Maybe we should forget about what the source of human behavior is and instead focus carefully on cases in which we hold people accountable and those cases where we do not, refining if we can some distinguishing principles of our practices. Although some of the very best writing on responsibility follows just this tack, this is not an approach we can be comfortable with either. It does matter how people come to have the views and values they have, but not in a way that has been clearly articulated. This is recognized in liberal and radical political theory, and it is certainly a recurring theme in the social sciences and of late in the cognitive sciences; only to a lesser extent is it appreciated by philosophers,[8] for whom abstract rational capacity seems to be nearly all that is required for fully responsible choice. Inquiring into how people learn and evaluate is important to our assessments of levels of accountability, but we are only at the beginning stages of sorting these things out in a way that goes beyond commonsense presumptions that are by and large uninformed by recent research. Unfortunately, some of the most imaginative literature on responsibility has suggested that we announce to the world that there is not any real problem there waiting to be solved.[9] Compatibilism, as a philosophical position, has become complacent.

What characterizes the essays contained in this collection is that the writers are, if anything, sensitive to the subtleties of the job that lay ahead of us in coming to understand different dimensions of respon-

---

[6] For a contemporary defense of the position that we are accountable for satisfying a standard even if we cannot meet it, see Robert Adams, "Involuntary sins," *Philosophical Review* 96 (1985), 3–32.

[7] I believe most writers follow H. L. A. Hart in saying that unless one had a fair opportunity to avoid doing something forbidden, our notion of moral responsibility does not extend to that case.

Thus a primary vindication of the principle of responsibility could rest on the simple idea that unless a man has the capacity and a fair opportunity or chance to adjust his behavior to the law its penalties ought not to be applied to him. ["Punishment and the elimination of responsibility," *Punishment and Responsibility* (Oxford, 1968), p. 181]

[8] A notable exception is Paul Feyerabend in *Against Method* (London: Verso, 1975).

[9] Daniel Dennett, *Elbow Room* (Cambridge, MA: MIT Press, 1984), esp. chap. IV.

sibility. Cognitive, emotional, motivational, cultural, and political limitations of full rational operation are not glossed over, but stressed. Locating the domain of responsible behavior is sought within these limitations, not in spite of them. Identifying the relationship between the impediments to human flourishing and the responsibility perspective is an underlying theme in many of the chapters in this book. The paradigm of a psychologically integrated and causally independent being seeking understanding is replaced by a paradigm of a socially enmeshed and rationally limited being that at any point in his or her life finds internal and external barriers on what he or she can practically think about and become.

As Aristotle observed, we do hold people accountable for their character, as well as for their behavior. We notice ourselves and others trying to do something about the kind of people we/they are and the kinds of dispositions we/they have. Some efforts at change are more successful than others. For any trait of character, we know that some people who wish to alter it succeed and others fail.

Although we know that some traits are more difficult to change than others, still it seems that for all we can tell there is little difference between some of those who succeed and some of those who do not. In this kind of situation we are tempted to say that the difference is up to the individual. We might look at it differently if all and only persons with background characteristics *A, B, C, D,* and *E* succeeded in changing. What we find is that some who succeed have *less* going for them than some who fail, in terms of the factors that we believe promote success.

Why should the presence of background characteristics matter? If all and only people with characteristics *A–E* succeeded, it would seem as if those without any of them could not succeed, *however hard they tried.* This would mean it was not up to them to change. Changing this characteristic would not be within the power, or under the control, of those without these identified characteristics.

If *A–E* were certain kinds of characteristics over which an agent could not exercise self-control, we would agree with this assessment; but what about factors that are not background factors, such as "tries very hard to deal with personality characteristics, even entrenched ones, that are morally troublesome" that we also know to be associated with success at moral improvement? It would not surprise us if people who lacked this drive did not succeed at ameliorating problems with their own characters. Would we say that those who are complacent about themselves were at fault?

This would depend on how we view the structure of motivational factors. If we thought that all and only persons with *X, Y,* and *Z* came to lack motivation, and *X, Y,* and *Z* were themselves factors over which an individual had no control, then we would not fault the agent for lacking drive. Alternatively, if there were no invariable and uncontrollable background pattern associated with lack of motivation, then even though the agent was not motivated, we would not regard this lack as outside the agent's control because we could not see that anything, internal or external, would stop this person from acquiring the ambition if he or she sought assiduously to acquire it. *Can* someone unmotivated assiduously seek to become highly motivated? We could think of ways in which external influences might work on someone unmotivated to make that person eventually seek to become motivated in a certain direction – but what if these environmental factors are not present?[10]

In fact, we have many statistically relevant factors, but few that are completely determinative of successful efforts at changing oneself. How unlikely does someone's prospects for effective change have to be, in light of certain background conditions, before we judge that this person did not have a fair opportunity to change, and consequently judge him or her less harshly than we would others?[11]

Suppose we find out that about 70 percent of the youths in a disadvantaged neighborhood end up with a police record by the time they turn 16? Suppose further that we find out this figure is five to ten times higher than the comparable police record rate for persons brought up in middle-class neighborhoods. What are we to say morally if we want to focus on the character of people who end up in prison from this environment? It is hard to avoid concluding that the environment has influenced them more than others to engage in criminal behavior. If we inquire how it is that people learn and come to care about various things, we will have to take diverse social factors into account. We are talking about things that powerfully influence the formation of the motivational, cognitive, and moral structure of

[10] The British documentary film *28UP*, directed by Michael Apted (Great Britain: Granada Productions, 1985), follows numerous children at seven-year intervals, from the time they are 7 till (at present) they are 28 years old. It is troubling as well as astounding to see the extent to which ambition in life is correlated with the early environment of these people.
[11] Of course, it will matter a lot in answering this question what we permit ourselves to conditionalize upon. For our purposes, we should restrict the conditions we can conditionalize on to factors that are background factors, meaning not ones the agent can or at one time could control.

personality. Patently, more stands in the way of these people ending up with a responsible and constructive approach to life than stands in the way of others. Given these impediments, how can we blame people who end up with less responsible attitudes if we can attribute much of their character to socially corrupting forces?[12]

When we think about the past, we recognize the moral relevance of socialization. We think advocates of slavery, racism, and sexism to be more objectionable in our surroundings than in some previous times, and more so in some contemporary societies than in others. We would think worse of someone who actively opposed integration of schools today than we would someone similarly active fifty years ago. It is not because we have access to relevant facts today that people previously lacked; rather, there are gestalt differences in how we and they put things together. This is so despite the fact that many people back then saw it as we do today and that some today see it as people then did. This last acknowledgment shows that when we judge our predecessors less harshly than our contemporaries we are not basing our evaluation on what we regard as possible, but on what we regard as feasible, given what we know about how people learn and perceive. To take another example of our practical dealings with this topic, we know that people trying to deal with addictions will more likely succeed in supportive environments than in environments that encourage them to revert to old patterns. The differences between the two environments are not informational, but motivational. Even as we think about ourselves as academics, we want to be in certain kinds of settings because we think we might really become better philosophers in some contexts than in others. We think this even though we are aware there are souls who would not be kept from their theoretical potential by hostile surroundings.

There is a problem, though, in assessing which factors effectively impede moral development to the extent that they can be treated as mitigating. Philosophers, like others, tend to be largely a prioristic about what they think influences people and to what extent. Some of the recent work in attribution theory points to this tendency in assessing others. People may not be good judges about what influences them, how the influences work, and how difficult some of these influences can be to counteract. To the extent that common sense wrongly assesses these factors, common sense will result in mistaken judgments. How should we come to judge what it is fair and reasonable to

---

[12] For an illuminating discussion of the issues socialization and deprivation raise for a theory of responsibility, see Jeffrie Murphy, "Marxism and retribution," in *Philosophy and Public Affairs* 2 (1974), 217–43.

expect of individuals? This question obviously relates four central and interrelated issues in the domain of responsibility:

1. What sense can be made of holding people responsible for themselves, for their basic character?
2. How do our theories of character and our theories of excuses inform one another?
3. What can we learn from the social sciences about how judgments are made and how values are adopted that inform our attributional practices?
4. What range of emotionally charged reactions – including judgments – to human shortcomings, whether or not avoidable, makes conceptual and moral sense?

I now turn to the chapters that make up this anthology. In Chapter 2, "Identification and Wholeheartedness," **Harry Frankfurt** tackles one of the most stubborn and pressing problems that arises in thinking about responsibility for character: In what sense can we be responsible for ourselves when we at any point find ourselves with values and habits that dispose us to certain ways of viewing what we might become? Isn't what we want to become biased by what we are? And if so, how can we be responsible for the way we develop our character? Are we not just acting out a program that has been imprinted on us, but that does not really stem from us?

Frankfurt distinguishes simply *having* a value, on the one hand, and *identifying* with the value, on the other. This distinction is important for Frankfurt because he is trying to show how one can have a higher-order desire that reflects oneself as a responsible agent, and not just as a being structured by an arbitrary and ordered set of desires. One of the roles of introducing higher-order desires for Frankfurt is to provide an agent with a basis of evaluation for the particular first-order concerns that agent finds himself or herself with. But even with higher-order desires furnished, one can wonder whether the higher-order desires are not analogously arbitrary parts of our psychic structure. Frankfurt wants to address this question by showing how our relationship to these higher-order desires can involve our activity as agents, and not just reflect our embodiment of some arbitrarily given set of concerns.[13]

---

[13] See Frankfurt, "Freedom of the will and the concept of a person," *Journal of Philosophy* 68 (1971), 5–20, and Gary Watson, "Free agency," *Journal of Philosophy* 72 (1975), 205–20. Both papers are reprinted in Gary Watson, *Free Will* (Oxford: Oxford University Press, 1982), and in John M. Fischer, *Moral Responsibility* (Ithaca, NY: Cornell University Press, 1986).

What is to be shown is that making a commitment to a value consists in more than a refusal or unwillingness to question the value at a higher level. Frankfurt uses the analogy of doing a calculation, displaying different attitudes toward the outcome, to clarify the distinction in relationships to desires. One can just quit after a calculation, not really caring much if one's result is correct; alternatively, one can labor over a result, working it out in different ways to detect blunders. If the person checks and rechecks the result and it comes out the same, accepting this answer is accepting it for a reason and it is doing so with some assurance that however often he or she were to recheck it, the outcome would coincide with the result obtained already. Terminating the sequence of checks and accepting the outcome as correct as a result of this process precludes the charge that our acceptance of the result is arbitrary.

Frankfurt argues that committing oneself to a higher-order desire is analogous to this process of checking and rechecking a result. When a person decides to accept a desire as his own, after consideration, he does not hold himself apart from the value, but makes it fully his own. In accepting the value after consideration one is not choosing arbitrarily; one's acceptance is based on a reason. In this process one identifies with this value, and if it does not conflict with other values one holds, then the person's relationship to the value is said to be wholehearted. The value embraced in this fashion is not just to be seen as something that happens to an agent, but as something a person does. The procedures of ordering and rejecting values are the processes by which one creates an integrated self out of the raw materials of inner life. The emphasis here is not with the origin of the desire, but with the agent's taking responsibility for it through the process of integration and rejection. Our relationship to our values need not be limited to just finding ourselves embodying them. Our values may represent the result of an inquiring and evaluative process that resonates at every higher level.

Susan Wolf also seeks a way of distinguishing the responsible from the nonresponsible agent, but does so in a way that does not presuppose that we are positioned to make choices at the most fundamental level of our being. In Chapter 3, "Sanity and the Metaphysics of Responsibility," Wolf argues that the mundane recognition that sanity is a condition of responsibility has important implications for theories of responsibility. What is an impossible requirement of some standard accounts of responsibility – that the agent be able to self-create – is to be replaced by a considerably weaker thesis – that the agent be sane.

Wolf begins her discussion with a review of a line of analysis according to which being responsible presupposes an ability to create the type of selves we are. Proponents of this view recognize that the creation of selves must rest on some deepest level on attitudes that give direction and substance to a person's evaluational scheme. The problem with this view, in part, is that we can always ask about the deepest-level self, "What is responsible for *it?*" The answer to that will have to be in terms of something outside the deepest self.

One of the strengths of the deep-self view is alleged to be its account of the difference between someone like the kleptomaniac and the ordinary person. The problem with the kleptomaniac is not that the compulsion to steal is *caused,* but that it stems from a desire that is not in turn governed by something deeper in agent. However, since by definition the deepest self of the ordinary, responsible person is itself not governed by something deeper in the agent, and thus must be accounted for causally by something outside the agent, we seem to be confronting a collapse in the distinguishing powers of the deep-self view. Both the kleptomaniac and the ordinary person have basic features of themselves that cannot be accounted for by looking for anything deeper in the agents themselves.

Wolf points out that another problem with the standard deep-self view is that there are examples of people who choose to be the types of selves that they are, but who are not responsible – namely, the insane, the morally blind. So at least part of what is wrong with the standard deep-self interpretation of responsibility is that it leaves out the requirement of sanity. Even though being sane is not ordinarily a quality one can determine for oneself, it is still a prerequisite for responsibility. Wolf then argues that a sufficient condition of responsibility is that an agent's acts are controlled by the agent's desires. that the agent's desires are themselves features of the self the agent can control, and that the agent is sane.

What separates the sane from the insane is not that the sane can control their deepest desires whereas the insane cannot: What is required for responsibility is that one is able to understand and appreciate whatever reasons there are to correct oneself, and one is able to act on this basis. These factors distinguish the sane from the insane and the responsible from those not responsible.

As we just saw, Susan Wolf argues that one does not have to be able to create one's deepest self in order to be thought responsible for one's character or for behavior flowing from this character. **Patricia Greenspan** argues that the view of behavior as following from one's character – with or without the assumption of "self-creation" – can capture only a limited notion of responsibility: a notion properly applied "after the fact" of action, and detachable from the "forward-looking" considerations of *freedom* that enter into full-blown responsibility.

In Chapter 4, "Unfreedom and Responsibility," Greenspan focuses on actions performed out of rage to exemplify behavior that is unfree, but for which the agent is still in some sense responsible. Greenspan uses variations on this example to explore some subtle relationships between freedom and responsibility, explaining their connection by reference to overlapping practical norms, both rational and moral.

For Greenspan, calling someone free to perform a certain act in a given context amounts to making a claim about the reasonableness of expecting it of that person, in the sense that it involves a demand for *future* performance. Freedom is thus made out in terms of a judgment of responsibility – but not the judgment presupposed by treating a person as responsible for what he or she *has* done. There can be times when we think an agent could not have acted differently, but nevertheless regard that agent as responsible in the sense of blameworthy. Where a wrong act has its source in the agent's character, he or she may be said to be "at fault" for it, even though there may be little practical point in condemning the person's behavior. This aspect of responsibility is at least arguably part of the common understanding of the notion, in Greenspan's view; but it is not sufficient for full-blown responsibility, of the sort that implies freedom.

Greenspan introduces intense anger as an example of something tending to make one *un*free with respect to certain ranges of behavior. Anger has this tendency because its affective component makes containment difficult. Intense anger may narrow a person's alternatives to overt aggression, to the extent that it makes those alternatives so uncomfortable – or so hard to recognize *as* alternatives to aggression – that it would be unreasonable to require them of that person during the rage state. But even where the agent acting out of rage is not free, that person may be responsible for his or her behavior for a variety of reasons. For one thing, he or she may have cultivated the disposition to exhibit rage.

This last case poses difficulties for the interpretation of free behavior as behavior that stems from the agent's character. An agent may be seen as responsible for the relevant aspects of his (or her) character – and even for behavior, in a sense sufficient to justify blame – just insofar as he *made* himself unfree. However, this is not sufficient for full-blown responsibility, taken as implying freedom at the *time* of action on Greenspan's view.

Greenspan sketches a complex account of freedom and responsibility, in terms of two normative presuppositions: (1) a judgment about the importance of the *reasons for* a certain practical demand; and (2) a judgment about the reasonableness of expecting the agent to come to *recognize* the reasons. The first judgment is meant to allow for cases of freedom *and* responsibility, where special "high stake" circumstances raise our expectations beyond what is standard. The second judgment – taken as a hypothetical condition on freedom, whose satisfaction would yield responsibility – is meant to allow for cases of freedom where the agent is not responsible for an action, simply because no reasons for it are "accessible" to the agent in time for the influence to be practical.

An agent is said to be free to perform an act, in short, as long as it would be reasonable to expect that agent to perform it if he or she had reason to – with the reason assumed to be at least as strong as those (if any) that justify our requirement of action in the case at hand. In this account, besides the cases we have already considered, where a person can be responsible but not free, there can be cases where a person is free but not responsible.

Moreover, since Greenspan takes recognition of the reasons for action to involve seeing that they *are* reasons, her notion of full-blown responsibility will not apply to a person who has no moral aptitude for a certain range of considerations. If there were nothing he (or she) could have done to make himself sensitive to these considerations, then he is not responsible for failing to acting on them. But in some such cases we may also suppose that *if* he had these considerations in mind, he would not find it too difficult to conform his behavior to the right standard; and here he would come out as free. The analysis thus yields a view of "sociopaths," and other agents deficient in moral understanding, as less than fully responsible, even where their freedom is not in question – and even though they *may* still be responsible in the limited sense that implies accountability for action.[14]

Like Greenspan's essay, Chapter 5 seeks an analysis of the ordinary notion of responsibility; it differs from Greenspan's effort in approaching the analysis somewhat more exclusively metaphysically. In "Responsiveness and Moral Responsibility," **John Martin Fischer** introduces the notion of reasons-responsiveness as one that tracks our ordinary distinctions between contexts permitting attribution and ones precluding it. An agent is said to be responsible for a given act

[14] I wish to thank Professor Greenspan for suggesting revisions in my statement of her position.

insofar as the mechanism that actually gives rise to the act is reasons-responsive. Fischer differentiates a strong and a weak manner of being reasons-responsive. Strong reasons-responsiveness obtains when the mechanism giving rise to behavior is such that had there been sufficient reason to act otherwise, the mechanism that led to the actual behavior would have led the agent to recognize that there was sufficient reason to do otherwise, would have resulted in the choice to do otherwise, and would have resulted in the appropriate behavior. Fischer argues that being strongly reasons-responsive is a sufficient, but not a necessary, condition for moral responsibility.

Weak reasons-responsiveness obtains if the mechanism that led to action would have led to a different action under some, but not necessarily all, conditions where there would be adequate reason to act otherwise. Fischer argues that this weak form of reasons-responsiveness is all that is required for moral responsibility. Fischer takes considerable effort to analyze what kind of mechanism would be required to count as reasons-responsive, and why the approach he adopts deals with cases more adequately than alternative accounts of responsibility.

Focusing on historical figures for insight into accountability for one's own character, **Lenn E. Goodman** has contributed a study entitled "Determinism and Freedom in Spinoza, Maimonides, and Aristotle: A Retrospective Study" (Chapter 6). Although Goodman adeptly shows the significant steps each of these figures takes in relating freedom to character, he focuses on Spinoza's treatment of the metaphysics of character. Unlike Aristotle and Maimonides, Spinoza locates the essence of each thing in its own individual nature, and not in a universal form. In acting as it must, a thing can still be expressing its own individual character. Because Spinoza is a rigorous determinist, acting from character does not imply that there is any real contingency or even logically possible alternatives open to the agent. Freedom for Spinoza does not come from having one's behavior uncaused, but from being relatively self-caused or autonomous.

Goodman unpacks and clarifies the connections between being self-caused, on the one hand, and being possessed of understanding and having an active relationship to one's emotions, on the other. Emotions are passive for Spinoza when they render us capable of only automatic and relatively uncontrolled responses. The more active emotions are those that put us in control of ourselves and less under the control of external events. In order to make sense of these distinctions and explicate human freedom in terms of them, Goodman finds it necessary to distinguish the empirical self from the rational self. Not all that acts through an individual is an act of the individual. For example, the real self for Spinoza is always self-preserving, even though people at times do what is self-destructive. One's freedom rests on one's accessibility to one's higher self.

The point of understanding for Spinoza is not to prevent unpleasant emotions from occurring in oneself, but to free the mind from the debilitating grip of those passive emotions. Whenever emotions gain the sort of power over the mind that limits a person's effectiveness as a human agent, it is because of the person's failure to scrutinize the ground for the emotion. When overwhelmed by an emotion, we feel it controls us even though it is more appropriate to have an interactive view of vulnerability to our emotions.

We saw that Susan Wolf argued that being positioned to determine one's own character was not a condition of being held responsible. Taking an even more radical position, social psychologists **John Sabini** and **Maury Silver** argue in Chapter 7, "Emotions, Responsibility, and Character," that a necessary condition of being responsible is that we are vulnerable emotionally in ways we cannot fully control. Sabini and Silver are concerned with the problem of grounding objective judgments about an individual's character when we recognize that only some aspects of personality are under the agent's control. The authors begin by rejecting Kant's attitude toward emotions because he saw them as having at best a corrupting influence. They also reject more recent psychological approaches to the emotions that treat them as unmediated physiological phenomena. The emotions, Sabini and Silver argue, are bound up with judgments of values and facts in a way that makes them both cognitively and morally charged.

Sabini and Silver offer an alternative approach that recognizes the connections of emotions to desires, plans, values, and reasons. Nevertheless, even though emotions are connected to reasons, values, and facts, they also have a passive or unwilled aspect. Despite this, we give weight to the emotions in deciding the worth of a person. This conflicts with the view that moral evaluations relate to factors over which an individual can exercise control or express choice. Sabini and Silver argue that part of what is involved in being a creature worthy of sympathy includes a level of vulnerability to emotions we cannot control. The fact that we are vulnerable to emotions we cannot control and are hence worthy of regard and sympathy establishes the connection between the passive aspects of character and the realm of the moral. The authors bring out the elements of passivity that make us the proper objects of moral caring.

We judge people on the basis of their emotions even when the orthodox requirements of responsibility are not met. We withdraw from someone with an ugly character even if the person is not at fault for it. We shun that person for being such, not for becoming such. This resembles aesthetic judgment but maintains its objectivity in being detached from our own idiosyncratic interests and perspectives. Even though our emotions are not completely under our control, they morally elevate or degrade our characters.

Thus far we have focused our attention on responsibility as it relates specifically to character. Another dimension of responsibility is concerned with degrees of culpability and the role of the retributive emotions. As several of the essays illustrate, there are important but problematical connections between character and morality on the one hand, and emotions on the other. Not the least of these issues is the extent to which one can be held accountable for having emotional responses of a given sort, especially given their relative intractability. The retributive emotions in particular have been as difficult to defend as they are common. Given that they involve anger, resentment, condemnation, and gratification in the suffering of another for what is essentially a bygone, and given the fact that the appropriateness of these attitudes is not internally or essentially connected to promoting good consequences, this range of emotions can come to seem gratuitous, primitive, sadistic, and thus misaligned with the rest of morality. Nevertheless it would be difficult to think about responsibility without simultaneously believing that resentment toward someone who performs below standard is fitting. If the behavior is very bad, we are disposed to think that unless we are willing to see the transgressor suffer, we must not regard the violation with the appropriate sense of gravity.

The essays in Part II offer alternative and at times opposing approaches to the role of the retributive emotions in resolving the level of culpability. The chapters by Moore, Morris, von Hirsch and Jareborg, and Watson explore the sense or point of guilt or resentment for the moral insight they offer. The paper by Burgh calls into question the moral legitimacy of the retributive emotions and offers in their place socially constructive and compensatory rationales for our responses to violations of important social norms. My own contribution to the volume investigates standard ways and suggests some new ways in which social practices affect our judgment of the level of accountability. The paper by Dworkin offers a rational-contractual model for why we differentiate levels of accountability between agents that directly intend some harm and agents that knowingly cause, but do not directly intend, the same amount of harm.

Michael Moore's essay, "The Moral Worth of Retribution" (Chapter 8), is devoted to unpacking the moral sense that underlies retributive emotions. Moore characterizes retributivism as the position that moral culpability is a sufficient and necessary condition of liability to punitive sanctions. Moore argues that we have an obligation to structure our institutions so that retributivism is achieved. Many people are suspicious of their retributive responses to grievous crimes even though they experience no difficulties with other intuitive notions related to justice, such as the judgment that it is wrong to punish the guilty. Many of the arguments people use to undercut the justice of punishing the guilty work equally effectively against the injustice of punishing the innocent. For instance, if someone suggests that when we punish a person we are "playing God," assuming that we know what others morally deserve, Moore points out that when we judge it wrong to punish the innocent, no one expresses the same kind of modesty about our understanding of desert.

Most of Moore's paper is devoted to an evaluation of the emotions associated with retributivism, inquiring whether they represent moral pathologies on the one hand or provide moral insights on the other. Moore distinguishes substantive and epistemic connections between emotions and morals. The epistemic connection relates to the issue of the insight into moral truths that emotions offer. The substantive connection relates to an appraisal of emotions themselves as being virtuous or defective. Moore argues that there is a connection between these two standards of evaluation; namely, that we use the virtue of possessing an emotion as a criterion of whether the emotion itself is a source of moral insight in a particular case.

After extensively discussing retributive emotions, Moore argues that many of them emerge as moral strengths we could recognize as such if we focus on the actual harm people inflict on others. We cannot identify with, or have respect or compassion for, others without feeling certain ways when they are violated. This response is connected to the feelings of guilt we would experience were we the ones who perpetrated the violation. Moore concludes that this shows the retributive emotions to be not pathological, but rather morally insightful. Moore also contends that because punishment is a social

institution, many of the genuinely worrisome aspects of the retributive emotions, which were brought out in his discussion, can be
controlled. By recognizing the dangers of retributive attitudes giving
rise to sadism and hatred, we can design our justice system to minimize the expression of these factors.

Moral philosophers have explicitly argued or taken for granted that
culpable wrongdoing is a necessary condition for guilt and for appropriate emotions connected with a sense of guilt. In his essay entitled
"Nonmoral Guilt" (Chapter 9), **Herbert Morris** argues that this position is distorted. Like Michael Moore, Morris explores the emotion of
guilt as a means of deriving psychological and moral insight. According to Morris, certain factors suggest that common feelings of guilt
without fault are appropriate: widespread acceptance of, and respect
for, these feelings in the absence of special explanations. Morris introduces three types of situation in which we commonly accept guilt and
associated emotions without fault: (1) states of mind over which we
have no control; (2) survivor guilt; and (3) identification with others
who have acted wrongly, but where there is no culpable relationship
to the wrongdoer. I will sketch Morris's treatment of these situations.
    As an example of guilt for a state of mind over which we have no
control, Morris cites wishing harm to another with whom we have an
intimate relationship. People typically do feel guilty for such involuntary thoughts, and rather than thinking that such a feeling is inappropriate, one might think there is something really damaging to an
important relationship to feel gratification upon imagining harm to
the other. Furthermore, one might realize in fantasizing about harm
to someone close to oneself that one has failed to be the kind of
person one aspired to become, and that one has fallen short of one's
own standard. Morris reminds us that often morality is contrasted
with legality specifically to permit reference to states of mind and
conditions of character in our moral evaluation of a person. It is legal,
not moral, evaluation that is allegedly restricted to overt, typically
voluntary, acts. This point seems to be ignored by those who dismiss a
sense of guilt for states of mind or thoughts over which one had no
control.
    The second range of cases Morris considers relates to survivor guilt
and fortuitous enrichment. A person might feel guilty just because
he, unlike others with whom he identifies, benefited from a distribution that cannot be defended as fair or deserved. To many this gives
rise to a sense of obligation to redress the imbalance. The adage
noblesse oblige captures this attitude. Furthermore, feeling guilty in

these contexts signifies an attachment to principles of fairness and manifests one's sense of solidarity with others. Rather than thinking a sense of guilt occasioned by fortuitous benefit is gratuitous or pathological, we typically admire people for expressing such a disposition.

The final type of case Morris considers involves vicarious guilt – guilt experienced because of transgressions on the part of others with whom one identifies. Morris begins his discussion here with some observations. We typically feel indignant and personally attacked when someone we are close to is attacked by another. We see what happens to another as happening to ourselves. Analogously, if someone we identify with engages in wrongdoing, we can feel ourselves caught up in evil because another has chosen it. We imagine what our own reaction would be to ourselves if we were the wrongdoer. We can even feel guilty because those one identifies with have no sense of remorse for what they have done. As a result of defining oneself in a certain way, for instance as an American, individuals may assume a sense of responsibility for what they see themselves as being – for instance, part of a group that has caused a massacre. As a result of such identification, one may feel specially connected with, and indebted to, those who have been injured, and consequently feel called upon to make amends. Once again, this is an attitude we can admire and respect. The appropriateness of the emotion suggests the legitimacy of attributions of guilt even in the absence of fault.

Also exploring retributive emotions for their moral content, two legal theorists, **Andrew von Hirsch** and **Nils Jareborg,** elaborate how retributive emotions can come to have moral and legal significance in the case of provocation. Chapter 10, "Provocation and Culpability," is addressed to the question of why provocation diminishes the extent of culpability. The problem in seeing provocation as an excuse is that the provoked defendant is not to be seen as defending himself (or herself), but as retaliating in anger. Since he would not have suffered from exercising restraint, it was inappropriate to act as he did. So why should we recognize provocation as an excuse?

After discussing various theories they judge to be inadequate, von Hirsch and Jareborg introduce their principle of resentment. This principle affords extenuation when the agent acts in anger that stems from a misdeed committed against him (or someone close to him) by the provoker. When one is wronged, anger is an appropriate response, reflecting a sense of one's self-worth. It is the sense of right and wrong that gives legitimacy to the anger. The sense of moral self-worth encourages certain hostile responses toward the provoker, but discourages others. Our appreciation for the ambivalent role of conscience in this context leads us to recognize mitigating circumstances for the person who acts out of provoked anger. Since the actor transgressed *because of*, rather than despite, a sense of right and wrong, blame for the transgression should be mitigated.

Gary Watson's contribution to the volume, an essay entitled "Responsibility and the Limits of Evil: Variations on a Strawsonian Theme" (Chapter 11), also focuses on the retributive emotions. This project is undertaken in the context of discussing Peter Strawson's seminal account of what it is to hold someone responsible and the adequacy of this account in dealing with excusing and exempting conditions. Strawson's thesis in his paper "Freedom and Resentment" is that "reactive" attitudes – blame, resentment, disappointment – toward wrongdoing are not collateral effects of beliefs in accountability of people, but rather are constitutive of treating a person as responsible. For Strawson, the idea that we are accountable is to be understood by the practice of insisting upon certain reactions. Ultimately this stance is rooted in the fact that the character of will as displayed in deference for others is a matter of concern. When we blame another we do more than note that a condition of good character is lacking; the reactive responses involve emotional engagement, along with a demand that general principles of human regard be met.

According to Watson, Strawson introduces various pleas that inhibit or modify negative reactive attitudes: excuses that work by showing that a basic demand has not in fact been violated, and exempting conditions that work by showing that the agent is exempt from ordinary moral requirements because of factors like immaturity, mental illness, or unfortunate formative circumstances. These exempting conditions exhibit constraints built into our requirements of legitimate moral address directed at a person.

Watson argues that while working well for excusing conditions, Strawson's thesis provides a less adequate account for the range of exempting conditions. Strawson sees basic moral demands as expressible only to a moral agent – someone who shares our basic framework for practical reasoning and who is potentially susceptible to understanding the point of moral discourse. This requirement has the paradoxical consequence of disqualifying from moral censure people who are extremely evil because they show no vulnerability to moral persuasion. Another problem with Strawson's approach, according to Watson, is that by focusing on an agent's current moral attitudes, it does not seem to show why "unfortunate formative circumstances" is relevant to exempting conditions. Watson himself then explores the ambivalence in reactive attitudes we experience when confronting someone who was brutalized as a child, but who as an adult victimizes others. Once attention is paid to unfortunate formative circumstances as an exempting condition, it is difficult to prevent all factors of character formation that are outside an agent's control from counting as exempting.

Watson ends by challenging another central feature of Strawson's account: the identification of a disposition for reactive attitudes toward another with the disposition to recognize the moral character of another. Watson cites figures, like Gandhi and M. L. King, Jr., who eschew blame and condemnation, but still clearly engage others as moral agents.

Over the past few decades the field of social psychology has given rise to a descriptive theory about what factors are germane to human attribution practices. By an attribution of an act to an agent what is meant is a measure of accountability (either causal and/or moral) the agent is seen as possessing. This area of research is labeled attribution theory. More recently, some attribution theory psychologists have turned to more normative objectives and have offered critical theories about when attributions are fitting and when they are based on misconceptions. In my own contribution to this volume – Chapter 12, "Statistical Norms and Moral Attributions," I discuss some of this literature. We have a tendency to think that if a social norm permits or promotes a certain attitude, then the person who acts in accordance with the norm is personally less causally responsible when acting according to the norm than when acting in violation of the norm. When it comes to assessing causal contribution, we are disposed to think that the more distinctive an individual's behavior, the more the behavior is attributable to that individual as opposed to being attributable to his or her surroundings. One of the questions addressed in this paper is what moral implications can be drawn from this practice.

Some psychologists who have studied personality theory criticize ordinary tendencies to underestimate the impact of situational factors and overestimate the role of dispositional factors in controlling behavior. This tendency is labeled the fundamental attribution error. Some of these same psychologists have argued that in addition to errors in the causal understanding of behavior, this tendency gives rise to errors in moral assessments. For instance, Nisbett and Ross, in their highly influential book on human inference,[15] argue that if the base rate for specific behavior in a given context is high, then the behavior cannot be correctly credited to the agent, but should be credited to the environment. I criticize this position. I use the Milgram obedience to authority study, and attribution theorists' writings about this study, in my analysis of how attribution theorists draw completely unwarranted and morally naive judgmental inferences from their causal theories. I argue that attribution theorists demonstrate a complete misunderstanding of the relationship between excuse and causal theories of behavior.

Even though attribution theorists often botch the assessment of moral implications from observed practices, I argue that there is an underlying point to their perspective that in large part has been ignored by philosophers concerned with responsibility. This underlying point relates to appreciation of human judgmental limitations and to principles of moral learning. If, in a wide range of cases, the best that most people can do is employ simplifying strategies of moral assessment, then the fact that others – either those one takes as authorities or those one sees little reason to question – do things in a given way may be seen as morally warranting conforming behavior or at least as providing an excusing condition for behavior that falls below some objective standard. The notion of entrapment is introduced and extended to cover cases where though a person acted wrongly, because of the quasi-authoritative inducement to substandard behavior, blame is attenuated.

In Chapter 13, "Guilt, Punishment, and Desert," **Richard Burgh** expresses skepticism about the moral legitimacy of the retributive emotions and offers in their place a new way of conceptualizing our responses to wrongdoers. After pointing out that no satisfactory theory of penal desert has resulted from either retributive or utilitarian theory, Burgh offers a compensatory theory that he argues introduces coherence into the field. Compensatory theory captures the backward-looking intuitions that culpable offenders deserve to be punished, and the forward-looking intuition that the infliction of suffering for its own sake is evil and can be justified only by good consequences.

Under compensatory theory, the wrongfully injured party deserves

---

[15] Richard Nisbett and Lee Ross, *Human Inference: Strategies and Shortcomings of Social Judgment* (Englewood Cliffs, NJ: Prentice-Hall, 1980).

to be made whole again, and the party responsible for the harm deserves to be held liable for making the injured party whole. The wrongdoer is imposed upon in order to make the victim whole. Here the suffering or deprivation of the wrongdoer must be connected to the reparation of the victim.

Burgh argues that this is just what punishment for crimes accomplishes when the victim is seen as the society and the harm is seen as the repudiation of socially central values. Crimes are to be viewed as public or social harms and punishment as social reparation. Burgh argues that crimes characteristically involve social harms by contrasting criminal law and tort law. Certain excuses that are allowed in criminal law have no place in torts because the objective of tort law is to preclude diminishment of the individual's interests and these are diminished independent of the intention of the tortfeasor. Excuses are permitted in the area of the criminal law, however, because some of the interests being protected are core social values, and these are only repudiated by intentional crimes. This repudiation is a social harm because it threatens the values that hold the society intact. Rectification involves a reaffirmation of these values, and this is accomplished by making the offender suffer. The wrongdoer's suffering is a way of condemning his or her repudiation and thereby restoring society's core values in the social scheme of things.

In the final contribution, Chapter 14, "Intention, Foreseeability, and Responsibility," **Gerald Dworkin** probes the problem of assessing differing levels of accountability when comparing knowingly doing something that has harmful consequences, on the one hand, and intending to bring about those consequences, even for a good objective, on the other. Dworkin is interested in analyzing the moral difference between directly intending harm to another as a means to some good and being prepared to act to bring about this same good even though a consequence of one's efforts will result in harm to others. What role does such a distinction play in our system of responsibility?

Dworkin argues that from a consequentialist as well as from a nonconsequentialist perspective, a mere difference in causal relationships will not itself make a moral difference. For the consequentialist, the results are the same whether the harm was a means to the end or merely a consequence of the process. For the nonconsequentialist, what must be relevant is how the agent views, or reasons about, what he or she is doing, and not the causal relationships.

In his constructive approach, Dworkin points out that everyone agrees an agent is accountable for what he or she indirectly intends, so the difference between what is directly intended and indirectly intended is one of degree, and not of kind. His approach to explaining this difference in degrees rests on the strategy of justifying to victims of the indirect harm how in his or her own role as an agent he or she must see the point of differentiating directly and indirectly intended harms. As an agent, we all have some interest in being free from some of the consequences of our acts. But as potential victims, we have an interest in others taking responsibility for the consequences of their acts. We seek a way of balancing our interests in ourselves as agents and our interests in ourselves as potential victims of others' good or bad intentions. Diminishing the degree of responsibility for harms indirectly intended lets us balance these interests by giving ourselves scope for action, even if it imposes harm on others.

Dworkin ends his analysis in terms of a "quality of will" account for the difference between the levels of accountability. He points out that it does not show *more* disregard for the interests of others to harm them as a consequence of what one intends than it does to harm them as a means to accomplishing what one intends. Rather, when one contemplates the harmful but unintended consequences to another of one's acts, it offers one more flexibility and reason actively to care about others than when the harm is itself a means to one's objective. The distinction between intended and unintended consequences represents a compromise that permits us to act as agents, working for good effects without totally ignoring the harms this agency may occasion.

Part I

Responsibility and character

2

Identification and wholeheartedness

HARRY FRANKFURT

I

The phrase "the mind–body problem" is so crisp, and its role in philosophical discourse is so well established, that to oppose its use would simply be foolish. Nonetheless, the usage *is* rather anachronistic. The familiar problem to which the phrase refers concerns the relationship between a creature's body and the fact that the creature is conscious. A more appropriate name would be, accordingly, "the consciousness–body problem." For it is no longer plausible to equate the realm of conscious phenomena – as Descartes did – with the realm of mind. This is not only because psychoanalysis has made the notion of unconscious feelings and thoughts compelling. Other leading psychological theories have also found it useful to construe the distinction between the mental and the nonmental as being far broader than that between situations in which consciousness is present and those in which it is not.

For example, both William James and Jean Piaget are inclined to regard mentality as a feature of all living things. James takes the presence of mentality to be essentially a matter of intelligent or goal-directed behavior, which he opposes to behavior that is only mechanical:

The pursuance of future ends and the choice of means for their attainment are the mark and criterion of the presence of mentality in a phenomenon. We all use this test to discriminate between an intelligent and a mechanical performance.[1]

Piaget similarly, but with even greater emphasis, construes the difference between the mental and the nonmental in terms of purposefulness:

There is no sort of boundary between the living and the mental or between the biological and the psychological. . . . [Psychology] is not the science of

[1] William James, *The Principles of Psychology* I (Cambridge, MA: Harvard University Press, 1983), p. 21.

consciousness only but of behavior in general . . . of conduct. . . . [Psychology begins] when the organism behaves with regard to external situations and solves problems.[2]

Powerful currents of thought, then, lead away from the supposition that being conscious is essential to mentality. The psychoanalytic expansion of the mind to include unconscious phenomena does not itself actually require, of course, that mentality be attributed to creatures who are entirely *incapable* of consciousness. On the other hand, the conceptions of James and Piaget do entail that mentality characterizes the lives of vast numbers of creatures – not only animals but plants as well – which enjoy no conscious experience at all.[3]

Now what is this *consciousness,* which is distinct from mentality and which we generally suppose to be peculiar to human beings and to the members of certain relatively advanced animal species? Anthony Kenny offers the following view:

I think that consciousness . . . is a matter of having certain sorts of ability. To be conscious is, for instance, to see and hear. Whether somebody can see or hear is a matter of whether he can discriminate between certain things, and whether he can discriminate between certain things is something that we can test both in simple everyday ways and in complicated experimental ways.[4]

Kenny's suggestion is that to be conscious is to be able to discriminate. But what is it to discriminate? It would seem that discriminating between two things is in the most fundamental sense a matter of being affected differently by the one than by the other. If my state remains exactly the same regardless of whether a certain feature is present in my environment or absent from it, then I am not discriminating between the presence and the absence of that feature. If my state does differ according to the presence or absence of the feature, then that is a mode of discriminating between its presence and its absence. To discriminate sounds, colors, levels of temperature, and the like just means – in its most general sense – to respond differentially to them.

It does seem indisputable that discrimination is central to consciousness: Seeing necessarily involves responding to differences in color, hearing to differences in sound, and so on. By no means, however, does this effectively grasp what we ordinarily think of as consciousness. The usual way of identifying the state of being conscious is by contrasting it to unconsciousness; and one way of being uncon-

---

[2] J.-C. Bringuier, *Conversations with Piaget* (Chicago: University of Chicago Press, 1980), pp. 3, 4.
[3] Piaget himself cites the behavior of sunflowers as indicative of mentality.
[4] Anthony Kenny et al., *The Nature of Mind* (Edinburgh: University Press, 1972), p. 43.

scious is to be asleep. But even while they are asleep, animals respond to visual, auditory, tactile, and other stimuli. Otherwise it would be difficult to wake them up. To be sure, the range of responses when they are sleeping is narrower than when they are awake. But they do not while asleep entirely lack the ability to discriminate, and Kenny cannot therefore regard them as being at that time altogether unconscious.

Now it might well be acceptable to consider sleep as consistent with a certain level of consciousness – lower than that of wakefulness, but above zero. In the view Kenny proposes, however, it is not only sleeping animals that are conscious – so is everything else in the world. After all, there is no entity that is not susceptible to being differentially affected by something. If the notion of consciousness is understood as having merely the very general and primitive sense allotted to it by Kenny's account, then a piece of metal is conscious of the ambient temperature to the extent that it becomes hotter and colder, or expands and contracts, as that temperature changes. Consciousness so construed is a state to which the contrasting state is clearly not unconsciousness, understanding unconsciousness to be what we ordinarily attribute to those who are deeply asleep or anesthetized or in a coma. Rather, the state to which consciousness in this sense contrasts is causal isolation.

Consciousness in the everyday sense cannot be exclusively a matter of discrimination, then, since all sorts of discriminating responses may occur (so to speak) in the dark. One might perhaps avoid this difficulty by saying that consciousness is the ability to discriminate *consciously*, but that would not be helpful. In any event, I wish to consider another feature, distinct from discrimination, which is essential to ordinary consciousness: *reflexivity*. Being conscious necessarily involves not merely differentiating responses to stimuli, but an awareness of those responses. When I am awake on a hot day, the heat raises the temperature of my skin; it also raises the surface temperature of a piece of metal. Both the metal and I respond to the heat, and in this sense each of us is aware of it. But I am also aware of my response, while the metal is not. The increase in the temperature of my skin is itself something which I discriminate, and this is essential to the mode of being conscious that consists in feeling warm.

Of course the fact that a creature responds to its own responses does not entail that it is conscious. It goes without saying that the second response may be no more conscious than the first. Thus, adding reflexivity to discrimination does not provide an explanation of how consciousness arises, nor of how it and unconsciousness differ.

Nonetheless, being conscious in the everyday sense does (unlike un-consciousness) entail reflexivity: It necessarily involves a secondary awareness of a primary response. An instance of exclusively primary and unreflexive consciousness would not be an instance of what we ordinarily think of as consciousness at all. For what would it be like to be conscious of something without being aware of this consciousness? It would mean having experience with no awareness whatever of its occurrence. This would be, precisely, a case of unconscious experience. It appears, then, that being conscious is identical with being self-conscious. Consciousness *is* self-consciousness.[5]

The claim that waking consciousness is self-consciousness does not mean that consciousness is invariably dual in the sense that every instance of it involves both a primary awareness and another instance of consciousness which is somehow distinct and separable from the first and which has the first as its object. That would threaten an intolerably infinite proliferation of instances of consciousness. Rather, the self-consciousness in question is a sort of *immanent reflexivity* by virtue of which every instance of being conscious grasps not only that of which it is an awareness, but also the awareness of it. It is like a source of light which, in addition to illuminating whatever other things fall within its scope, renders itself visible as well.

II

There is a baffling problem about what consciousness is *for*. It is equally baffling, moreover, that the function of consciousness should remain so baffling. It seems extraordinary that, despite the per-vasiveness and familiarity of consciousness in our lives, we are uncer-tain in what way (if at all) it is actually indispensable to us.[6] Be this as it

---

[5] What I am here referring to as "self-consciousness" is neither consciousness of a self — a subject or ego — nor consciousness that there is awareness. Both require rational capacities beyond what would seem to be necessary for consciousness itself to occur. The reflexivity in question is merely consciousness's awareness of itself. To hear a sound consciously, rather than to respond to it unconsciously, involves being aware of hearing it or being aware of the sound as heard.

[6] Thus the Nobel laureate physiologist John Eccles says: "I would like to . . . [ask] as a neurophysiologist, why do we have to be conscious at all? We can, in principle, explain all our input–output performances in terms of activity of neuronal circuits; and, conse-quently, consciousness seems to be absolutely unnecessary. I don't believe this story, of course; but at the same time I do not know the logical answer to it. In attempting to answer the question, why do we have to be conscious? it surely cannot be claimed as self-evident that consciousness is a necessary requisite for such performances as logical argument or reasoning, or even for initiative and creative activities." In J. Eccles, ed., *Brain and Conscious Experience* (New York, 1966). Perhaps, despite Eccles's reluctance to admit it, the inwardness of human life is an ontological absurdity — something that takes itself enormously seriously, but that actually has no important role to play at all.

may, the importance of *reflexivity* to those in whose lives it occurs is readily apparent. A creature's sensitivity to its own condition – whether it is by way of the inwardness or immanent reflexivity of waking consciousness, or by way of a less dazzling variety of secondary responsiveness – is essential for purposeful behavior.

The metal does not change in any purposeful way when it becomes hot; on the other hand, under certain conditions a sunflower turns toward the light. Both the metal and the sunflower respond to what goes on around them. Each is affected by, and hence discriminates, environmental stimuli. But the sunflower, unlike the metal, makes second-order as well as primary discriminations. This contributes essentially to its capacity for purposeful change. The metal lacks this capacity, since it is insensitive to its own responses – which is to say that it is altogether unresponsive or indifferent to what happens to it. A creature engaged in secondary responsiveness is monitoring its own condition; to that extent the creature is in a position, or at least is closer to being in a position, to do something about its condition.

Thus reflexivity has a point, just as action itself does, in virtue of the riskiness of existence. It enables a creature, among other things, to respond to the circumstance that its interests are being adversely affected. This makes reflexivity an indispensable condition for behavior that is directed purposefully to avoiding or to ameliorating circumstances of this kind, in which there is a conflict between the interests of a creature and forces that are endangering or undermining them.

There is also another sort of reflexivity or self-consciousness, which appears similarly to be intelligible as being fundamentally a response to conflict and risk. It is a salient characteristic of human beings, one which affects our lives in deep and innumerable ways, that we care about what we are. This is closely connected both as cause and as effect to our enormous preoccupation with what other people think of us. We are ceaselessly alert to the danger that there may be discrepancies between what we wish to be (or what we wish to seem to be) and how we actually appear to others and to ourselves.

We are particularly concerned with our own motives. It matters greatly to us whether the desires by which we are moved to act as we do motivate us because we want them to be effective in moving us, or whether they move us regardless of ourselves or even despite ourselves. In the latter cases we are moved to act as we do without it being the case that we want wholeheartedly to be motivated as we are. Our hearts are at best divided, and they may even not be in what we are doing at all.

This means, moreover, that we are to some degree passive with respect to the action we perform. For in virtue of the fact that we do not unequivocally endorse or support our own motive, it can appropriately be said that what we want – namely, the object of our motivating desire, and that desire itself – is in a certain ordinary sense not something which we *really* want. So while it may be that we perform our action on account of the motivating force of our own desire, it is nonetheless also true that we are being moved to act by something other than what we really want. In that case we are in a way passive with respect to what moves us, as we always are when we are moved by a force that is not fully our own.

It is possible for a human being to be at times, and perhaps even always, indifferent to his own motives – to take no evaluative attitude toward the desires that incline him to act. If there is a conflict between those desires, he does not care which of them proves to be the more effective. In other words, the individual does not participate in the conflict. Therefore, the outcome of the conflict can be neither a victory for him nor a defeat. Since he exercises no authority, by the endorsement or concurrence of which certain of his desires might acquire particular legitimacy, or might come to be specially constitutive of himself, the actions engendered by the flow and clash of his feelings and desires are quite wanton.

III

Now what conceptualization of this range of phenomena fits its contours in the most authentic and perspicuous way? My own preference has been for a model that involves levels of reflexivity or self-consciousness. According to this schema, there are at the lowest level first-order desires to perform one or another action. Whichever of these first-order desires actually leads to action is, by virtue of that effectiveness, designated the will of the individual whose desire it is. In addition, people characteristically have second-order desires concerning what first-order desires they want; and they have second-order volitions concerning which first-order desire they want to be their will. There may also be desires and volitions of higher orders.

This makes it rather natural to distinguish two ways in which the volitional aspects of a person's life may be radically divided or incoherent. In the first place, there may be a conflict between how someone wants to be motivated and the desire by which he is in fact most powerfully moved. An example of this sort of inner conflict is provided by the situation of a person who wants to refrain from smoking – that is, who wants the desire to refrain from smoking to be what effectively motivates his behavior – but whose desire for a cigarette proves to be so strong that it becomes his will despite the fact that he prefers not to act upon it and even struggles against it. Here there is a lack of coherence or harmony between the person's higher-order volition or preference concerning which of his desires he wants to be most effective and the first-order desire that actually is the most effective in moving him when he acts. Since the desire that prevails is one upon which he would prefer not to act, the outcome of the division within him is that he is unable to do what he really wants to do. His will is not under his own control. It is not the will he wants, but one that is imposed upon him by a force with which he does not identify and which is in that sense external to him.

Another sort of inner division occurs when there is a lack of coherence within the realm of the person's higher-order volitions themselves. This does not concern the relation between volitions and will. It is not a matter of volitional strength, but of whether the highest-order preferences concerning some volitional issue are *wholehearted*. It has to do with the possibility that there is no unequivocal answer to the question of what the person really wants, even though his desires do form a complex and extensive hierarchical structure. There might be no unequivocal answer because the person is *ambivalent* with respect to the object he comes closest to really wanting: In other words, because, with respect to that object, he is drawn not only toward it, but away from it too. Or there might be no unequivocal answer because the person's preferences concerning what he wants are not fully integrated, so that there is some *inconsistency* or *conflict* (perhaps not yet manifest) among them.

Incoherence of the first kind (the kind that afflicts the smoker) might be characterized as being *between* what the person really wants and other desires – like the rejected but nonetheless inescapably preemptive desire to smoke – that are *external* to the volitional complex with which the person identifies and by which he wants his behavior to be determined. The second kind of incoherence is *within* this volitional complex. In the absence of wholeheartedness, the person is not merely in conflict with forces "outside" him; rather, he himself is divided.

One advantage of this model is that it provides a convenient way of explaining how, as in the case of the reluctant smoker, passivity or impaired autonomy may be due to the force of what are in some basically literal sense the individual's own desires. The model also lends itself in fairly obvious ways to the articulation and explication of a variety of useful concepts pertaining to structural features of the mind (e.g., weakness of the will, ego-ideal, and so on). However, the model's central notion of a hierarchy of desires seems not to be entirely adequate to its purpose. For it appears to be impossible to ex-

plain, using the resources of this notion alone, in what way an individual with second-order desires or volitions may be less wanton with
respect to *them* than a wholly unreflective creature is with respect to its
first-order desires.[7]

Someone does what he *really wants* to do only when he acts in accordance with a pertinent higher-order volition. But this condition could
not be sufficient unless the higher-order volition were *itself* one by
which the person *really wanted* to be determined. Now it is pretty clear
that this requirement cannot be satisfied simply by introducing *another* desire or volition at the next higher level. That would lead to a
regress which it would be quite arbitrary to terminate at any particular point. The difficulty bears on both types of volitional incoherence
I have distinguished above. A characterization of either type of incoherence requires construing some of a person's desires as integral
to him in a way in which others are not. Yet it is not obvious what
account to give of the distinction between volitional elements that are
integrated into a person and those that remain in some relevant sense
external to him.

The mere fact that one desire occupies a higher level than another
in the hierarchy seems plainly insufficient to endow it with greater
authority or with any constitutive legitimacy. In other words, the assignment of desires to different hierarchical levels does not by itself
provide an explanation of what it is for someone to be *identified* with
one of his own desires rather than with another. It does not make
clear why it should be appropriate to construe a person as *participating*
in conflicts within himself between second-order volitions and first-
order desires, and hence as vulnerable to being defeated by his own
desires, when a *wanton* is not to be construed as a genuine participant
in (or as having any interest in the outcomes of) conflicts within himself between desires all of which are of the first order. Gary Watson
has formulated the issue succinctly:

Since second-order volitions are themselves simply desires, to add them to the
context of conflict is just to increase the number of contenders; it is not to give
a special place to any of those in contention.[8]

---

[7] The notion of reflexivity seems to me much more fundamental and indispensable, in
dealing with the phenomena at hand, than that of a hierarchy. On the other hand, it is
not clear to me that adequate provision can be made for reflexivity without resorting to
the notion of a hierarchical ordering. While articulating volitional life in terms of a
hierarchy of desires does seem a bit contrived, the alternatives – such as the one
proposed by Gary Watson in "Free Agency" (*Journal of Philosophy*, 1975) – strike me as
worse: more obscure, no less fanciful, and (I suspect) requiring a resort to hierarchy in
the end themselves.

[8] Watson, op. cit., p. 218.

It appears that the hierarchical model cannot as such cope with this difficulty. It merely enables us to describe an inner conflict as being between desires of different orders. But this alone is hardly adequate to determine – with respect to that conflict – where (if anywhere) the person himself stands.[9]

I tried some time ago to deal with this problem, in the following passage:

When a person identifies himself *decisively* with one of his first-order desires, this commitment "resounds" throughout the potentially endless array of higher orders. . . . The fact that his second-order volition to be moved by this desire is a decisive one means that there is no room for questions concerning the pertinence of volitions of higher orders. . . . The decisiveness of the commitment he has made means that he has decided that no further questions about his second-order volition, at any higher order, remain to be asked.[10]

The trouble with what I wrote in this passage is that the notions I invoked – namely, "identification," "decisive commitment," "resounding" – are terribly obscure. Therefore, the passage left it quite unclear just how the maneuver of avoiding an interminable regress by making a decisive commitment can escape being unacceptably arbitrary. Thus, Watson says:

We wanted to know what prevents wantonness with regard to one's higher-order volitions. What gives these volitions any special relation to "oneself"? It is unhelpful to answer that one makes a "decisive commitment", where this just means that an interminable ascent to higher orders is not going to be permitted. This *is* arbitrary.[11]

Now in fact Watson is in error here. As I shall attempt to explain, making a decisive commitment does not consist merely in an arbitrary *refusal* to permit an interminable ascent to higher orders.

IV

Consider a situation somewhat analogous to that of a person who is uncertain whether to identify himself with one or with another of his own desires, but which is rather more straightforward: the situation of someone attempting to solve a problem in arithmetic. Having per-

[9] The problem of explaining identification is not, of course, peculiar to the hierarchical model. It must be dealt with by any account of the structure of volition. Accordingly, it is not a fault of the hierarchical model that it requires an explanation of identification.

[10] "Freedom of the Will and the Concept of a Person," *Journal of Philosophy*, 1971, p. 16.

[11] Watson, op. cit., p. 218.

formed a calculation, this person may perform another in order to check his answer. The second calculation may be just the same as the first, or it may be equivalent to it in the sense that it follows a procedure which is different from the first but which must yield the same result. In any case, suppose the first calculation is confirmed by the second. It is possible that both calculations are faulty, so the person may check again. This sequence of calculations can be extended indefinitely. Moreover, there is nothing about the position of any particular item in the sequence that gives it definitive authority. A mistake can be made at any point, and the same mistake may be repeated any number of times. So what is to distinguish a calculation with which the person can reasonably terminate the sequence? How does the person avoid being irresponsible or arbitrary when he ends at some particular point a sequence of calculations that he might extend further?

One way in which a sequence of calculations might end is that the person conducting it simply quits, negligently permitting the result of his last calculation to serve as his answer. Perhaps he just loses interest in the problem, or perhaps he is diverted from further inquiry by some compelling distraction. In cases like these, his behavior resembles that of a wanton: He allows a certain result to stand without evaluating its suitability or considering the desirability of allowing it to be his answer. He does not *choose* a result, nor does he *endorse* one. He acts as though it is a matter of complete indifference to him whether there is in fact adequate support for the acceptability of his answer.

On the other hand, a sequence of calculations might end because the person conducting it *decides for some reason* to adopt a certain result. It may be that he is unequivocally confident that this result is correct, and therefore believes that there is no use for further inquiry. Or perhaps he believes that even though there is some likelihood that the result is not correct, the cost to him of further inquiry – in time or in effort or in lost opportunities – is greater than the value to him of reducing the likelihood of error. In either event there may be a "decisive" identification on his part. In a sense that I shall endeavor to explain, such an identification resounds through an unlimited sequence of possible further reconsiderations of his decision.

Suppose the person is confident that he knows the correct answer. He then expects to get that answer each time he accurately performs a suitable calculation. In this respect, the future is transparent to him, and his decision that a certain answer is correct resounds endlessly in just this sense: It enables him to anticipate the outcomes of an indefinite number of possible further calculations. Now suppose he is not entirely confident which answer is correct, but is convinced that it would nonetheless be most reasonable for him to adopt a certain answer as his own. Then he cannot with full confidence expect this answer to be confirmed by further inquiry; he acknowledges that accurate calculation might produce a different result. But if he has made a genuinely unreserved commitment to the view that adopting the answer is his most reasonable alternative, he can anticipate that *this* view will be endlessly confirmed by accurate reviews of it.

The fact that a commitment resounds endlessly *is* simply the fact that the commitment is *decisive*. For a commitment is decisive if and only if it is made without reservation. And making a commitment without reservation means that the person who makes it does so in the belief that no further accurate inquiry would require him to change his mind. It is therefore pointless to pursue the inquiry any further. This is, precisely, the resonance effect.[12]

Now what leads people to form desires of higher orders is similar to what leads them to go over their arithmetic. Someone checks his calculations because he thinks he may have done them wrong. It may be that there is a conflict between the answer he has obtained and a different answer which, for one reason or another, he believes may be correct; or perhaps he has merely a more generalized suspicion, to the effect that he may have made some kind of error. Similarly, a person may be led to reflect upon his own desires either because they conflict with each other, or because a more general lack of confidence moves him to consider whether to be satisfied with his motives as they are.

Both in the case of desires and in the case of arithmetic a person can without arbitrariness terminate a potentially endless sequence of evaluations when he finds that there is no disturbing conflict, either between results already obtained or between a result already obtained and one he might reasonably expect to obtain if the sequence were to continue. Terminating the sequence at that point – the point at which there is no conflict or doubt – is not arbitrary. For the only reason to continue the sequence would be to cope with an actual conflict or with the possibility that a conflict might occur. And given that the person does not have this reason to continue, it is hardly arbitrary for him to stop.

---

[12] I am here agreeing with the suggestion concerning the relation between resonance and decisive commitment made by Jon Elster, in his *Ulysses and the Sirens: Studies in Rationality and Irrationality* (Cambridge: Cambridge University Press, 1979), p. 111, n. 135. My own treatment of these matters owes much to Descartes's discussion of clear and distinct perception.

Perhaps it will be suggested that there remains an element of arbitrariness here, in the judgment that no pertinent conflict can be found: This judgment is also subject to error, after all, and it would be possible to reassess it endlessly without any of the reassessments being inherently definitive or final. Whatever the merit of this point, however, it does not imply a deficiency specific to the principle that a person is justified in terminating a sequence of calculations or reflections when he sees no conflict to be avoided or resolved. For the point is quite general. It is *always* possible, in the deployment of any principle whatever, to make a mistaken or an unwarranted judgment that the conditions for applying the principle correctly have been satisfied. It should go without saying that no criterion or standard can guarantee that it will be wielded accurately and without arbitrariness.

V

The etymological meaning of the verb "to decide" is "to cut off." This is apt, since it is characteristically by a decision (though, of course, not necessarily or even most frequently in that way) that a sequence of desires or preferences of increasingly higher orders is terminated. When the decision is made without reservation, the commitment it entails is a decisive one. Then the person no longer holds himself at all apart from the desire to which he has committed himself. It is no longer unsettled or uncertain whether the object of that desire – that is, what he wants – is what he really wants: The decision determines what the person really wants by making the desire upon which he decides fully his own. To this extent the person, in making a decision by which he identifies with a desire, *constitutes himself.* The pertinent desire is no longer in any way external to him. It is not a desire that he "has" merely as a subject in whose history it happens to occur, as a person may "have" an involuntary spasm that happens to occur in the history of his body. It comes to be a desire that is incorporated into himself by virtue of the fact that he has it *by his own will.*

This does not mean that it is through the exercise of the will that the desire originates; the desire may well preexist the decision made concerning it. But even if the person is not responsible for the fact that the desire *occurs,* there is an important sense in which he takes responsibility for the fact of having the desire – the fact that the desire is in the fullest sense his, that it constitutes what he really wants – when he identifies himself with it. Through his action in deciding, he is responsible for the fact that the desire has become his own in a way in which it was not unequivocally his own before.

There are two quite different sorts of conflicts between desires. In conflicts of the one sort, desires compete for priority or position in a preferential order; the issue is which desire to satisfy *first*. In conflicts of the other sort, the issue is whether a desire should be given *any* place in the order of preference at all – that is, whether it is to be endorsed as a legitimate candidate for satisfaction or whether it is to be rejected as entitled to no priority whatsoever. When a conflict of the first kind is resolved, the competing desires are *integrated* into a single ordering, within which each occupies a specific position. Resolving a conflict of the second kind involves a radical *separation* of the competing desires, one of which is not merely assigned a relatively less favored position, but extruded entirely as an outlaw. It is these acts of ordering and of rejection – integration and separation – that create a self out of the raw materials of inner life. They define the intrapsychic constraints and boundaries with respect to which a person's autonomy may be threatened even by his own desires.[13]

Aristotle maintained that behavior is voluntary only when its moving principle is inside the agent. This cannot be correct if "inside" is construed in its literal sense: The movements of an epileptic seizure are not voluntary, but their moving principle or cause is spatially internal to the agent. The location of a moving principle with respect to the agent's body is plainly less relevant than its "location" with respect to the agent's volition. What counts, even with respect to a moving principle that operates as an element of his psychic life, is whether or not the agent has constituted himself to include it. On the one hand, the principle may be internal, in the sense pertinent to whether the behavior to which it leads is voluntary, by virtue of the fact that the person has joined himself to what moves him by commitment through which he takes responsibility for it. On the other hand, the moving principle of his behavior may remain external to the person in the pertinent sense because he has not made it part of himself.

This suggests another respect in which Aristotle's theory is unsatisfactory. He maintains that a person may be responsible for his own character on account of having taken (or having failed to take) measures that affect what his habitual dispositions are. In other words, a person acquires responsibility for his own character, according to Aristotle, by acting in ways that are causally instrumental in

[13] The determining conditions that are pertinent here are exclusively *structural* arrangements. I mention this, although I do not pursue the point, since it bears on the familiar issue of whether *historical* considerations – especially causal stories – have any essential relevance to questions concerning whether a person's actions are autonomous.

bringing it about that he has the particular set of dispositions of which his character is comprised. I think that Aristotle's treatment of this subject is significantly out of focus because of his preoccupation with causal origins and causal responsibility. The fundamental responsibility of an agent with respect to his own character is not a matter of whether it is as the effect of his own actions that the agent *has* certain dispositions to feel and to behave in various ways. That bears only on the question of whether the person is responsible for having these *characteristics*. The question of whether the person is responsible for his own *character* has to do with whether he has *taken responsibility for* his characteristics. It concerns whether the dispositions at issue, regardless of whether their *existence* is due to the person's own initiative and causal agency or not, are characteristics with which he identifies and which he thus by his own will incorporates into himself as constitutive of what he is.

When someone identifies himself with one rather than with another of his own desires, the result is not necessarily to eliminate the conflict between those desires, or even to reduce its severity, but to alter its nature. Suppose that a person with two conflicting desires identifies with one rather than with the other. This *might* cause the other – the desire with which the person does not identify – to become substantially weaker than it was, or to disappear altogether. But it need not. Quite possibly, the conflict between the two desires will remain as virulent as before. What the person's commitment to the one eliminates is not the conflict between it and the other. It eliminates the conflict *within the person* as to which of these desires he prefers to be his motive. The conflict between the *desires* is in this way transformed into a conflict between *one* of them and the *person* who has identified himself with its rival. That person is no longer uncertain which side he is on, in the conflict between the two desires, and the persistence of this conflict need not subvert or diminish the wholeheartedness of his commitment to the desire with which he identifies.

VI

Since it is most conspicuously by making a decision that a person identifies with some element of his psychic life, deciding plays an important role in the formation and maintenance of the self. It is very difficult to articulate what the act of deciding consists in – to make fully clear just what we do when we perform it. But while the nature of deciding is aggravatingly elusive, at least it is apparent that making a decision is something that we do *to ourselves*. In this respect it differs fundamentally from making a choice, the immediate object of which is not the chooser, but whatever it is that he chooses. This difference between deciding and choosing accounts for the fact that deciding to make a certain choice is not the same as actually making it (after all, the time or occasion for doing that may not yet have arrived), while deciding to make a particular decision (that is, deciding to decide things a certain way) cannot be distinguished from making the decision himself.

In some languages, the reflexivity of deciding – the fact that it is an action done to oneself – is indicated in the form of the pertinent verb. Thus, the French verb is *se décider*. The closest parallel among English synonyms for "to decide" is the phrase "to make up one's mind," in which there is an explicit representation of the reflexive character of deciding. Now what are we to make of the rather protean metaphor this phrase invokes? Is making up one's mind like "making up a story," or is it like "making up a bed"? Is it like "making up one's face," or is it rather like "making up a list of things to do"? Or is it, perhaps, more like "making up after a quarrel"? What is the difference, in these various instances, between what is made up and what is not? And which of these differences corresponds most closely to the difference between a mind that is made up and one that is undecided?

The use of cosmetics pertains to a contrast between what a person looks like naturally and how the person may contrive to appear. A similar contrast is implicit in the idea of making up a story, which resembles making up a face in that the outcome is in both cases something artificial or fictitious; it does not simply exhibit the way things really are. One difference between using makeup and making up a story is, of course, that there is a face before it is made up – something to which being made up happens. This has no ready analogue in the case of a story, which is not transformed by being made up, but which comes into existence only as it is contrived. In this respect, making up a face more closely resembles making up a bed. As for making up a list, it plainly has nothing to do with the fictitious or the contrived; it is more a matter of establishing certain relationships among the items listed, or of recording relationships among them that already exist.

What appears to be fundamentally common in all occurrences of the notion of making something up is not the contrast between fiction and reality or between the natural and the artificial, but the theme of creating an orderly arrangement. It seems to me that in this light the closest analogue to a situation in which someone makes up his mind is,

rather surprisingly perhaps, a situation in which two people make up
their differences. People who do that after a quarrel pass from a
condition of conflict and hostility to a more harmonious and well-
ordered relationship. Of course people do not always make up when
their quarrel ends; sometimes their hostility continues even after the
conflict that was its original cause has been resolved. Moreover, people who have been quarreling may restore harmony between themselves even though their disagreement continues. Making up concerns healing a relationship disrupted by conflict, and it has nothing
directly or necessarily to do with whether or not the conflict has
ended.

Construed on this analogy, the making of a decision appears to
differ from the self-reparative activities of the body, which in some
other ways it resembles. When the body heals itself, it *eliminates* conflicts in which one physical process (say, infection) interferes with
others and undermines the homeostasis or equilibrium in which
health consists. A person who makes up his mind also seeks thereby to
overcome or to supersede a condition of inner division and to make
himself into an integrated whole. But he may accomplish this without
actually eliminating the desires that conflict with those upon which he
has decided, as long as he dissociates himself from them.

A person may fail to integrate himself when he makes up his mind,
of course, since the conflict or hesitancy with which he is contending
may continue despite his decision. All a decision does is to create an
intention; it does not guarantee that the intention will be carried out.
This is not simply because the person can always change his mind.
Apart from inconstancy of that sort, it may be that energies tending
toward action inconsistent with the intention remain untamed and
undispersed, however decisively the person believes his mind has
been made up. The conflict the decision was supposed to supersede
may continue despite the person's conviction that he has resolved it.
In that case the decision, no matter how apparently conscientious and
sincere, is not wholehearted: Whether the person is aware of it or not,
he has other intentions, intentions incompatible with the one the decision established and to which he is also committed. This may become
evident when the chips are down and the person acts in a way ostensi-
bly precluded by the intention upon which he thought he had settled.

VII

But why are we interested in making up our minds at all? It might
seem that the point of deciding is to provide for the performance of
an action that would otherwise not be performed. Suppose I make up

my mind to show anger more openly the next time I am gratuitously insulted by an arrogant functionary. This might be thought of as establishing a connection, which did not previously exist, between insulting behavior of a certain kind and the sort of response upon which I have now decided – a connection such that the response will ensue if the provocation occurs. In fact, however, people often decide to do things which – whether they themselves realize it or not – they would do in any case. The connection between the provocation and the response, which the decision appears to establish, may already exist: I would have shown my anger openly even if I had not previously formed the intention to do so. The point of making up one's mind is not, accordingly, to ensure a certain action.

Nor is it to ensure that one will act well. That is the function of deliberation, which is designed to increase the likelihood that decisions will be good ones. Hobbes suggests that the word "deliberation" connotes an activity in which freedom is lost.[14] It is, after all, *deliberation*. This may seem paradoxical, since we customarily regard deliberation as paradigmatically connected to the exercise of autonomy. The difficulty disappears when we recognize that the liberty with which deliberation interferes is not that of the autonomous agent, but that of someone who blindly follows impulse – in other words, of the wanton. A person who is deliberating about what to do is seeking an alternative to "doing what comes naturally." His aim is to replace the liberty of anarchic impulsive behavior with the autonomy of being under his own control.

One thing a deliberate decision accomplishes, when it creates an intention, is to establish a constraint by which other preferences and decisions are to be guided. A person who decides what to believe provides himself with a criterion for other beliefs: Namely, they must be coherent with the belief upon which he has decided. And a person who makes a decision concerning what to do similarly adopts a rule for coordinating his activities to facilitate his eventual implementation of the decision he has made. It might be said, then, that a function of decision is to integrate the person both dynamically and statically. Dynamically, insofar as it provides – in the way I have just mentioned – for coherence and unity of purpose over time; statically, insofar as it establishes – in the way discussed earlier – a reflexive or hierarchical structure by which the person's identity may be in part constituted.

In both respects, the intent is at least partly to resolve conflict or to avoid it. This is not achieved by eliminating one or more of the con-

[14] *Leviathan*, Part I, Chapter 6: "And it is called *deliberation* because it is a putting an end to the *liberty* we had of doing, or omitting, according to our own appetite, or aversion."

flicting elements so that those remaining are harmonious, but by endorsing or identifying with certain elements which are then authoritative for the self. Of course, this authority may be resisted and even defeated by outlaw forces – desires or motives by which the person does not want to be effectively moved, but which are too strong and insistent to be constrained. It may also turn out that there is conflict within the authority itself – that the person has identified himself inconsistently. This is the issue of *wholeheartedness.*

Wholeheartedness, as I am using the term, does not consist in a feeling of enthusiasm, or of certainty, concerning a commitment. Nor is it likely to be readily apparent whether a decision which a person intends to be wholehearted is actually so. We do not know our hearts well enough to be confident whether our intention that nothing should interfere with a decision we make is one we ourselves will want carried out when – perhaps recognizing that the point of no return has been reached – we come to understand more completely what carrying it out would require us to do or to sacrifice doing.

In making up his mind a person establishes preferences concerning the resolution of conflicts among his desires or beliefs. Someone who makes a decision thereby performs an action, but the performance is not of a simple act that merely implements a first-order desire. It essentially involves reflexivity, including desires and volitions of a higher order. Thus, creatures who are incapable of this volitional reflexivity necessarily lack the capacity to make up their minds. They may desire and think and act, but they cannot decide. Insofar as we construe the making of decisions as the characteristic function of the faculty of volition, we must regard such creatures as lacking this faculty.

In "Freedom of the Will and the Concept of a Person" I asserted that being wanton does not preclude deliberation. My thought then was that although a creature might be wanton with respect to goals, he might nonetheless engage in calculation or reasoning about technical questions concerning how to get what he wantonly desires. But reasoning involves making decisions concerning what to think, which appear no less incompatible with thoroughgoing wantonness than deciding what one wants to do. Making a decision does seem different from figuring out how to implement it, but it is unclear that the latter activity can be accomplished without making up one's mind in ways structurally quite similar to those entailed in the former.

We are accustomed to thinking of our species as distinguished particularly by virtue of the faculty of reason. We tend to suppose that volition or will is a more primitive or a cruder faculty, which we share

with creatures of lesser psychic complexity. But this seems dubious
not only because of the reflexivity that volition itself requires, but also
to the extent that reasoning requires making up one's mind. For to
that extent the deliberate use of reason necessarily has a hierarchical
structure, requiring higher-order elements that are unavailable to a
genuine wanton. In this respect, then, reason depends upon will.

3

Sanity and the metaphysics of responsibility

SUSAN WOLF

Philosophers who study the problems of free will and responsibility have an easier time than most in meeting challenges about the relevance of their work to ordinary, practical concerns. Indeed, philosophers who study these problems are rarely faced with such challenges at all, since questions concerning the conditions of responsibility come up so obviously and so frequently in everyday life. Under scrutiny, however, one might question whether the connections between philosophical and nonphilosophical concerns in this area are real.

In everyday contexts, when lawyers, judges, parents, and others are concerned with issues of responsibility, they know, or think they know, what in general the conditions of responsibility are. Their questions are questions of application: Does this or that particular person meet this or that particular condition? Is this person mature enough, or informed enough, or sane enough to be responsible? Was he or she acting under posthypnotic suggestion or under the influence of a mind-impairing drug? It is assumed, in these contexts, that normal, fully developed adult human beings are responsible beings. The questions have to do with whether a given individual falls within the normal range.

By contrast, philosophers tend to be uncertain about the general conditions of responsibility, and they care less about dividing the responsible from the nonresponsible agents than about determining whether, and if so why, any of us are ever responsible for anything at all.

In the classroom, we might argue that the philosophical concerns grow out of the nonphilosophical ones, that they take off where the nonphilosophical questions stop. In this way, we might convince our students that even if they are not plagued by the philosophical worries, they ought to be. If they worry about whether a person is mature enough, informed enough, and sane enough to be responsible, then they should worry about whether that person is metaphysically free enough, too.

The argument I make here, however, goes in the opposite direction. My aim is not to convince people who are interested in the apparently nonphilosophical conditions of responsibility that they should go on to worry about the philosophical conditions as well, but rather to urge those who already worry about the philosophical problems not to leave the more mundane, prephilosophical problems behind. In particular, I suggest that the mundane recognition that *sanity* is a condition of responsibility has more to do with the murky and apparently metaphysical problems which surround the issue of responsibility than at first meets the eye. Once the significance of the condition of sanity is fully appreciated, at least some of the apparently insuperable metaphysical aspects of the problem of responsibility will dissolve.

My strategy is to examine a recent trend in philosophical discussions of responsibility, a trend that tries, but I think ultimately fails, to give an acceptable analysis of the conditions of responsibility. It fails due to what at first appear to be deep and irresolvable metaphysical problems. It is here that I suggest that the condition of sanity comes to the rescue. What at first appears to be an impossible requirement for responsibility – the requirement that the responsible agent have created her- or himself – turns out to be the vastly more mundane and noncontroversial requirement that the responsible agent must, in a fairly standard sense, be sane.

Frankfurt, Watson, and Taylor

The trend I have in mind is exemplified by the writings of Harry Frankfurt, Gary Watson, and Charles Taylor. I will briefly discuss each of their separate proposals, and then offer a composite view that, while lacking the subtlety of any of the separate accounts, will highlight some important insights and some important blind spots they share.

In his seminal article "Freedom of the Will and the Concept of a Person,"[1] Harry Frankfurt notes a distinction between freedom of action and freedom of the will. A person has freedom of action, he points out, if she (or he) has the freedom to do whatever she wills to do – the freedom to walk or sit, to vote liberal or conservative, to publish a book or open a store, in accordance with her strongest desires. Even a person who has freedom of action may fail to be

---

[1] Harry Frankfurt, "Freedom of the Will and the Concept of a Person," *Journal of Philosophy* LXVIII (1971), 5–20.

responsible for her actions, however, if the wants or desires she has
the freedom to convert into action are themselves not subject to her
control. Thus, the person who acts under posthypnotic suggestion,
the victim of brainwashing, and the kleptomaniac might all possess
freedom of action. In the standard contexts in which these examples
are raised, it is assumed that none of the individuals is locked up or
bound. Rather, these individuals are understood to act on what, at
one level at least, must be called *their own desires*. Their exemption
from responsibility stems from the fact that their own desires (or at
least the ones governing their actions) are not up to them. These cases
may be described in Frankfurt's terms as cases of people who possess
freedom of action, but who fail to be responsible agents because they
lack freedom of the will.

Philosophical problems about the conditions of responsibility naturally focus on an analysis of this latter kind of freedom: What *is*
freedom of the will, and under what conditions can we reasonably be
thought to possess it? Frankfurt's proposal is to understand freedom
of the will by analogy to freedom of action. As freedom of action is the
freedom to do whatever one wills to do, freedom of the will is the
freedom to will whatever one wants to will. To make this point clearer, Frankfurt introduces a distinction between first-order and second-
order desires. First-order desires are desires to do or to have various
things; second-order desires are desires about what desires to have or
what desires to make effective in action. In order for an agent to have
both freedom of action and freedom of the will, that agent must be
capable of governing his or her actions by first-order desires *and*
capable of governing his or her first-order desires by second-order
desires.

Gary Watson's view of free agency[2] – free and responsible agency,
that is – is similar to Frankfurt's in holding that an agent is responsible for an action only if the desires expressed by that action are of a
particular kind. While Frankfurt identifies the right kind of desires as
desires that are supported by second-order desires, however, Watson
draws a distinction between "mere" desires, so to speak, and desires
that are *values*. According to Watson, the difference between free
action and unfree action cannot be analyzed by reference to the logical form of the desires from which these various actions arise, but
rather must relate to a difference in the quality of their source.
Whereas some of my desires are just appetites or conditioned responses I find myself "stuck with," others are expressions of judg-

[2] Gary Watson, "Free Agency," *Journal of Philosophy* LXXII (1975), 205–20.

ments on my part that the objects I desire are good. Insofar as my actions can be governed by the latter type of desire – governed, that is, by my values or valuational system – they are actions that I perform freely and for which I am responsible.

Frankfurt's and Watson's accounts may be understood as alternate developments of the intuition that in order to be responsible for one's actions, one must be responsible for the self that performs these actions. Charles Taylor, in an article entitled "Responsibility for Self,"[3] is concerned with the same intuition. Although Taylor does not describe his view in terms of different levels or types of desire, his view is related, for he claims that our freedom and responsibility depends on our ability to reflect on, criticize, and revise our selves. Like Frankfurt and Watson, Taylor seems to believe that if the characters from which our actions flowed were simply and permanently *given* to us, implanted by heredity, environment, or God, then we would be mere vehicles through which the causal forces of the world traveled, no more responsible than dumb animals or young children or machines. But like the others, he points out that, for most of us, our characters and desires are not so brutely implanted – or, at any rate, if they are, they are subject to revision by our own reflecting, valuing, or second-order desiring selves. We human beings – and as far as we know, only we human beings – have the ability to step back from ourselves and decide whether we are the selves we want to be. Because of this, these philosophers think, we are responsible for our selves and for the actions that we produce.

Although there are subtle and interesting differences among the accounts of Frankfurt, Watson, and Taylor, my concern is with features of their views that are common to them all. All share the idea that responsible agency involves something more than intentional agency. All agree that if we are responsible agents, it is not just because our actions are within the control of our wills, but because, in addition, our wills are not just psychological states *in* us, but expressions of characters that come *from* us, or that at any rate are acknowledged and affirmed *by* us. For Frankfurt, this means that our wills must be ruled by our second-order desires; for Watson, that our wills must be governable by our system of values; for Taylor, that our wills must issue from selves that are subject to self-assessment and redefinition in terms of a vocabulary of worth. In one way or another, all these philosophers seem to be saying that the key to responsibility

---

[3] Charles Taylor, "Responsibility for Self," in A. E. Rorty, ed., *The Identities of Persons* (Berkeley: University of California Press, 1976), pp. 281–99.

lies in the fact that responsible agents are those for whom it is not just the case that their actions are within the control of their wills, but also the case that their wills are within the control of their *selves* in some deeper sense. Because, at one level, the differences among Frankfurt, Watson, and Taylor may be understood as differences in the analysis or interpretation of what it is for an action to be under the control of this deeper self, we may speak of their separate positions as variations of one basic view about responsibility: the *deep-self view*.

The deep-self view

Much more must be said about the notion of a deep self before a fully satisfactory account of this view can be given. Providing a careful, detailed analysis of that notion poses an interesting, important, and difficult task in its own right. The degree of understanding achieved by abstraction from the views of Frankfurt, Watson, and Taylor, however, should be sufficient to allow us to recognize some important virtues as well as some important drawbacks of the deep-self view.

One virtue is that this view explains a good portion of our pre-theoretical intuitions about responsibility. It explains why kleptomaniacs, victims of brainwashing, and people acting under posthypnotic suggestion may not be responsible for their actions, although most of us typically are. In the cases of people in these special categories, the connection between the agents' deep selves and their wills is dramatically severed – their wills are governed not by their deep selves, but by forces external to and independent from them. A different intuition is that we adult human beings can be responsible for our actions in a way that dumb animals, infants, and machines cannot. Here the explanation is not in terms of a split between these beings' deep selves and their wills; rather, the point is that these beings *lack* deep selves altogether. Kleptomaniacs and victims of hypnosis exemplify individuals whose selves are *alienated* from their actions; lower animals and machines, on the other hand, do not have the sorts of selves from which actions *can* be alienated, and so they do not have the sort of selves from which, in the happier cases, actions can responsibly flow.

At a more theoretical level, the deep-self view has another virtue: It responds to at least one way in which the fear of determinism presents itself.

A naive reaction to the idea that everything we do is completely determined by a causal chain that extends backward beyond the times of our births involves thinking that in that case we would have no control over our behavior whatsoever. If everything is determined, it is thought, then what happens happens, whether we want it to or not. A common, and proper, response to this concern points out that determinism does not deny the causal efficacy an agent's desires might have on his or her behavior. On the contrary, determinism in its more plausible forms tends to affirm this connection, merely adding that as one's behavior is determined by one's desires, so one's desires are determined by something else.[4]

Those who were initially worried that determinism implied fatalism, however, are apt to find their fears merely transformed rather than erased. If our desires are governed by something else, they might say, they are not *really* ours after all – or, at any rate, they are ours in only a superficial sense.

The deep-self view offers an answer to this transformed fear of determinism, for it allows us to distinguish cases in which desires are determined by forces foreign to oneself from desires which are determined *by* one's self – by one's "real," or second-order desiring, or valuing, or deep self, that is. Admittedly, there are cases, like that of the kleptomaniac or the victim of hypnosis, in which the agent acts on desires that "belong to" him or her in only a superficial sense. But the proponent of the deep-self view will point out that even if determinism is true, ordinary adult human action can be distinguished from this. Determinism implies that the desires which govern our actions are in turn governed by something else, but that something else will, in the fortunate cases, be our own deeper selves.

This account of responsibility thus offers a response to our fear of determinism; but it is a response with which many will remain unsatisfied. Even if my actions are governed by my desires and my desires are governed by my own deeper self, there remains the question: Who, or what, is responsible for this deeper self? The response above seems only to have pushed the problem further back.

Admittedly, some versions of the deep-self view, including Frankfurt's and Taylor's, seem to anticipate this question by providing a place for the ideal that an agent's deep self may be governed by a still deeper self. Thus, for Frankfurt, second-order desires may themselves be governed by third-order desires, third-order desires by fourth-order desires, and so on. Also, Taylor points out that, as we can reflect on and evaluate our prereflective selves, so we can reflect on and evaluate the selves who are doing the first reflecting and

[4] See, e.g., David Hume, *A Treatise of Human Nature* (Oxford: Oxford University Press, 1967), pp. 399–406, and R. E. Hobart, "Free Will as Involving Determination and Inconceivable Without It," *Mind* 43 (1934).

evaluating, and so on. However, this capacity to recursively create endless levels of depth ultimately misses the criticism's point.

First of all, even if there is no *logical* limit to the number of levels of reflection or depth a person may have, there is certainly a psychological limit – it is virtually impossible imaginatively to conceive a fourth-, much less an eighth-order, desire. More important, no matter how many levels of self we posit, there will still, in any individual case, be a last level – a deepest self about whom the question "What governs it?" will arise, as problematic as ever. If determinism is true, it implies that even if my actions are governed by my desires, and my desires are governed by my deepest self, my deepest self will still be governed by something that must, logically, be external to myself altogether. Though I can step back from the values my parents and teachers have given me and ask whether these are the values I really want, the "I" that steps back will itself be a product of the parents and teachers I am questioning.

The problem seems even worse when one sees that one fares no better if determinism is false. For if my deepest self is not determined by something external to myself, it will still not be determined by *me*. Whether I am a product of carefully controlled forces or a result of random mutations, whether there is a complete explanation of my origin or no explanation at all, *I* am not, in any case, responsible for my existence; I am not in control of my deepest self.

Thus, though the claim that an agent is responsible for only those actions that are within the control of his or her deep self correctly identifies a necessary condition for responsibility – a condition that separates the hypnotized and the brainwashed, the immature and the lower animals from ourselves, for example – it fails to provide a sufficient condition of responsibility that puts all fears of determinism to rest. For one of the fears invoked by the thought of determinism seems to be connected to its implication that we are but intermediate links in a causal chain, rather than ultimate, self-initiating sources of movement and change. From the point of view of one who has this fear, the deep-self view seems merely to add loops to the chain, complicating the picture but not really improving it. From the point of view of one who has this fear, responsibility seems to require being a prime mover unmoved, whose deepest self is itself neither random *nor* externally determined, but is rather determined *by* itself – who is, in other words, self-created.

At this point, however, proponents of the deep-self view may wonder whether this fear is legitimate. For although people evidently can be brought to the point where they feel that responsible agency requires them to be ultimate sources of power, to the point where it seems that nothing short of self-creation will do, a return to the internal standpoint of the agent whose responsibility is in question makes it hard to see what good this metaphysical status is supposed to provide or what evil its absence is supposed to impose.

From the external standpoint, which discussions of determinism and indeterminism encourage us to take up, it may appear that a special metaphysical status is required to distinguish us significantly from other members of the natural world. But proponents of the deep-self view will suggest this is an illusion that a return to the internal standpoint should dispel. The possession of a deep self that is effective in governing one's actions is a sufficient distinction, they will say. For while other members of the natural world are not in control of the selves that they are, we, possessors of effective deep selves, are in control. We can reflect on what sorts of beings we are, and on what sorts of marks we make on the world. We can change what we don't like about ourselves, and keep what we do. Admittedly, we do not create ourselves from nothing. But as long as we can revise ourselves, they will suggest, it is hard to find reason to complain. Harry Frankfurt writes that a person who is free to do what he wants to do and also free to want what he wants to want has "all the freedom it is possible to desire or to conceive."[5] This suggests a rhetorical question: If you are free to control your actions by your desires, and free to control your desires by your deeper desires, and free to control those desires by still deeper desires, what further kind of freedom can you want?

The condition of sanity

Unfortunately, there is a further kind of freedom we can want, which it is reasonable to think necessary for responsible agency. The deep-self view fails to be convincing when it is offered as a complete account of the conditions of responsibility. To see why, it will be helpful to consider another example of an agent whose responsibility is in question.

JoJo is the favorite son of Jo the First, an evil and sadistic dictator of a small, undeveloped country. Because of his father's special feelings for the boy, JoJo is given a special education and is allowed to accompany his father and observe his daily routine. In light of this treatment, it is not surprising that little JoJo takes his father as a role model and develops values very much like Dad's. As an adult, he does

5 Frankfurt, p. 16.

many of the same sorts of things his father did, including sending people to prison or to death or to torture chambers on the basis of whim. He is not *coerced* to do these things, he acts according to his own desires. Moreover, these are desires he wholly *wants* to have. When he steps back and asks, "Do I really want to be this sort of person?" his answer is resoundingly "Yes," for this way of life expresses a crazy sort of power that forms part of his deepest ideal.

In light of JoJo's heritage and upbringing – both of which he was powerless to control – it is dubious at best that he should be regarded as responsible for what he does. It is unclear whether anyone with a childhood such as his could have developed into anything but the twisted and perverse sort of person that he has become. However, note that JoJo is someone whose actions are controlled by his desires and whose desires are the desires he wants to have: That is, his actions are governed by desires that are governed by and expressive of his deepest self.

The Frankfurt–Watson–Taylor strategy that allowed us to differentiate our normal selves from the victims of hypnosis and brainwashing will not allow us to differentiate ourselves from the son of Jo the First. In the case of these earlier victims, we were able to say that although the actions of these individuals were, at one level, in control of the individuals themselves, these individuals themselves, qua agents, were not the selves they more deeply wanted to be. In this respect, these people were unlike our happily more integrated selves. However, we cannot say of JoJo that his self, qua agent, is not the self he wants it to be. It *is* the self he wants it to be. From the inside, he feels as integrated, free, and responsible as we do.

Our judgment that JoJo is not a responsible agent is one that we can make only from the outside – from reflecting on the fact, it seems, that his deepest self is not up to him. Looked at from the outside, however, our situation seems no different from his – for in the last analysis, it is not up to any of us to have the deepest selves we do. Once more, the problem seems metaphysical – and not just metaphysical, but insuperable. For, as I mentioned before, the problem is independent of the truth of determinism. Whether we are determined or undetermined, we cannot have created our deepest selves. Literal self-creation is not just empirically, but logically impossible.

If JoJo is not responsible because his deepest self is not up to him, then we are not responsible either. Indeed, in that case responsibility would be impossible for anyone to achieve. But I believe the appearance that literal self-creation is required for freedom and responsibility is itself mistaken.

The deep-self view was right in pointing out that freedom and responsibility requires us to have certain distinctive types of control over our behavior and our selves. Specifically, our actions need to be under the control of our selves, and our (superficial) selves need to be under the control of our deep selves. Having seen that these types of control are not enough to guarantee us the status of responsible agents, we are tempted to go on to suppose that we must have yet another kind of control to assure us that even our deepest selves are somehow up to us. But not all the things necessary for freedom and responsibility must be types of power and control. We may need simply to *be* a certain way, even though it is not within our power to determine whether we are that way or not.

Indeed, it becomes obvious that at least one condition of responsibility is of this form as soon as we remember what, in everyday contexts, we have known all along – namely, that in order to be responsible, an agent must be *sane*. It is not ordinarily in our power to determine whether we are or are not sane. Most of us, it would seem, are lucky, but some of us are not. Moreover, being sane does not necessarily mean that one has any type of power or control an insane person lacks. Some insane people, like JoJo and some actual political leaders who resemble him, may have complete control of their actions, and even complete control of their acting selves. The desire to be sane is thus not a desire for another form of control; it is rather a desire that one's self be connected to the world in a certain way – we could even say it is a desire that one's self be *controlled by* the world in certain ways and not in others.

This becomes clear if we attend to the criteria for sanity that have historically been dominant in legal questions about responsibility. According to the M'Naughten Rule, a person is sane if (1) he knows what he is doing and (2) he knows that what he is doing is, as the case may be, right or wrong. Insofar as one's desire to be sane involves a desire to know what one is doing – or more generally, a desire to live in the real world – it is a desire to be controlled (to have, in this case, one's *beliefs* controlled) by perceptions and sound reasoning that produce an accurate conception of the world, rather than by blind or distorted forms of response. The same goes for the second constituent of sanity – only, in this case, one's hope is that one's *values* be controlled by processes that afford an accurate conception of the world.[6] Putting

---

[6] Strictly speaking, perception and sound reasoning may not be enough to ensure the ability to achieve an accurate conception of what one is doing and especially to achieve a reasonable normative assessment of one's situation. Sensitivity and exposure to certain realms of experience may also be necessary for these goals. For the purpose of this essay, I understand "sanity" to include whatever it takes to enable one to develop an adequate conception of one's world. In other contexts, however, this would be an implausibly broad construction of the term.

these two conditions together, we may understand sanity, then, as the minimally sufficient ability cognitively and normatively to recognize and appreciate the world for what it is.

There are problems with this definition of sanity, at least some of which will become obvious in what follows, that make it ultimately unacceptable either as a gloss on or an improvement of the meaning of the term in many of the contexts in which it is used. The definition offered does seem to bring out the interest sanity has for us in connection with issues of responsibility, however, and some pedagogical as well as stylistic purposes will be served if we use sanity hereafter in this admittedly specialized sense.

The sane deep-self view

So far I have argued that the conditions of responsible agency offered by the deep-self view are necessary but not sufficient. Moreover, the gap left open by the deep-self view seems to be one that can be filled only by a metaphysical, and, as it happens, metaphysically impossible addition. I now wish to argue, however, that the condition of sanity, as characterized above, is sufficient to fill the gap. In other words, the deep-self view, supplemented by the condition of sanity, provides a satisfying conception of responsibility. The conception of responsibility I am proposing, then, agrees with the deep-self view in requiring that a responsible agent be able to govern her (or his) actions by her desires and to govern her desires by her deep self. In addition, my conception insists that the agent's deep self be sane, and claims that this is *all* that is needed for responsible agency. By contrast to the plain deep-self view, let us call this new proposal the *sane deep-self view*.

It is worth noting, to begin with, that this new proposal deals with the case of JoJo and related cases of deprived childhood victims in ways that better match our pretheoretical intuitions. Unlike the plain deep-self view, the sane deep-self view offers a way of explaining why JoJo is not responsible for his actions without throwing our own responsibility into doubt. For, although like us, JoJo's actions flow from desires that flow from his deep self, unlike us, JoJo's deep self is itself insane. Sanity, remember, involves the ability to know the difference between right and wrong, and a person who, even on reflection, cannot see that having someone tortured because he failed to salute you is wrong plainly lacks the requisite ability.

Less obviously, but quite analogously, this new proposal explains why we give less than full responsibility to persons who, though acting badly, act in ways that are strongly encouraged by their societies – the slaveowners of the 1850s, the Nazis of the 1930s, and many male chauvinists of our fathers' generation, for example. These are people, we imagine, who falsely believe that the ways in which they are acting are morally acceptable, and so, we may assume, their behavior is expressive of or at least in accordance with these agents' deep selves. But their false beliefs in the moral permissibility of their actions and the false values from which these beliefs derived may have been inevitable, given the social circumstances in which they developed. If we think that the agents could not help but be mistaken about their values, we do not blame them for the actions those values inspired.[7]

It would unduly distort ordinary linguistic practice to call the slaveowner, the Nazi, or the male chauvinist even partially or locally insane. Nonetheless, the reason for withholding blame from them is at bottom the same as the reason for withholding it from JoJo. Like JoJo, they are, at the deepest level, unable cognitively and normatively to recognize and appreciate the world for what it is. In our sense of the term, their deepest selves are not fully *sane*.

The sane deep-self view thus offers an account of why victims of deprived childhoods as well as victims of misguided societies may not be responsible for their actions, without implying that we are not responsible for ours. The actions of these others are governed by mistaken conceptions of value that the agents in question cannot help but have. Since, as far as we know, our values are not, like theirs, unavoidably mistaken, the fact that these others are not responsible for their actions need not force us to conclude that we are not responsible for ours.

But it may not yet be clear why sanity, in this special sense, should make such a difference – why, in particular, the question of whether someone's values are unavoidably *mistaken* should have any bearing on their status as responsible agents. The fact that the sane deep-self view implies judgments that match our intuitions about the difference in status between characters like JoJo and ourselves provides little support for it if it cannot also defend these intuitions. So we must consider an objection that comes from the point of view we considered earlier which rejects the intuition that a relevant difference can be found.

Earlier, it seemed that the reason JoJo was not responsible for his

---

[7] Admittedly, it is open to question whether these individuals were in fact unable to help having mistaken values, and indeed, whether recognizing the errors of their society would even have required exceptional independence or strength of mind. This is presumably an empirical question, the answer to which is extraordinarily hard to determine. My point here is simply that *if* we believe they are unable to recognize that their values are mistaken, we do not hold them responsible for the actions that flow from these values, and *if* we believe their ability to recognize their normative errors is impaired, we hold them less than fully responsible for the relevant actions.

actions was that although his actions were governed by his deep self, his deep self was not up to him. But this had nothing to do with his deep self's being mistaken or not mistaken, evil or good, insane or sane. If JoJo's values are unavoidably mistaken, our values, even if not mistaken, appear to be just as unavoidable. When it comes to freedom and responsibility, isn't it the unavoidability, rather than the mistakenness, that matters?

Before answering this question, it is useful to point out a way in which it is ambiguous: The concepts of avoidability and mistakenness are not unequivocally distinct. One may, to be sure, construe the notion of avoidability in a purely metaphysical way. Whether an event or state of affairs is unavoidable under this construal depends, as it were, on the tightness of the causal connections that bear on the event's or state of affairs' coming about. In this sense, our deep selves do seem as unavoidable for us as JoJo's and the others' are for them. For presumably we are just as influenced by our parents, our cultures, and our schooling as they are influenced by theirs. In another sense, however, our characters are not similarly unavoidable.

In particular, in the cases of JoJo and the others, there are certain features of their characters that they cannot avoid *even though these features are seriously mistaken, misguided, or bad.* This is so because, in our special sense of the term, these characters are less than fully sane. Since these characters lack the ability to know right from wrong, they are unable to revise their characters on the basis of right and wrong, and so their deep selves lack the resources and the reasons that might have served as a basis for self-correction. Since the deep selves *we* unavoidably have, however, are sane deep selves – deep selves, that is, that unavoidably *contain* the ability to know right from wrong – we unavoidably do have the resources and reasons on which to base self-correction. What this means is that though in one sense we are no more in control of our deepest selves than JoJo et al., it does not follow in our case, as it does in theirs, that we would be the way we are, even if it is a bad or wrong way to be. However, if this does not follow, it seems to me, our absence of control at the deepest level should not upset us.

Consider what the absence of control at the deepest level amounts to for us: Whereas JoJo is unable to control the fact that, at the deepest level, he is not fully sane, we are not responsible for the fact that, at the deepest level, we are. It is not up to us to *have* minimally sufficient abilities cognitively and normatively to recognize and appreciate the world for what it is. Also, presumably, it is not up to us to have lots of other properties, at least to begin with – a fondness for purple, perhaps, or an antipathy for beets. As the proponents of the plain deep-self view have been at pains to point out, however, we do, if we are lucky, have the ability to revise our selves in terms of the values that are held by or constitutive of our deep selves. If we are lucky enough both to have this ability and to have our deep selves be sane, it follows that although there is much in our characters that we did not choose to have, there is nothing irrational or objectionable in our characters that we are compelled to keep.

Being sane, we are able to understand and evaluate our characters in a reasonable way, to notice what there is reason to hold on to, what there is reason to eliminate, and what, from a rational and reasonable standpoint, we may retain or get rid of as we please. Being able as well to govern our superficial selves by our deep selves, then, we are able to change the things we find there is reason to change. This being so, it seems that although we may not be *metaphysically* responsible for ourselves – for, after all, we did not create ourselves from nothing – we are *morally* responsible for ourselves, for we are able to understand and appreciate right and wrong, and to change our characters and our actions accordingly.

Self-creation, self-revision, and self-correction

At the beginning of this chapter, I claimed that recalling that sanity was a condition of responsibility would dissolve at least some of the appearance that responsibility was metaphysically impossible. To see how this is so, and to get a fuller sense of the sane deep-self view, it may be helpful to put that view into perspective by comparing it to the other views we have discussed along the way.

As Frankfurt, Watson, and Taylor showed us, in order to be free and responsible we need not only to be able to control our actions in accordance with our desires, we need to be able to control our desires in accordance with our deepest selves. We need, in other words, to be able to *revise* ourselves – to get rid of some desires and traits, and perhaps replace them with others on the basis of our deeper desires or values or reflections. However, consideration of the fact that the selves who are doing the revising might themselves be either brute products of external forces or arbitrary outputs of random generation made us wonder whether the capacity for self-revision was enough to assure us of responsibility – and the example of JoJo added force to the suspicion that it was not. Still, if the ability to revise ourselves is not enough, the ability to create ourselves does not seem necessary either. Indeed, when you think of it, it is unclear why any-

one should want self-creation. Why should anyone be disappointed at
having to accept the idea that one has to get one's start somewhere? It
is an idea that most of us have lived with quite contentedly all along.
What we do have reason to want, then, is something more than the
ability to revise ourselves, but less than the ability to create ourselves.
Implicit in the sane deep-self view is the idea that what is needed is the
ability to *correct* (or improve) ourselves.

Recognizing that in order to be responsible for our actions, we have
to be responsible for our selves, the sane deep-self view analyzes what
is necessary in order to be responsible for our selves as (1) the ability
to evaluate ourselves sensibly and accurately, and (2) the ability to
transform ourselves insofar as our evaluation tells us to do so. We may
understand the exercise of these abilities as a process where by we *take*
responsibility for the selves that we are but did not ultimately create.
The condition of sanity is intrinsically connected to the first ability;
the condition that we be able to control our superficial selves by our
deep selves is intrinsically connected to the second.

The difference between the plain deep-self view and the sane deep-
self view, then, is the difference between the requirement of the capacity for self-revision and the requirement of the capacity for self-
correction. Anyone with the first capacity can *try* to take responsibility
for himself or herself. However, only someone with a sane deep self –
a deep self that can see and appreciate the world for what it is – can
self-evaluate sensibly and accurately. Therefore, although insane
selves can try to take responsibility for themselves, only sane selves
will properly be accorded responsibility.

Two objections considered

At least two problems with the sane deep-self view are so glaring as to
have certainly struck many readers. In closing, I shall briefly address
them. First, some will be wondering how, in light of my specialized
use of the term "sanity," I can be so sure that "we" are any saner than
the nonresponsible individuals I have discussed. What justifies my
confidence that, unlike the slaveowners, Nazis, and male chauvinists,
not to mention JoJo himself, we are able to understand and appreciate the world for what it is? The answer to this is that nothing justifies
this except widespread intersubjective agreement and the considerable success we have in getting around in the world and satisfying our
needs. These are not sufficient grounds for the smug assumption that
we are in a position to see the truth about *all* aspects of ethical and
social life. Indeed, it seems more reasonable to expect that time will

reveal blind spots in our cognitive and normative outlook, just as it has revealed errors in the outlooks of those who have lived before. But our judgments of responsibility can only be made from here, on the basis of the understandings and values that we can develop by exercising the abilities we do possess as well and as fully as possible.

If some have been worried that my view implicitly expresses an overconfidence in the assumption that we are sane and therefore right about the world, others will be worried that my view too closely connects sanity with being right about the world, and fear that my view implies that anyone who acts wrongly or has false beliefs about the world is therefore insane and so not responsible for his or her actions. This seems to me to be a more serious worry, which I am sure I cannot answer to everyone's satisfaction.

First, it must be admitted that the sane deep-self view embraces a conception of sanity that is explicitly normative. But this seems to me a strength of that view, rather than a defect. Sanity *is* a normative concept, in its ordinary as well as in its specialized sense, and severely deviant behavior, such as that of a serial murderer or a sadistic dictator, does constitute evidence of a psychological defect in the agent. The suggestion that the most horrendous, stomach-turning crimes could be committed only by an insane person – an inverse of Catch-22, as it were – must be regarded as a serious possibility, despite the practical problems that would accompany general acceptance of that conclusion.

But, it will be objected, there is no justification, in the sane deep-self view, for regarding only horrendous and stomach-turning crimes as evidence of insanity in its specialized sense. If sanity is the ability cognitively and normatively to understand and appreciate the world for what it is, then *any* wrong action or false belief will count as evidence of the absence of that ability. This point may also be granted, but we must be careful about what conclusion to draw. To be sure, when someone acts in a way that is not in accordance with acceptable standards of rationality and reasonableness, it is always appropriate to look for an explanation of why he or she acted that way. The hypothesis that the person was unable to understand and appreciate that an action fell outside acceptable bounds will always be a possible explanation. Bad performance on a math test always suggests the possibility that the testee is stupid. Typically, however, other explanations will be possible, too – for example, that the agent was too lazy to consider whether his or her action was acceptable, or too greedy to care, or, in the case of the math testee, that he or she was too occupied with other interests to attend class or study. Other facts about the agent's history will help us decide among these hypotheses.

This brings out the need to emphasize that sanity, in the specialized sense, is defined as the *ability* cognitively and normatively to understand and appreciate the world for what it is. According to our commonsense understandings, having this ability is one thing and exercising it is another – at least some wrong-acting, responsible agents presumably fall within the gap. The notion of "ability" is notoriously problematic, however, and there is a long history of controversy about whether the truth of determinism would show our ordinary ways of thinking to be simply confused on this matter. At this point, then, metaphysical concerns may voice themselves again – but at least they will have been pushed into a narrower, and perhaps a more manageable, corner.

The sane deep-self view does not, then, solve all the philosophical problems connected to the topics of free will and responsibility. If anything, it highlights some of the practical and empirical problems, rather than solves them. It may, however, resolve some of the philosophical, and particularly, some of the metaphysical problems, and reveal how intimate are the connections between the remaining philosophical problems and the practical ones.

4

Unfreedom and responsibility

PATRICIA GREENSPAN

In what follows, I want to examine a case of action out of rage, where the agent seems to be unfree and yet responsible – at least on widespread views of responsibility, stressing the relation between an act and the agent's "character" (in some sense). Often these views, or variants of them, are reflected in compatibilists' suggestions for understanding *freedom* – or at any rate, that sort of freedom that entails responsibility.[1] They also have been represented as yielding an alternative account of other apparent cases of responsibility without freedom – where freedom is assumed, as it is (especially) by *in*compatibilists, to involve the ability to do otherwise.[2] However, I shall argue that the proposals fail to capture our intuitions on my own case, except as applied to a limited notion of responsibility – one on which it does not entail *freedom*. I shall give freedom a somewhat different interpretation, along lines I have indicated elsewhere.[3] The essential condition of freedom, on this view, is that it be *reasonable to expect* the agent to do otherwise; but it also implies that alternative action is not too much to *require* of the agent, under the circumstances. It therefore has some normative content – and I shall go on to argue that it seems to be quite pervasively normative when spelled out further in application to

For helpful discussion of my initial treatment of the main case in this paper, I owe thanks to Ferdinand Schoeman and Michael Slote.
[1] See esp. Harry G. Frankfurt, "Freedom of the Will and the Concept of a Person," *Journal of Philosophy*, LXVIII (January 14, 1971), 5–20, and "Coercion and Moral Responsibility," in T. Honderich (ed.), *Essays on Freedom of Action* (London: Routledge & Kegan Paul, 1973), pp. 63–86; see also Wright Neely, "Freedom and Desire," *Philosophical Review*, LXXXIII (January 1974), 32–54; Gary Watson, "Free Agency," *Journal of Philosophy*, LXXII (April 24, 1975), 205–20; and Michael A. Slote, "Understanding Free Will," *Journal of Philosophy*, LXXVII (March 1980), 136–51.
[2] See esp. Frankfurt, "Alternate Possibilities and Moral Responsibility," *Journal of Philosophy*, XLVI (December 1969), 329–39; cf. John Martin Fischer, "Responsibility and Control," *Journal of Philosophy*, LXXIX (January 1982), 24–40.
[3] See "Behavior Control and Freedom of Action," *Philosophical Review*, LXXXVII (April 1978), esp. p. 233. The article is reprinted in J. M. Fischer (ed.), *Moral Responsibility* (Ithaca, NY: Cornell University Press, 1986).

my case – but "control" (or some related property) may be thought of as representing the *factual core* of this rough notion of freedom.[4]

Even as so far described, however, the notion suggests one sort of *responsibility*. Calling someone free, on the view I shall defend here, amounts to a claim about the reasonableness of making certain practical *demands* on that person. The demands are oriented toward future action – an action the person is held responsible for performing *later* – so when we endorse them as reasonable, we might be thought of as ascribing responsibility "before-the-fact." This contrasts with the ascription of responsibility "after-the-fact," taken as imputing *fault*, and as indicating the reasonableness of blame, punishment, demands for reform or restitution, and similar responses to an action the agent is held responsible for *already having* performed. The distinction may sound more familiar if it is expressed in terms of "forward-looking" and "backward-looking" *judgments* of responsibility; but its application will not always depend on the temporal standpoint from which such a judgment is made. Even where we ascribe responsibility in advance of some wrong action, for instance, *what* we ascribe may be thought of as emerging with the action – and as compatible with the agent's failure to satisfy some earlier conditions of full-blown responsibility. In effect, then, if my argument succeeds, it should isolate an element of full-blown responsibility that is often ignored in current discussions of freedom. It may also suggest a way of recasting the problem of freedom and determinism. But I shall not draw any metaphysical morals here; instead, my discussion will proceed by way of detailed spadework, mainly exploratory, on the case of action out of rage.

Responsibility without freedom

My case is a fairly simple one, though I shall complicate it, and construct a number of variants on it, as I proceed. Initially, just suppose that *X*, in a state of intense anger at an insult, throws a punch at the source of the insult. The question is: Was *X*'s action free? Another question is: Was *X* free with respect to this action at the time when he performed it? Further subquestions might be disentangled; but I shall myself feel free, for the sake of naturalness of idiom, to treat them as more or less equivalent in most of my discussion, abandoning idiom

---

[4] See Daniel C. Dennett, *Elbow Room: The Varieties of Free Will Worth Wanting* (Cambridge, MA: MIT Press, 1984), esp. chap. 3; cf. my review of Dennett in *Philosophical Review*, XCV (April 1986), 257–61. Despite many objections to Dennett's detailed discussion, I was greatly influenced by it in my choice of general topics and questions here; see notes 6 and 11.

only where a distinction seems to make a difference. The second question does a better job of exhibiting our focus on the agent (as needed for a direct comparison of freedom with responsibility), along with the time at which the agent acted (as needed for reasons to emerge below). However, on an appropriate understanding of either question, the answer might well be "No" – that X "could not help himself," given the state he was in, whether or not he really should have been in it.

Our answer also requires some clarification, though, in light of various further distinctions, on the nature of motivational *un*freedom. First of all, unless we take a rather simpleminded view of emotion as *causing* action, "the" action with respect to which X was unfree may sometimes have to be described a bit more broadly, covering other possibilities besides the one that was realized.[5] For it is not clear that X, even in a state of "overpowering" anger, could satisfy his anger *only* by throwing a punch. Attacking the source of the insult with a knife, say, might have been at least as satisfying; and we might suppose that a knife was readily available. It is not that X did not *know* of this alternative, let us grant. Though there are epistemic conditions on freedom, some of which will be brought in later, this case is meant to center on a loss of *control*. Nor do we want, then, to say that X simply failed to think of any alternatives to throwing a punch. What we want to say is that he *could* not think of any – at any rate, in time to affect his action – or that, strictly speaking, he was unfree only with respect to a more inclusive action, punching-or-stabbing.

The first interpretation might well be defended for a "pressuring" emotion like anger, in a case where it is intense enough to affect the agent's ability to deliberate, or to postpone action until after deliberation. Perhaps X was so "blinded" by rage, for instance, that he could not think *beyond* the first action that occurred to him. Or perhaps he had to *act* on that first thought, given the "urgency" of his need to discharge anger. For that matter, we might suppose that, because of his moral upbringing, rather than his rage, stabbing someone was "unthinkable," in some fairly strong sense, for X at the time of action. This might be interpreted along either of the two lines sketched just above – as a claim that stabbing was viewed by X as too horrible even to contemplate as an option in these circumstances; or as a claim that, if it did come to mind, an emotional reaction would force X to turn it

---

[5] For a fuller treatment of emotional motivation, which I hope will answer at least some of the many questions left open here, see my *Emotions and Reasons: An Inquiry into Emotional Justification* (New York: Routledge & Kegan Paul, forthcoming), esp. chap. 6.

down. Here X would be seen as pressured by some emotion other than *anger* – a moral variant of fear, perhaps, or repugnance; or perhaps some combination of the two – but compounding this with anger would serve to narrow X's options in response to the insult. In some versions of the case, however, X might have exercised a degree of dispassionate moral judgment, even in the heat of anger, so that throwing a punch would count as an action based partly on deliberation, however hasty or habitual; but we should also note that this is not incompatible with a claim that X's action was unfree – under some description. Our intuitions would naturally focus on the narrower description that picks out the action we see X as having done; but more precisely, as the case is currently described, we should say that what X "had" to do was to "lash out" at the other party in some way or other – in some *physical* way, let us suppose, given some further assumptions about the case.

Further assumptions are necessary in order to explain why x turned down various less extreme alternatives. There are other ways of discharging anger, at least when the emotion is less extreme. We often can content ourselves with aggressive verbal action (an insult in return, say), or mental action (a fantasized punch); or physical action either undirected or directed at some fantasy-object (pounding the table, with or without a thought of punching the source of the insult, or someone else). Even if anger *limits* our freedom, then – in the sense of limiting us to these (or similar) options, along with physical aggression, as ways of relieving emotional pressure – it usually leaves us some degree of choice. Why should we say that the extreme case, the case of *intense* anger, or rage, is any different, at least in general form? We might grant that the agent still *has* all these options, that is, while allowing that he also has a more intense need to choose one of them – not some particular one, but one-or-another. In that case, it seems, the agent would be no more unfree that the rest of us, with respect to the particular option he chooses, but only with respect to this *range* of options for discharging anger. Doing nothing – simply putting up with emotional pressure – represents a further option for us, but not for him. So X is unable to control his anger completely; but it might not be strictly true to say, with respect to his physical attack on the source of the insult, that he "cannot help himself."

To move toward an adequate account of X's case, though, we must also ask what we mean by the various modal expressions underlying our admission that rage does make him unfree, even if only in this broad sense. He cannot restrain himself from expressing anger *somehow* – I take it that we do want to make at least this rather weak claim

– but what does "cannot" mean here? If the difference between his anger and ours is a matter of degree – of intensity of affect, in the first instance – it would seem that we ought to take the ascription of inability to him as ascribing something also present, though in lesser degree, in our own case. But what can this be? Simple *impossibility* does not seem to have degrees: In ordinary cases, it is not "somewhat" impossible to restrain oneself from expressing anger. Rather, it is somewhat *difficult* – at least partly because the affective component of anger is uncomfortable, in a way that exerts pressure toward more or less immediate discharge in action, if only mental action. At the very least, then, rage makes it extremely difficult to avoid some form of discharge. We might say, in *X*'s case, that control would be "impossibly" difficult; but I see no real point in interpreting this claim strictly either. For one thing, I can think of no way of distinguishing it, in practice, from a claim about the nonoccurrence of something "extraordinarily" difficult. Disconfirmation would seem to depend on the discovery of "similar" cases with a different behavioral outcome; but an adequate criterion of similarity would seem to be limited to the agent's actual circumstances, including his unrepeatable personal history.[6] In any case, my later attempt to explain unfreedom in general will not require reference to impossibility.

With a rough explanation of the sort just sketched, though, we may now return to our original, narrower account of *X*'s unfreedom, in the case I began with. Even in cases of ordinary anger, some of our optional responses are more satisfying than others. Typically, for instance, the more overt and direct responses discharge anger to a greater degree than their covert, or indirect, alternatives. It therefore may be difficult, even if it is not impossible, to avoid attacking the object of anger (with an insult, say), rather than simply imagining doing so, or lashing out in some other (or in no particular) direction. For *X*, we may say, this is *extremely* difficult – and extremely difficult, let us now add, to manage by less-than-physical means. His intense discomfort exerts pressure toward immediate discharge; and as his patterns of thought are in fact set up, physical attack is the first, or the only, alternative that occurs to him. Alternatively, it is the only one that occurs to him as something he can manage with reasonable hope of success; or it simply is the only one that would satisfy his rage, by relieving its component of discomfort. In short, we may appeal back to reasons like those suggested earlier, as ways of explaining why we might sometimes grant that *X* has to take one sort of action in particu-

6 Cf. Dennett, *Elbow Room*, op. cit., esp. pp. 130–9.

lar. However, the list of reasons is now extended by the interpretation of "has to," and similar modal expressions, in terms of the difficulty of doing otherwise. For simplicity's sake, I shall now return to that narrower version of the case itself, letting this discussion serve to broaden its interpretation, and to indicate how more familiar cases may be interpreted in light of what follows. As with ordinary action out of anger, X's action rests on a choice; but his choice is made under *extra*ordinary pressure.

I have purposely left open, just above, some questions about precisely how it is that X's thought patterns make it so difficult for him to refrain from physical attack – or, we may now say, from throwing a punch – in response to "overpowering" rage. These may bear importantly on the issue of responsibility, in conjunction with some further questions about X's personal history, questions I have not even raised. We might want to ask how much control X had over the *formation* of his options in response to rage states – and for that matter, over the fact that he got into such a state on this occasion. However, my discussion up to this point pertains only to the issue of X's freedom, with respect to a particular action – and indeed as restricted to the time when X decides to take action. This last may be construed to include those moments right before action when alternatives to it are or might have been contemplated; but it does not include, say, earlier times when X might possibly have controlled a tendency to react to insults with rage. In short, I have applied a (dated) "control model" of freedom to a case of action *out of* (present) rage, and not to rage itself – either its occurrence on this particular occasion, or the general disposition which led to it. Without departing from the control model, though, we might change our view of x's freedom if we evaluated his action from an earlier temporal standpoint. For at times when X could still have avoided getting into a rage state, in response to the latter insult, he could thereby have avoided the limitations imposed by rage on his options for *action* in response. However, let us bypass such complicating factors for the moment, and simply grant that X was limited to a single option while in a given state of rage. From at least one temporal standpoint, then, he was unfree with respect to some action.

On a "character model" of freedom, however, we may reach a different conclusion – even without appealing to considerations of the sort just bypassed. I use the term "character" to cover a number of related conceptions of an agent's "core self," sometimes without the suggestion of moral significance, or of significant temporal duration, but with reference only to the central internal sources of motivation.

An action is said to be free, on the character model, when it stems from such sources – from the agent's "higher-order volitions," or unconflicting desires, for instance; or from the agent's values; or from these or similar features which actually *originate* in the agent.[7] But it is not clear that emotions should be viewed as peripheral or external sources of motivation, especially where they are not "out of character," but are based on long-standing dispositions of the agent, by now accepted as *personality* features. They may interfere with freedom, though, in the sense of self-control, without limiting "autonomy," in the sense suggested by the views summed up just above.

We may satisfy all the above conditions on freedom, it seems, by supposing that X, in the case of action out of rage, has *cultivated* in himself a tendency to react to insults with rage and physical aggression. He sees himself as "the man of towering passions," say; and he values rage and physical aggression as essential to any such "self-respecting" man who has just been subjected to an insult. Indeed, we may grant that his particular action on this occasion – throwing a punch – is something he unambivalently wanted to do. Even if not picked out precisely by his earlier desires, it was the *sort* of action they required – without conflict, and with no more "outside" origin or influence than is typical of responses to perception, as mediated by physiological factors and by habit. Later, too, let us suppose, X looks back upon his action without the slightest stirrings of regret. So his action is in no way, and at no time, unfree – if freedom amounts to conformity with, or causation by, the agent's "core self." Nor was X unfree "with respect to" the action – and similarly, as far as I can tell, for X's "will."[8] But surely this is counterintuitive, at least as applied to the time when X's will was exercised – under the pressure of extreme anger.

The case of X resembles some familiar cases of self-induced lack of control, such as drunkenness, where an agent may be held responsible for resulting unfree actions, apparently on the assumption that the initial action was free. But what is induced in such cases is normally a *surrender* of control to something else – with the physiological effects of alcohol viewed as external to the self – and the resulting action is normally not the sort of thing the agent *independently* wanted

---

7 The various sources summed up here are taken, in order, from the authors cited in note 1. The final clause attempts to capture Slote's suggestion for a further necessary condition of freedom, sufficient in combination with the others; see "Understanding Free Will," op. cit., p. 150; cf. p. 149.

8 I include this to attempt to cover alternative terminological conventions, including the one made out as "canonical" in Slote, "Understanding Free Will," op. cit., p. 137, n. 2.

to do. Still, we might imagine a case where the agent uses alcohol to "bring out" some qualities of his own – to generate "Dutch courage," say, by removing his usual ambivalence about anger – just in order to force himself to act in accordance with his "higher-order volitions." By the time this person throws a punch, though, whether or not the action is "in character," it might be something he cannot help doing. If so, it would seem to be *unfree* on the control model sketched above; and I think this accords with our intuitions. However, the agent still might be held *responsible* for the action – even if his initial action of drinking seemed intuitively *un*free, but came out as free on the character model. Suppose that the agent was deeply *addicted* to alcohol, for instance, but independently wanted to drink, on this occasion and others, in order to carry out the plan of action just sketched.[9] In that case, both the rage the plan was meant to stir up and its outcome in behavior would seem to be fully attributable to *him*, despite their mediation by external "influence."

Something similar seems to be true of X's case, at least if we confine ourselves to *one* sort of attribution of responsibility. My denial that X is free while acting out of rage should not be taken as *exonerating* him for the action or its consequences – even apart from doubts about his earlier freedom, in the sense of self-control, with respect to the rage state itself. He is an appropriate locus of *blame*, it would seem – whether or not the only one – as long as the action has its sources in qualities X rightly accepts as his own. They may sometimes need to be brought out by external stimuli, including "provocation" by other agents. However, the blame does not shift entirely to others, though his share of it may be lessened, where his reaction to them is understandable *only* in light of his own psychological makeup. I take it as an essential condition of *responsibility*, on this view, that the agent's character is in some sense a *first cause* of action. It may rest on causes of its own, of course, so it need not be "first" in order of time; but it is assumed to stand out, as a cause of action, against the usual *background* causes of character *formation*.[10]

This condition would not be satisfied if a tumor caused the agent's rage states, say, along with either a set of coherent desires and supporting beliefs, or the sort of radical personality disintegration which would not allow for a locus of blame at all. On the other hand, it would seem to be satisfied if the agent's psychological makeup, as

[9] Cf. Don Locke, "Three Concepts of Free Action," *Proceedings of the Aristotelian Society,* Suppl. IL (1975), 95–112, pp. 99–100.
[10] This represents my own attempt to spell out assumptions I take to be implicit in Slote's condition; see note 7 above.

formed in a relatively normal childhood, caused both the rage states and internal conflict about them. Conflict bears on responsibility as a *sign* of external causation, in short, but by no means an infallible sign, on suitable formulations of the character model. To the extent that the model picks out the responsible agent by appeal to "the usual" causal background, moreover, it may involve some implicit reference to norms – of reasonable treatment of children, for instance. If the agent's tendency toward rage-plus-guilt, say, resulted from confinement to a closet for childhood misdeeds, we *might* transfer responsibility back to his parents – depending, among other things, on the gravity of the later misdeeds. However, here we introduce a kind of normative *weighting* that will also figure in our application of the *control* model – eventually to cases like these, but seen from a rather different standpoint. I now want to return to the control model, and to show how, on closer examination, it seems to make quite *pervasive* reference to norms. Indeed, it suggests another sort of attribution of responsibility.

Unfreedom and reasonable expectation

I think that the last point may best be put negatively, by noting that a claim that X is *un*free, on the control model, seems to function as a kind of excuse – though it may not excuse him "after-the-fact," most notably from *blame* for his past actions. "Excusing" someone may also involve simply ceasing to impose on that person a demand for *future* action – in the way in which one might "forgive" a debt, or release someone from a promise he cannot keep, without necessarily forgiving him for failing to make good on it. A person may be excused *from* an obligation, in "forward-looking" terms, that is, without being excused, in "backward-looking" terms, *for* the nonfulfillment of it. Even if a person is *unable* to fulfill it, at the time when we release him from it, he may still be subject to blame – for the later inaction, as well as the current inability – if we see him as responsible for the inability. If we suppose, for instance, that the addicted drinker is unable to abstain just by his own efforts, so that we cannot hold him to a pledge of abstinence, we might still hold him responsible for drinking, where he is in some sense the cause of the addiction. However, I doubt whether inability, though it does provide an excuse "before-the-fact," provides the only possible excuse, in the sense relevant to the control model. I now want to take a closer look at the use of that model to explain why X is unfree, exploring some complications in its appeal to norms of "reasonable expectation."

I have explained X's unfreedom, at the time when he acts out of rage, in terms of the *difficulty* of doing otherwise; but not all acts with "difficult" alternatives, or agents who perform them, are unfree. In a case of ordinary anger, for instance, it may be hard to restrain oneself from lashing out verbally; but silence is still a real option. It is not *so* difficult that it cannot reasonably be expected of an agent – under circumstances, say, where verbal attack would have bad enough consequences to be *worth* avoiding, even at some cost in emotional discomfort. On the other hand, it would *not* be reasonable to expect the agent to avoid even mental manifestations of anger – except under rather special circumstances, where the cost of control is strongly outweighed by the bad consequences of losing it. While delivering an important lecture, for instance, one might sometimes be expected to do more than usual to keep from being distracted by anger – at rudeness from someone in the audience, say. Even in a rage, for that matter, an agent might sometimes be held to an abnormally high standard – assuming that he is *able* to live up to it, but only by making an enormous effort. When insulted by a hemophiliac with glasses, for instance, one might be expected to find some alternative to physical aggression, even in a rage no less intense than the rage that makes X, in my central case, unfree.

In determining *how much* difficulty is enough to make X unfree, then, we seem to appeal to a normative standard whose application varies with "the stakes," as well as with features of X's personal history and psychological makeup. The standard is normative on several levels, in fact – in the first instance, by its use of a normative notion of "expectation." There are epistemic conditions on freedom, as I have granted; but they apply to *the agent's* state of knowledge, in complex ways that will need to be examined shortly. For the moment, let us just note that a reference to knowledge would not explain the sense in which *we* reasonably "expect" more control of someone whose anger is less intense than the rage which makes X unfree. For it would not distinguish unfreedom from other states of an agent which provide us with adequate grounds for predicting his behavior. If someone is known to be unusually lazy, say, or simply to dislike a certain kind of action – cleaning up, for instance – it might not be reasonable for us to "expect" that person to perform it, in the sense of predicting that he *will;* but it might still be reasonable to think that the person *ought* to perform it – to expect it *of* him, in the sense of holding him to a standard which requires it. We might have no grounds for thinking it any *harder* for him than for other agents, that is – or enough so to make him unfree – even supposing that its performance is very *unlikely* in this case.

If we do not require inability, how then do we determine what degree of difficulty *is* enough for unfreedom? My claim is that there is no definite standard, but simply a normative appeal to "reasonable" expectation, whose application also depends on the *importance* of the act in question. The addicted drinker, for instance, may be held to a higher standard where someone's life depends on his exercising control – as in the case where rage is directed toward a hemophiliac. A general denial of an agent's freedom, then, assumes the typical circumstances of action, and may be modified in particular cases to reflect unusual features of "the stakes." It also assumes – let us now note, to bring out some complications in our "reasonable expectation" requirement – that the agent's failure to exercise control does not rest on deficiencies in his *knowledge* of the circumstances. However, we must be sure to distinguish between the agent's knowledge of the *alternatives* for exercising control and his knowledge of the *reasons* for thinking he ought to.

Deficiencies in the former involve not knowing *how* to do otherwise, so they do seem to rule out freedom;[11] but deficiencies in the latter need not make an action unfree, though they may make its alternatives "unreasonable to expect" of the agent – simply because we could not expect him to know that they are *required,* quite apart from problems about control. In short: The "reasonable expectation" requirement has to be qualified to filter out reference to norms affecting responsibility but not freedom.[12] Someone insulted by a hemo-

---

[11] For suggested epistemic *interpretations* of modal terms, see Dennett, *Elbow Room*, op. cit., pp. 107–30, and pp. 144–52. In an unpublished extension of this general approach to modality and free will, Dennett and Slote focus on the expression "having it in one's power," which evidently makes reference to knowing *how* to do something.

[12] Here I focus on epistemic norms, partly because of the particular questions about them raised by views such as those cited in note 11; but partly, too, in the hope of illustrating a general way of handling norms of expectation that do not bear directly on the issue of control. My own suggestion for a normative account of freedom differs from others I know of in its appeal to "our" reasonable expectations of an agent; so it may also have to rule out reference to norms of *fairness,* of the sort that apply to an "external" judgment of responsibility.

Complications of this further sort seem to emerge from a detailed answer to the following set of questions on another issue, raised by an anonymous reviewer for Cambridge University Press:

> Does what it is reasonable to require vary from person to person? What about someone accustomed to heroics who on a given occasion decides not to bother and allows a robber to take his money and that of his companions? Is it unreasonable to require him to do otherwise, so that his act of allowing the robber to rob is not free?

My general answer to the first question here is "Yes"; and it also holds for freedom, particularly on the assumption which I take to be implicit in the second question: that becoming "accustomed" to something ordinarily makes it easier to manage. However, it would then seem that my answer to the third question should be "No." If the action of resisting the robber is so easy for *this* agent that he may be described as simply

philiac, for instance, and contemplating physical aggression in ignorance of the other's condition, might not be expected to *exercise* control if it would be unreasonable to expect him to know why he should; but his ignorance does not affect the *capacity* for self-control. As in the case where our own knowledge was at issue, control may be unlikely, but not particularly hard for him to manage. In this case, presumably, the agent would not be responsible for controlling himself; but we need not therefore see the agent as unfree – any more than someone who fails to clean up simply because he has no idea that visitors are about to drop in.

I think we can handle such cases by taking the "reasonable expectation" requirement to involve an implicit epistemic assumption which functions as an unasserted *condition on* its use as the essential condition of freedom. An agent is free to perform a certain action – let us say for short – as long as it would be reasonable to expect him to perform it *if* he had reason to. An unqualified judgment of reasonable expectation *asserts* the "if"-clause extracted from it here; but an explanation of the "if"-clause would seem to introduce another judgment of the same sort, spelling out the sense in which the agent is taken to "possess" the reason in question. "The reason" should be thought of as *some* sufficient reason for action – sufficient under normal circumstances, but at least as strong as *the* reason, in cases where there is one, that applies to the agent under circumstances where "the stakes" are abnormally high. The agent need not actually have this in mind,

---

simply deciding "not to bother," then it would seem to come out as *reasonable* to require of him – and his omission of it, on this occasion, as *free* – for an illustration of the requisite sort of variability.

In holding this agent responsible for resisting the robber, however, we impose on him more than the immediate task of action; for the action may have burdensome *long-range* consequences that do not affect its present difficulty. Suppose, for instance, that the agent in this case, in contrast to his companions, can act without the slightest fear of the likely consequences of his action – a gunshot wound, let us say. He still would suffer as much from the wound as they would. So even if "the stakes" were higher, and his failure to act would subject his companions to similar suffering, picking *him* out for subjection to it might seem to impose an unfair burden on him. In some such cases, we might want to say that it would be *un*reasonable for us to require the requisite heroics of him, despite the fact that he is *free* to perform them. Perhaps it would be reasonable for him to expect no less of himself; but "our" corresponding expectation would still be excessive.

There may be more than one way of handling such complications – and I expect to deal with them more fully in another place – but for the moment we may content ourselves with the qualification illustrated for epistemic norms just below. Making out the account of freedom as implicitly hypothetical, with an "if"-clause bringing in our "reasonable expectation" *that* the agent *recognize* the "external" reason in question, allows us to say that he may be free in cases where factors other than difficulty make action "too much" to expect of him.

though, to be reasonably expected to act on it. The agent "has" a reason, in the requisite sense, in cases where it is *accessible* to him without further information.

This gloss on "having a reason" demands more than the mere *existence* of a reason – even one that the agent might come to recognize more or less by accident – but less than the agent's actual *recognition* of it, in current terms. The assumption of "accessibility," as implied by the reasonable expectation of action, should be taken as granting that the agent may reasonably be *expected* to come to recognize a reason for action, simply by reflecting on the information now available to him. On its hypothetical application to freedom, though, it should not be taken as limited to the time span remaining for action. For we want to rule out as *un*free, in current terms, cases where the pressure of rage simply keeps an agent from *attending to* some reason he "has" in time to affect what he does. Since they cannot *influence* an earlier action, reasons an agent is kept from discerning until later may be covered by our epistemic assumption without yielding counterintuitive cases of freedom. In fact, with this complication of our account, some questionable cases may be excluded.

The "reasonable expectation" requirement now also rules out as unfree, that is, cases where an agent lacks practical *responsiveness* to the reasons – access to them *as* reasons, as distinct from simple awareness of their factual content – *within* the time span remaining for action. Thus, if X, in my central case above, were unable, while in a "blind" rage, to appreciate the *significance* of the degree of harm which he recognized as resulting from a given response, we would still count him as unfree, just as we would if he could think of no alternatives to that response. *Moral* blindness of this sort would indeed seem to undermine his capacity for self-control, since it involves not knowing *how* – how to reason practically in light of the facts within his "possession," conforming his behavior to their evaluative content as *reasons*. Even if he recognized that a punch might cause death, X might be unable to *take* that fact as a reason for controlling aggression against a hemophiliac; and if so, he would seem to come out, once again, as unfree. For the full requirement on freedom to be satisfied, then, it must be reasonable to expect the agent to act *on* some hypothetically "accessible" reasons for action. Where it is not, though, the agent may still be *responsible* for what he does – sometimes even "before-the-fact," but with reference to an earlier time, when the accessibility assumption was itself satisfied.

The accessibility assumption introduces a further level of reference to norms; and in some cases, its reference to *practical* norms will allow for freedom without responsibility, as well as the reverse, even where *factual* blindness is not in question. Its implications may be best glimpsed, I think, if we take another look at some of the questions left open in my previous discussion of the nature and development of X's rage response. We might suppose, for instance, that X is unable to "think past" physical aggression, in response to an insult, partly because of "blind spots" induced by a morally impoverished upbringing, and preceding the state of rage. Even without time pressure, on this version of the case, his coming to appreciate the significance of the consequences of aggression is something that would require either outside help or an enormous effort. But if he did have access to the reasons for control, let us suppose, it would not be particularly difficult for him to *act* on them. He would seem to come out as free, then, at least at times when awareness of the reasons would still have allowed for behavioral control – by allowing him to avoid the rage state, say. He was free, that is, with respect to a particular action – throwing a punch – though we might not have held him responsible for alternative action, in view of the deeply ingrained limitations on his moral reasoning. With respect to the latter, he might *not* have been free – if his background offered so little exposure to others' reasoning in similar situations, for instance, that he could not have been expected, even over an extended time span, to *learn* the value of control. This case at first may seem improbable; but assumptions something like those behind it do seem to figure in our assessments of individuals in earlier states of *society* — lacking due regard for the feelings of slaves, say, or for members of competing tribes.

An agent's freedom, and his responsibility "before-the-fact," will thus depend on overlapping but nonidentical normative considerations. Both will vary with "the stakes," conceived as the importance of an object of "reasonable expectation," weighed against the difficulty of fulfilling it. However, the notion of responsibility apparently takes awareness of the reasons for action as a further object of reasonable expectation, with a further weighting – of the importance and the difficulty of *discerning* the reasons – imposed only hypothetically on freedom. The applicability of either notion will therefore depend, though in different ways, on temporal considerations; for it also rests on variable facts – including hypothetical facts – about the agent's developing patterns of reasoning and response. It does not seem to rest primarily, though, on support for the claim that the agent "caused" his character – the claim that, on a character model, might seem to yield a less time-bound account of responsibility. I shall now bring back some details of my central case above, contrasting it with variant cases, to conclude my overall argument by exhibiting some of the virtues of its suggested alternative account. Though these clearly do not include simplicity, I think they do include the possibility of a more adequate treatment of cases. I have in mind especially cases like some of those just sketched, where character development is abnormal at the outset, to a degree that supports conflicting intuitions on guilt and "victimhood."

In its most elaborate form, illustrating responsibility on several different versions of the character model, my central case above was one where X actually *cultivated* in himself the tendencies, toward rage and physical aggression, that led to his unfree action. So here we might grant that, despite his lack of freedom *while in* the state of rage – or even, perhaps, when just subjected to an insult – X may be taken as responsible at earlier times, in a sense apparently relevant to the control model as well. For he helped to *shape* his patterns of reasoning and response – "caused" his character in some sense, even if not from the outset. We might even strengthen the case by supposing that he was at any rate the initial cause of the particular traits in question here – that his tendency toward rage and physical aggression was not encouraged by early childhood experiences, but resulted entirely from decisions made in later life. Even as it stands, though, the case does seem to involve responsibility – and indeed responsibility at *some* time before-the-fact. However, I doubt whether the latter point really turns on the assumption of character causation, unless the assumption has only minimal content.

For we might pare away X's actual contribution to the formation of his character, in this case, and still be left with a case where he has a chance to *block* the development (or the maintenance) of some or all of its aspects, but simply fails to take advantage of the opportunity. The case will yield responsibility only on certain epistemic assumptions – roughly, that it would be reasonable to expect X to *recognize* the opportunity he passes up, perhaps in a way that involves some awareness of its moral significance. I think it would be enough, though, if he were able see its implications for his future social behavior – in promoting conventional interaction, say. He need not refer – even if he did take advantage of the opportunity for change – to a notion of character development, any more than to a clear-cut notion of morality. In passing up the opportunity, moreover, he certainly need not see himself as choosing *to* become (or to remain) a certain sort of person – one who flouts morality, or the like. He would seem to be responsible – before- *and* after-the-fact – even if he simply takes the line of least resistance, and avoids change, but in the knowledge that his future behavior will continue to take a certain form. Where we make no stronger assumption, however – and indeed we need only assume that he *should* see the implications of his choice – it will be stretching things greatly to claim that his passive acceptance of patterns of response amounts to "shaping his character."

Let me illustrate some of these points – initially in negative form – by working with one of the cases that emerged just above, where my argument suggested that unfreedom, even on the control model, might sometimes allow for responsibility before-the-fact, assuming an earlier stage of freedom. The case involved unfreedom while in a rage state, on the basis of a kind of practical unresponsiveness to the harm caused by aggression. Let us now suppose, though, that X did *not* initially *cultivate* this practical failing in himself. Rather, he was uniformly encouraged in early life – by adults' treatment of him and by their responses to his own treatment of others – to be indifferent (at best) to others' suffering, taking responsiveness as a sign of humiliating weakness. Furthermore, the deficiencies of his early childhood training were so extreme, let us grant, that this aspect of his character was quite solidly formed, and resistant to modification, by the time he was exposed to contrasting models of social behavior. In school, or even on television, X either saw only models of the same sort or had contrasting models explained away, by his parents or his peers, as unworthy of emulation. At some point, however, he *was* in a position to absorb new information on his own.

In many such cases, of course, X might by then be too far gone to be expected to *reevaluate* what he sees – perhaps not because such reevaluation would be impossible, or even impossibly difficult, but just because he would not know how to process the information differently. Nor would he have access, in time to affect his action, to the reason that *would* result from *learning* how to process it differently. However, then our forward-looking judgment of "reasonable expectation" would not apply to his alternative action; so he would not be responsible – before-the-fact, that is. A claim that he is responsible after-the-fact, though, might still be defended by reference to *further* forward-looking considerations – those that look *beyond* the action in question – as combined with some backward-looking version of the character model.[13] If blame would improve his *later* character, for

[13] The reference here to "*further* forward-looking considerations" should indicate one of my reasons for bringing in less familiar terminology: Responsibility "after-the-fact" implies that the fact looked *toward,* in bringing such considerations to bear on a given action, *is* the fact of *action.* By itself, the desirability of changing the agent's character does not make him responsible *either* for doing something himself or for something he

instance, then it may be imposed, if only in mitigated form, even where we acknowledge that his prior character was not of his making. That the action flowed from *him,* moreover – indeed, let us say, from a self he now accepts without qualms, even if not one that he helped to create – also seems sufficient for at least some degree of responsibility after-the-fact. However, let us focus on the question of responsibility before-the-fact – of the reasonableness of holding the agent to a requirement of alternative action – and note that, in this case, it would seem to be ruled out *well* before action. It would not be reasonable to expect *X,* given his earlier character, to control physical aggression in response to a later insult. The reasons for control, on our assumptions, were simply not accessible to him earlier; and at this point, access to them would not affect his action. Either way (free or unfree), he would not be responsible – in past or in current forward-looking terms.

Now let us change our assumptions about the case. We might grant that *X* – or even, perhaps, that *any* agent whose childhood was not so traumatic as to block the normal development of social perception – would have been capable, at an earlier stage, of improvement on his own. He could have overcome his insensitivity to others' suffering – on the basis of later information, say, about the importance society placed on it – once he was exposed to a wider circle of acquaintances, and to other (at least conventional) notions of importance. Yet in fact he continually passed up any such opportunities for improvement – just out of a kind of inertia, rather than a project of building or maintaining a certain sort of character; and not, on the other hand, because it would have been particularly difficult to do otherwise. We should then grant, I think, that he *was* responsible for his later action as seen from this earlier standpoint – even though he did not shape his character, even to the extent of striving to preserve it. Indeed, for

has done. Nor does it yield *full-blown* responsibility, on the view I presuppose here, even as appropriately *combined* with a view of the agent's causal contribution, on the character model, to some past action. What I do allow – though it might be taken concessively, for more critical discussion elsewhere – is that an element of full-blown responsibility is involved here, just insofar as a wrong act is "chargeable" to the agent. However, this does not imply that the agent was previously in a position to be "charged" with the task of avoiding it – an attribution of responsibility "before-the-fact." The latter is worth isolating as the likely source of even apparent conflict with determinism – with the caution that it *seems* to cover certain intermediate cases. Contrary-to-duty obligation sometimes requires action *preceding* the violation of duty – warning someone, for instance, that one cannot keep an appointment – but the obligation really should be seen as contingent on a prior *inability*, not on the *act* of violation, if we are to avoid paradox. See my argument in "Conditional Oughts and Hypothetical Imperatives," *Journal of Philosophy,* LXXII (May 22, 1975), 259–76.

5

Responsiveness and moral responsibility

JOHN MARTIN FISCHER

Introduction

We distinguish between creatures who can legitimately be held morally responsible for their actions and those who cannot. Among the
actions a morally responsible agent performs, we distinguish between
those actions for which the agent is morally responsible and those for
which he is not.

An agent is morally responsible for an action insofar as he is rationally accessible to certain kinds of attitudes and activities as a result
of performing the action. The attitudes include resentment, indignation, respect, and gratitude; and the activities include moral praise
and blame, and reward and punishment.[1] With this approach, an
agent can be a rational candidate for praise or blame, even though he
is neither praiseworthy nor blameworthy. For instance, an agent can
be morally responsible for a morally "neutral" act. A theory of moral
responsibility sets the conditions under which we believe that an individual is a *rational candidate* for praise or blame on account of his
behavior. This theory needs to be supplemented by a further moral
theory that specifies which agents, among those who are morally responsible, *ought* to be praised or blamed (and to what extent) for their
actions. Whereas both kinds of theory are obviously important, I
focus here on the first sort of theory – one that explains rational
accessibility to the pertinent attitudes and activities.

What I present here is really just a sketch of a theory. It needs to be
elaborated and defended much more carefully and explicitly. But I
hope that enough of its content will be presented to see that it is a
worthwhile approach to develop. The kind of theory I present is
certainly not radically new and entirely different from its predeces-

I have benefited greatly from comments on previous versions of this paper by Sarah
Buss, Anthony Brueckner, and Ferdinand Schoeman. I also benefited from reading a
version of this paper at Birkbeck College, University of London.

[1] Strawson calls the attitudes involved in moral responsibility the "reactive attitudes":
P. F. Strawson, "Freedom and Resentment," *Proceedings of the British Academy* 48 (1962),
pp. 1–25.

sors.[2] But I hope to develop the theory in a way that avoids some of the objections to similar approaches, and I will draw out some implications that have so far gone unnoticed.

A sketch of a theory of moral responsibility

A theory of moral responsibility should capture our intuitive judgments about clear cases. That is, I assume there is at least fairly wide agreement about certain cases in which an agent can reasonably be held morally responsible for what he does and certain cases in which an agent cannot be held responsible. Considered opinions about these sorts of situations are important data to be explained by a theory of moral responsibility. In order to generate a principle that might underlie our reactions to relatively clear cases, it is useful to begin by considering examples in which we are inclined to think that an agent cannot legitimately be held morally responsible.

Imagine that an individual has been hypnotized. The hypnotist has induced an urge to punch the nearest person after hearing the telephone ring. Insofar as the individual did not consent to this sort of hypnotic suggestion (perhaps he has undergone hypnosis to help him stop smoking), it seems unreasonable to hold him morally responsible for punching his friend in the nose upon hearing the telephone ring.

Suppose similarly that an evil person has got hold of Smith's television set and has wired it so as to allow him to subject Smith to a sophisticated sort of subliminal advertising. The bad person systematically subjects Smith to subliminal advertising that causes Smith to murder his neighbor. Because of the nature of the causal history of the action, it is apparent that Smith cannot be held morally responsible for the lamentable deed.

We feel similarly about actions produced in a wide variety of ways. Agents who perform actions produced by powerful forms of brainwashing and indoctrination, potent drugs, and certain sorts of direct

[2] Some contemporary versions of similar theories are found in Alasdair MacIntyre, "Determinism," *Mind* 56 (1957), pp. 28–41; Jonathan Glover, *Responsibility* (New York: Humanities Press, 1970); Herbert Fingarette, *The Meaning of Criminal Insanity* (Berkeley: University of California Press, 1972); Wright Neely, "Freedom and Desire," *Philosophical Review* 83 (1974), pp. 32–54; Timothy Duggan and Bernard Gert, "Free Will as the Ability to Will," *Nous* 13 (1979), pp. 197–217; Lawrence Davis, *A Theory of Action* (Englewood Cliffs, NJ: Prentice-Hall, 1979); Michael Levin, *Metaphysics and the Mind-Body Problem* (Oxford: Clarendon Press, 1979); Robert Nozick, *Philosophical Explanations* (Cambridge, MA: Harvard University Press, 1981); and Daniel Dennett, *Elbow Room: The Varieties of Free Will Worth Wanting* (Cambridge, MA: MIT Press, 1984). For an excellent survey of some aspects of these approaches, see David Shatz, "Free Will and the Structure of Motivation," *Midwest Studies in Philosophy* X, Peter French et al. (eds.), University of Minnesota Press, 1985, pp. 444–74.

manipulation of the brain are not reasonably to be held morally responsible for their actions. Imagine, for instance, that neurophysiologists of the future can isolate certain key parts of the brain, which can be manipulated in order to induce decisions and actions. If scientists electronically stimulate those parts of Jones's brain, thus causing him to help a person who is being mugged, Jones himself cannot reasonably be held morally responsible for his behavior. It is not to Jones's credit that he has prevented a mugging.

Also, if we discover that a piece of behavior is attributable to a significant brain lesion or a neurological disorder, we do not hold the agent morally responsible for it. Similarly, certain sorts of mental disorders – extreme phobias, for instance – may issue in behavior for which the agent cannot reasonably be held responsible.

Many people feel there can be genuinely "irresistible" psychological impulses. If so, then these may result in behavior for which the agent cannot be held morally responsible. Drug addicts may (in certain circumstances) act on literally irresistible urges, and we might not hold them morally responsible for acting on these desires (especially if we believe they are not morally responsible for acquiring the addiction in the first place).

Also, certain sorts of coercive threats (and perhaps offers) rule out moral responsibility. The bank teller who is told he will be shot unless he hands over the money might have an overwhelming and irresistible desire to comply with the threat. Insofar as he acts from such an impulse, it is plausible to suppose that the teller is not morally responsible for his action.[3]

Evidently, the causal history of an action matters to us in making moral responsibility attributions. When persons are manipulated in certain ways, they are like marionettes and are not appropriate candidates for praise or blame. Certain factors issuing in behavior are, intuitively, "responsibility-undermining factors."

We can contrast such cases – in which some responsibility-undermining factor operates – with cases in which there is the "normal," unimpaired operation of the human deliberative mechanism. When you deliberate about whether to give 5 percent of your salary to the United Way and consider reasons on both sides, and your decision to give the money is not induced by hypnosis, brainwashing, direct manipulation, psychotic impulses, and so on, we think you can legitimately be praised for your charitable action. Insofar as we can identi-

[3] I contrast this kind of bank teller with one who, in exactly the same circumstances, does not have an irresistible impulse to comply with the threat. Such a teller might be morally responsible (though not necessarily *blameworthy*) for handing over the money.

fy no responsibility-undermining factor at work in your decision and action, we are inclined to hold you morally responsible.

Now it might be thought that there is a fairly obvious way of distinguishing the clear cases of moral responsibility from the clear cases of lack of it. It seems that, in the cases in which an agent is morally responsible for an action, he is free to do otherwise, and in the cases of lack of moral responsibility, the agent is not free to do otherwise. Thus, it appears that the actual operation of what is intuitively a responsibility-undermining factor rules out moral responsibility because it rules out freedom to do otherwise.

The point could be put as follows. When an agent is (for example) hypnotized, he is not sensitive to reasons in the appropriate way. Given the hypnosis, he would still behave in the same way, no matter what the relevant reasons were. Suppose, again, that an individual is hypnotically induced to punch the nearest person after hearing the telephone ring. Now given this sort of hypnosis, he would punch the nearest person after hearing the telephone ring, even if he had extremely strong reasons not to. The agent here is not responsive to reasons – the behavior would be the same, no matter what reasons there were.

In contrast, when there is the normal, unimpaired operation of the human deliberative mechanism, we suppose that the agent *is* responsive to reasons. So when you decide to give money to the United Way, we think that you nevertheless would not have contributed had you discovered that there was widespread fraud within the agency. Thus it is very natural and reasonable to think that the difference between morally responsible agents and those who are not consists in the "reasons-responsiveness" of the agents.

But I believe that there are cases in which an agent can be held morally responsible for performing an action, even though that person could not have done otherwise (and is not "reasons-responsive").[4] Here is a graphic example. Imagine that an evil person has installed a device in Brown's brain which allows him to monitor Brown's mental activity and also to intervene in it, if he wishes. He can electronically manipulate Brown's brain by "remote control" to induce decisions, and let us imagine that he can also ensure that Brown acts on the

---

[4] John Locke presented an interesting example of a man who voluntarily stays in a room which, unbeknown to him, is locked: John Locke, *Essay Concerning Human Understanding*, Bk. II, Ch. xxi, Secs. 8–11. For a number of examples of agents who are morally responsible for actions, although they could not have done otherwise, see Harry Frankfurt, "Alternate Possibilities and Moral Responsibility," *Journal of Philosophy* 46, n. 23 (1969), pp. 829–39. Also see John Martin Fischer, "Responsibility and Control," *Journal of Philosophy* 79, n. 1 (1982), pp. 24–40.

decisions so induced. Now suppose that Brown is about to murder his neighbor, and that this is precisely what the evil person wishes. That is, let us imagine that the device simply monitors Brown's brain activity, but that it plays no role in Brown's actual decision and action. Brown deliberates and behaves just as he would have if no device had been implanted in his brain. But we also imagine that had Brown begun to decide not to murder his neighbor, the device would have been activated and would have caused him to choose to murder the neighbor (and to do so) anyway. Here is a case where an agent can be held morally responsible for performing an action, although he could not have done otherwise.[5] Let us call such a case a "Frankfurt-type" case.

In a Frankfurt-type case, the actual sequence proceeds in a way which grounds moral responsibility attributions, even though the alternative scenario (or perhaps a range of alternative scenarios) proceeds in a way which rules out responsibility. In a Frankfurt-type case, no responsibility-undermining factor occurs in the actual sequence, although such a factor occurs in the alternative scenario. Such cases impel us to adopt a more refined theory of moral responsibility – an "actual-sequence model" of moral responsibility. With such an approach, we distinguish between the kinds of mechanisms that operate in the actual sequence and in the alternative sequence (or sequences).

In a Frankfurt-type case the kind of mechanism that actually operates is reasons-responsive, although the kind of mechanism that would operate in the alternative scenario is *not*.[6] In the case discussed above, Brown's action issues from the normal faculty of practical reasoning, which we can reasonably take to be reasons-responsive. But in the alternative scenario, a different kind of mechanism would have operated – one involving direct electronic stimulation of Brown's brain. And this mechanism is not reasons-responsive. Thus, the actual-sequence mechanism can be reasons-responsive, even though the *agent* is not reasons-responsive. (*Brown* could not have done otherwise.)

The suggestion, then, for a more refined way of distinguishing the relatively clear cases of moral responsibility from cases of the lack of it is as follows. An agent is morally responsible for performing an action

[5] For a vigorous and interesting criticism of this description of the case, see Peter van Inwagen, "Ability and Responsibility," *The Philosophical Review* 87 (1978), pp. 201–24, reprinted in Peter van Inwagen, *An Essay on Free Will* (Oxford: Clarendon Press, 1983), pp. 161–82. Although it is inappropriate to pursue the details of the debate here, I defend the claim that there are cases in which an agent is morally responsible for performing an action, although he couldn't have done otherwise; see Fischer, "Responsibility and Control."

[6] I owe this way of describing the Frankfurt-type cases to Sydney Shoemaker.

insofar as the mechanism that actually issues in the action is reasons-responsive. When an unresponsive mechanism actually operates, it is true that the agent is not free to do otherwise; but an agent who is unable to do otherwise may act from a responsive mechanism and can thus be held morally responsible for what he does.

So far I have pointed to some cases in which it is intuitively clear that a person cannot be held morally responsible for what he has done and other cases in which it is intuitively clear that an agent can be held responsible. I have suggested a principle that might distinguish the two types of cases. This principle makes use of two ingredients: reasons-responsiveness and the distinction between actual-sequence and alter-native-sequence mechanisms. But I have been somewhat vague and breezy about formulating the principle. It is now necessary to explain it more carefully, beginning with the notion of reasons-responsiveness.

Reasons-responsiveness

I wish to discuss two kinds of reasons-responsiveness: strong and weak. Let's begin with strong reasons-responsiveness. Strong reasons-responsiveness obtains when a certain kind K of mechanism actually issues in an action and if there were sufficient reason to do otherwise and K were to operate, the agent would recognize the sufficient reason to do otherwise and thus choose to do otherwise and do otherwise. To test whether a kind of mechanism is strongly reasons-responsive, one asks what would happen if there were sufficient reason for the agent to do otherwise and the actual-sequence mechanism were to operate. Under circumstances in which there are suffi-cient reasons for the agent to do otherwise and the actual type of mechanism operates, three conditions must be satisfied: The agent must take the reasons to be sufficient, choose in accordance with the sufficient reason, and act in accordance with the choice. Thus, there can be at least three sorts of "alternative-sequence" failures: failures in the connection between what reasons there are and what reasons the agent recognizes, in the connection between the agent's reason and choice, and in the connection between choice and action.

The first kind of failure is a failure to be *receptive* to reasons. It is the kind of inability that afflicts certain delusional psychotics.[7] The sec-ond kind of failure is a failure of *reactivity* – a failure to be appropri-ately affected by beliefs. Lack of reactivity afflicts certain compulsive

---

[7] Here I am indebted to Duggan and Gert, op. cit.

or phobic neurotics.[8] Finally, there is the failure successfully to translate one's choice into action; this failure is a kind of impotence. If none of these failures were to occur in the alternative sequence (and the actual kind of mechanism were to operate), then the actually operative mechanism would be strongly reasons-responsive. There would be a tight fit between the reasons there are and the reasons the agent has, the agent's reasons and choice, and choice and action. The agent's actions would fit the contours of reasons *closely*.[9]

I believe that, when an action issues from a strongly reasons-responsive mechanism, this suffices for moral responsibility; but I do not believe that strong reasons-responsiveness is a necessary condition for moral responsibility. To see this, imagine that as a result of the unimpaired operation of the normal human faculty of practical reasoning, I decide to go (and go) to the basketball game tonight, and that I have sufficient reason to do so; but suppose that I would have been "weak-willed," had there been sufficient reason *not* to go. That is, imagine that had there been a sufficient reason not to go, it would have been that I had a strict deadline for an important manuscript (which I could not meet, if I were to go to the game). I nevertheless would have chosen to go to the game, even though I would have recognized that I had sufficient reason to stay home and work. It seems to me that I actually go to the basketball game freely and can reasonably be held morally responsible for going; and yet the actual-sequence mechanism that results in my action is not reasons-responsive in the strong sense. The failure of strong reasons-responsiveness here stems from my disposition toward weakness of the will.

Going to the basketball game is plausibly thought to be a morally neutral act; in the approach to moral responsibility adopted here, one can be morally responsible for an action, even though the act is neither praiseworthy nor blameworthy. The phenomenon of weakness of will also poses a problem for intuitively clear cases of moral responsibility for *commendable* acts. Suppose, for example, that I devote my afternoon to working for the United Way (and my decision and action proceed via an intuitively responsibility-conferring mechanism). And imagine that, if I had a sufficient reason to refrain, it would (again)

---

[8] *Ibid.*

[9] Robert Nozick requires this sort of close contouring of action to value for his notion of "tracking value": see Nozick, op. cit., pp. 317–62. In this respect, then, Nozick's notion of tracking value corresponds to strong reasons-responsiveness. Nozick claims that an agent who tracks value displays a kind of moral virtue, but he does not claim that tracking value is a necessary condition for moral responsibility.

have been my publication deadline. But imagine that I would have devoted my time to charity, even if I had such a reason not to. Here it seems that I am both morally responsible and praiseworthy for doing what I do, and yet the actual mechanism is not strongly reasons-responsive.

Further, it is quite clear that strong reasons-responsiveness cannot be a necessary condition for moral responsibility for morally blame-worthy and/or imprudent acts. Suppose that I steal a book from a store, knowing full well that it is morally wrong for me to do so and that I will be apprehended and thus that it is not prudent of me to do so. Nevertheless, the actual sequence may be intuitively responsibility-conferring; no factors that intuitively undermine moral responsibility may actually operate. (Of course, I assume that there can be genuine cases of weak-willed actions that are free actions for which the agent can be held responsible.) Here, then, is a case in which I am morally responsible for stealing the book, but my actual-sequence mechanism is not strongly reasons-responsive: There actually is sufficient reason (both moral and prudential) to do otherwise, and yet I steal the book.

All three cases presented above provide problems for the claim that strong reasons-responsiveness is necessary for moral responsibili-ty. Strong reasons-responsiveness may be both sufficient and neces-sary for a certain kind of praiseworthiness − it is a great virtue to connect one's actions with the contours of value in a strongly reasons-responsive way. Of course, not all agents who are morally responsible are morally commendable (or even maximally prudent). I believe that moral responsibility requires only a looser kind of fit between reasons and action: "weak reasons-responsiveness."

Under the requirement of strong reasons-responsiveness, we ask what would happen if there were a sufficient reason to do other-wise (holding fixed the actual kind of mechanism). Strong reasons-responsiveness points us to the alternative scenario in which there is a sufficient reason for the agent to do otherwise (and the actual mecha-nism operates), which is *most similar* to the actual situation. Put in terms of possible worlds, the nonactual possible worlds that are ger-mane to strong reasons-responsiveness are those in which the agent has a sufficient reason to do otherwise (and in which the actual kind of mechanism operates) that are most similar to the actual world. (Perhaps there is just one such world, or perhaps there is a sphere of many such worlds.) In contrast, under weak reasons-responsiveness, there must exist *some* possible world in which there is a sufficient reason to do otherwise, the agent's actual mechanism operates, and the agent does otherwise. This possible world need not be the one (or ones) in which the agent has a sufficient reason to do otherwise (and the actual mechanism operates), which is (or are) *most similar* to the actual world.[10]

Consider again my decision to go to the basketball game. In this situation, if I were to have a sufficient reason to do otherwise, this would be a publication deadline; and I would under such circumstances be weak-willed and still go to the game. However, there certainly exists *some* scenario in which the actual mechanism operates, I have sufficient reason not to go the the game, and I don't go. Suppose, for instance, that I am told that I will have to pay $1,000 for a ticket to the game. Even though I am disposed to be weak-willed under some circumstances, there are some circumstances in which I would respond appropriately to sufficient reasons. These are circumstances in which the reasons are considerably *stronger* than the reasons which would exist, if I were to have sufficient reason to do otherwise.

Consider, similarly, my commendable act of working this afternoon for the United Way. Even though I would do so anyway, even if I had a publication deadline, I certainly would *not* work for the United Way if to do so I would have to sacrifice my job. Thus, the actual mechanism issuing in my action is weakly reasons-responsive. Also, when an agent wrongly (and imprudently) steals a book (i.e., there actually is sufficient reason not to), the actual mechanism might be responsive to at least some logically possible incentive not to steal. To the extent that it is so responsive, he is properly held morally responsible for stealing the book. Even an agent who acts against good reasons can be responsive to *some* reasons.

I believe that the agent's actual-sequence mechanism *must* be weakly reasons-responsive, if he is to be held morally responsible. If (given the operation of the actual kind of mechanism) he would persist in stealing the book even knowing that by so acting he would cause himself and his family to be killed, then the actual mechanism would seem to be inconsistent with holding that person morally responsible for an action.

An agent whose act is produced by a strongly reasons-responsive mechanism is commendable; his behavior fits tightly the contours of value. But a weakly responsive mechanism is all that is required for moral responsibility. In my approach, actual irrationality is compatible with moral responsibility (as it should be). Perhaps Dostoyevsky's

[10] Here I adopt the constraint that the possible worlds pertinent to the weak reasons-responsiveness of the actual-sequence mechanism must have the same *natural laws* as the actual world.

underground man is an example of an actually irrational and yet morally responsible individual. Similarly, certain kinds of hypothetical irrationality are compatible with moral responsibility; a tendency toward weakness of the will need not point to any defect in the actual mechanism leading to action. Moral responsibility requires *some* connection between reason and action, but the fit can be quite loose.[11]

In this section I have distinguished two kinds of responsiveness. I have argued that an agent is morally responsible for an action insofar as the action is produced by a weakly reasons-responsive mechanism. In the next section, I discuss an analogy between this theory of moral responsibility and a parallel sort of theory of knowledge. This analogy will help to refine our understanding of the "actual-sequence" nature of moral responsibility. In the following section, I further sharpen the formulation of the theory by rendering more precise the key idea of a "kind of mechanism issuing in action."

Knowledge and responsibility

I have sketched an "actual-sequence" model of moral responsibility. In this approach, an agent can be morally responsible for performing an action, although he is not free to do otherwise. It is sufficient that the actual-sequence mechanism be responsive to reasons in the appropriate way. There is an analogy between this sort of theory of moral responsibility and an "actual-sequence" model of knowledge. In this approach to knowledge, an agent may have knowledge of a certain proposition, even though he lacks the pertinent discriminatory capacity. It is sufficient that the actual-sequence mechanism be "sensitive to truth" in the appropriate way.

[11] Ferdinand Schoeman has brought to my attention a kind of example that threatens my claim that weak reasons-responsiveness is sufficient for moral responsibility. Imagine someone who is apparently insane. This person commits a barbarous act, such as killing a number of persons on the Staten Island Ferry with a saber. And suppose that this individual would have killed the persons under all possible circumstances except one: He would have refrained if he believed that it was Friday and thus a religious holiday. Intuitively, the individual is highly irrational and should not be considered morally responsible, and yet he seems to satisfy the condition of acting from a reasons-responsive mechanism. Weak reasons-responsiveness obtains by virtue of the agent's responsiveness to a "bizarre" reason, even though the agent is not responsive to a wide array of "relevant" reasons.

I am aware that this sort of example poses a problem for the theory of responsibility I present here. At this point, I see two possible responses. First, one might claim that in this kind of case there would be a different mechanism operating in the alternate scenario (in which the agent is responsive) than in the actual sequence. Alternatively, one might restrict the reasons that are pertinent to weak reasons-responsiveness. I hope to discuss such examples and to develop an adequate response in future work.

In order for a person to know that p, it is clear that the person must believe that p, and that p must be true; but this is surely not enough, and there are various strategies for providing further requirements.[12] One "externalist" approach claims that the person's belief that p must be a "reliable indicator" of p's truth – or perhaps, that it must "track" p's truth. Very roughly, one might say that, in order for an agent to have knowledge that p, it must be the case both that (1) the agent would not believe that p if p were not true, and (2) under various conditions in which p were true, the agent would believe that p. One asks here about the agent's beliefs in a sphere of worlds which are relatively similar to the actual world – both worlds in which p is true and worlds in which p is false.[13]

So suppose that as you are driving along, you see what you take to be a barn in a field, and that you conclude that it is a barn in the field; and it is an ordinary barn in a field. Unknown to you, had it not been a barn, a demonic farmer would have installed a papier-mâché replica of a barn. In this case you truly believe that it is a normal barn in the field, but your belief does not "track truth": Had there been no barn in the field, you still would have believed there to be a barn in the field. In this case you lack a discriminatory capacity that might seem required for knowledge.

Let us contrast this case with another in which you see a banana in a supermarket, and you conclude that there is a banana on the shelf. We suppose here that there is no demonic supermarket manager poised to fool you, and that if there were no banana on the shelf, you would not believe that there is a banana on the shelf. Presumably, in this case your belief tracks truth, and you might be said to know that there is a banana on the shelf. Furthermore, this is so even though *there exists* a logically possible scenario in which a demonic supermarket manager has placed a plastic banana on the shelf and you still conclude that it is a banana. In this account, what is pertinent to knowledge are the scenarios in which p is false that are *most similar* to

[12] Roughly, one might distinguish between "internalist" and "externalist" accounts of knowledge. An internalist proceeds by requiring that the agent have a certain sort of *justification* for his belief. The externalist abandons the search for refined kinds of justification and requires certain kinds of causal connections between the fact known and the agent's belief.

[13] I am obviously presenting only a sketch of a theory of knowledge here. Further, I do not here suppose that this is obviously the *correct* account of knowledge. I am merely pointing to an analogy between my approach to moral responsibility and the externalist conception of knowledge. The approach to knowledge presented here follows those of, among others, Dretske and Nozick: F. Dretske, "Conclusive Reasons," *The Australasian Journal of Philosophy* 49 (1971), pp. 1–22; and Nozick, op. cit., pp. 167–98. Nozick also discusses the analogy between moral responsibility and knowledge.

the actual world; that there are more remote possibilities in which the proposition p is false is not taken by the approach to be germane to whether the individual has knowledge.[14]

The cases described above might suggest that an agent has knowledge that p only if he has the ability to discriminate the conditions that would obtain if p were true from those that would obtain if p were false. However, consider the following examples (due to Nozick):

A grandmother sees her grandson is well when he comes to visit; but if he were sick or dead, others would tell her he was well to spare her upset. Yet this does not mean she doesn't know he is well (or at least ambulatory) when she sees him.[15]

S believes a certain building is a theater and concert hall. He has attended plays and concerts there. . . . However, if the building were not a theater, it would have housed a nuclear reactor that would so have altered the air around it (let us suppose) that everyone upon approaching the theater would have become lethargic and nauseous, and given up the attempt to buy a ticket. The government cover story would have been that the building was a theater, a cover story they knew would be safe since no unmedicated person could approach through the nausea field to discover any differently. Everyone, let us suppose, would have believed the cover story; they would have believed that the building they saw (but only from some distance) was a theater.[16]

These examples are epistemological analogues to Frankfurt-type cases in which an agent is morally responsible for performing an action, although he could not have done otherwise. In these cases an agent knows that p, although he lacks the pertinent discriminatory capacity. Just as we switched from demanding agent-responsiveness to demanding mechanism-responsiveness for moral responsibility, it is appropriate to demand only mechanism-sensitivity to truth, in order for an agent to have knowledge.

As Nozick points out, it is possible to believe that p via a truth-sensitive mechanism, and thus know that p, even though an insensitive mechanism would have operated in the alternative scenario (or scenarios). Thus, we want an actual-sequence theory of knowledge, just as we want an actual-sequence theory of responsibility. We need to distinguish between actual-sequence and alternative-sequence mechanisms and focus on the properties of the actual-sequence mechanism. But whereas there is a strong analogy between the theories of responsibility and knowledge sketched above, I now want to point to two important differences between responsibility and knowledge.

[14] Nozick claims that this fact helps to refute a certain kind of epistemological skeptic: Nozick, op. cit., pp. 197–247.
[15] Nozick, op. cit., p. 179.
[16] Ibid., pp. 180–1. Nozick attributes this example to Avishai Margalit.

First, in the theory of responsibility presented above, if an agent acts on a mechanism of type M, there must be *some* possible scenario in which M operates, the agent has sufficient reason to do otherwise, and he does do otherwise, in order for the agent to be morally responsible for his action. The possible scenario need not be the one that would have occurred if M had operated and the agent had sufficient reason to do otherwise. That is, the scenario pertinent to responsibility ascriptions need not be the scenario (or set of them) in which an M-type mechanism operates and the agent has sufficient reason to do otherwise that are *most similar* to the actual scenario. In contrast, in the theory of knowledge presented above, if an agent believes that p via an M-type mechanism, then it must be the case that if an M-type mechanism were to operate and p were false, the agent would believe that p is false, if the agent is to know that p.

Roughly speaking, the logical possibilities pertinent to moral responsibility attributions may be more remote than those pertinent to knowledge attributions. I believe, then, that the connection between reasons and action that is necessary for moral responsibility is "looser" than the connection between truth and belief that is necessary for knowledge. Of course, this point is consistent with the claim that both knowledge and moral responsibility are "actual-sequence" notions; it is just that actual-sequence truth-sensitivity is defined more "strictly" (i.e., in terms of "closer" possibilities) than actual-sequence reasons-responsiveness.

But I believe there is a second difference between moral responsibility and knowledge. I have claimed that, just as moral responsibility does not require freedom to do otherwise, knowledge does not require the capacity to discriminate; what is sufficient in the case of responsibility is reasons-responsiveness, and in the case of knowledge, truth-sensitivity. Thus both notions are "actual-sequence" notions. But I wish to point out a stronger sense in which moral responsibility (and not knowledge) depends only on the actual sequence.

I claim that an agent's moral responsibility for an action is "supervenient on" the actual physical causal influences which issue in the action, whereas an agent's knowledge that p is *not* supervenient on the actual physical causal influences which issue in the belief that p. First, let me explain the supervenience claim for moral responsibility. It seems to me impossible that there be cases in which there are two agents who perform actions of the same type as a result of exactly the same kind of actual causal sequence, but in which one agent is morally responsible for the action and the other is *not*. Differences in responsibility ascriptions must come from differences in the actual physical factors resulting in action; mere differences in alternate scenarios do not translate into differences in responsibility ascriptions. That is, differences in responsibility ascriptions must come from differences in the actual histories of actions, and not mere "possible" histories.

Suppose you and I both heroically jump into the lake to save a drowning swimmer, and everything that actually happens in both cases is relevantly similar – except that whereas you could have done otherwise, I could not have. (I could not have done otherwise by virtue of the existence of a mechanism in my brain that would have stimulated it to produce a decision to save the swimmer, had I been inclined not to.) Insofar as the actual physical sequences issuing in our behavior are the same, we are equally morally responsible.

However, here is an epistemological example of Nozick's:

Consider another case, of a student who, when his philosophy class is cancelled, usually returns to his room and takes hallucinogenic drugs; one hallucination he has sometimes is of being in his philosophy class. When the student actually is in the philosophy class, does he know he is? I think not, for if he weren't in class, he still might believe he was. . . . Two students in the class might be in the same actual situation, having (roughly) the same retinal and aural intake, yet the first knows he is in class while the other does not, because they are situated differently subjunctively – different subjunctives hold true of them.[17]

The two students have exactly the same actual physical factors issue in beliefs that they are in class. However, one student does not know he is in class: If he were not in class (and he were to employ the method of introspection, which was actually employed), then he would (or at least might) still believe that he is in class (as a result of the drug). The other student – who is not disposed to use the drug – does know that he is in class. Thus knowledge is not supervenient on actual physical facts in the way that moral responsibility is.

I have claimed above that there is a certain parallel between moral responsibility and knowledge: The reasons-responsiveness of the actual mechanism leading to action suffices for responsibility, and the truth-sensitivity of the actual mechanism leading to belief suffices for knowledge. How exactly is this claim of parallelism compatible with the further claim that moral responsibility attributions are supervenient on actual physical causal factors, whereas knowledge attributions are *not*? I think the answer lies in our intuitive way of individuating "mechanisms." We tend to individuate mechanisms more finely in action theory than in epistemology.

In the case of the first student, we take the relevant mechanism

17 Ibid., p. 191.

issuing in belief to be "introspection." Of course, the same sort of mechanism would have operated had the student taken the drug. With this "wide" kind of individuation of mechanisms, it turns out that the mechanism that issues in the one student's belief is *not* truth-sensitive, whereas the mechanism of the other student *is*.

However, in the case in which I save the drowning child ("on my own"), it is natural to suppose that if I had been stimulated by the scientists, this would have been a *different* kind of mechanism from the one that actually operates. Similarly, had I been injected with a drug that issued in an irresistible desire to save the drowning swimmer, this would have constituted a *different* kind of mechanism from the actual one. With this "narrow" kind of individuation of mechanisms, it turns out that the mechanism that issues in my action of saving the child *is* reasons-responsive (just as yours is).

The asymmetry of supervenience is compatible with the symmetrically actual-sequence nature of knowledge and moral responsibility. The asymmetry of supervenience is generated by the intuitively natural tendency to individuate mechanisms issuing in belief more broadly than mechanisms issuing in action.[18]

Mechanisms

I have suggested that an agent is morally responsible for performing an action insofar as the mechanism that actually issues in the action is reasons-responsive; but this suggestion needs to be refined in light of the fact that various different mechanisms may actually operate in a given case. Which mechanism is relevant to responsibility ascriptions?

Suppose that I deliberate (in the normal way) about whether to donate 5 percent of my paycheck to the United Way, and that I decide to make the donation and act on my decision. We might fill in the story so that it is intuitively a paradigmatic case in which I am morally responsible for my action; and yet consider the actually operative mechanism, "deliberation preceding donating 5 percent of one's salary to the United Way." If *this* kind of mechanism were to operate, then I would give 5 percent of my paycheck to the United Way in any

---

[18] I have left extremely vague the crucial notion of "same mechanism." There are certainly very disturbing problems with this notion in epistemology. For a discussion of some of these problems, see Robert Shope, "Cognitive Abilities, Conditionals, and Knowledge: A Response to Nozick," *Journal of Philosophy* 81, n. 1 (1984), pp. 29–48. And there may well be similar problems in action theory. Here I am simply relying on some intuitive way of individuating kinds of mechanisms issuing in action, for the purposes of moral responsibility ascriptions. A defense of the sketch of a theory that I am presenting would involve saying more about the individuation of mechanisms.

logically possible scenario. Thus, this kind of actually operative mechanism is *not* reasons-responsive.

However, a mechanism such as "deliberating prior to giving 5 percent of one's salary to the United Way" is not of the kind that is relevant to moral responsibility ascriptions. This is because it is not a "temporally intrinsic" mechanism. The operation of a temporally extrinsic or "relational" mechanism "already includes" the occurrence of the action it is supposed to cause.

Note that the operation of a mechanism of the kind "deliberating prior to giving 5 percent of one's paycheck to the United Way" *entails* that one give 5 percent of one's paycheck to the United Way. In this sense, then, the mechanism already includes the action: Its operation entails that the action occurs. Thus, it is a necessary condition of a mechanism's relevance to moral responsibility ascriptions (on the theory proposed here) that it be a "temporally intrinsic" or "nonrelational" mechanism in the following sense: If a mechanism M issues in act X, then M is relevant to the agent's moral responsibility for performing X only if M's operating does not entail that X occurs. I believe that the requirement that a mechanism be temporally intrinsic is an intuitively natural and unobjectionable one. Of course, we have so far only a necessary condition for being a relevant mechanism; there may be various different mechanisms that issue in an action, all of which are temporally intrinsic. Which mechanism is "the" mechanism pertinent to moral responsibility ascription?

I do not have a theory that will specify in a general way how to determine which mechanism is "the" mechanism relevant to assessment of responsibility. It is simply a presupposition of this theory as presented above that, for each act, an intuitively natural mechanism is appropriately selected as *the* mechanism that issues in action, for the purposes of assessing moral responsibility.

I do not think this presupposition is problematic. But if there is a worry, it is useful to note that the basic theory can be formulated without such a presupposition. As so far developed, the theory says that an agent is morally responsible for performing an action insofar as the (relevant, temporally intrinsic) mechanism issuing in the action is reasons-responsive. Alternatively, one could say that an agent is morally responsible for an action insofar as there is no actually operative temporally intrinsic mechanism issuing in the action that is not reasons-responsive. This alternative formulation obviates the need to select one mechanism as the "relevant" one. In what follows I continue to employ the first formulation, but the basic points should apply equally to the alternative formulation.

I wish now to apply the theory to a few cases. We think intuitively that irresistible urges can be "psychologically compulsive" and can rule out moral responsibility. Imagine that Jim has a literally irresistible urge to take a certain drug, and that he does in fact take the drug. What exactly is the relevant mechanism that issues in Jim's taking the drug? Notice that the mechanism, "deliberation involving an irresistible urge to take the drug," is not temporally intrinsic and thus not admissible as a mechanism pertinent to moral responsibility ascription: Its operation entails that Jim takes the drug. Consider, then, the mechanism "deliberation involving an irresistible desire." Whereas this mechanism *is* temporally intrinsic, it is also reasons-responsive: There is a possible scenario in which Jim acts on this kind of mechanism and refrains from taking the drug. In this scenario, Jim has an irresistible urge to *refrain* from taking the drug. These considerations show that neither "deliberation involving an irresistible desire for the drug" nor "deliberation involving an irresistible desire" is the relevant mechanism (if the theory of responsibility is to achieve an adequate "fit" with our intuitive judgments).

When Jim acts on an irresistible urge to take the drug, there is some physical process of kind P taking place in his central nervous system. When a person undergoes this kind of physical process, we say that the urge is literally irresistible. I believe that what underlies our intuitive claim that Jim is not morally responsible for taking the drug is that the relevant kind of mechanism issuing in Jim's taking the drug is of physical kind P, and that a mechanism of kind P is not reasons-responsive. When an agent acts from a literally irresistible urge, he is undergoing a kind of physical process that is not reasons-responsive, and it is this lack of reasons-responsiveness of the actual physical process that rules out moral responsibility.[19]

Consider again my claim that certain sorts of "direct manipulation of the brain" rule out moral responsibility. It is clear that not all such manipulations would rule out moral responsibility. Suppose, for instance, that a scientist manipulates just one brain cell at the periphery of my brain. This kind of manipulation need not rule out responsibility insofar as this kind of physical process can be reasons-responsive. It is when the scientists intervene and manipulate the brain in a way which is *not* reasons-responsive that they undermine an agent's moral responsibility for action.[20]

[19] The claim, as stated, relies on the intuition that the physical process P is the relevant mechanism. Alternatively, one could simply point out that in Jim's case *there exists* an actually operative mechanism (of kind P) that is temporally intrinsic and not reasons-responsive.

[20] Daniel Dennett says: "The possibility of short-circuiting or otherwise tampering with an intentional system gives rise to an interesting group of perplexities about the extent of responsibility in cases where there has been manipulation. We are generally absolved

Similarly, not all forms of subliminal advertising, hypnosis, brain-washing, and so on are inconsistent with moral responsibility for an action. It is only when these activities yield physical mechanisms that are not reasons-responsive that they rule out moral responsibility. Thus, the theory that associates moral responsibility with actual-sequence reasons-responsiveness can help to explain our intuitive distinctions between causal influences that are consistent with moral responsibility and those that are not.

Consider also the class of legal defenses that might be dubbed "Twinkie-type" defenses. This kind of defense claims that an agent ought not to be punished because he ate too much "junk food" (and that this impaired his capacities, etc.). In the approach presented here, the question of whether an agent ought to be punished is broken into two parts: (1) Is the agent morally responsible (i.e., rationally accessible to punishment), and (2) if so, to what degree ought the agent to be punished? The theory of moral responsibility I have presented allows us to respond positively to the first question in the typical "Twinkie-type" case.

Even if an individual has eaten a diet composed only of junk food, it is highly implausible to think that this yields a biological process that is not weakly reasons-responsive. At the very most, such a process might not be strongly reasons-responsive, but strong reasons-responsiveness is *not* necessary for moral responsibility. Our outrage at the suggestion that a junk food eater is not morally responsible may come from two sources. The outrage could be a reaction to the "philosophical" mistake of demanding strong rather than weak reasons-responsiveness; or the outrage could be a reaction to the implausible suggestion that junk food consumption yields a mechanism that is not weakly reasons-responsive.

Thus the theory of responsibility supports the intuitive idea that "Twinkie-type" defendants are morally responsible for what they do. Of course, the question of the appropriate *degree* of punishment is a separate question; but it is important to notice that it is *not* a consequence of the theory of responsibility that an agent who acts on a mechanism that is weakly but not strongly reasons-responsive is properly punished to a *lesser* degree than an agent who acts on a mechanism that is strongly reasons-responsive. This may, but need not be, a part of one's full theory of punishment.

of responsibility where we have been manipulated by others, but there is no one principle of innocence by reason of manipulation." Daniel Dennett, "Mechanism of Responsibility," reprinted in Dennett (ed.), *Brainstorms* (Montgomery, VT: Bradford Books, 1978), pp. 233–55, esp. p. 248. My suggestion provides a way of distinguishing responsibility-undermining manipulation from manipulation that is consistent with responsibility.

Temporal considerations

I wish to consider a problem for the theory of responsibility that I have been developing. This problem will force a refinement in the theory. Suppose Max (who enjoys drinking but is not an alcoholic) goes to a party where he drinks so much that he is almost oblivious to his surroundings. In this state of intoxication he gets into his car and tries to drive home. Unfortunately, he runs over a child who is walking in a crosswalk. Although the actual-sequence mechanism issuing in Max's running over the child is plausibly taken to lack reasons-responsiveness, we may nevertheless feel that Max *is* morally responsible for running over the child.

This is one case in a class of cases in which an agent acts at a time T_1 on a reasons-responsive mechanism that causes him to act at T_2 on a mechanism that is *not* reasons-responsive. Further, Max ought to have known that getting drunk at the party would lead to driving in a condition in which he would be unresponsive. Thus, Max can be held morally responsible for his action at T_2 by virtue of the operation of a suitable sort of reasons-responsive mechanism at a prior time T_1. When one acts on a reasons-responsive mechanism at time T_1 and one ought to know that so acting will lead to acting on an unresponsive mechanism at some later time T_2, one can be held morally responsible for so acting at T_2. Thus, the theory of moral responsibility should be interpreted as claiming that moral responsibility for an act at T requires the actual operation of a reasons-responsive mechanism at T or some suitable earlier time. (For simplicity's sake, I suppress mention of the temporal indexation below.)

An individual might cultivate dispositions to act virtuously in certain circumstances. It might even be the case that when he acts virtuously, the motivation to do so is so strong that the mechanism is not reasons-responsive. But insofar as reasons-responsive mechanisms issued in the person's cultivation of the virtue, that person can be held morally responsible for his action. It is only when it is true that at no suitable point along the path to the action did a reasons-responsive mechanism operate that an agent will not properly be held responsible for an action.

Semicompatibilism

I have presented a very sketchy theory of responsibility. The basic idea would have to be developed and explained much more carefully in order to have a fully adequate theory of responsibility, but enough of the theory has been given to draw out some of its implications. My claim is that the theory sketched here leads to compatibilism about moral responsibility and such doctrines as God's foreknowledge and causal determinism.

Let us first consider the relationship between causal determinism and moral responsibility. The theory of moral responsibility presented here helps us to reconcile causal determinism with moral responsibility, even if causal determinism is inconsistent with freedom to do otherwise. The case for the incompatibility of causal determinism and freedom to do otherwise is different from (and stronger than) the case for the incompatibility of causal determinism and moral responsibility.

Causal determinism can be defined as follows:

> *Causal determinism* is the thesis that, for any given time, a complete statement of the facts about the world at that time, together with a complete statement of the laws of nature, entails every truth as to what happens after that time.

Now the "basic argument" for the incompatibility of causal determinism and freedom to do otherwise can be presented. If causal determinism obtains, then (roughly speaking) the past together with the natural laws entail that I act as I do now. So if I am free to do otherwise, then I must either have power over the past or power over the laws of nature. But since the past and the laws of nature are "fixed" – for instance, I cannot now so act that the past would have been different from what it actually was – it follows that I am not now free to do otherwise.[21]

This is obviously a brief presentation of the argument; a more careful and detailed look at the "basic argument" is beyond the scope of this presentation.[22] It should be evident, however, that a compatibilist about causal determinism and freedom to do otherwise must either deny the fixity of the past or the fixity of the laws. That is, such

---

[21] For some contemporary developments of the "basic argument" for incompatibilism, see Carl Ginet, "Might We Have No Choice?", in K. Lehrer (ed.), *Freedom and Determinism* (New York: Random House, 1966); David Wiggins, "Towards a Reasonable Libertarianism," in T. Honderich (ed.), *Essays on Freedom of Action* (Boston: Routledge and Kegan Paul, 1973); J. W. Lamb, "On a Proof of Incompatibilism," *Philosophical Review* 86 (1977); and Peter van Inwagen, "The Incompatibility of Free Will and Determinism," *Philosophical Studies* 27 (1975), and *An Essay on Free Will* (Oxford: Clarendon Press, 1983), esp. pp. 55–105.

[22] I have discussed the argument in John Martin Fischer, "Incompatibilism," *Philosophical Studies* 43, (1983), pp. 127–37; "Van Inwagen on Free Will," *Philosophical Quarterly* 36 (1986), pp. 252–60; and "Freedom and Miracles," forthcoming, *Nous*. For a classic discussion of the argument, see David Lewis, "Are We Free to Break the Laws?", *Theoria* 47 (1981), pp. 113–21.

a compatibilist must say that an agent can have it in his power at a time so to act that the past would have been different from what it actually was, or that an agent can have it in his power so to act that a natural law that actually obtains would not obtain.[23] Even if these compatibilist claims are not obviously false, they are certainly not easy to swallow.

The approach to moral responsibility developed here allows us to separate compatibilism about causal determinism and moral responsibility from compatibilism about causal determinism and freedom to do otherwise. The theory says that an agent can be held morally responsible for performing an action insofar as the mechanism actually issuing in the action is reasons-responsive; the agent need not be free to do otherwise. As I explain below, reasons-responsiveness of the actual-sequence mechanism is consistent with causal determination. Thus a compatibilist about determinism and moral responsibility can *accept* the fixity of the past and the fixity of the natural laws. He need not accept the unappealing claims to which the compatibilist about causal determinism and freedom to do otherwise is committed. If it is the "basic argument" that pushes one to incompatibilism about causal determinism and freedom to do otherwise, this need not also push one toward incompatibilism about causal determinism and moral responsibility.

The theory of responsibility requires reasons-responsive mechanisms. For a mechanism to be reasons-responsive, there must be a possible scenario in which the same kind of mechanism operates and the agent does otherwise; but, of course, sameness of kind of mechanism need not require sameness of all details, even down to the "micro" level. Nothing in our intuitive conception of a kind of mechanism leading to action or in our judgments about clear cases of moral responsibility requires us to say that sameness of kind of mechanism implies sameness of micro details. Thus, the scenarios pertinent to the reasons-responsivenes of an actual-sequence mechanism may differ with respect both to the sort of incentives the agent has to do otherwise and the particular details of the mechanism issuing in action. (Note that if causal determinism obtains and I do X, then one sort of mechanism which actually operates is a "causally determined to do X" type of mechanism. But of course this kind of mechanism is not germane to responsibility ascriptions insofar as it is not temporally

---

23 For an interesting alternative challenge to certain formulations of the "basic argument," see Michael Slote, "Selective Necessity and the Free-Will Problem," *Journal of Philosophy* 82 (1982), pp. 5–24.

intrinsic. And whereas the kind, "causally determined," is temporally intrinsic and thus may be germane, it is reasons-responsive.)

If causal determinism is true, then any possible scenario (with the actual natural laws) in which the agent does otherwise at time T must differ in *some* respect from the actual scenario prior to T. The existence of such possible scenarios is all that is required by the theory of moral responsibility. It is not required that the agent be able to bring about such a scenario (i.e., that the agent have it in his power at T so to act that the past, relative to T, would have been different from what it actually was). Furthermore, the existence of the required kind of scenarios is compatible with causal determinism.

The actual-sequence reasons-responsiveness theory of moral responsibility thus yields "semicompatibilism": Moral responsibility is compatible with causal determinism, even if causal determinism is incompatible with freedom to do otherwise. Compatibilism about determinism and responsibility is compatible with *both* compatibilism and incompatibilism (as well as agnosticism) about determinism and freedom to do otherwise.[24]

Often incompatibilists use the example discussed above of the demonic scientists who directly manipulate one's brain. They then pose a challenge to the compatibilist: In what way is this sort of case *different* from the situation under causal determinism? There is clearly the following similarity: In both the cases of manipulation and determination, conditions entirely "external" to the agent causally suffice to produce an action. Thus, it may be that neither agent is free to do otherwise. However, as I argued above, there seems to be a crucial difference between the case of direct manipulation and "mere" causal determination. In a case of direct manipulation of the brain, it is likely that the process issuing in the action is not reasons-responsive, whereas the fact that a process is causally deterministic does not in itself bear on whether it is reasons-responsive. The force of the incompatibilist's challenge can be seen to come from the plausible idea that in neither case does the agent have freedom to do otherwise; but it can be answered by pointing to a difference in the actual-sequence mechanisms.

---

[24] I believe that Frankfurt is a compatibilistic semicompatibilist. I am an agnostic semicompatibilist, although I am perhaps a latently incompatibilistic semicompatibilist. In "Responsibility and Control" I pointed out that Frankfurt-type cases do not in themselves establish the consistency of causal determinism and moral responsibility. Thus, Frankfurt-type cases leave open the position of "ultra-incompatibilism": Causal determinism is incompatible with moral responsibility, even if moral responsibility does not require freedom to do otherwise. Here I have preferred agnostic (or perhaps incompatibilistic) semicompatibilism to agnostic (or incompatibilistic) ultra-incompatibilism.

The same sort of considerations show that moral responsibility is consistent with God's foreknowledge, even if God's foreknowledge is incompatible with freedom to do otherwise. Let us suppose that God exists and thus knew in the past exactly how I would behave today. If I am free to do otherwise, then I must be free so to act that the past would have been different from what it actually was (i.e., so to act that God would have held a different belief from the one He actually held). However, the past is fixed, and so it is plausible to think that I am not free to do otherwise, if God exists.

God's existence, however, is surely compatible with the operation of a reasons-responsive mechanism. God's belief is not a part of the mechanism issuing in my action (on a standard view of the nature of God). His belief is not what causes my action; rather, my action explains His belief. Thus there are possible scenarios in which the actual kind of mechanism operates and issues in my doing otherwise. (In these scenarios, God believes correctly that I will do other than what I do in the actual world.) Again, the cases for the two sorts of incompatibilism – about divine foreknowledge and responsibility and about divine foreknowledge and freedom to do otherwise – are *different*, and the actual-sequence reasons-responsiveness theory yields semi-compatibilism.[25]

Structure and history

In this section I wish to contrast my approach to moral responsibility with a class of theories that might be called "mesh" theories of responsibility. My approach is a historical theory.

Consider first a "hierarchical" model of moral responsibility. In this

[25] I have here sketched an approach that attempts to reconcile moral responsibility *for action* with causal determinism and God's foreknowledge. My approach relies on the claim that moral responsibility for an action does not require freedom to do otherwise. Elsewhere I have argued that, whereas an agent can be morally responsible for performing an action although he could not have done otherwise, an agent cannot be held responsible for *not* performing an action he could not have performed: John Martin Fischer, "Responsibility and Failure," *Proceedings of the Aristotelian Society* 86 (1985–6), pp. 251–70. If this "asymmetry thesis" is true, then I still have not reconciled moral responsibility *for omissions* (or perhaps, for "not-doings") with causal determinism (and divine foreknowledge).

I do not have the space here fully to develop my theory of responsibility for not performing actions. But I can say that, even if an agent is not responsible for failing to do something he could not do, an agent may be held morally responsible for *something* (perhaps, a "positive" action). And so he will be accessible to praise or blame. I believe that such a theory of moral responsibility can be developed so as to reconcile causal determinism (and divine foreknowledge) with the moral attitudes we think are intuitively appropriate.

model, a person is morally responsible for an action insofar as there is a mesh between a higher-order preference and the first-order preference that actually moves him to action. On one version of this theory, which is suggested by some remarks by Harry Frankfurt, an agent is morally responsible for an action if there is conformity between his "second-order volition" and "will" (the first-order desire that moves the person to action).[26]

In another version of the theory, moral responsibility for an action is associated with conformity between "identification" and will.[27] According to Frankfurt's suggestion, one way of identifying with a first-order desire would be to formulate an unopposed second-order volition to act on it, together with a judgment that no further reflection would cause one to change one's mind.

The problem with such hierarchical "mesh" theories, no matter how they are refined, is that the selected mesh can be produced via responsibility-undermining mechanisms. After all, a demonic neurophysiologist can induce the conformity between the various mental elements via a sort of direct electronic stimulation that is not reasons-responsive. I believe that the problem with the hierarchical mesh theories is precisely that they are purely structural and ahistorical. It matters what kind of process issues in an action. Specifically, the mechanism issuing in the action must be reasons-responsive.

The "multiple-source" mesh theories are also purely structural. Rather than positing a hierarchy of preferences, these theories posit different sources of preferences. One such theory is that of Gary Watson, according to which there are "valuational preferences" (which come from reason) and motivational preferences.[28] Employing Watson's theory, one could say that an agent is morally responsible for an action insofar as there is a mesh between the valuational and motivational preference to perform the action.[29]

Again the problem is that such a theory is purely structural. The mesh between elements of different preference systems may be induced by electronic stimulation, hypnosis, brainwashing, and so on.

[26] Harry Frankfurt, "Freedom of the Will and the Concept of a Person," *Journal of Philosophy* 68 (1971), pp. 5–20, esp. p. 15.
[27] Frankfurt discusses the notion of identification in Harry Frankfurt, "Identification and Externality," in A. O. Rorty (ed.), *The Identities of Persons* (Berkeley: University of California Press, 1976); and "Identification and Wholeheartedness," Chapter 2 of this book.
[28] Gary Watson, "Free Agency," *Journal of Philosophy* 72 (1975), pp. 205–20.
[29] I am not sure whether Watson himself is committed to the sufficiency of the mesh for moral responsibility. He is committed to the claim that an agent is free insofar as he has the power to effect a mesh between the valuational and motivational systems: ibid., p. 216.

Moral responsibility is a *historical* phenomenon; it is a matter of the kind of mechanism that issues in action.[30]

Conclusion

I have presented a sketch of a theory that purports to identify the class of actions for which persons are rationally accessible to moral praise and blame, and reward and punishment. I have claimed that this theory captures our clear intuitive judgments about moral responsibility, and that it helps to reconcile moral responsibility with causal determinism. I certainly have not *proved* that moral responsibility is compatible with causal determinism. Rather, my strategy has been to argue that the approach presented here allows the compatibilist about moral responsibility and determinism to avoid the commitments of the compatibilist about freedom to do otherwise and determinism. There might be other sorts of challenges to compatibilism about determinism and moral responsibility that my approach does not, in itself, answer.

The theory I have presented builds upon and extends the approaches of others. It avoids some of the most pressing objections to similar types of theories. These objections might seem convincing if one fails to "hold fixed" the actual-sequence mechanism, or if one employs strong rather than weak reasons-responsiveness, or if one does not suitably temporally index the theory.

I wish to end with a few suggestions about the relationship between the theory of moral responsibility presented here and punishment. A theory of moral responsibility needs to explain why cerain creatures (and not others) are appropriate candidates for punishment. Punishment, of course, involves treating an individual "harshly" in some manner. It affects the desirability of performing a certain action. That is, punishment involves reacting to persons in ways to which the mechanisms on which they act are sensitive. My suggestion is that punishment is appropriate only for a creature who acts on a mechanism "keyed to" the kind of incentives punishment provides.

My point here is not that the justification of punishment is "consequentialist" – that it alters behavior. (Of course, this kind of justification does not in itself distinguish punishment from aversive condi-

---

[30] Moral responsibility is in this respect like such notions as justice and love for a particular person. Nozick argues in *Anarchy, State, and Utopia* (New York: Basic Books, 1974) that justice and love are historical rather than "current time-slice" notions. Purely structural approaches to moral responsibility are inadequate in a way that is parallel to the inadequacy of current time-slice approaches to justice.

tioning.) Indeed, it is metaphysically possible that an individual's total pattern of choices and actions throughout life be "unalterable" by virtue of a continuous string of Frankfurt-type situations. (It is even possible that *no* human's behavior is alterable, because it is possible that all human beings are subject to Frankfurt-type "counterfactual interventions".) My justification is nonconsequentialist and "direct": Punishment is an appropriate reaction to the actual operation of reasons-responsive mechanisms. When it is justified, punishment involves a kind of "match" between the mechanism that produces behavior and the response to that behavior.

The theory of moral responsibility, then, provides some insight into the appropriateness of punishment for certain actions. But it does not in itself provide a full account of the appropriate *degrees* of punishment. For instance, it may be the case that the appropriate degree of severity of punishment for a particular action is less than (or greater than) the magnitude of the incentive to which the actual-sequence mechanism is responsive. This is entirely compatible with saying that punishment – being a "provider of reasons" – is appropriately directed to agents who act on reasons-responsive mechanisms.

6

Determinism and freedom in Spinoza, Maimonides, and Aristotle
A retrospective study
LENN E. GOODMAN

Determinism is the belief that things must be as they are. Three types of determinism are distinguishable: logical, theological, and causal. Logical determinism rests on the notion that a thing cannot be other than it is without somehow violating the universal rule that each thing must preserve its own identity. For a thing to depart from being as it is is interpreted in one sense or another as a departure from its being *what* it is. Theological determinism is founded on the belief that God makes all things as they are. Causal determinism is the belief that things must be as they are because their causes make them so.

The three determinisms overlap not only because their advocacy may coexist in the same thinker, but because their terms of reference are often interpreted in one another's senses and their claims are often made dependent on one another's assertions. Thus God is treated as a cause or as a cause of causes in most varieties of theological determinism; in some, the work of causes or the fabric of causality is interpreted as an act of God. When the divine is assimilated to fate and fate to the underlying nature of things or character of reality, causal, theological, and logical determinism may coincide. Similarly, when efforts are made to analyze the necessity affirmed in any of the three versions of determinism, causality, via essentialism, can be made a matter of identity; and the metaphysical requirement of identity (that a thing be what it is) is readily interpreted as a requirement of logic. The same movement between logic and metaphysics, via identity, can be traced in some varieties of theological determinism – those that regard God Himself as determined and argue that God cannot be other than He is or do other than He does.[1]

[1] For some recent discussions of determinism, see Douglas Odegard, "Analytical Approaches to Determinism," in *Dialogue* (Canada) 23 (1984), 271–80; Daniel Dennett, "I Could Not Have Done Otherwise – So What?" *Journal of Philosophy* 81 (1984), 553–65 and *Elbow Room: The Varieties of Free Will Worth Wanting* (Cambridge: MIT, 1984). And indeterminism: Charles Hartshorne, "Indeterministic Freedom as Universal Prin-

This chapter examines the affirmation of human freedom in three philosophers who were cornerstones of the Western tradition of moral philosophy and metaphysics historically and who were all committed to determinism in one or several of our three senses. The philosophers in question are Aristotle, Maimonides, and Spinoza. I believe that an examination of the sense these philosophers gave to their affirmations of determinism – specifically, the manner in which they made conceptual distinctions that gave place to human freedom – can be instructive for present-day philosophical inquiries.

What I propose is to proceed at first chronologically, to examine the sense given to necessity in each of these three thinkers, noting the philosophic rationales that give credibility to each position and especially the linkages between the causal, logical, and theological considerations. Then I think we should thread our way back from Spinoza to Maimonides to Aristotle, considering Spinoza's view that man is free to the extent that he is the adequate cause of his own actions, Maimonides' voluntaristic account of choice and character, and finally

---

cipal," *Journal of Social Philosophy* 15 (1984), 5–11. Augustine Schutte, "The Refutation of Determinism," *Philosophy* 59 (1984), 481–90. It is sometimes claimed that determinism can be stated without the use of modal categories. This I would question. If it is said that determinism is the belief that all true propositions are true in all possible worlds, where the modality of possibility is dissolved by defining possible worlds as combinations of facts it is not self-contradictory to deny, I would argue that the reductive account of possibility employed here does not define but only sketches in formal and inevitably somewhat distorted terms the rather richer notion of determination that determinists employ. For the formalized account in which modality is dissolved at once says more and less than determinists in general intend. Not all determinists intend the equation of causal with logical necessity, which the reduction brings in train. (It was to save the distinction between natural and logical necessity that Leibniz introduced the idea of possible worlds. And subsequent possible worlds theorists similarly preserve the distinction between logical and natural necessity by applying further restrictions than those of self-consistency to the universe of possible worlds. Such material restrictions play the role of Leibniz's idea of *compossibility* in preserving the thrust of the modal concept.) Again, causal determinists do not claim that all actual events must take place under all logically possible circumstances (i.e., will occur in all possible worlds), but that each must take place (will occur) in all and only those worlds that contain its causes in suitable combination. Logical atomism is not adequate to the mapping of this claim when it seeks to define necessity truth conditionally. Consider a Laplacean universe. The state of such a universe at any given time can be described by a (long) number, an ordered set indicating the positions and velocities of all particles at that time. Given one number and time, one could deduce the state (number) for any prior or subsequent time, *provided* one knew the laws of physics: The state of the universe at time t is necessary, but not in itself; it is necessary relative to the laws of physics, which relate it to antecedent states of the identical set of particles – that is, to its causes. The modal element is not dissolved when the universe is described as occupying a series of states that have a determinate mathematical relationship to one another. It is preserved (albeit perhaps concealed) in the modal force of the propositions describing the relationship. Without modality, those propositions would not uniquely specify the state of the universe at any given time, given its state at any other.

Aristotle's subtle account of the manner in which knowledge works and fails to work in making us morally free. All three thinkers are rationalists – intellectualists, in fact, in one sense or another. So Aristotle's conception of the limits of the contribution thought can make to action is critical to the project on which all three are embarked. In this project, Aristotle lays the foundation on which Maimonides and Spinoza build their conceptions of human freedom. And examination of the accomplishments of Maimonides and Spinoza in developing some of the key Aristotelian commitments will in turn enhance our appreciation of what we might be inclined to call Aristotle's theory of excuses.

Aristotle's determinism

Aristotle's commitment to determinism is rooted in his logic, grows to metaphysical stature in his essentialism, and flowers in his theory and practice of scientific observation and speculation.[2] The heritage is Parmenidean. For Parmenides had founded logic and metaphysics on the recognition that a thing must be what it is and cannot be anything else. Parmenides interpreted the notion of identity as an implication of the law of the excluded middle and understood it to imply in turn the impossibility of all change. Not distinguishing facts from things, Parmenides took any negation for the absolute negation (affirmation of pure nullity) which his primary metaphysical insight (nonbeing is unthinkable) took to be impossible. The disjunction expressed within the law of contradiction, interpreted materially in favor of affirmation and against "unthinkable" negation, seemed to imply that plurality was as impossible as process or (finitizing) predication, for all differentiation depends upon negation.[3]

There was much for Aristotle's analysis to clear up. His crucial first move, the opening shot in the *Categories,* which sets forth his theory of predication, was to pinion the fallacy of equivocation. If diverse senses of the verb "to be" can be distinguished, then it can be shown that what is affirmed when one identifies Socrates is not negated

[2] For the scope and character of Aristotle's work in the empirical natural sciences, see G. E. R. Lloyd, *Aristotle: The Growth and Structure of His Thought* (Cambridge: Cambridge University Press, 1977, first ed. 1968), 68–93.

[3] See Parmenides, Fragments 6, 7, 8 ap. Simplicius *Phys.* 117, 4; Plato *Sophist* 237a/ Sextus *Adv. Math* VII 114; 145–46, items 345–52 in G. S. Kirk and J. E. Raven, *The Presocratic Philosophers* (Cambridge: Cambridge University Press, 1962). For the continuing conflict between logic of the "strict" or Parmenidean type and the nonextensional (ultimately, intensional) notions of time (tense) and modality, see Alan Code, "Aristotle's Response to Quine's Objections to Modal Logic," *Journal of Philosophical Logic* 5 (1976), 159–86.

when one denies that Socrates is Plato or when one affirms that Socrates grows musical. Substances are differentiated from their accidents by Aristotle in the interest of predication, plurality, and change. At the same time, it must be recognized that the differentiation of the categories is effectuated by Aristotle in the interest of sustaining what he intuitively found true in Parmenides' claims: Absolute nonbeing and absolute genesis or destruction remain impossible. A particular can become what it is not, either accidentally (Socrates becomes musical) or essentially (Socrates dies). But no particular can become what is not absolutely (none can be annihilated), and none can come to be from nothing (there is no absolute creation).

A primary reason for Aristotle's differentiating substance from accident and assigning a certain ontic primacy to *secondary* substance (that is, species)[4] is Aristotle's fidelity to what he saw as true in the logic cum metaphysics of Parmenides: the thesis that what is (at least in the most primary way) cannot not be. Essences express the identity of things not as individuals, but as members of natural classes, and essences (just as in Plato) do not change. Indeed, it is because individuals come and go that essences are necessary – both for science and for nature. Thus individuals (primary substances) can persist through change. This is necessary if any sort of change (viz., alteration) is to be interpreted as consistent with identity and the very logic of change itself is not be regarded as implying absolute negation of the subject term. Species exist eternally and unchangingly – unchangeably. So what is and what is known to be, at least in the rock bottom sense, cannot be otherwise.

Now Aristotle is not averse to what we would call a somewhat statistical approach to natural laws. He knows of sports of nature and his approach to all sorts of anomalies is far more open, say, than that of Hume, who founds his expectations on what is customary and familiar.[5] Natural necessity for Aristotle is what is true always or for the most part. Yet there is a striking excrescence of Aristotle's Parmeni-

---

[4] For Aristotle's position and the conflicting factors that sway him, see Edward Booth, *Aristotelian Aporetic Ontology in Islamic and Christian Thinkers* (Cambridge: Cambridge University Press, 1983), and my review in *Philosophy East and West* 37 (1987).

[5] For nature as made up of events that hold always or for the most part, see Aristotle *Physics* II 5, 196b 10 and II 8, 198b 32; *Metaphysics* Epsilon 2, 102b 26–34; *Prior Analytics* I 13, 32a 18–21. Contrast the Peripatetic empiric interest in collecting accounts of rare, unlikely and unique events with Hume's assertion that certain types of events are so unprecedented that he would not believe accounts of them (even though beliefs about the past have no logical bearing upon beliefs about the future): Compare the Peripatetic *De Mirabilibus Auscultationibus* and Aristotle's *De Divinatione per Somnum* with Hume's *Of Miracles*.

dean heritage in his thesis that there are no unrealized possibilities.[6] In his polemic with the Megarian heirs of Eleatic monism, Aristotle defends real possibility against the Megarian denial. To accept what seems the overstringent Megarian interpretation of the law of the excluded middle (as applied to judgments about the future) would lead to the rejection of time and change and the complete undoing all of Aristotle's good work on predication. Potentiality is the bulwark of that work: A is not negated when it is claimed that the A that was ϕ is not longer ϕ but ψ, because A *was* ψ *potentially*. Aristotle's affirmation of real potentiality would seem to commit him to the assertion that some potentialities are unrealized. For surely the potential of A to be ψ before A was so was unrealized. But in the universal perspective of cosmic time, the Parmenidean logic takes over: If there is no time at which A is or will be ψ, then it is senseless, Aristotle argued, to say that A is ψ potentially. The concession plays into the hands of later Megarians like Diodorus Cronus, yielding a premise of his celebrated master argument. But Aristotle takes this route nonetheless, because (like many logicians since) he inclines to equate necessity with universal tense quantification. It is his rationalism that leads him to admit the identity of what will never be with the impossible: If a thing will never be, then it has no cause in nature. Here we see the obverse of Aristotle's causal determinism: Since all things that are have definite causes, all things that have no definite causes can never be.

Despite the "statistical" expression of Aristotle's naturalism, his notion of natural necessity is founded in logic – that is, it is founded in the logical necessity of things being what they are, which he interprets by reference to the idea of things remaining true to their essences.[7] Species are not merely natural groups, they are natural groups held together by sets of intelligible characteristics in terms of which the members most truly are what they are and act and suffer as they do. These characteristics, the essential properties of things, are the subject matter of science. They found the immutable principles which are the steady, conceptual content that scientific understanding requires – for there is no science of the unique as unique, or of the changeable qua changing.[8] Natural, essential properties ground natural necessity in the logic it requires. For the goal of Aristotelian science is the

---

[6] See *De Caelo* I 10–12, cf. *Physics* III 4, 203b 30 and *Metaphysics* Theta 8, 1050b 9–24; but Aristotle qualifies this view at *Metaphysics* Theta 3, 1047a.

[7] Thus Aristotle can say of necessity in mathematics and in nature that they are "almost the same." *Physics* II 9, 200a 15.

[8] *Metaphysics* Epsilon 2, Lambda 4, 1078b 16–17. See also *Posterior Analytics* I 31, 87b 28 33, 88b 31–2, I 13, 32b 18–20, *Metaphysics* Zeta 6, 1031b 6–7, alpha 6, 1003a 14–15; *Nicomachean Ethics* VI 6, 1140b 31–2.

discovery of why things must be as they are,[9] and the key to that discovery is the conceptual understanding of specific essences, which are nothing more than the natural expressions of the specific characters of natural kinds.[10]

We have shown that Aristotle grounds his causal determinism in a doctrine of logical determinacy which derives from his preservation and refinement of the Parmenidean principle of identity, and ultimately from Aristotle's refinement of Parmenides' law of contradiction from a principle which excludes all change to a principle which marks the boundaries of possible change. For when Aristotle specifies that the law of contradiction requires that a thing cannot both be and not be at a given time, in a given sense and respect, he is differentiating self-identical composite substances as the persistent substrates of change and subjects of predication and marking as the enduring constants that logic (metaphysically interpreted) seems to require the underlying matter or essential form by which those substances are identified through alteration, or understood, even through generation and corruption. For Aristotle, the continuity of causes is also the continuity of matter, form, time, and change. There are no interruptions in the causal fabric because there are no gaps in nature, no spots of nullity in being. The approach is naturalistic; but the thrust of Aristotle's naturalism always bears a distinctive, rationalistic, and ultimately theological component. Violation of the causal rhythm (as by absolute creation of destruction) is for Aristotle violation of the intelligible order that distinguishes the cosmos as divine from a mere chaos or Democritean whirligig.[11]

Accordingly we find a theological determinism in Aristotle – not a doctrine of predestination, of course, still less any idea of special (that is, individual) providence, but a thesis that the divine intelligence guides all things for the best: The passing-away of this is the coming-to-be of that, so coming-to-be and passing-away will always be continuous, "For in all things, as we affirm, Nature always strives after the better." Being is better than not being, but particulars cannot have unqualified being. "God therefore adopted the remaining alternative and fulfilled the perfection of the universe by making coming-to-be uninterrupted . . . because that coming-to-be should itself come-to-be

[9] See *Posterior Analytics* I 2, 71b 9.
[10] See *Metaphysics* Iota 2, 1053b 25–1054a 12 and *Physics* I 2, 185b 20–5, as applied in Ibn Rushd (Averroes) *Incoherence of the Incoherence*, ed. M. Bouyges (Beirut, 1930), 520–1, trans. S. Van Den Bergh (London, 1954), 318, quoted at note 26 below.
[11] See *De Gen. et Corr.* II 10, 336b–337a; *Metaphysics* Alpha 3, Delta 1, 1013a 22, Lambda 1075a 12–24.

perpetually is the closest approximation to eternal being" (*De. Gen et Corr.* I 3, 318a, 13–318b, 13).

When Aristotle reaffirms Socrates' disappointment with the work of Anaxagoras for promising to show how all things are ruled by nous but failing to show how nous (as intelligence would require) governs all things for the best, Aristotle lays claim for his own metaphysic of nous (as it will unfold in the climax of the *Metaphysics*) to have overcome the weaknesses he cites.[12] Aristotle's charge is that nous in Anaxagoras has the character of a *deus ex machina*. It does not operate organically within the action of nature, as, say, in a tragedy a hero's character, working within the logic or dynamic of the action, brings about (and does not merely foreshadow) the inevitability of his fall.[13] Aristotle's nous is not tacked on to nature, to account for what the natural principles themselves cannot explain. It works in and through the natural principles, as the ultimate cause, the goal of all change: As the principle of pure actuality and perfection, Aristotle's nous directs all things toward the good. In Aristotle, this inevitably means *their* good, just as being means the being of each thing and kind of thing and is not an abstract and adventitious notion, externally stuck on, as it were, by a deus ex machina. Mechanically all things in nature are moved by other things and in some measure by their own natures and the supervenient motions of the spheres. The order of the cosmos is directed by the train of causation from the spheres to the meteora and the changing seasons of growth, reproduction, and decay. But the spheres are moved telically by the divine intelligences, as the expression of the recognition in those intelligences of the divine perfection of pure intelligence. All change (insofar as movement is a progress from potency to act) is a mimesis of perfection, each being pursuing its own good or persisting in its own nature and its own act and thereby pursuing realization of its own character as a member of its species. And each species enacts (rather than merely pursuing) the perfect realization of its nature as a species. It may no longer be possible for Aristotle to repeat Plato's gnomic identification of time as

---

[12] See *Metaphysics* Alpha 3, 984b, 985a 18 *De Part. An.* IV 10, 687a 7 ff.; cf. Plato *Phaedo* 97–99 (cf. *Laws* 967c); but Aristotle makes the same charge against Plato himself: see *Metaphysics* Alpha 9, 991a 12–14, 991b 1. Guthrie translates: "The Forms are of no assistance either to our knowledge of other things . . . or to their existence, if they are not inherent in the objects which are said to participate in their being. . . . How can the Forms be essences when they exist apart? . . . Granted there are Forms, the things that 'share in them' cannot be produced without a motive cause." *A History of Greek Philosophy*, vol. 6, 244; cf. 1080a 2.

[13] See *Poetica* 15, 1454a 26–b 8; 9, 1452a 4–5; 35; 14, 1453b 1–2; cf. 9, 1450b 36, 1451b 34.

the moving image of eternity (*Timaeus* 37d), but Aristotle's cosmic choric dance vividly projects the naturalistic sense he gives to Plato's image.

Maimonides' determinism

Maimonides (1135–1204), one of the great theological rationalists of the Middle Ages, grafts a scriptural predestinarianism and a Neoplatonic emanationism to the naturalism and essentialism of Aristotle, as developed and made more rigorous in the post-Aristotelian Peripatetic tradition down to the time of Maimonides' Muslim contemporary Averroes (Ibn Rushd). The expected effect might be to make determinism more oppressive, shifting from bonds of inner logic and nature to those imposed by divine causality, without relaxing their stringency. Yet, as we shall see, Maimonides maintains the Aristotelian balance and mutual interpretability of the logical, theological, and natural dimensions of determinism. When we come to consider Maimonides' celebrated voluntarism, we shall see that, like Aristotle, he was unfazed by the notion that there might be a contradiction between determinism and human freedom. For the moment we focus on Maimonides' affirmations of determinism. These are too readily glossed over even by scholars well familiar with his work, and it is necessary to comprehend the groundings of these affirmations if we are to gain an understanding of how Maimonides, like Aristotle and Spinoza, judged human freedom to be compatible with determinism.

In the *Guide to the Perplexed*, Maimonides sees his task as a philosopher to be one of interpreting the statements of the Hebrew Bible in light of the requirements of the Neoplatonic Aristotelianism, which represented in his view the most adequate, mature, and responsible historical development of philosophy. No faith-straining dogmas were to be found in scripture, for the Torah (if it was to be appropriated as a timeless law, founded on wisdom for all ages) must be open to constant reinterpretation, by the probing of its own dynamic[14] and by the exploration of its interactions with the requirements of reason, the findings of science, and the contrasting and complementary values and ideas of cultures alien to its own.[15] Philosophy, for its part, and the natural science it included, was not to be regarded as a closed

[14] Maimonides, *Guide to the Perplexed*, Epistle Dedicatory; I 2, II 2, cf. I 50; Goodman, *RAMBAM, Readings in the Philosophy of Moses Maimonides* (New York: Viking, 1976), 210, 77.
[15] See *Guide*, e.g., I 34, III 29–32; *RAMBAM*, 413–24.

book. Just as "the sages of the nations" (as Maimonides echoes the Talmudic phrase) rightly triumph when natural science dismisses the idea of the music of the spheres,[16] so the findings of such science might be wanting – as the Ptolemaic model, weighed down with epicycles, seemed increasingly to be.[17] Just as even the idea of creation must be yielded up and allegorized away as poetry (as most Neoplatonists had allegorized it when they found it in the *Timaeus*) if philosophy could demonstrate its untenability,[18] so it must be recognized that the dogmatic pretensions of some philosophers against creation do not constitute demonstrations. Aristotle knew as well or better than anyone the difference between apodeictic and non-apodeictic arguments, and his use of persuasive language when arguing in behalf of the eternity of the cosmos is his admission that he lacked proof.[19]

Neither scripture nor philosophy, then, is a dead corpus. Both are living, and either may inform the other. It is the usage of the Torah, Maimonides observes, that all events are ascribed to God, whether these are events of nature, acts of will, or outcomes of pure chance.[20] All, in fact, are causal. For nature is governed by causal law, wills are motivated by the ends they choose, and what we denominate as chance is a superfluity of causes; it is, as Aristotle explained, a mere confluence of normally unrelated causal streams.[21] If we were to accept the Bible literally, we might feel moved to adopt some species of occasionalism, as developed by the numerous schools of *mutakallimun* (*loquentes*) or dialectical theologians who flourished in the early centuries of Islam and who in one way or another ascribed all events directly to the act of God. For the idiom of the Bible routinely omits reference to proximate causes. Such extreme versions of theological determinism are untenable, however. Theologically, Maimonides argues, if there is no horizontal causality, then God's creation of apparent causes as the mere occasions of their effects (our perceptions, our nourishment) is otiose and unbefitting the divine.[22] Philosophically, Maimonides refutes the notions of continuous creation and atomic time and space as incompatible with the principles of geometry and mechanics and at odds even with the continuity of bodies, let alone the possibility of science.[23] Accordingly, the biblical

[16] *Guide* II 8; *RAMBAM*, 340.   [17] *Guide* II 11.   [18] *Guide* II 25.
[19] *Guide* II 15–19; *RAMBAM*, 183–96.   [20] *Guide* II 48.
[21] *Guide* II 12, *RAMBAM*, 343–6; and see note 79 below.
[22] *Guide* II 17, 13; *RAMBAM*, 311–18, 262–77.
[23] *Guide* I 73–76; *RAMBAM*, 124–55.

idiom of divine ominificence must be interpreted as referential to the ultimate causality of God: God is the cause of all things, but not to the exclusion of the proximate causes we encounter in experience and study in the natural sciences. The metaphysics of emanation explains such seeming overdetermination. For this metaphysics identifies the vehicle of divine causality as the being or perfection (Aristotle's old actuality, now treated Neoplatonically as an imparted character or specific nature) that is the active essence of each thing. God's providence and governance are exercised through the flow of forms to things, and even the special providence shed by God's grace on prophets takes place by the bestowal upon them of the mind and imagination – form and material receptivity/schematic facility – by which prophecy is made possible.[24]

It is a central teaching of the Torah, clearly articulated by the Rabbinic sages, according to Maimonides, that the world's existence is tripartite, or as he puts it, that there are three kinds of created beings: (1) prime matter and the natural bodies we encounter here on earth; (2) celestial matter, the bodies of the spheres; and (3) the disembodied intellects, natural forms or essences, energizing forces or principles that mediate between God and nature. These last form the link through which the nonphysical and illimitable God governs finite, physical, changeable bodies. In biblical parlance they are called angels; but since scripture and the Rabbis take the reality of angels as unproblematic, indeed axiomatic, Maimonides infers that the reference is not to some anthropomorphic figure but to the forms – some temporal and unique, others recurrent and thus properly construed as universal. Maimonides bolsters his naturalistic gloss of angelology with biblical and Rabbinic proof texts about the "angel appointed over lust" and the like.[25] The thrust of his argument is the appropriation of the Neoplatonic intermediary ontology. It is this that keeps medieval metaphysics from collapsing into the lifeless mechanism of the post-Cartesian world, where only ghosts seem able to animate the dead machine. Here what gives life, consciousness, and form is the divinely imparted reality of each thing. This is the very principle by which each is governed, causally, by God; but governed they are – all has been and continually is determined. The rejection of arbitrary divine intervention is not a rejection of determinism, but is accomplished only by the consummation of a perfect, emanative causal determination.

Causal and theological determinism are reconciled, then, by way of

[24] *Guide* II 12; 343–50; II 48, III 23, with III 17.5, II 37–8, 45.
[25] *Guide* II 2–7, 10; *RAMBAM*, 330–40.

emanation, and logical determinism follows suit. For the being that emanates to all things, giving them their determinate characters and dispositions, is the formal being of their essences, which we study in the sciences.[26] Prior to the bestowal of those essences there is, of course no inner necessity to their character. Only formal logic provides absolute boundaries to necessity and possibility. However, once the natures of things are given by the divine choice in the act of creation, there is a settled order of nature,[27] and it is possible to infer soundly that things must behave in accordance with their given natures.[28] For humans, empirical study of nature is necessary because there is no necessity beyond that of logic to constrain the divine choice in its selection of underlying natural principles. Our natural sciences are therefore necessarily a posteriori, attendant on the settled order of nature, which is itself a radically contingent fact. Yet such sciences hold in the settled order of nature. The "logic" they discover is not one of categorical necessity, but an a posteriori logic of respect for the consequences of natural givens. God's knowledge, by contrast is a priori, like the inventor's knowledge of a clock before it has been built. God knows the natures He will posit and thus knows timelessly all that will follow from things' essences and identities. The thought owes something to al-Ghazali's meditations on the interface of temporality with eternity and is therefore fittingly complemented with a related thought elaborated by al-Ghazali's metaphysical adversary Ibn Rushd: that it is in terms of God's a priori conception of the forms of things that philosophers can conceive of what theologians picture as continuous creation – that is, emanation, the vehicle of God's authorship and governance of the world.[29]

Spinoza's determinism

Spinoza argues vehemently in behalf of a doctrine of strict determinism and carries forward the trend represented in his predecessors, Aristotle and Maimonides, of conflating logical, causal, and the-

---

[26] Cf. Averroes: "It is evident that things have essences and attributes which determine the actions specific to each. These are the characteristics in terms of which the natures of things are differentiated, and their names and definitions assigned. For if each being did not have its own specific mode of action, then it would not have its own specific nature, and if it did not have its own specific nature it would not have its own specific name or definition – all things would be one and the same thing, and not one and the same thing. . . ." *The Incoherence of the Incoherence*, ed. M. Bouyges, 521 ll. 10–15; trans. Van den Bergh, 318.

[27] *Guide* II 17; *RAMBAM*, 186–9.

[28] See al-Ghazali ap. Ibn Rushd, ed. Bouyges, 525 ll. 7–16, 533 ll. 12–15, 536 ll. 2–21.

[29] *Guide* III 21; *RAMBAM*, 305–8.

ological determinisms. Yet Spinoza's cosmology is less constrained by essentialism than is Aristotle's, and his denial of what he calls free will does not prevent him from affirming a remarkable doctrine of human freedom at the very climax of his philosophic exposition in the *Ethics*. What is the meaning of Spinoza's determinism, and on what basis does he suppose his affirmations of human freedom to be compatible with his categorical assertion that all events are determined?

Like other rationalists – Descartes for example[30] – Spinoza treats causal determinism as an axiom (*Ethics* I, Ax. 3, 4) and relates the principle of causality with that of identity to establish a thoroughgoing assertion of the intelligibility of all things: "What cannot be conceived through something else must be conceived through itself" (*Ethics* I, Ax. 2): Each thing can be conceptualized and thus understood, either in its own terms or in terms of the complex of external causes which condition its character. Causality is comprehensive: It necessitates, either from within or from without (*Ethics* I, Prop. 8, Sch. 2, theses 3 and 4), or so the axiom requires. The complementarity of internal and external causality fully determines the nature of each thing.

As in Aristotle, so in Spinoza, it is the law of identity, construed as a principle of logic, which lays the foundation of causality and thus of determinism. That is to say, determinism rests on the concept of determinacy in the existence of all things. God Himself is both the subject and the object of causal determination. The absoluteness of His being and omnipotence of His power do not exempt Him from the logic of determinacy. On the contrary, God's eternal and necessary production of all that expresses reality is the sole and sufficient manifestation of divine power. Spinoza adopts the emanative conception of the Neoplatonists, down to the inclusion of their usage which refers to God's acts as "following from" His nature – using the language of geometry – as the properties of a triangle follow from its definition.[31] The value of this imagery for Spinoza lies in the link it

---

[30] Thus, "it is manifest by the natural light that there must be at least as much reality in the efficient and total cause as in its effect." *Meditations* III, in E. S. Haldane and G. R. Ross, trans., *The Philosophical Works of Descartes*, vol. 1, 162.

[31] Compare Spinoza's usage of *sequitur* at *Cogitata Metaphysica* II viii, ed. Gebhardt, vol. 1, 264, ll. 6–7, and *Ethics* I, Prop. 15, ed. Gebhardt, vol. 2, 60, ll. 10–12; Prop. 16, ll. 17–19, Prop. 36, p. 77, l. 13; Pt. II, Prop. 49, Schol., p. 136, ll. 10–12: "Omnia ab aeterno Dei decreto eadem necessitate sequuntur, ac ex essentia trianguli sequitur, quod tres ejus anguli sunt aequales duobus rectis," etc., with the usage of Proclus, who also organized his metaphysics in Euclidean style. See Proclus, *Elements of Theology*, ed. E. R. Dodds (Oxford: Clarendon Press, 1964, first ed., 1933): Neoplatonic principles (*archai*) are both ontically and intellectually primary; they both produce and explain the effects that participate in them. Proclus in fact interprets geometry itself metaphysically (see

enables him to forge between causality and intelligibility. We can understand God through "what follows from Him," as we can understand a triangle through study of the implications of its essence;[32] or (taking a more cosmic perspective), causes serve as principles of explanation, allowing a perfect intelligence to comprehend nature a priori, from the underlying principles of being (see *Ethics* I, Props. 16, 25–30).

Here causal determinism is elegantly fused with logical determinism, as in Aristotle by way of essentialism, now coupled with a newly energized rationalism which looks to causes (not merely internal essences) as essential principles of explanation and is thus more emphatically interactive than was Aristotle.[33] Two other features of Spinoza's essentialist determinism are new at least in thrust, and both were put to telling use by Leibniz.

1. In keeping with the nominalism of Renaissance philosophy, Spinoza has cut clear of Aristotle's dependence on Platonic universals. Spinoza defines the essence of each thing as its *conatus in suo esse perseverare*, its striving to persist in its own being. He writes: "Conatus quo unaquaeque res in suo esse perseverare conatur, nihil est praeter ipsius rei actualem essentiam" (*Ethics* III, Prop. 7, Gebhardt vol. 2, p. 146, ll.20–21) – "The striving by which each and every particular endeavors to persist in its own being is none other than the actual essence of that particular." Essences are no longer defined in terms which make unavoidable reference to species or other natural groups. Determinism, accordingly, is dissociated from logical dependence on the notion of natural classes. Things behave the way they do because of what each and every one of them is individually and what all of

his Commentary on the first book of Euclid's *Elements,* trans. Glenn R. Morrow (Princeton: Princeton University Press, 1970). So the geometric organization of Proclus's *Elements* is no more a mere metaphor than that of Spinoza's *Ethics.* Maimonides too adopts the idea that God's effects (i.e., His works) are what follow from Him. He glosses the biblical notion of God's back accordingly: Moses is enabled to see God's back (i.e., "all the objects of My creation"); see *Guide* I 38, 54, *RAMBAM,* 70, 86–89. However, Maimonides modifies the sense, rejecting the idea that what follows from God follows automatically or mechanically; see *Guide* II 22, *RAMBAM,* 201.

[32] Maimonides similarly argues that although we cannot know God directly ("see His face") and although He has no proper essence or attributes distinct from His identity, we can know God through His works, in which we can recognize what we apprehend as God's "attributes" relative to our finite perspectives: in the mercy, wisdom and concern upon which nature is founded. These we can imitate. We model ourselves not on God's impersonality, but on those aspects of nature that manifest what would be perfections in us.

[33] Spinoza fuses causal and logical determinism with theological determinism in *Ethics* I, Prop. 33, and Scholium. The interactive character of his view of causality is perhaps most evident in *Ethics* II, Ax. 7, where individuals are found wherever (and insofar as) there is concatenated action.

them are interactively. Causality stems not from the fatality of species membership, but from the active nature of all particulars.[34]

2. Partly as a result of the disentanglement of essence (as *conatus*) from the idea of species, Spinozistic essences are more dynamic than Aristotle's. What stays constant in Spinoza is a mode of organization. Thus an organism (as in Aristotle) can grow (or metamorphose) without losing its essential form — and the universe as a whole can "vary in infinite ways without any change in the individual as a whole" (*Ethics* II, Ax. 3 concerning the body, Lemma 7, Schol.). Looking to Spinoza's predecessors, we can see this thesis as the triumphant conclusion to a refutation of the antideterminist claim that essentialist determinism renders change and variation impossible. Spinoza has refined Aristotle's essentialism to allow temporal variation within nature at large without changing the essential face of nature, just as he has refined Parmenides' monism to allow unity in nature without compromising the variety of existents (*Ethics* II, Ax. 7). In terms highly relevant to Spinoza's contemporaries and successors (Descartes himself was a "discreet" evolutionist),[35] Spinoza's more dynamic essentialism leaves room for evolution, which Aristotelian essentialism precludes as a matter of logic. For there are many forms that a thing may take, or that a mode of organization may pursue, in its striving to persist in its own being.

Theological determinism is, of course, again conflated with the causal cum logical determinism of Spinoza. Since God is the whole of nature, including both the physical and the mental aspects of reality and an infinitude of other manifestations that surpass our understanding because we have nothing in common with them, and since God or nature is not exempt from the universal law by which each thing is what it is and does what it does, God's infinite expressive power and claim upon reality are fully actual at all times. Everything that can be is, and the very laws of nature — the principle of determinacy itself — are the manifestations of God's power. God is not interpreted as that which acts — or to whom appeal must be made — when all else fails; for there is nothing else. God's infinity precludes

---

[34] In the *Tractatus Theologico-Politicus* Spinoza writes: "The universal power of nature at large is none other than the power of all individuals at once . . . and the highest law of nature is that by which each and every thing, insofar as in it lies, strives to persist in its own state — ruled by no other principle than its own accustomed one." Here Spinoza fuses his determinist essentialism once again with his particularism/individualism — and with his doctrine of political liberty, for he infers: "Whence it follows that each individual thing has the highest right to do this, that is, as aforesaid, to exist and act as it is naturally so determined." *TTP*, cap. 16, Gebhardt, vol. 3, 189, ll. 21–30.

[35] See *Principles of Philosophy* III 54, 61, 140, 146, IV 1, 2, 14, 44, 71

all other being and action. God's necessity of existence, as the sole substance, the sole self-sufficient existent, lays down the necessity of all existents that express God's diverse aspects. For God is the cause of their essences (*conatus*) as well as their existence, and God's essence is His existence (*Ethics* I, Prop. 25, 16, 7).

Spinoza's defense of human freedom

Unlike Aristotle and Maimonides, Spinoza argues vociferously and repeatedly against the notion of free will. By free will, he understands an unconditioned mode of thought – a clearly incoherent notion (*Ethics* I, Prop. 32; II, Prop. 48). In the tradition of Averroes's interpretation of Peripatetic causality, Spinoza equates the assertion that a being might have done other than it does with the specious claim that an existent thing might be other than the thing it is. What is undetermined, Averroes had argued, having no cause, has no definite nature; in other words, it does not exist.[36] Contingency is an illusion based on ignorance.[37] There is no contingency in nature. All is determined because all is determinate. Determinacy is the condition of existence, and the actions of all beings are expressions of that determinacy.[38] Free will is just a special case of the illusion of contingency – application to our choices or our ignorance as to their determining grounds and motives, treating them speciously as though they were groundless, and assigning human unpredictability not to our ignorance of the unseen springs of human action, but to an imagined power of arbitrary, uncaused, and unconditioned choice. Misconceiving arbitrariness as power, we project the same ignorance into our anthropomorphic notions of God, assigning to God an arbitrary will and inventing a realm of unrealized possibilities over which the divine indeterminacy may range. But in fact, will is a mode of thought, and like all modes it is determinate in each of its instances. There is no faculty or power of will in general. Such notions are mere hypostatizations, reifying and blurring the various instances of volitional thought, each of which is conditioned fully by the infinite array of other thoughts (mental processes) with which it comes in contact.[39] Although infinite in infinite ways, God is as determinate as actuality

---

[36] See *Ethics* II, Prop. 17, Cor. and Schol., Prop. 32–33; Ibn Rushd, ed. Bouyges, 34–6, trans. Van den Bergh, 18–20.
[37] *Ethics* I, Appendix.
[38] Cf. *Ethics* I, Prop. 35.
[39] *Ethics* I, Prop. 32; II, 48; 49 Corol., Gebhardt 131, 1. 2; Schol., esp. 134–6.

and as determined as the world – because, of course, God is the world.[40]

Our penchant for investing God, ourselves, and one another with free will stems from our proneness to various passive emotions – regret, vainglory, guilt, and shame, to name a few. Whatever we perceive as causing us pain or pleasure, sorrow or joy, we think of as evil or good accordingly. We take a kind of perverse pleasure in focusing on such causes, isolating them from their concomitants and conditions, and investing them with independent powers, whose intensionalities and purposes, like their specious independence, are illusory, projections of our own anger or expectations, hopes, and fears. Our notion of free will is in part a figment of such emotions of ours. We flagellate ourselves or one another with the notion that we might have done better. Or we translate our wishes and anxieties into the idea that God ought to have done better by us – or still might if rightly wooed. We sense our own power of action and ignore its limits and predisposing factors. Seeking praise for ourselves and disparagement for our detractors, we assign to allies and enemies alike an arbitrary absoluteness in volitions that is purely mythic. That is, its affirmation and indeed presupposition in our thought are artifacts of the irrational, associative psychology of the emotions, unwarranted and indeed negated by the evidence of science.

Yet the discourse of the emotions and of subjective valuation runs deep. Is it possible to dispense with the language of free will? Confronting the standard objection that without free will there will be neither praise and blame nor punishment and reward, nor human dignity, Spinoza answers as follows:

1. Praise and blame are impertinent. Our task is not to bemoan the human condition nor to congratulate ourselves upon it, but to understand it and to think and act in accordance with that understanding.[41]

2. Punishment and reward do not logically require belief in arbitrary, uncaused choices. Indeed, punishment presupposes some measure of causal control over our actions. How else could we single out and differentiate whom to punish and whom to reward, and for what? But no notion of free will is required. We can (in keeping with the idea more recent philosophers label as that of "strict liability") punish or reward persons for what they have done, without regard for what we may take to be the ultimate source of their motives.[42] The

[40] *Ethics* I, Props. 31–2.
[41] See *Ethics* III, Preface.
[42] Punishment, Spinoza argues, may be justified by the rule of pestilence: "You may ask at this point, 'Why then are the wicked punished, for they act by their own nature and according to the divine decree.' But I respond: 'It is equally at the divine decree that they are punished. And if only those ought to be punished whom we deem to have

overriding concern of law, it can be argued, is not with motives or intentions in any case, but with actions. It is these we rightly punish and reward, and to do so we do not need to know that an individual had free will or was (as medieval philosophers might have put it) the sole and sufficient creator of his acts.

3. As for human dignity, it can well be argued that human dignity does not stand or fall with the affirmation of uncaused volitions, any more than the dignity of God profits from the imputation of arbitrariness. To please their fancies, human beings have abstracted from the little that they know about the causes that underlie their conscious motives. Just as we artificially abstract an item from the causally interactive surroundings in which it is embedded when we call a finite mode a *substance,* so we artificially abstract ourselves and our volitions from their thought environment when we call them *free* and mean *unconditioned* (*Ethics* I, Prop. 36). The effect of such illogic (treating modes as substances) is naturally a paradox. We make our choices appear simultaneously more rational and more irrational than they are, and we are left with no criterion by which to judge their rationality. Then we compound the affront to the determinacy of nature by projecting the same faulty model of human choices onto God, inventing a teleology in which God is made to act in the design of nature with the same pettish and arbitrary emotions that we imagine constitute freedom in ourselves. The pettiness and passions of our fancied deity (who wants only to be honored by ourselves and jolts nature about to accommodate our every flattery or affront) reflect, on a grotesquely enlarged scale, the pettiness and passions of His creators. It can come as no surprise that this specious deity's chief concern is imagined to rest upon ourselves.[43]

It is after this denunciation of free will has been laid as a groundwork that Spinoza returns to the idea of freedom, which he has defined at the very outset of his *Ethics* (Def. 7) as belonging to that thing "which exists solely by the necessity of its own nature and is determined to action solely by itself." For the entire fifth part of the *Ethics* is devoted to delineating a path of human freedom by which we can release ourselves from the control of the passions and indeed transcend the conditions of finitude and temporality. The means by which Spinoza can affirm human freedom after categorically rejecting the

---

offended by their own free will, then why do men strive to extirpate poisonous snakes – for they too offend only by their own nature and cannot do otherwise." *Cogitata Metaphysica* II cap. 8, Gebhardt, vol. 1, 265, ll. 18–24; cf. *Ethics* IV, Prop. 51, Scholium. Criminals need not, of course, be extirpated. What the rule justifies is their constraint, by whatever means prove most appropriate.
[43] *Ethics* I, Appendix; cf. Maimonides *Guide* III 13, *RAMBAM,* 262–70.

very notion of free will and most of its familiar bastions of defense in psychology, theology, law, and morals are most instructive for contemporary discussions of freedom and responsibility and too often neglected or misunderstood.

To begin with, what Spinoza rejects is not the same as what he reaffirms. It is characteristic of Spinoza that he dissolves classic conundrums of philosophy by means of the careful distinctions he embeds within his definitions. It is by insistence upon rigorous and unflinching application of the Aristotelian and Cartesian definitions of substance, which he combines, that he reaches his monistic interpretation of reality and obviates the embarrassing, fudging notion of his predecessors that there is a relative self-sufficiency in finite substances, which are thus contingent in themselves, but necessary with reference to their Cause or causes.[44] He similarly eliminates anthropocentric and anthropomorphic teleology, to replace it with a more objective and universal teleology in which each being carries and develops in itself the goals focused as its *conatus*.[45] He inveighs against projective notions of good and bad, order and disorder, even perfection and imperfection, only to displace them with a more objective conceptualization that identifies perfection with reality, introducing a new version of the Neoplatonists' hierarchically graded reality as an ontic and ethical scale.[46] Spinoza's keen analytic sense is reflected in his definition of the freedom he accepts as self-necessitation. This freedom is not and does not call for an exception to the universal causal law and the governance of nature by the determinacy (not fixedness) of all things' essences. Freedom is autonomy, self-causedness, and self-determination, not indeterminacy or causelessness. Clearly God is free, since God is self-determined. Spinoza is prepared to argue that freedom as autonomy is worthier of God than free will. God is more nobly and dispassionately conceived as self-sufficing than as arbitrary (even if sense could be made of divinely perfect arbitrariness), and human choices are more nobly and dispassionately planned when related to an idea of necessity than when related to an idea of abstract and arbitrary positivity (a fiat, rule, or mere isolated fact).[47] But ethically, the question is, Is anyone free besides God?

---

[44] *Ethics* I, Prop. 10, Corol. and Schol.

[45] The key to Spinoza's shift is his recognition that "the perfection of things [if it is to be taken in an objective sense] must be evaluated solely in terms of their own nature and capability." *Ethics* I, Appendix, Gebhardt, vol. 2, 83, ll. 22–3; cf. Maimonides, *Guide* III 13, 268–9. See also *De Intell. Emend.*, Gebhardt, vol. 2, 8, l. 22; 9. ll. 12–15; 12, ll. 23–4.

[46] *Ethics* I, Prop. 11; II, Def. 6.

[47] See *Ethics* V, Props. 5–9. The polemical point, that God is more nobly conceived as self-constrained than as arbitrary, is of course made in the Appendix to Part I, by way

Plainly, only God is free in an absolute sense, for only God is clear of all possibility of interference. But from the very outset Spinoza lays the groundwork for a partial or relative human freedom as well. Human beings are free to the extent that they are self-determined in their actions – that is to say, self-determining. In defining that branch of necessity which excludes freedom, Spinoza identifies those agents as coerced or constrained (*coacta*) "which are determined to be and to behave in a certain way by another" – by some thing or some one other than themselves (*Ethics* I, Def. 7). All things, of course, are necessary, so Spinoza substitutes the term *coacta* here for *necessaria*, writing "necessaria . . . vel potius coacta" (necessary or, more properly, constrained) to distinguish as constrained that class of necessary actions which are externally determined. He thus leaves room for those necessary actions whose causal determination is internal.

The latter are properly called free. It is true that the actions of finite beings (modes) are never self-determined absolutely, but always externally conditioned in an infinitude of interactions. However, the fact remains that each determinate mode makes its own causal contributions to the interactive system and can be called free to the extent that its own character and identity are the determinants of its actions, rather than the mere effects of the actions of others upon it. The *conatus* of each thing, be it remembered, is that thing's essence and identity. *Conatus* of which the subject is conscious is desire. It is called appetite when it pertains to mind and body alike. But considered as a mental affection, it is called the will (*Ethics* III, Prop. 9). Each of us is determined to action by a personal *conatus*, interacting with the impacts upon us of all other things; and our *conatus* is conditioned by all that we have undergone – conditioned, but not determined or created, for we are not the mere products of our history, reducible to what we have been. Each being participates in making itself what (or who) it is, and it is from what or who we are (from our *conatus*, not our history) that our actions flow.

Spinoza thus subscribes to a rigorous and unexceptioned determinism in all three of the senses we have identified, while maintaining human freedom. He adopts a strong version of the metaphysical reading of the law of identity that we have labeled logic-grounded determinism. He links this with his causal determinism via a modified (dynamic and individual) essentialism, setting all beings and events in thoroughgoing causal interaction. He sums up the whole in a classic

of the reference to the projection of ignoble emotions upon God. The point was a standard piece of Averroistic invective against the notion of God as "an Oriental despot," and it is rooted in the natural theology of Aristotle and Alexander of Aphrodisias.

reformulation of theological determinism worthy of being set along-side any other produced by a natural theologian when he argues that nothing occurs contrary to God's nature and that God Himself ex-presses His power not in arbitrary invasions of nature, but by the flowing forth from His nature of all that takes place. This occurs with a necessity as regular and as intellectually transparent to absolute intel-ligence as the necessity of geometrical implication, and without any essential change in God or nature. Spinoza preserves freedom in the context of determinism by the simple but elegant expedient of dis-tinguishing between uncaused and self-caused actions. The former are an illusion, and a rather pernicious one at that. The latter are real and are no exception to determinism, but a necessary component in it.

It has long been commonplace in discussions of free will for propo-nents to cite the self-evidence of human intentions, while opponents cite the concealment and uncertainty of our inner motives as evidence of the lack of rational control. Awareness of the hidden dimensions of the inner life does not begin with Freud, after all, but runs back through Kant and his Pietist predecessors into the Middle Ages and ultimately to the biblical footings of Western spirituality.[48] In histor-ical perspective, the triumphant observations of a Paul Edwards, dis-covering to his readers or listeners that human motivations have ge-netic and environmental precursors that can be read or pled as their determinants,[49] inevitably looks somewhat superficial if not soph-omoric. Clarence Darrow's archetypical defense speech, canonized and almost parodied in dramatic representations of his summation in the Loeb–Leopold trial or transmogrified by Hollywood in the fa-mous summing up in the film *Knock on Any Door* – arguing that any member of the jury, given the wrong background, might have been the prisoner in the dock – has antecedents going back to the legal practice of the ancient Sophists. Modern sciences like psychology, sociology, genetics, and endocrinology add props but alter little in the structure of the argument.[50] If the notion is that we can be victims of

---

[48] See my "Bahya (and Kant) on the Antinomy of Free Will and Predestination," in *Journal of the History of Ideas* 44 (1983), 115–30. And see, for example, Bahya Ibn Paquda, *Kitab al-Hidaya ila Fara2id al-Qulub*, ed. A. S. Yahuda (Leiden: Brill, 1912), 163, ll. 4–6, corresponding to *The Book of Direction to the Duties of the Heart*, trans. M. Mansoor (London: Routledge and Kegan Paul, 1973), 210.

[49] See Paul Edwards, "Hard and Soft Determinism," in Sidney Hook, ed., *Determinism and Freedom in the Age of Modern Science* (New York: Macmillan, 1974, first ed., 1958), 117–25.

[50] For evidence against biological determinism of the external sort which excludes participation by the self, see M. J. Goodman and L. E. Goodman, *Sex Differences in the Human Life Cycle* (Los Angeles: Gee Tee Bee, 1986, first ed., 1980); for external and reductionistic determinism as an artifact of the scientific quest, see Goodman and

our past circumstances, Spinoza offers little disagreement; but if the price of understanding (which Spinoza does not believe entails exoneration) is adoption of a metaphysical denial of human freedom in the sense of self-direction, then Spinoza vigorously dissents. What Spinoza contributes here is the exposition of a dynamic by which individuals can be seen as causally, rationally responsible for their own actions in some varying measure, dependent in part on their fortunes (the natural given), but dependent in part on choices over which we can exercise some measure of control. For in the complex array of determinants, one is oneself an actor.

Modern sociological accounts of human agency tend to overlook this feature. They tend to treat the human person as a product of heredity and environment whose every choice and motivating value is the determined outcome of external forces. Such an analysis, as I argued in the early 1970s in what I called the Point Zero argument, is self-undermining to the extent that it assumes other persons to be agents of the effects that it holds to determine a subject's choices.[51] That is, the familiar types of social and behavioral determinism presume upon the very kind of active agency they deny. The problem is that all causal agency is assumed to be external. However, if persons cannot act, much of the agency relied upon in the deterministic theory is vitiated or dissipated. We receive inputs but pass them on essentially unmodified by any distinctive contribution of our own. If that were possible, we would be unique in nature. Indeed, our identity would vanish to a point, to nullity. In Spinoza's terms (to express the reduction in his language of comprehensibility), nothing would be contributed to an understanding of our actions by an understanding of ourselves. Otherwise expressed: There would be only passivities, no actions. The spurious determinism founded on such a farrago defeats its own intention, if the intention was the Lucretian one of knowing the causes of things: It does not count human beings as causes, but only as the butts of causal effects.

Goodman, "Is There a Feminist Biology?" *International Journal of Women's Studies* 4 (1981), 393–413.
[51] See L. E. Goodman, *Ibn Tufayl's Hayy Ibn Yaqzan* (Los Angeles: Twayne, 1972), 17–21; cf. 72–86. The presupposition of determinism in accounts of freedom was pointed out by Kant when, in the Thesis of the Third Antinomy, he assigned to freedom "another causality" (*Critique of Pure Reason* A444/B472). The point zero argument goes somewhat further, claiming that freedom is presupposed in determinism – at least when determinism adopts a social perspective and presumes some persons to be causes of the responses of others. Even if we slide to the nonpersonal level of organization or stage of history, an equivalent assumption will be found: All particulars are assumed to exert an action of their own which can be understood fully only by taking into account their distinctive, individual contributions.

Only the pragmatic and dramatic (rhetorical) uses of the spurious determinism keep it operative: Its images and appeals to external causation (whether of stars and lots and destinies in ancient times or of genes, hormones and Oedipal conflicts in the more recent mythologies) serve our passion for exoneration, just as the equally specious indeterminism of complete moral backgroundlessness serves our passion for vituperation. The truth lies in the middle ground: Human beings are partially responsible for their own acts and choices, and much of the strength of Spinoza's psychology lies in its ability to show how this can be so. His position is like that of the Eastern sage in the fable who was able to comfort a group of foolish monks who thought they had lost one of their number in crossing a river. He pointed out that in counting heads after crossing, each one of the monks had forgotten to count himself.

Three features of Spinoza's metaphysics make possible his discovery of a power of action counterpoised against passivity within individuals:

1. In logic there is the fact that Spinoza's essentialism is not static, but dynamic. This leaves room for a reflexive or reflective moment in the action of human individuals, allowing us to be conceived as in some measure the authors of our own choices.
2. In theology there is the fact that Spinoza's God is immanent, not *transeunt*. *Transeunt,* as Spinoza uses the term, does not mean "transient." It means external to the world – hit and run – corresponding to the deus ex machina that Aristotle, Plato, and Socrates, by Plato's account, rejected in the thinking of Anaxagoras.[52]
3. Causally there is Spinoza's interactionism, his recognition that the thoroughgoing interconnectedness of all things does not preclude but on the contrary presupposes the activity of each particular. Crucial here is the psychophysical parallelism Spinoza salvages from the dualism of Descartes. This prevents the reduction of mental events to physical causes that has shortcircuited so much of modern deterministic psychology – seeking physical explanations for psychological events whose internal activeness has not been adequately credited or understood.

1. Just as Aristotle recognized that the principle of identity would freeze reality in immobility unless a distinction between essence and

---

[52] See *Ethics* I, Prop. 18 Letter 73, Gebhardt, vol. 4, 307, ll. 5–11.

accident were allowed, so Spinoza saw that essences must be dynamic and in some measure self-constituting if provision is to be made for the organic complexity of life[53] and for the reflexivity of consciousness.[54] This I take to be the real thrust for the problem of freedom, of Spinoza's transformation of Aristotelian essence into the more dynamic notion of the *conatus*. For Aristotelian essences were already related to process, but they did not change. It was Aristotle's belief that the life cycle of a plant or the changing purposes of a person could be accounted for by way of the varying material encounters of an invariant specific essence with diverse situations as a program of development unfolds. However, in Spinoza's view essences are not externally bestowed or Platonically static: The plan (or "face") of nature as a whole is what does not change, and essences themselves, as *conatus*, can be what unfolds – or rather, self-constructs. Nowhere is this clearer than where *conatus* becomes self-conscious as desire.[55] Human consciousness, like all other things in nature, existentiates itself. Granted, it does so within a causal context, but like all other things it expresses a nature that is not merely given to it. In some measure consciousness is self-creative – and that on a level higher than other things because of its reflexivity and self-transparency. It does not merely know, but it knows that it knows. That gives it some measure of control. Consciousness is not, Spinoza insists, like some picture painted on a screen.[56] Not even like a moving picture on a screen, we might add. It is not merely a set of objective presentations whose subject must be sought somewhere else, in the back of the theater; the subject is present in the representations. They are subjective. As Descartes had urged,[57] they never appear without the I. What this means, insofar as consciousness is capable of choosing its own focus and attitude, is that consciousness constitutes itself.

Spinoza's account of the possibility of freedom rests on his distinction between adequate and inadequate ideas, active and passive emotions. Indeed, his account of freedom rests upon acceptance of his account of determinism. A principal source of passive emotions (as Stoic and Pietist advocates of resignation had long argued in their own terms) is the notion that other individuals and external events

---

[53] Thus the *conatus* of a living being is its endeavor to persist in its own organic arrangement. See *Ethics* II, Gebhardt vol. 2, 98–102.

[54] *Ethics* II Prop. 22, cf. V Props. 29, 30, 31.

[55] *Ethics* III Prop. 9, Schol.; Defs. 1, '*cupiditas*'; cf. *Cogitata Metaphysica* I cap. 6, Gebhardt vol. 1, 248. l. 6.

[56] *Ethics* II Prop. 43, Scholium.

[57] See Descartes, *Meditations* II; cf. Augustine, *De Trinitate* X iii, 5; John Philoponus in *De Anima* III 2, 425b 12, ed. Hayduck (Berlin, 1897), 13 ff., trans. in F. Rahman, *Avicenna's Psychology* (Westport, CT: Hyperion, 1981, first printed, 1952), 111–14.

freely or arbitrarily – at any rate, noncausally – conspire in behalf of or against one's imagined interests. Understanding the causes of events gives one freedom (as in the teachings of the Buddha) by freeing the mind of passions – passionate desires and fears that enslave us to external things.[58] To understand a thing adequately is to understand it in relation to its causes, and such understanding (in terms of adequate ideas) necessarily dissolves the passions (passive emotions). This renders us more free, more adequately the cause of our own actions, which are then to be understood more in terms of our nature and identity – the nature and identity we ourselves define and make by our own acts and choices.

It remains nonsense for Spinoza (except as a species of refined and rather misleading abstraction) to say that an individual can choose or act other than he or she does; but it is equally nonsensical and misleading to pretend that we are in no measure the cause of our own actions, for that is to make all actions passive. Spinoza, to be sure, does not draw the line between active and passive just where we might place that between coercion and noninterference. Nor does he identify an act as free merely because it bears the mark of individuality or idiosyncrasy. An ax murderer does not grow freer as he develops his own unique style or modus operandi; he remains a victim of compulsions. For Spinoza we are free to the extent that we act on the basis of adequate ideas. This is what makes us adequate causes of our own actions. Nothing can be other than what it is or do other than as the causes of its acts require. But the program of the self is not simply static and externally imposed; it is in some measure self-created.

2. Spinoza's God is not external to the world, but identical with nature, conceived as broadly as infinite conception will allow. So God does not interfere with the world. The traditional problems of miracles and predestination are dissolved, along with the more specifically Cartesian problems of the creation and governance of physical nature by an immaterial spirit. Neoplatonic emanationism and Aristotelian immanentism are here culled for the benefits they provide in resolving the age-old problems theologians even today would rather ignore than confront. Spinoza's God, like Aristotle's, works in and through the natures of all things, *as* the natures of all things, omnipresently, irrefragably, impersonally, and intelligibly, not as an external engine, thus not at all as a deus ex machina, but as the distinctive essence (*conatus*) in which each thing simultaneously manifests its own nature and (one determinate aspect of) that of God.

In medieval scholastic theology and *kalam,* the boundaries of the

[58] *Ethics* V, Props. 2–10.

dispute between voluntarists and determinists were generally marked out by the recognition that to assign more liberty to God was to give less to man and nature. In Spinoza, where the human being is part of nature and nature is identical with God, there is, of course, no such competition: God acts when each being acts.[59] God loves humans when they love themselves and one another.[60] To know nature (as in Aristotle) is to know God, since each thing in nature manifests God — that is, each is a small epiphany.[61]

Our autonomy or relative independence is, of course, a part of the authenticity[62] of our being, our being in God and God's being in us. In medieval terms it can be asked whether God's act of creation is real if God does not impart real being to His creatures. In Spinozistic terms the authenticity of our being and thus of the divine creative act is guaranteed by the fact that our being is God's presence in us, that God's being is His manifestation in us and in all other things. In medieval terms one could say that human autonomy mirrors the divine aseity, that morally at least it is clear why humans are said to be created in God's image. In Spinozistic terms the analogy between human and God is preserved, as Wolfson showed,[63] in Spinoza's preservation of the image of the anthropic microcosm in his portrait of nature. For nature stands here in the place of God. Thus the mind–body problem as bequeathed by Descartes is resolved by Spinoza in parallel with the Maimonidean problem of the nexus between God and nature, and by way of the Maimonidean theory of the attributes of God.[64] Human freedom (as relative autonomy) is identical in kind and different only in degree from the absolute self-determiningness of nature as a whole.

3. Brilliant as Descartes was, Spinoza argues, he betrayed his own fundamental insight when he attempted to relate mind and body (thought, spirit, or idea, with matter, extension, the mechanical) as cause and effect. That we conceive of the two distinctly, one as (subjective) consciousness, the other as (objective) extension, does not demonstrate that they are separate substances (for as determinacies, even if

[59] *Ethics* I, Prop. 16, Corol. 1.
[60] *Ethics* V, Prop. 36 and Corol.
[61] *Ethics* V, Prop. 31, 38–9, with Props 7–9; cf. Aristotle *Nicomachaean Ethics* X 7–8; Maimonides, *Guide* I 54, 59.
[62] For this theme, see my commentary on Saadiah Gaon's translation and commentary on the Book of Job (New Haven, CT: Yale University Press, in press).
[63] See H. A. Wolfson, *The Philosophy of Spinoza: Unfolding the Latent Process of His Reasoning* (New York: Schocken, 1969, first ed., 1934), vol. 2, 7 ff.
[64] See my essay, "Matter and Form as Attributes of God in the Philosophy of Spinoza," in R. J. Long and C. Manekin, eds., *A Straight Path: Essays in Honor of Arthur Hyman* (Washington, DC: Catholic University Press, in press).

infinite they are not conceivable as wholly self-sufficient). It does demonstrate, however, that they cannot causally delimit (determine or condition) one another, for they have nothing in common in terms of which their connection can be conceived. Their unity must be conceived in terms of their parallelism, as dual manifestations of the infinite exuberance of the divine. Neither can be the cause of the other or provide the explanation of the other's determinations. Mind cannot make contact with matter, and matter cannot impinge on mind or even locate it. If it could, then the same gearbox through which perceptions are transmitted from the body to the mind, or volitions from the mind to the body, could be used as reduction gear by which the body could be made to force the mind.[65] However, we know from experience, and from the example both of martyrs and of stubborn people, that it is simply not possible to posit this as a necessary relation. Thus while there is a necessary parallelism between the states of the human body and the states of the human mind, there is no possibility of reductively explaining the behavior of either in terms of the principles of the other. Just as each is conceived in its own terms, each must be explained by its own principles. The reductive presumption that gives color of scientific authority to the notion that mental acts must be wholly passive to the affects of the body is systematically dismissed: Both mind and body can be either active or passive; and, in all finite beings, each aspect will be *both* active and passive in some degree. We act not to the extent that we escape the sway of causal determinations, but to the extent that we integrate our thoughts well enough to allow the dissolution of our passions and direction of our acts and thoughts by our adequate ideas.

Since the distinction between adequate and inadequate ideas is crucial to Spinoza's account of human freedom, a word more is in order about this: What is the relation between adequate or inadequate ideas on the one hand, and active or passive emotions on the other? How are we liberated from passivity to the extent that we are guided by our adequate ideas? To begin with, of course, adequate ideas do not free us of all passivity. They do not, for example, directly and in themselves free us from illness, poverty, or cold. They free us from passivity by freeing us from the hold of passive emotions. It is in this sense that they make us more adequately the causes of our own ac-

[65] See *Ethics* V, Preface, Gebhardt, vol. 2, 278 l. 3–280 l. 21 with III Preface, p. 137 l. 25–138 l. 5; cf. Descartes, *Principles of Philosophy* I 64. The latter work was rightly dedicated to Princess Elizabeth, for it was through his correspondence and conversation with her that Descartes came to adopt a far subtler position than that in which the denouement of the *Meditations* had thrust him. See John Blom, ed., *Descartes: His Moral Philosophy and Psychology* (New York: NYU Press, 1978), where the letters are translated.

tions and less the victims of external circumstance. For Spinoza it is a truth of reason that adequate ideas dissolve the corresponding passive emotions. Rationalists from Plato to Freud have held a faith corresponding to Spinoza's thesis that to understand a passion is to dissolve it; but few have succeeded, as Spinoza has, in spelling out the grounds that underlie this faith.

Spinoza argues that a passive emotion is nothing more than a confused idea. To say that such ideas cease when they are clearly thought through and thus subsumed within an adequate idea is thus an analytic statement. It follows that "In proportion as we know an emotion better it is more within our control" (*Ethics* V, Prop. 3 and Cor.). Rage, jealousy, and spite, timidity, arrogance, groundless hate, servility, vindictiveness, cruelty, and self-contempt – all passive emotions – are rooted in, or rather identical with, confusion of ideas (compare the Hebrew expression *timahon levav*). Cruelty, for example, is defined by Spinoza (*Ethics* III, Defs. of the Emotions, 38) as a desire to harm one whom we pity. Now the origin of such an emotion can be accounted for in Spinoza's associative psychology as a projection of our own discomfort: We identify with the object of our pity, dislike the disturbance that emotion produces in ourselves, and project the dislike upon the object of our pity (or perhaps on others we associate with that person), whom we conceive associatively as the *cause* of our discomfort. Cruel thoughts or actions are the result. If we understand the source and basis of our emotions, the linkage that promotes them is perceived to be irrational. When such understanding, rather than irrational, merely reactive associative responses founds our feelings, they are no longer malicious. When understanding rather than the projective responses of passive emotions informs our actions, they are no longer cruel. The same model can be followed for all the passive emotions.

The mere ability to recite such a model does not, of course, dissolve the passions. Actual understanding must be ours in order for it to dissolve the nexus of our passions and displace them as foundations of our actions. It will take an Aristotle (as we will see when we turn to his account of human freedom) fully to lay bare the divergence of mere formulaic or sentential knowledge from the sort of embedded or imbibed dispositional knowledge that is relevant in ethics. But what Spinoza has accomplished, I believe successfully, is to show (as almost all philosophers have somehow hoped to show) that the calmer, wider, rationally grounded form of thought is not merely an anodyne to the passions, but an antidote to the loss of control, the loss of freedom, which those emotions represent.

Spinoza says that to the extent that we are freed from the control of the passions, we are more adequately the causes of our own actions; our actions become more truly our own. What exactly does this mean? In Spinoza's highly interactive universe, every act of every particular is both the cause and the effect of countless other events. No finite mode is ever wholly self-determining, and no act of a finite mode can be understood without reference to the individual nature of that mode. When an animal hunts or two chemicals react, they are expressing their own natures. What does it mean for a person to be more free? If there is a monster – a beast of a certain type, or some moral monster with strange and perverse desires or needs – does it not act out of the necessity of its own nature? In what sense is a moral agent more free?

Clearly, all things in some minimal sense act out of the necessity of their own nature. What consciousness makes possible, through its reflexivity, is some degree of self-control. A rock thrown in the air can only rise and then fall. Its trajectory is determined by its nature and the nature of the things around it. A human being's actions too are determined by his or her nature and environment, but in some measure the human is capable of altering both. A beast pursues the dictates of its appetites and other stimuli and cues. A moral monster is the victim of such appetites and cues. His or her emotions are passive in the sense that this person is (qua monster) powerless to modify the manner of his or her response to external stimuli. It is in this sense that they can be said, metaphorically, to act through him or her. It is not (we have observed) the idiosyncrasy of our actions that makes them uniquely our own. (Imagining that this is so was the mistake of Plato's tyrant, who supposed that only through perversity could he manifest his presence and his power.) Rather, our actions are our own to the extent that our nature is in our own control, to the extent that our *conatus* is self-conscious, self-reflective, self-critical – in some degree self-made. The key to Spinoza's insight here is the recognition that the passions do not constitute an identity in the same sense that the active emotions do. Those emotions Spinoza calls passive are those that render us capable only of automatic, mechanical, or relatively uncontrolled responses like those of grief, rage, pity, complacency, concupiscence, and scorn. The more reflective emotions are those that place us on a higher plane of action, in which we are more in control of ourselves, less under the control of external events and thus more active and less passive – more undertakers and less undergoers of events. They have this character because of their reflective nature, because of their foundation upon adequate ideas and displacement of the inadequate ideas that render human behavior, to the extent that they are its determinants, as mechanical and unreflective as the behavior of mechanisms or brutes.

When we speak of human actions as capable of being raised to a less mechanical level and thus being less externally determined, we raise several problems that can be readily dispelled: Like other rationalists, Spinoza does not believe we are free when we act viciously. He does not, however, fall into the trap of denying that we are causally responsible for our vicious acts. For Spinoza separates freedom (in the sense that he affirms it) from volition in general: The mind is volitionally responsible for actions that arise both from its confused or inadequate ideas and from its clear or adequate ideas. In both cases we express our own nature – our own *conatus* and will (*Ethics* III, Prop. 9 and Cor.); but we are more adequately the cause of our own actions when that *conatus* is informed by adequate ideas. It is true that the moral wretch is more to be pitied than censured and also true that there is no hindrance to the wretch being punished or controlled. Such a person's actions still bear the mark of a unique, perhaps complex, variety of wretchedness. The sense in which they are not his or hers is simply that in which more thought or better thought might have rendered them abhorrent to him or her.

What are we to make of this "might have"? Does Spinoza believe in the possibility of alternative futures? This is certainly not the sort of language he approves. However, in keeping with our analysis, a distinction should be made (as in Aristotle it was made) between futures whose determinants are given, and futures whose determinants have not yet emerged. Spinoza's account of the dynamic and reflexive character of *conatus* clearly allows this and in turn allows a Bergsonian rather than Laplacean account of determination. That is, things on Spinoza's account must act in accordance with what they are; but they have not always been what they are, and they contribute through their own actions to the making of what they are. Laplacean causality would be criticized Spinozistically not for being too deterministic, but for being too linear, not allowing feedback or recursion. Bergson's idea of an open future, based on giving a new emphasis to the idea of time, would be more welcome. For what Laplace ignores is that we act in the present, although we have been acted on in the past. In Maimonides, where divine omniscience might be called upon to play the same role as Laplacean predictability, the issue is more clear-cut, since what God knows (and creates) is a volitional being, with polyvalent capabilities of choice. I am extending the notions offered by Spinoza's philosophy here, but in a direction that he need not have disapproved. The basis of the extension is the Aristotelian distinction between the specious notion of alternative pasts and the legitimate notion of alternative futures. To paraphrase the words of one of our great athletic coaches: A decision isn't made until it's made.

In an argument of much apparent rigor, Jonathan Bennett seems to propose that Spinoza's claims in behalf of autonomy are to be interpreted either as a plea in behalf of independence of all things external to the organism, or as an appeal to independence of all things external in the Stoic sense – that is, of all that is not dictated by our own will.[66] But surely, Bennett argues, we cannot literally ignore the data of the senses, despite Spinoza's evident fondness for medieval-sounding denigrations. Nor can we simply ignore the opinions of others or merely cower within ourselves, rejecting any great under taking because its success may lie outside our mastery. What Bennett seems to think Spinoza *ought* to mean in urging relative self-sufficiency is the value of making ourselves *volitionally* autonomous – that is, making our own will the cause of our actions. "It is a pity, therefore, that this revised theory" – the theory of "completeness of voluntary control" Bennett supplies to smooth over Spinoza's confusions and "incoherence" – "was perfectly unavailable" to Spinoza. For one thing, Bennett continues, it undercuts Spinoza's argument for egoism based on the idea that an individual's destruction cannot proceed from its essence. Bennett has already (pp. 234 ff.) dismissed this argument of Spinoza's: "Since the conclusion is false, the argument is faulty." Bennett does not believe that "a purely endogenous cancer" is impossible, nor does he believe that suicide should be described as other than self-destruction. To this he adds, by way of criticizing Spinoza's notion that beings express their own essences and that such essences cannot produce their own destruction, "it is hard to know what 'essence' means in this context, but there is no chance of making it mean 'will' or having anything to do with voluntary control" – presumably because individuals may voluntarily destroy themselves. Moreover, taking Spinoza's internal–external distinction volitionally "abolishes most of the demonstrations in Part 4: their appearance of being arguments at all depends on the morality's being based on the dictates of 'reason,' with this understood in terms of causal self-sufficiency; take away that last concept, and the elaborate structure of mostly invalid arguments collapses into a shapeless pile of rubble." I'm not sure just where the vitriol here is coming from, or where it is directed, but it seems pretty clear, since Bennett has already ruled out

---

[66] See Jonathan Bennett, *A Study of Spinoza's Ethics* (Hackett, 1984), esp. chaps. 13–14.

the nonvolitional interpretations of the internal–external distinction as well, that the shapeless pile of rubble is not just a rhetorical threat, but an intended description of the actual outcome of Spinoza's efforts in this area. I am not convinced, however, that the outcome of Bennett's exceedingly painstaking analyses is as destructive as he seems to fear or hope.

First, the notion of sensory deprivation, which Bennett invokes, is a red herring. When Spinoza proposes less reliance on the senses, he is speaking germanely to the issue of passivity, insofar as the senses are understood traditionally as the avenues through which the passions make their appeal. The point is not to exclude sensory information from our deliberations, but to avoid the sort of merely reactive behavior observable in organisms for which sensory inputs are determinative of response. Further, it is part of Spinoza's program to articulate insights that describe the means by which the wise overcome other, equally reactive modes of behavior, in which our human reflective capabilities are employed only to echo, amplify, blindly associate, or otherwise nonrationally manipulate the sensory data, allowing it, as passively modified, to determine our responses.

Second, there is no "purely endogenous cancer" because no finite cause is ever "purely endogenous." This is a major theme in Spinoza. As for suicide, Spinoza does not consider it a form of self-expression just because it may be the choice of a human will. Suicide cannot express the essence or identity (that is, the self) of a human being, because that essence, like all essences, is self-affirmatory, a striving to preserve and promote its own reality. Accordingly, suicide is not an action, it is a passion. The suicide is a victim, not a free chooser. If Bennett or Marsha Norman wishes to dispute this thesis of Spinoza's they are of course welcome to do so, but when they do, I think it will be readily observed that they do so not by discovering an incoherence in Spinoza's claims, but by removing themselves (not bodily or volitionally but conceptually) from the ambit of his central premises. The Spinozistic thesis is not that suicide is impossible, but that suicide is not a means of self-fulfillment.

Third, as to "complete volitional control." This is, of course, not a project of Spinoza's. A sound goal of human action, inasmuch as we are rational beings, lies in our maximizing our freedom. But this does not mean getting what we want or think we want as often as possible; rather, it entails having more adequate notions of what is worth wanting. The acquisition of more adequate ideas is, by Spinoza's account, both possible and desirable. It is not automatic. Acquisition of adequate ideas is possible in part because we are not required to invent or discover for ourselves de novo every idea we may entertain. As cultural beings who read books and (at least as important) encounter the trials and outcomes of many and varied moral experiments, we have rich experiential and imaginatively developed materials available to us among which to choose, refine, and develop the working hypotheses of our moral lives. As conscious beings, we both order and appropriate the mental premises on which those lives are conducted.

A crucial difficulty in Spinoza's account of freedom, by Bennett's account, is the apparent gap between Spinoza's concept of will and the idea of essence Spinoza employs in arguing that an individual's destruction cannot proceed from its essence: "It is hard to know what 'essence' means in this context, but there is no chance of making it mean 'will' or having anything to do with voluntary control" (p. 328). Yet Spinoza does define the essence of a thing as its *conatus* – that is, its striving for self-preservation (and, by implication, self-expression – self-fulfillment); and he defines "will" as *conatus* relative to the mind, "appetite" as *conatus* relative to the mind–body complex, and "desire" as self-conscious appetite.

If the question is asked, then, how characters are to be informed and trained so that the exercise of human freedom in Spinoza's sense becomes actual rather than a mere virtuality (that is, how do we break the cycle of moral ignorance and bad example that seems to lock the doors against the moral advance of all but the most fortunate?), Spinoza's answer is intellectual and cultural – very much of a piece with the tradition of Aristotle, Plato, and Socrates from which his thought is sprung: To begin with, as I have indicated, we are not as ideationally deprived as we sometimes like to make out. The point is Aristotle's, as we shall urge further, but it is certainly not inaccessible to Spinoza. A rich array of exemplars of human strengths and weaknesses stands and moves before our eyes in every human environment; and logic, imagination, and personal reaction readily ring the changes on what we observe directly, generating an infinite array of moral possibilities for emulation or rejection. The mind is the theater in which this array is projected, but it is not just a theater: It is also the observer and the chooser – it is the self.

What I think is sound at the root of Bennett's analysis is the recognition that Spinoza uses a shifting notion of human identity when he expresses the idea of pursuing our own best interest. That is, the self, which is the subject of human freedom, its author and its beneficiary, is not identifiable with the empiric ego or with the empirically volitional self. When Spinoza speaks of choices we can make that make us more the author or more the victim of our acts, he is following a well-established tradition of Pietist moral philosophy that thinks of a higher and a lower self, only one of which at any given moment can be identified with the empiric self of choice. When I choose wisely, in these traditional schemes, the higher self is said to act – in that I am choosing as I would have done had I known my own best interest. When I choose unwisely, the lower self, sometimes called spirit or by some other distinguishing term, is said to act: I was not the real chooser because I did not choose what I really would have wanted (what I ultimately did and do want in the Aristotelian sense that regards it as an axiom that all men desire their own objective felicity, although they may conceive it adequately or inadequately). I did not choose my own best interest as I would have conceived it had I been adequately informed. The empiric self acts in the foreground, but a second self, higher or lower than that of the empiric self which chooses, remains virtual in the background, as the object created by the choices of the empiric self. For wise and foolish choices form the character: They make me a better or a lesser person, more capable or less capable of choice, in fact, in the dynamic and reflexive Mu'tazilite model of human freedom Spinoza inherits from Maimonides and Saadiah Gaon. Thus the fact that I am the author of an act in the common law sense that the event was uniquely modified by my participation does not imply my being the author of the same act in Spinoza's sense. I am active or passive on a relative scale that depends not on the extent to which I momentarily appropriate a given choice, but on the extent to which that choice contributes to the formation of an identity which may never empirically be mine but which I would recognize as my best self if my ideas were adequate enough to allow me to perceive its virtuality within me.

In fairness to Bennett, be it said, Spinoza does not feel the need to spell out this curious (but to moralists of the tradition all too familiar) piece of dialectic. He did entail it, however, when he equated the essence or identity of each thing not with what that thing was (statically, empirically, in the past), but with a tendency, the tendency of each thing to persist in, express, promote, and develop its own being. The key assumption of Spinoza's scheme, as of the traditional literature whose categories he adapts, is that I am not necessarily who I think I am. I am also who I might become, a better (i.e., more perfect) or a lesser being, whose identity I acquire and indeed define in the appropriation of the choices I make, and whose identity I entrench in the habituation of those choices. My freedom rests on the intellectual access I have to the conception of what traditionally was called a higher self, but what Spinoza prefers to call (via the notion of wiser choices) adequate ideas.

Human consciousness is, by Spinoza's account, a reflexive and self-transparent idea, dynamic rather than static, and capable of access to its own content in practical and speculative ways. To deny this is to deny the mind's activity, and the burden of proof in such a case passes to the critic to explain in other terms (that is, without reference to an active and reflexive mind) the phenomena of consciousness and volition. However, Spinoza's account is anything but a heap of rubble. Does this mean that the house, although habitable, is perfect? Spinoza died young, and it would be foolish to pretend that he left his system flawless. There are many points at which the account could be criticized, ranging from the radical rejection of his premises to the detailed quibbles that might no more than add a nuance to his terminology or to the critic's understanding. To develop fully each major or minor point and to be fully candid about which criticisms reflected lacunae in Spinoza's philosophy, which projected values or perceptions at variance from his own – which were constructive relative to his project and which relative to our larger philosophic interests – would take us far beyond the scope afforded by the present context. Some misapprehensions can be readily cleared up. One begins and persists, at least in part, as a result of a persistent mistranslation: The two key emotions, upon which love and hate and all the more complex emotions are founded, are *laetitia* and *tristitia*. These terms, as any Latin student knows, mean joy and sorrow, not pleasure and pain – still less pleasure and unpleasure. They are defined by Spinoza as transitions of the mind to a greater or lesser state of perfection. As mere transitions, both are passive; they happen to the mind, although in the special case of the joy that we can bring about through developing our adequate ideas, joy involves an activation (self-awakening) as well.

Spinoza has a name for pleasure and pain. These are *titillatio* and *dolor*, also regularly mistranslated to cover up the mistranslation of *laetitia* and *tristitia* and preserve the fiction that the naturalism of Spinoza resolves to some form of hedonism. Spinoza defines *titillatio* and *dolor* as a localized joy or sorrow, referential to some particular part of the mind–body complex (see *Ethics* III, Prop. 11, Schol; Defs 2–3). Readers who doubt that *laetitia* and *tristitia* are joy and sorrow should attempt to explain why Spinoza defined pleasure or pain as a transition of the mind to a state of greater or lesser perfection. This is a question of moral experience and perhaps development, not of sensation. Those who doubt that *titillatio* and *dolor* mean what the Latin says they do, pleasure and pain, should endeavor to explain how these feelings could be localized, as Spinoza says they are, unless they had the nature of pleasures and pains.[67]

Spinoza did not imagine that adequate ideas make us proof against pain, as some faith healers or exponents of positive thinking propose that illness can be held at bay by "good thoughts" or "visualization." Nor was it Spinoza's hope to banish passions in the sense of neutering the mind to joy, grief, or anger. Finite beings in an interactive world will experience passive emotions whether they like it or not, regardless of the mental strategies they adopt. The project of the *Ethics* is not to create an immunity to emotions, but to free the mind from the grip of those passive emotions over which we can exercise control on an intellectual level in virtue of their flawed intellectual nature as expressions of inadequate ideas. Thus although adequate ideas are not some kind of mental novocaine that dissolves or numbs our human feelings, they do provide us (in much the way that the Epicurean, Stoic, and medieval monotheistic moralists claimed they do) with a means of liberating ourselves from the obsessive grip of those passions whose tight hold derives from the passive collaboration of our own mental powers. Spinoza's brief is less to show that this is so than to provide a theoretical basis for explaining the possibility of this well-known (if less systematically practiced) power of the mind.

The model is this: When I nurse my wrath to keep it warm, harbor a grudge, cultivate my anger, yield to my prejudices, fail to master my appetites or fears, or otherwise become a victim to my emotions and show signs of what earlier philosophers had no compunction in calling vices – that is, moral flaws – I am being less active and less adequate as a person (Spinoza argues) because I am not subjecting certain of my thoughts – irrational thoughts based on inadequate ideas – to the rational scrutiny that would dissolve them. This is readily seen in the case of prejudice: When one harbors malice toward a person because that person is arbitrarily associated with some negative quality or experience – with my own discomfort at the thought of weakness, poverty, victimhood, for example – one is investing the object of one's prejudice with properties whose actual origin is one's own error. The harm to oneself of such emotions (for they are never harmful solely to their object) is a direct consequence of perhaps remediable negligence. One ought to scrutinize the grounds of

---

[67] We are fortunate that Edwin Curley has now corrected the hundred-year-old misapprehension, one may hope decisively, in his translation of *The Collected Works of Spinoza* (Princeton: Princeton University Press, 1985), p. 642.

one's emotions, just as one should scrutinize the grounds of one's beliefs. An emotion such as prejudice or bigotry has much the same logical structure as an unwarranted belief.

However, given the metaphysical background of Spinoza's system and the critical role he expects acceptance of monism and determinism to play in that system, it is possible to say that whenever human emotions gain the sort of power over the mind that is likely to limit our effectiveness as human agents (in other words, whenever they are to be called passions or passivities in the sense that is ethically germane), we fall victim to a precise analog of prejudice: Fear becomes unwieldy when the mind flounders in its own fascination with an object of terror, viewing that object as the sole and sufficient controlling factor in a situation or in our lives. A more holistic perspective, Spinoza is confident, would be more wholesome. Hatred, sexual obsession, and power mania all share the same logical anatomy. Grudges, spite, grief, and regret commit the same fallacy in a dynamic framework; that is, they presume contingency – another way of falsely isolating a particular or a set of particulars or events from their causal environment. Monism and determinism, once adopted as the outlooks advised by reason, allow, indeed require, a more detached, objective viewpoint, a viewpoint in which we would not crudely identify the good with our own immediate goal and from which we would perceive our comrades' goals as well. The larger perspective, Spinoza argues, is inherently cooling to the passions. It is the perspective Marcus Aurelius strove to adopt when he pleaded with himself to remember with whom he had to deal. Even if to understand is not to forgive, at least it will dissolve the most vicious hold upon us of our inability to forgive, the paralyzing hatred, cruelty, anger, or remorse that grow demonstrably from lack of understanding.

Now there are two lines of criticism to which Spinoza's central thesis here is open. The first is that Spinoza's monism and determinism might not be true. This requires a reversion to metaphysics few ethicists feel desirous of undertaking, unless it is with the question-begging objective of establishing that determinism renders ethics impossible. But for our present purpose, the journey really is not necessary. Determinism need not be true or even believed in order to be useful in the moral tactics of mastering the passions. Bahya Ibn Paquda fields a superb version of the "philosophy of as if" in behalf of moral mastery, using determinism to minimize human regrets and wishfulness while simultaneously using the idea of human freedom to maximize the scope of our moral responsibility. Kant, developing and secularizing a related Pietist tradition, does something very similar, while avoiding commitment on the metaphysical issue almost as scrupulously as Bahya does. For ethics, the critical issue is not whether determinism is true or false, but whether belief in determinism or monism, or to generalize, any intellectual notion we may hold, can actually give us power over our emotions. Spinoza, to be sure, is far too earnest a philosopher to rely on any notion he does not take to be true categorically, and in this I think he is right. Besides, the pragmatic value of a mere posture rather than commitment of belief is questionable, and Spinoza would not be the philosopher to recommend inuring ourselves to a belief, as Pascal and James do, for the sake of its reputed benefits. However, the monism and determinism required by Spinoza's ethical prescription in some respects amount to little more than the recognition of the interconnectedness of all things in a single scheme or system and the correlative recognition that the events that harm or aid us did not conspire to do so, but follow a logic and dynamic of their own. That is the heart of the recognition that Spinoza is confident will give us peace of mind. Do we in fact battle against a determinism of the emotions that makes such peace of mind impossible?

Most modern critics of rationalism are romantics in the precise sense that they believe the power of the emotions to be primary, perhaps insuperable, certainly inaccessible to the pleas of reason. The Spinozistic model, which relies upon a continuum between reason and emotion (since all are really only thoughts), is accordingly dismissed as bad psychology. A form of romanticism founded in knowing appeals to the power of the emotions lies behind much of the oversubtle and overinterpretive efforts at critique to be found in the recent literature on Spinoza. Appeals to the power of the passions and their sui generis character provide the intuitive kernel of subjective verisimilitude in which the sophisticated critics ultimately but repeatedly rest their case. Spinoza, of course, does not deny the power of the emotions; the burden of his intellectualism and indeed of much of his monism and determinism is to deny their omnipotence.

The second line of criticism, then – and to my way of thinking it contains all the most germane critiques of Spinozistic ethics – rests on psychodynamics. Spinoza, like Freud, assumes that we have access through our conscious minds to all of the un-self-conscious processes of association by which a blind striving for self-preservation might mask our intentions to us and trip up our higher interests. In other words (and this is his Mosaic heritage, as it is Freud's), Spinoza denies the inevitability of tragedy and affirms the power of rationality not merely to control the irrational within ourselves, but indeed to sublimate it, to transform it into reason. There is evidence for the possibility of such alchemy, but as individuals and as a species we are far from mastery of its techniques, and we have many reasons to doubt the completeness of any prescription for its practice. For we know that no mere mechanism or recipe, no mere combination of thoughts or words or sentiments, is adequate to guarantee the reform of human character. Our character is too complex, too mercurial, too capable of receding into its own depths, to allow doubts to be dispelled entirely. Complacency is just another of the protean traps which the mind, blindly seeking life, throws up about itself to defend itself from effort and liability to risk.

The evidence for the possibility of using consciousness to gain some measure of self-mastery and thus freedom in Spinoza's sense comes from the lives of ordinary and extraordinary individuals who achieve some degree of inner peace. The difficulty and depth of the process comes from the equally commonplace and extreme cases of moral weakness. The issue of moral weakness affects Spinoza's claims as it affects all rationalism in morals because it challenges the rationalist's model of the relationship between consciousness and action. Specifically, Spinoza must address the issues of recalcitrance surrounding the self-definition of character. In seeking the realization of intellectual patterns in our human dispositional matter, we must operate in a context that is anything but purely intellectual. Where Spinoza did not develop a full and circumstantial account – partly because he believed that human weakness, as exemplified, say, in the case of suicide, eludes the grasp of philosophy, and partly because he could rely on the work accomplished by his predecessors, whose insights he had no need to repeat.

In assaying the prospects of our gaining control of our own character, Spinoza follows in the footsteps of Aristotle and in the Maimonidean tradition, despite his sense of greater rigor in determinism and despite his outspoken disappointment and impatience with the flaws in the tradition. Just as we can use Spinoza to gain insight into what an Aristotelian can mean in calling the human subject a small prime mover, so we can use Maimonides to gain further insight into what it means for an individual to be responsible for the constitution of his or her own character, and Aristotle to gain further insight into the possibility of moral failure despite the seeming presence of the knowledge that intellectualist (Socratic) accounts of virtue seem to tell us renders such failure impossible.

Maimonides on character and freedom

Looking over his shoulder at the Islamic heritage of predestinarian theology, Maimonides thanked God that the premise of free choice had never been questioned within his own confession.[68] Human freedom, he argues, is an axiom of biblical law, implicit in the very syntax of the imperative mood in which Torah addresses its commands. The rejection of fatalism – that is, of the notion that human actions make no difference to the outcome of events – is presupposed, Maimonides argues, in the logic of the precautionary commandments in particular – the commandment, for example, to place a parapet on one's roof as a precaution against tragic accidents. How can there be a law of negligence without the assumption that human precautions prevent what would otherwise have occurred?[69]

God, Maimonides argues, is not determined by His own nature, not determined, for example, to create. Following the lead of al-Ghazali (who held all eternalists to be atheists), but mitigating al-Ghazali's stance, Maimonides argues that the doctrine of the world's creation is preferable to that of its eternity. The notion of God's authorship of nature, as Maimonides recasts the argument, is attenuated to irrelevance if God's choice (to create or not create, so or otherwise) has made no difference to the final outcome. God's absolute simplicity cannot create complexity if the divine creative act works solely by necessity.[70] Here Maimonides shores up the groundwork in an affirmation of choice for what will become Leibniz's and later Kripke's doctrine of alternative possible worlds.[71] Causal necessity, as we have seen, acquires the logical authority of essentialism when essences are given, but such is the case only within "the settled order of nature." And part of the settled order of nature, part of the human essence, is human choice.

Maimonides, then, is a voluntarist within the context of his determinism. Is he a soft determinist? He certainly does not go easy on the *mutakallimun* who attempted to combine their occasionalism with an affirmation of human freedom: The Mu'tazilite voluntarists were inconsistent in affirming that we are the authors of our own actions while maintaining that God is the cause of each particular atom, with all its accidents, at every instant. Maimonides calls occasionalism a

---

[68] *Guide* III 17, *RAMBAM*, 315.
[69] "Eight Chapters," 8, *RAMBAM*, 242–3.
[70] *Guide* II 21, 22.
[71] See my "Maimonides and Leibniz," *Journal of Jewish Studies* 31 (1980), 214–36. This includes my translation of Leibniz's Latin reading notes on the *Guide to the Perplexed*.

mockery of the divine creative act. The Ash'arite doctrine that we "appropriate" our actions by our choices (and thus acquire moral responsibility for them, a doctrine modeled on Stoic theory) he labels a piece of doubletalk, in view of the corresponding Ash'arite view that our acts of acquisition (like the Mu'tazilite created capacities for action) are directly created by God.[72]

A soft determinist, as defined in Paul Edwards's now-classic explication of William James's original notion, is one who is prepared to concede that the determinants of our choices are already predetermined by forces external to our control when we make those choices.[73] The "softness" consists in willingness to invoke moral categories – as of punishment and blame – despite the concession, in cases where overt constraints are not operative: Physical force and extreme threats of violence are taken as coercive, but inducements or even warnings coupled with the predispositions of our character are not, even though it is admitted that the combination predetermines choice. Strong blandishments and sanctions short of intimidation often remain in a somewhat murky or mushy area, of relative freedom (semidetermination?). Perhaps here too, there is some softness; but if so, it seems to be a logical softness – since all outcomes of choice are conceded to be predetermined by external factors. The intention (often overtly expressed) is simply to provide for the convenience of moral philosophers and social (e.g., penal) agencies by making a rather ad hoc distinction between remote or overwhelming determinants of choice or action, over which an individual is formally expected to exercise no control, and proximate determinants of choice, which leave room for social sanction, even though it is conceded that no real alternative futures can exist. The distinction between sanctioned and sanctionless determinants, then, is purely rhetorical, based on an emotive appeal to the immediacy or remoteness, laxity or intensity of factors which are causally no different in their outcome. In other words, it is a device useful for haranguing juries (and susceptible of use as readily in prosecution as in defense), but of limited earnestness in view of the universal (usually psychosocial) concession that accompanies it.[74] It is to the Rambam's credit that he steers clear of that concession, and it will be

---

[72] See *Guide* I 73.6, III 17.4 I 51.
[73] See Hook, pp. 121–2.
[74] I focus on Paul Edwards's definition of soft determinism because William James assigned at least three distinct notions of freedom to the persons he called soft determinists: "acting without external constraint," "acting rightly," and "acquiescing in the law of the whole." See "The Dilemma of Determinism," in W. James, *The Will to Believe and Other Essays in Popular Philosophy* (New York: Dover, 1959, lecture of 1884), 149. Our present exploration only tangentially concerns the ideas of freedom as acquies-

philosophically worthwhile for us to ascertain how he manages to do so.

Maimonides' assertion that human freedom had never been questioned within his religion is startling in view of the testimony of scripture, whose idiom, as he observes, is one of universal theistic determinism. Scripture, to be sure, could be quoted on both sides of the issue. The Rabbis address the problem gnomically: "Everything is overseen, and leave is given," or "All is in the hands of Heaven except the fear of Heaven."[75] Among Jewish philosophic rationalists, the two sayings were interpreted to imply that humans are delegated freedom of choice not only with regard to faith and devotion to God, but in all ethical areas, where our actions might express the tenor of our intentions. But how could God be a universal creator and governor of nature, while yet affording to His creatures independence of choice and action?

Maimonides answers this question by way of the same sort of causal account that he uses against occasionalism: God acts by way of intermediaries which include not merely the celestial intelligences that guide the spheres, but the substantial forms or essences in all things. In human beings the most distinctive expression of the divinely im-

---

cence and freedom as recognition of necessity. Nor does it centrally address the question whether only rightful acts are free – although it does conclude with some reflections on the problem which at least some rationalists have in calling wrongful acts free. But my essay is centrally concerned with the confinement of freedom to the absence of external coercion. This is the sense that Edwards singles out for attention, and this is the sense I find most commonly resorted to by soft determinists; that is, persons who wish to get on to the issues of responsibility (by which they usually mean social or legal accountability) and sidestep as rapidly as possible the relevant problems of human agency. The technique is to concede external determination of all human motives but to find sufficient grounds for accountability in the lack of overt coercion or of overwhelming constraints upon our choices.

Soft determinism was the position of Thomas Hobbes, and it is from Hobbes via Hume that it seems to acquire its peculiar hold on the minds of English-speaking philosophers, who are all too prone to confuse it with the positions of the Stoics, say, or Spinoza. "Liberty, or Freedom," Hobbes writes, "signifieth, properly, the absence of opposition; by opposition, I mean external impediments to motion . . . *Liberty* and *necessity* are consistent: as in the water, that hath not only *liberty*, but a *necessity* of descending by the channel; so likewise in the actions which men voluntarily do: which, because they proceed from their will, proceed from *liberty;* and yet, because every act of man's will, and every desire, and inclination proceedeth from some cause, and that from another cause, in a continual chain, whose first link is in the hand of God the first of all causes, proceed from necessity." As Ralph Ross succinctly sums up Hobbes's position: "A man may do as he wants, but he must want what he wants." See *Leviathan* Pt. 2, ch. 21 and "Of Liberty and Necessity" in Molesworth ed., 1839, vol. 4, pp. 239–78. Ralph Ross's remark is from his essay "Some Puzzles in Hobbes," in R. Ross et al., eds., *Thomas Hobbes in His Time* (Minneapolis: University of Minnesota Press, 1974), 43.

75 R. Akiba in Mishnah *Avot* 3:15, trans. Danby, 3:16, p. 452; cf. Jeremiah 10:23 with Deuteronomy 30:19. And *Berakhot* 33b; cf. Josephus, *Antiquities* XVIII i 3 and *Niddah* 16 b.

parted forms is represented in the rational soul, whose affinity with
God is manifest in its intellectual apprehension of the forms of things,
its governance of the body, and its reflection (in a finite way) of the
perfection and stability that reason teaches us belong absolutely only
to God.[76] The human subject chooses, as the Muʿtazilites argued, via a
"created capacity" – the proof is that an agent's divinely given power
to act is not impaired.[77] But the human capacity for action is not
monovalent and instantaneous (as the Ashʿarites proposed), but polyvalent and enduring, in keeping with the theory of character and
dispositions Aristotle developed from the ethical psychology of Plato:
Natural causes may have just one effect; choices confront several
possible alternatives.[78]

Dispositions are the key to any Aristotelian theory of human freedom because dispositions are the foundations of natural possibility,
what things or persons can and cannot do. This is the reason Aristotle
makes the crucial observation that human dispositions are polyvalent.
They involve choice. To establish freedom, it is necessary to show that
choice is rational – not merely calculative, but self-constituting, reflexive, and reflective as a mode of consciousness. Here the Spinozistic way of speaking and analysis inform and are informed by
Maimonides' Aristotelian contention that human consciousness creates multiple alternatives, where (other) natural dispositions find only
one. For Spinoza understood Maimonides as Aristotle understood
Plato or as Kant understood Hume, and the concepts of the later
philosopher shed light on the assumptions of his predecessor. Spinoza's reflective *conatus* stands in the place of Maimonides' polyvalent
dispositions. The original conception, of course, is Aristotelian.

Aristotle himself packs the rational criteria of freedom into his
operative definition of the term *prohairesis* (choice, but rational, considered, deliberative choice); as a result the word serves him rather
well. The drawback is a certain tendency to circularity or sup-
positiousness, at least in appearance, in the passages where Aristotle
seems most explicitly to discuss human freedom – that is, where he
speaks of voluntary and coerced actions. Guthrie remarks: "There is
nothing in Aristotle of the philosophical debate between free will and
determinism, which appears to have made its first entry with the

---

[76] *Guide* I 1, *RAMBAM*, 56–7.
[77] See *Guide* I 73.10, *RAMBAM*, 136–8, "Eight Chapters," 2, 8, cf. *Guide* III 17.4–5;
Saadiah, *Book of Beliefs and Convictions* IV 3, trans. Rosenblatt (New Haven: Yale University Press, 1947), 186.
[78] See Aristotle *Metaphysics* Theta 2, 1046b 1–24; 5, 1048a 8–12.

Epicureans. . . ."[79] Guthrie is right on two counts: (1) it was the Epicurean usage of *voluntas* (paired in the poetry of Lucretius with *voluptas*) that stuck in our vocabulary of volition; and (2) it was Epicurus' mistrust of the strict determinism of Democritus and of his own teacher Nausiphanes that made the debate between determinism and voluntarism a philosophic *topos*. Unlike Epicurus, Aristotle did not regard scientific determinism as posing a threat to voluntarism; but Aristotle was not unaware of freedom as an issue. In my view, Aristotle's subtlest and most valuable contributions to the discussion of human freedom come not in his discussions of the voluntary and involuntary, but in his discussion of *akrasia,* where he confronts the issue of self-conscious wrongdoing and the tenability or untenability of his teachers' views. As Guthrie explains: "Aristotle's whole discussion of voluntary and involuntary action is avowedly an attempt to come to terms with the Socratic and Platonic dictum that virtue is knowledge and ignorance the whole cause of wrongdoing" (p. 359). It is in regard to *akrasia* or moral weakness, the very area in which Spinoza confessed the insufficiency of his own rationalistic theory (*Ethics* II, Prop. 49, Schol., Gebhardt, vol. 2, 135, ll. 30–31), that this issue comes to a head. Yet in discussions of the voluntary and involuntary, or of choice and deliberation, the key Aristotelian theses may seem to be built into the definitions of the terms.

In general, Aristotle does not treat the idea of human freedom as problematic. Most commonly, he presumes it – as in the context of the Sea Battle, where he presumes but does not prove that we might choose other than as we do.[80] The dialectic of confessional debates

---

[79] Cf. W. K. C. Guthrie, *A History of Greek Philosophy,* vol. 6, 361. For Aristotle's account of voluntary motion and its bearing on human freedom and responsibility, see Martha Nussbaum, *The Fragility of Goodness* (Cambridge: Cambridge University Press, 1986), 283–9 and her earlier *Aristotle's De Motu Animalium* (Princeton, NJ: Princeton University Press, 1978). For *prohairesis* see *Nicomachaean Ethics* III 2, and for *boulesis* III 3.

[80] That Aristotle presumes rather than arguing in support of frèe will at *De Interpretatione* 9 is clear from the text (18b 5–17) and vividly shown in al-Farabi's commentary ad loc., *Sharh fī 2l-2Ibara,* ed. W. Kutsch and S. Marrow (Beirut: Catholic Press, 1960), 83 l. 24–84, l. 21, trans. F. W. Zimmermann (Oxford: Oxford University Press, 1981), 76–7; see my discussion in *IYYUN,* 23 (1973), 100–12. That Aristotle is committed to future contingency is evident also in the *Metaphysics* (VI 3), where he argues that not all things are of necessity, since for some their causes have not yet come to be. Yet he rejects indeterminism as well: Events are not fortuitous; they happen in accordance with their causes and as those causes require. Chance is the intervention of a causal train whose necessities are not regularly associated with those we are attending to. It is not an alternative to causality, but, as Maimonides put it, results from a superfluity of causes. See *Metaphysics* 1027a 30–b16; *Physics* II 6; Maimonides, *Guide* II 48, ed. Munk, vol. 2, 101a, ll. 2–8.

places Maimonides in the position of being more explicit. He opens his discussion of free will (which is directed to a broad, not esoteric public) with a rejection of the notions of original sin, and astral and physiological determinism. His treatment is in keeping with the Rabbinic rejection of hereditarian notions of destiny. It is argued in the Talmud (Sanhedrin 38a) that humanity was created from a single stock, "So that the righteous should not say, 'We are the descendants of a righteous ancestor,' and the wicked, 'We are the descendants of a wicked ancestor,'" grounding complacency in the one group and a sense of futility or irresponsibility in the other. Maimonides, similarly, outspokenly rejects appeals to the stars and their controlling influences on the humors, and all such appeals to overwhelming fate – whether derived from God, from nature, or from the presumptive nexus of divine rule over nature.

The stars afford no excuse to adulterers or fornicators, and human fate provides no excuse to criminals. Humans retain moral and legal accountability for their actions because they are responsible for them causally. Human beings are in control, by a delegated power, just as natural causes are in control of their (monovalent) effects: "When a stone is tossed in the air and falls, we say correctly that it fell in accordance with God's will. . . . But it is not the case that God wills this bit of earth to fall at the time it falls, as the *Mutakallimun* would have it . . . the willing took place during the six days of creation and all things continue forever in accordance with their natures. . . ." In the same way it is true "that for a man to sit or stand – all his movements – are according to the will of God and at His pleasure." What this means, however, is that human nature, as bestowed by God, gives us the power to sit or stand – to determine our own actions.[81]

Maimonides holds that the physiology of the humors predisposes but does not predetermine choice. The argument in support of this thesis is grounded in the Aristotelian analysis of virtue and vice as dispositions. The habits we single out for praise or blame are those in which choices are made that both manifest and entrench a certain tendency of character. It is the presence of habit that makes the tenor of our actions dependable, and perhaps predictable in a probabilistic way. It is the presence of rational consciousness that makes them free. All things are determined, but we ourselves are participants in the process of determination. We can reject and overcome our inner urges and tendencies, combat and conquer our own nature, re-

[81] "Eight Chapters," 8.

gardless of the depth, intensity, or direction of its thrust.[82] The course of ethical habituation – that is, the acculturation and psychic assimilation, appropriation in the proper sense – of an ethos is not comparable to what we in a post-Pavlovian spirit would call *conditioning*. Conscious alternatives are always present; we are never so secure or so lost that we cannot alter our moral status and heading for better or for worse. "Every human being is fit to become righteous as Moses or wicked as Jeroboam, wise or foolish, compassionate or cruel, niggardly or liberal, and so with all other moral qualities."[83] The story of Adam and Eve does not portend our long-consummated and therefore inevitable tragic fall from grace, but rather portrays the radical openness of the human future at every instant – we could reach out at this very moment and pluck eternity from the tree of life.[84]

A coward, like a courageous person, can confront danger, but partly because of habit, partly because of temperament (this means the humors, for which we might read the hormones, substituting adrenalin and its releasing factors, antagonists and analogues for the medieval sanguine, phlegmatic, melancholic, and bilious humors, which are assigned the same psychological roles), it is harder for a coward to be brave than it is for a courageous person. A courageous person can become a coward or a coward courageous. Either can make himself or herself into a model of the other through habit, by finding and imposing on the self the sorts of actions that conduce to courage (which is a habit of bravery) or to cowardice (which is a habit of timidity). The same is true of any moral trait. The claim should not be thought suppositious, for moral traits are those specifically which predispose us to making certain types of choices, about which encouragement and discouragement are deemed socially useful and appropriate. We make such choices readily when we have a more or less settled disposi-

---

[82] For the definition of heroism as the conquest of our (lesser) nature: Ben Zoma, "Who is mighty? He who overcomes his nature." *Avot* 4:1. Cf. the Muslim pietist traditions about self-conquest as the true *jihad*. The dialectic of Ben Zoma does not assume that human nature is evil, but only that natural inclination has been used as an excuse.

[83] See Maimonides *Code* I, *Sefer ha-Madaʿ, Hilkhot Teshuvah* 5.2, cf. 5.1 and 5.4 viii: "Just as it was the pleasure of the Creator that fire and air should rise upwards, earth and water descend downwards, and the sphere revolve in a circle, and that all other creatures should be in their accustomed ways, which it pleased Him to assign, so He was pleased that man should have leave in all the actions which a human being can perform, to act freely, of his own accord and God given reason, without being pushed or pulled." M. Hyamson, ed., *Maimonides: The Book of Knowledge* (Jerusalem: Feldheim, 1974), 86b–87b. I understand "pushed or pulled" as allusive to mechanistic determination and psychologic compulsion.

[84] "Eight Chapters," 8, *RAMBAM*, 246–7; Code I, ed. Hyamson, 86b, 5.1.

tion, not mechanically, but in accordance with the counsels of reason, yet spontaneously, noncalculatively, as an expression of the nature (habit, as in Aristotle, is second nature) that we continually acquire, modify, and manifest through our actions.

Maimonides models his Aristotelian theory of ethical dispositions (virtues and vices) vividly by glossing a celebrated locus of the biblical deterministic idiom, the passages where God reveals to Moses that He will harden Pharaoh's heart against the pleas of Israel. If God hardened Pharaoh's heart, the classic question is asked: Why was Pharaoh's punishment justified?[85] Maimonides' response is that Pharaoh's initial sin was the freely made choice to pursue a genocidal policy against the Israelites. This was a deliberate and coolly considered (if prejudicially initiated) decision: "Let us deal wisely with him" (Exod. 1:9–10). The stereotypic use of "him" to designate all Israelites clearly indicates the prejudice at the base of the proposal, and the phrase "lest he multiply . . . and he too be added to our enemies" reveals related passions of fear, suspicion, and isolation. However, the deliberative context equally clearly precludes the possibility that these motives were necessary determinants: The proposal might have been rejected. Other counsels might have been introduced or given greater weight. These counsels were chosen; conscious intelligence hid from its own criteria and took these to itself as exemplars of rationality. When it did so, there were consequences not only for the Israelites. Adoption of a policy or appropriation of a choice leads to the entrenchment of habits that become dispositions in an individual. In a nation or society habits become trends, and trends become institutions. Maimonides analyzes the outcome in keeping with the teaching of the second-century Tanna Ben Azzai: The wages of sin are sin, while those of duties fulfilled are the power to fulfill further duties.[86] As interpreted by Saadiah Gaon, this means that the abuse of freedom by the wicked causes the restriction of their degrees of freedom in the future.[87] God's hardening of Pharaoh's heart, as Maimonides understands the passage, refers to Pharaoh's progressively dimin-

---

[85] "Eight Chapters," 8, ad Exod. 14:4, Gen. 15:14.

[86] Ben Azzai defines the dynamic of habituation: "One commandment draws another after it, and one sin draws another after it. For the reward of a commandment fulfilled is another, and the price of a transgression is another transgression." *Avot* 4:2, Cf. *Mekhilta* ad. Exod. 15:26, ed. Lauterbach (Philadelphia: Jewish Publication Society, 1933), vol. 2, 97; cf. *Makkot* 10b, *Shabbat* 104a, *Yoma* 39a. Compare Ben Azzai at *Yoma* 38a.

[87] See *Book of Beliefs and Convictions* IV 5, 6.2, trans. Rosenblatt, 195, ad Proverbs 19:3, and 198 ad Isaiah 6:10, Deuteronomy 28:29, Job 5:13–14, 12:24–25. Saadiah's thesis is founded In Mu'tazilite (anti-Ash'arite) *Kalam*.

ished power to extricate himself psychologically and his nation politically from the dynamic of the events that his choices and their outcomes had wrapped and tightened about monarch and nation.[88]

Aristotle and *akrasia*

In a model speech that Gorgias wrote in defense of Helen of Troy, the famous Sophist argued that if Helen was persuaded into adultery, she was as guiltless as if she had been abducted by force.[89] Here, in its proper context of special pleading, is the central notion of soft determinism: that motives in a sense compel us and are determined ultimately by factors entirely beyond our control. Socrates, in his characteristically parodistic mode, was aping and inverting the contention of the Sophists when he argued that no man willingly does evil.[90] But the outcome of the Socratic claim, when it was subjected to the rigor of Socratic analysis rather than merely being used in one context and then ignored or reversed in polarity in another, was the recognition of a deeper sense of willing (and of knowing) than the Sophists had been prepared to grapple with: Wrongdoers plainly do not know what they are doing, although they may suppose they do. Right action always rests on knowledge, even when the understanding relied upon does not belong to the actor.[91]

For Aristotle, the elementary phases of the compatibility of freedom and determinism seemed clear. The Aristotelian account of potentiality seemed sufficient to unfreeze nature from the cast of logical determinism and allow change to proceed in a world of unchanging essences. The account of God's immanent action seemed sufficient to release nature from the hold of an arbitrary deus ex machina imposing external decrees. The account of human rational dispositions seemed sufficient to dissolve the idea that human character was unalterably fixed and fatally fixative of our whole future course. It was because Aristotle saw no fundamental problems in these areas of his solutions that we are forced to look to Spinoza for the recognition that *conatus* – essences themselves – can be dynamic and self-changing; to Maimonides for the refutation of fatalistic versions of the idea of divine determination, which transformed God from a deus ex ma-

---

[88] Cf. my argument in "Ibn Khaldun and Thucydides," *Journal of the American Oriental Society* 92 (1972), 250–70. The political case is powerfully instantiated today in South Africa.
[89] Fragment 11.
[90] See *Protagoras* 345e.
[91] See *Republic* IV 443–5, VI 484c, IX 589–90; cf. *Protagoras* 323–4 *Laws* VI 768b.

china to a deus mechanicus. We look to both Maimonides and Spinoza for the further spelling out of the dialectics of the emotions and human character beyond what Aristotle had worked out. For Aristotle is penetrating and subtle about the interactions of the ethical dispositions with social and cultural influences, but frustratingly elliptical about the inner psychology of ethical *hexeis* and the internal dynamics of the emotions – their relationships with one another and with duties.

Yet it is Aristotle who provides the richer and philosophically more critical account when it comes to the assumption built into the rationalistic idea of freedom, that a certain kind of knowledge is sufficient to our freedom, such that if we have that knowledge we are guaranteed control and not only can act freely, but in effect can do no wrong. Aristotle deals with the curious rationalist notion that free actions can never be wrong by way of a sophisticated reformulation of the Socratic paradox in unparadoxical terms in the context of his theory of *akrasia*, "incontinence" or moral weakness. It is in this context, having settled and dismissed the more elementary problems of human freedom, that Aristotle reverts to the issue on a higher level and contributes the necessary capstone to our account of Maimonides' and Spinoza's theories of the compatibility of freedom and determinism by revealing (where Spinoza and Maimonides had shown how knowledge makes us free) how knowledge can fail to be operative while we yet exercise the will. This final stage is crucial, for on it hinges the success of the response to the Sophist use of internal or soft determinism.

Aristotle accepted the Socratic thesis that knowledge of a sort underlies the exercise of virtue: He defines virtue as a disposition toward action in accordance with a mean (between excess and deficiency of certain prima facie goods and ills) as determined by right reason – that is, sound thinking, exemplified in the person of practical wisdom.[92] The cognitive component is essential if virtue is to refer to thoughtful moderation of action, rather than mere mechanical modulation of behavior. The middles that virtue finds can be ascertained only by good judgment as habitually applied in diverse and varying circumstances, either as a practical expression of one's own practical wisdom or as a result of the attunement of one's character to the standards of some common practical wisdom embedded in the mores of one's community (at the level of family, peers, or the culture at large). For the means virtue seeks and tends to find are not mathe-

---

[92] See *Nicomachean Ethics* (EN) II 6, 1106b 36–1107a 2.

matically calculable; they involve sensitivity, tact, and insight into what is appropriate in given circumstances – knowledge of roles, intentions, needs, and deserts, the consequences of alternative choices for oneself and others.[93] What is ostentatious in a private home may be only decorous in a public building or a monument. Proper pride in one circumstance is arrogance, hauteur, or superciliousness in another.[94] Insight is required into oneself and into one's social circumstances (for the human condition is always a social and thus always a cultural one) if one is to steer one's course evenly or even safely. Vices involve a corresponding lack of insight. It is for this reason that it is harder and rarer to live well than badly – since so many things must be adequately apprehended. Furthermore, it is because knowledge underlies the excellences (*aretai*) that lead to the good life (*eudaimonia*) that living well is like an art rather than an accident of fortune.

Aristotle's virtues, like those dealt with by Plato and implicitly by Socrates, are not merely bits of knowledge, however. They are habituations, dispositions of the practical side of character. This point is spelled out in Aristotle. Plato preferred only to suggest it, and Socrates apparently preferred to leave the matter tangled in *aporia*, as a trapdoor escape from verbal earnestness and full disclosure, lest he seem to preach or to attempt to teach excellence as the Sophists did, by selling recipes for success. It is because Aristotle has explicitly worked out the logic of the relationship between knowledge and virtue that he is capable of resolving the Socratic paradox, teasing out the senses of its discrete assertions to unsnarl the apparent contradiction between them.

It is clearly true in one sense that no one willingly does evil. For no one wittingly does what is bad for him, and it is clear from the great thrust of the *Republic* and from Aristotle's own conception of *eudaimonia* – that to live well is to live the life of the virtues, fulfilling our human social, moral, and intellectual nature. Wrong choices are not conducive to living well and are therefore not in our best interest. The vicious person does not know this, for he or she has given precedence to other, less worthy and less fulfilling goals, laying down habits of choosing founded on some kind of a misconstruction of the nature of the good life. One who gave as much thought to ends as to means (to express in Aristotle's terms an argument that Socrates uses[95] against Thrasymachus) would know that a vicious life is a fool's errand in pursuit of unexamined objects, ends that will not withstand scrutiny if

---

[93] EN II 6, 1106a 26–1106b 27.
[94] EN IV 2, 3.
[95] See *Republic* I, 344e; cf. *Apology* 38.

critically tested for their external consequences and inner implications or for their intrinsic worth. In that sense, all vice is self-deception, and the first onus on the morally unsound person is that of
negligence: One has not given thought to the worth of the goods
whose pursuit one's choices have engrained within the character,
compared with those one has habitually ignored or undervalued.
Such a life at best is self-impoverished, or in extreme cases, perverted.

Vice, however, is not the only human failing, and perhaps not even
the most common. Most people have some notion at least of the broad
outlines of right and wrong – enough that the values of the many are
as needful a canon in orienting moral discourse as the disquisitions of
the wise,[96] and enough that Aristotle can beg off on the expectation
that *he* will be a teacher of virtue: If your parents and your peers have
not taught you something of how to live, then formal moral discourse
will be of little value to you, and you are more to be pitied than
preached to.[97] Philosophy is of greater value in working out the syntax of the virtues (e.g., as dispositions) and of happiness (as a synthesis
of activities together making up a life) than it is at formulating the
actual modulations of right choice in every circumstance. That is better left to experience – to practical wisdom – culture and example, art
and poetry, rather than to theory. That is why Plato steadfastly refused to write formulaically about the good life and Aristotle argued
with regard to ethical and political discourse that a science should not
be more precise than its subject matter.[98] The common human goal
of happiness can orient us toward the life of virtue, because virtue is
the means to happiness, and we can observe in our own experience
and that of others what sorts of character and behavior seem most
likely to lead to human fulfillment and what sorts to self-frustration,
self-stultification, or the self-satisfaction of a moral solipsist's fool's
paradise.

Vice, we say, is not the only or the common human failing. If vice
were as common as moral weakness, human societies could scarcely
get by. Our common problem is that we do know at least what we are
supposed to do and find ourselves time and again doing something
else. Paul says: "For the good that I would I do not; but the evil that I

---

[96] Hence Plato's practice of opening his Socratic dialogues with ostensive (almost Ryle-
ian) lists of illustrations of the notion sought. Such a list does not ever constitute a
definition, since it is not a formula; but it does orient the discussion and provide a
steady source of test cases from the pool of common notions. Hence too Aristotle's
deference to the opinions of the many – in general, and as the repository of the ethos
from which (and not from theory) he expects our moral tendencies to be derived.
[97] See EN I 4, 1095b 5–14.
[98] I 3, II 1, X 6.

would not, that I do" (Rom. 7:19). As one who has known guilt, remorse, and moral conflict, Paul is an eloquent spokesman for the phenomenology of choice against conscience. As a trained rhetorician, adept in the methods of argument taught by the Sophists, Paul also offers a rationale not unlike the apology of Gorgias for Helen, but even more closely akin to the poetic plea put in the mouth of Agamemnon by Homer himself: "Not I was the cause of this act [appropriating Achilles' captive girl], but Zeus and my lot, and the Fury who walks in darkness. It was they who in council put wild desire in my understanding the day I took Achilles' prize from him."[99] Paul argues: "Now then it is no longer I that do it but sin that dwelleth in me. For I know that in me (that is in my flesh) dwelleth no good thing. For the will is present with me but how to perform that which is good I find not." And as the underlying explanation: "I am carnal, sold under sin. For . . . what I hate that I do" (Rom. 7:17–18, 14–15).

Paul's purpose is to demonstrate his utter helplessness before sin, the inability of the Law to save him, his need for an external eschaton. For salvation by way of grace depends on his recognition of his human powerlessness to find his way to right action. He is overwhelmed not because he does not know what is right – indeed he has been told (Mic. 6:8) – but because conscience does not rule in him. The point, the guilt, is crucial to Paul's argument. If it is necessary rhetorically to overstate his helplessness, as though it were categorical, and to write off the body utterly, as containing no good (at least in the present context, but see 1 Cor. 6:15, 19), Paul is prepared to do so. Rhetorically the body is only a haven of sinful desires. Rational will does not rule in us; we are victims of our passions, as Agamemnon was of the destiny that gave him his.

Aristotle's brief is to answer such appeals to the irrational. His thesis that the good life is possible for human beings depends on this rebuttal. So ultimately does Maimonides' monotheistic rejection of the notion of dark and evil powers determining human fate and suborning nature and our motives. So does Spinoza's affirmation of the liberative power of adequate ideas. If Aristotle is to succeed in treating rational choice as a capable determinant of human actions, then Aristotle must explain not the occasions where rational choice is not the basis of our actions, but the occasions where rational choice seems to break down – that is, where we say that we knew what was right, but somehow did not do it. Guilt, regret, remorse, mixed feelings, and

---

[99] *Iliad* 19:86, cited in E. R. Dodds, *The Greeks and the Irrational* (Berkeley: University of California Press, 1964), 3.

mixed motives are the common evidence of this fact.[100] We might regret an action, saying in a moral sense that we did not really know what we were doing; but remorse more often takes a different and perhaps more candid tack, admitting that we knew all along that what we chose was wrong. The remorse arises because we did it anyway, despite our better judgment. In Socratic terms — that is, within the framework of Aristotle's cognitive foundation for moral choice — how is this possible?[101]

Aristotle argues that we might "have" knowledge in the sense of being able to state propositions correspondent to what is the case (e.g., "My best choice is philosophy"), yet not have it in the sense that it does not provide the practical foundation for a given choice or sequence of choices.[102] This is not the case with vice. The vicious think they know a better maxim on which to act than the one virtue provides. They are, of course, mistaken.[103] However, one whose head is willing but whose will is weak makes no such pretension. What is the status of this person's knowledge?

Obviously, a distinction must be made between having knowledge and exercising it. Socrates might be loath to say that someone who did not use the knowledge he or she had was acting knowingly. Yet it would be a misrepresentation to pretend that a person who, shall we

---

[100] EN VII 1, 1145b 12–13; 8, 1150b 29–30.

[101] On the face of it, it is not possible. That is, if Socrates be taken strictly at this word, he held knowledge in us to be sovereign and therefore in effect denied the possibility of *akrasia*. But such a denial is in manifest contradiction to the facts (EN VII 2, 1145b 20–8). Yet Socrates often said strange and paradoxical things, overstating one point to suggest another. Aristotle sought the subtler truth behind the outspoken Socratic pronouncement.

[102] EN 1147b 6–19.

[103] Aristotle argues that the saying 'No one is voluntarily wicked' is false: "Otherwise . . . we shall have to deny that man is a moving principle or begetter of his actions, as of children . . ." EN III 5, 1113b 15–20. For Aristotle, the human being is in a sense a prime mover, in much the way that Maimonides makes us the (delegated) causes of our own acts, and Spinoza allows for autonomy in human choices. To deny this (whatever terminology is used) is to deny human agency — ultimately, to deny causal agency altogether. But at the same time Aristotle maintains the truthfulness of the other half of the same saying, which holds that no one is involuntarily happy. Happiness by Aristotle's standards proves to be an art or the product of an art, the art of living well. It cannot be achieved by accident. But can one be voluntarily unhappy? It would seem not. That is, unhappiness is a goal that no one would choose voluntarily (EN I 1). It follows that if viciousness can be an art, it cannot be an art of living well and wisely in accordance with human nature. For vices are weaknesses, not strengths of character. The vicious person, then, in a salvageable sense of the Socratic dictum, does not know what he (or she) is doing, for he does not know what he is choosing. Such a person is responsible for his actions (as a father is responsible for begetting children) inasmuch as he knows what actions he performs, but the vicious person does not choose them with full knowledge in the sense to which the Socratic dictum was allusive, because he mistakenly regards them as conducive to the good life.

say, had learned and not forgotten that high-cholesterol meats may be harmful to one's health was acting in ignorance when he or she ate such meats. A rather special sense of knowledge and ignorance would be necessary to make credible that Socratic type of claim. Differentiating common usage from such Socratic usage, Aristotle can resolve the Socratic paradox by saying that one who violates what he or she knows to be a healthful diet has not acted on his or her knowledge. This person remains responsible and aware, but if knowledge is taken to be fully actual or active only when it is maximally invoked in the formation of our decisions, a sense can be found in which *akrasia* does involve a rather special (and yet common) form of ignorance: acting without the full benefit of our knowledge, acting on the basis of ignorance even when we are, in the common acceptation, not ignorant at all.

One way of setting aside our knowledge (which the vicious person more systematically neglects and in a practical sense rejects in favor of false opinion) is failure to apply our principles to ourselves. This might be called the "Just this once" type of *akrasia*. I know that this sort of thing is good (or bad) for me, but I fail to apply that knowledge in my choices, refusing to act in recognition of the various appropriate minor premises that define the right course for me now. Such wrong choice is blameworthy, since I am responsible for focusing my general principles on concrete situations and remaining sensitive to every point of pertinent application for the principles of reason which serve to promote my human happiness or fulfillment, *eudaimonia*. Yet it is possible to see how in one sense I did not act with full knowledge: In choosing I did not give full weight to my recognition that high-cholesterol meats may contribute to arteriosclerosis. I cannot say that my judgment was overwhelmed, but it was overruled when I gave precedence to some other claims upon my action.

My failure to give due weight to what I knew was like an instance of the corresponding vice in that it set aside the relevant truth in favor of some distracting appetite or passion; but I did not (as with vice) substitute another maxim on the specious grounds of its superiority, foment and promote a habit of character expressive of this illusory notion, and ally my perceptions and associations as to pleasure and pain with a specious notion of advantage.[104] In *akrasia*, it is true to say that we know what we are doing in a sense of knowing that does not truthfully apply to vice. Yet in the intensified practical sense that Socrates gave to knowing we can still be said not to know at all: The

[104] See EN II 3, 1104b 3–13.

moral and material knowledge we have has not been replaced with ignorance, but it does not form the basis of our action.

To this calm variety of *akrasia*, Aristotle adds a special case that he compares with drunkenness or madness, where in an excess of passion one seems somewhat more literally not to know what he or she is doing. Outbursts of anger or responses to other powerful emotions may actually seem to blot out what we know – for instance, about the consequences and the implications of our acts. Indeed, such passions may seem to blot out all consciousness beyond that involved in the immediacy of the act they imperiously demand. In fact, however, consciousness is not obliterated, and such actions only superficially resemble those of madness, drunkenness, or sleepwalking, with which they are figuratively compared. What actually is blotted out is the weight assigned to moderating or mitigating considerations. No new analysis is required: We have knowledge when we act in what we call a fit of passion, but the knowledge that we have does not fully inform our decisions.

Maimonides' analysis of the failing of Moses[105] can profitably be read in the light of Aristotle's discussion of *akrasia*. For it would seem strange to assign a vice to one who was "the master of Antiquity but also of Posterity," as Maimonides calls Moses. Moses' failing, according to Maimonides, was his loss of patience with the Israelites "when he exclaimed, 'Hear me rebels!'" Moses failed to honor God in failing to retain his composure toward a people "the least woman of whom, as the Sages put it, was on a par with Ezekiel."[106] God was strict with Moses, Maimonides argues, because for a man like him to be angry was tantamount to blasphemy – especially since the people took him to have no faults and modeled their actions upon his. In deviating only slightly from the mean, Moses did not, of course, acquire the corresponding habit, the vice of irascibility. His action, then, might be accountable to *akrasia*. He knew what was right and how it applied to himself and others, but in this instance he did not act upon his knowledge. His Socratic ignorance did not diminish his responsibility, for Moses was responsible for allowing himself to reach a state where the pressures of the moment overruled his usually habitual better judgment. He gave vent to anger not from an uncontrollable rage (to be unable to control his rage would have been a weakness of character; that is, a vice), but from a momentary lapse of rational control – an instantaneous but conscious decision to express an emotion whose expression gave no place to the relevant considerations that might have controlled it.

[105] "Eight Chapters," 4, *RAMBAM*, 233, ad Exod. 20.
[106] Loc. cit., citing *Mekhilta* to Exod. 15:2.

Socrates presumes a close pragmatic integration between what we know and what we do. The Socratic man is very direct. If he deceives himself or holds his knowledge in abeyance, then he is presumed not to have given it sufficient weight, not to have regarded it or treated it as knowledge, really, but as mere opinion that could be set aside. Aristotle accepts this analysis on one level, but at the same time recognizes that what Socrates has to say can be misleading to people who persist in using the word "knowledge" in a less rarefied – or rather, we should say, a less down-to-earth sense.

The most distinctive feature of our ability to choose among alternative goods is our ability to determine for ourselves what premises to adopt or emphasize in our moral deliberations, what syllogisms to pursue with practical intent, what to deemphasize or drop. In building his analysis of *akrasia* on his recognition of this fact, Aristotle succeeds, where many other analysts of human agency have failed, in accounting for the possibility of wrong choices as well as right ones. The tendency in rationalist accounts from Socrates to Kant is to describe freedom in terms so rational that free choice of improper ends seems virtually impossible. That clearly was the suggestive tenor of the Socratic paradox, and of Spinoza's normatized definition of freedom as liberation from the passions as well. Spinoza adopted a spiritualized definition of freedom, whereas Socrates employed an almost private conception of knowledge. Aristotle's account has no quarrel with either of these, but insists on preserving their distinctness from the common conceptions of knowledge and freedom. For the common conceptions are still viable. Spinoza himself retains what is needful and valid from the common idea of freedom under the name of volition. And Aristotle is prepared to retain the common notion of knowledge as well, once that notion has been properly reined in. Allowed its head, the intellectualist notion of freedom, like the Socratic notion of knowledge which feeds into it, will undercut the very applicability of the idea of freedom in the moral and legal spheres, vitiating its usefulness most in the areas where moral or legal accountability are in question.

The Aristotelian analysis of virtue and vice (choice always stands at the helm of the causal linkage that governs the formation of character) is vital;[107] but Aristotelian deliberative choice (*prohairesis*) is so

---

[107] "It is stupid not to recognize that states of character are the product of individual actions," EN III 5, 1114a; and cf. Maimonides' view: No person is born innately virtuous or vicious. To imagine that such is possible is to misconstrue the notion of virtue (as a habit and therefore only to be acquired – and as a habit of rational choosing, which cannot be automatic or mechanical). It is also to misconstrue the force of moral discourse at large – for moral discourse addresses those aspects of character that are susceptible of improvement or decline.

Socratically rational that the analysis does run the risk of suggesting that wrong choices are never free (in the common sense), because those who made them did not fully know what they were doing. This consequence does not square with Aristotle's conception of human nature as inextricably social: Culture without some moral notions is impossible, and for that reason we always have at least some rudiments of moral knowledge and some reference by which our own intelligence can orient itself vis-à-vis its social environment and the ethos and range of ethical choices it presents.

Wrong choices in practice have as much to do with the application of major premises – that is, of values – as they have to do with our appropriation of styles and modulation of passions and desires. The recognition that this is so is a necessary part of Aristotle's account of moral freedom and responsibility. We are responsible for our character because it is by our choices that we appropriate the tendencies of action by which we form our character and give it definition in its social setting; but we do not do so oblivious of cognitive pronouncements regarding right and wrong. If we took absolutely seriously all the sound moral notions we encountered, wrong choices would be virtually impossible. If we scoffed at all of them, our viciousness would preclude the possibility of right choices (for virtuous action does not occur by accident, but presupposes the right motive).[108]

Socrates was right in regarding the vicious person as in way morally blind – although the Aristotelian analysis shows this person crucially to be *self*-blinded. Most wrong choices, however, result not from blindness, but from a tendency we have to close our eyes or blink when confronting powerful appetites or emotions: We forget ourselves, we say, when we are, figuratively speaking, overcome by appetite or anger. That is, we neglect to act upon our principles, although they remain our principles – in much the way that we might neglect to apply a rule of grammar or arithmetic that we know very well and have not rejected, when we are distracted in our work by some extraneous concern. In living, as in other arts, not only speed but also excellence is of importance. It is for this reason that Aristotle says the incontinent person may be clever but does not have practical wisdom:[109] This person does not lose the ability to deliberate about means and ends and pursue what is taken to be the goal, but he or she does keep steadily in view the rightly identified goal of human life. It is in this sense that such a person soundly can be said to be unwise.

---

[108] EN VI 12, 1144a 13–20.
[109] EN VII 9.

Conclusion

We have considered three philosophers who are central figures in the tradition of Western rationalism that is the spine of Western philosophy. All three are committed to varieties of determinism on logical, causal, and theological grounds. None is a soft determinist in Paul Edwards's sense. Yet each upholds a version of human freedom as a central thesis of his philosophy. None is willing to compartmentalize as Kant or Bahya did,[110] or to make freedom a pure postulate of morality or law. Each grounds the idea of freedom in a naturalistic psychology.

And each in his own way shows that human freedom is not incompatible with every variety of hard determinism. If every human action is antecedently determined by external forces, so that there can be no present control by the self over our choices, then there is, of course, no human freedom. But Spinoza, who is zealously protective of the individual effectiveness of each interactive mode, is careful to say that all actions of modes are externally conditioned, not externally determined. The causes of an action include those that are contributed by the self, which is capable of formulating rational foundations for its own action that extend directly to the present determination of choice. Similarly, Aristotle and Maimonides, in arguing that we are responsible for the constitution of our own character, sustain both a universal causal determinism and a clear commitment to voluntarism. Human selves in the Aristotelian scheme can act in some measure as a kind of volitional prime movers – not unconditioned by external givens, but undetermined by them, capable of rational, self-determining choice.

Human freedom is, however, incompatible with soft determinism. For in conceding that all our motives are externally determined and treating motives as the monovalent causes of our actions (while pretending that such external determinations are irrelevant to questions of responsibility – by which it means accountability), soft determinism has in fact closed the door on human freedom. Aristotle is particularly telling in his exposure of soft determinists' favorite evasive haunts. His affirmation of our freedom and responsibility is expressed most importantly not in his well-known and rather strenuous exclusion from the realm of the involuntary of all actions over whose outcomes we exercise some measure of control,[111] nor in any discussion of the term will, which scholars have observed is an issue for

[110] See note 47.
[111] EN III 1.

Epicurus and Lucretius in a sense that never arises as a problem in the
works of Aristotle, but rather in his insistence that the objects of our
passions and our appetites are not by themselves the determinants of
our actions. The point is made in the context of Aristotle's discussion
of *akrasia,* which functions, in effect, as an argument against the
claims of soft determinism, holding, contrary to the pleas of Helen,
Paul, and Agamemnon, that we can be responsible for our own
motives, even when they seem overwhelming.

Aristotle holds that all things in nature act out their specific essences, but that human nature gives us rational choice over a variety
of alternatives whose modulation will modulate our character in turn.
Maimonides, following and filling in the insight of Aristotle and syn-
thesizing it with the biblical and Rabbinic tradition as read by his great
philosophic and exegetical predecessor Saadiah Gaon, finds the authenticity of God's governance and creation in the bestowal of natures
upon things, which can then act in their own behalf,[112] monovalently
in the case of inanimate objects, polyvalently in the case of persons.
Emanation of form upon all things (including intelligence in human
beings) is both the vehicle of God's governance and the gift of independent action in nature and liberty in human subjects. Spinoza's
contribution to the discussion of freedom is perhaps the most valuable – not only because his determinism is the most uncompromising
and his affirmation of freedom the most outspoken, but because his
account of the possibility of freedom within the context of determinism is the most circumstantial, clearly and explicitly stating the assumptions necessary to others in the same tradition: Essences must be
construed as dynamic and in the human case reflective; divine
causality should be immanent, not hit and run; and, above all, natural
causality should not be construed exclusively as external. We too,
along with all other things, are actors in the drama in which we are
cast.

[112] *Guide* III 13.

7

Emotions, responsibility, and character

JOHN SABINI AND MAURY SILVER

The aim of this chapter is to find a place for both emotion and responsibility in our assessment of character. We find that in the course of our everyday lives, we judge people on the basis of their emotions – their warmth, spontaneity, and so on – as well as on the basis of their actions. Furthermore, these judgments seem objective; we treat them as if they were about the worth of the people we judge. However, it seems there are parts of our emotional selves that are not within our control, even with intense, long-range effort.

The problem is how to ground objective judgments about character that appreciates that much is under our control, but that some is not. Unfortunately, the tradition that has found the most sensible location for choice, responsibility, and objectivity, the Kantian, precludes an honorable place for these unchosen feelings. We argue that this difficulty can be repaired once we see that Kant's exclusion of emotion relies on a faulty psychological model of the emotions working with an overly narrow conception of character. We wish to give the emotions a home in judgments of character without evicting responsibility. Let us start with why Kant attempted the eviction.

Kantian thought on emotion

A Kantian chapter on emotion and responsibility is easy to write and quick to read: The domain of the moral is the domain of the will expressed in action; it is the domain of that for which we are responsible. Emotions are beyond the will, and for this reason have no intrinsic moral value. We know nothing of moral significance about a person if we know that person's emotions. People neither gain worth by having appropriate emotions nor lose worth by having inappropriate ones. Indeed, insofar as emotions play a role in moral life, it is an ignoble one; they distract us from attending to moral principles and doing our duty.

Kant's moral theory and the psychology of emotion

Kant's attitude toward emotions and morality presupposes a psychology: Emotions are brute forces unconnected with higher mental functions. Pain is the obvious model. Pain is a brute force; it is beyond the will; it is, or at least typically is, independent of reason. Our feeling pain when our trigeminal nerve is stimulated is a fact about us unconnected to our values or any other important aspect of our characters. Furthermore, pain can overwhelm reason. We might, for example, give in to an addiction because of the pain of withdrawal, even though reason dictates that we resist. It can even erode or distort reason itself: It is hard to think straight with a toothache. The closer the psychology of emotion fits the model of pain, the better prepared it is to play the role in moral life, or in our judgments of character, that a Kantian offers it.

The psychology of the emotions

A painlike conception of emotion does not want for supporters within psychology. Robert Zajonc (1980), in a widely cited paper, has proposed that emotions are precognitive; that is to say, independent of reason, and thus of values, character, and the like. His is not a novel position; indeed, as we shall see, much of the psychology of emotion in this century trivializes them in this way.

James (1884/1968) argued that emotions were the perception of various unspecified bodily states. This confuses how we know we are in an emotional state with what it is to be in an emotional state. Nonetheless, James gave birth to much of the psychological study of the emotions, especially to the attempt to understand emotions by finding their location. The search began in the gut. The view was that the various emotional states were constituted by different reactions of the viscera. Thus, to be afraid was to perceive one's viscera reacting in one way; to be angry was to feel different things there, and so on. Because we experience sensations there when in strong emotional states, this was an attractive lead for those interested in localizing emotions; but it was soon learned that the gut is too undifferentiated in its responses to support the range of emotions we are capable of feeling. So attention shifted to a structure closely related to the gut, but less obviously undifferentiated, the sympathetic nervous system.

The attempt to localize emotion there also came under attack: The strongest line derived from Maranon (1924) and was developed by Schachter and Singer (1962). These attacks attempted to show either that reactions of the sympathetic nervous system are too undifferentiated to underlie the variety of emotions we feel (which attacks the view that the emotions are sympathetic nervous system reactions), or that people in the same state of sympathetic arousal report different emotions (attacking the view that we know our emotional state from the state of our sympathetic nervous system). There are still, however, some who hold out hope for the sympathetic nervous system as the locus of emotion (Frankenaeuser, 1975).

Other psychologists, such as Silvan Tomkins (1962, 1981) and most recently Zajonc (1985), also following remarks of James, have focused on facial feedback as the locus of emotion: The face, unlike the gut or sympathetic nervous system, is capable of a remarkable range of expressions; and we do look to other people's faces to help us determine their reactions. Research in this tradition has proceeded to describe – with extraordinary sophistication – the facial reactions people show when in particular emotional states. However, this research is an analysis of the emotions only if one believes that patterns of facial expressions of the emotions *are* the emotions. This research too has run into trouble. People can experience emotions different from the expressions they show on their faces. (See, for example, Tourangeau and Ellsworth, 1979, Ellsworth and Tourangeau, 1981, and also see rejoinders from Tomkins, 1981, and Izard, 1981.) Facial expressions, while they might be important signs of emotion, seem to be detachable from the experience of emotions.

Another attempt to localize emotion involves importing techniques from the psychophysics of the perception of sensation to the study of the experience of emotion; see Plutchick (1962) for an approach that draws its inspiration from models of color vision. Unfortunately, emotions lack an accessory, crucial for psychophysics, that sensations have: detectors that respond precisely to emotional provocations of various types, as there are receptors for ranges of wavelengths of colors. Emotions are not qualia.

Misplaced concreteness and the psychology of emotion

These different, but related, research traditions all suffer from the same defect: the fallacy of misplaced concreteness. Emotions are not just reactions of the viscera, though such reactions may accompany them. They are not just facial expressions, though they may have such expressions accompanying them, and they are not just qualia, though perhaps there are such things. If they were just visceral reactions, facial feedback, or qualia, emotions could not play the role they do in our lives especially in our judgments of character. On the other hand, they would be perfectly suited to the role Kant assigns them in moral life.

To see this, imagine two people alike in every way except that one feels anger just where the other feels sympathy, and vice versa. Thus, for example, one experiences anger at the 5-year-old who has been the victim of a rape, while the other experiences sympathy. This surely is an important difference between them – it would be a reason for picking one as a friend and avoiding the other – but what does this difference consist in for the various views of emotions we have been describing?

Were emotions disturbances of the gut (or sympathetic nervous system, or whatever), the difference would be nothing but a difference in the tweaks, twinges, and pangs these two people feel – and what about *that* would lead us to select one over the other as a friend? In the facial expression view, they would look quite different in the same circumstance, but is this a reason to pick a friend or to shun someone? In the qualia view, the difference is even less significant: They have different contents of consciousness while in the same circumstance. Why in the world would this matter in choosing a friend – even if we could know it?

A richer view is needed to do justice to the emotions. Could Kant have his way with such a richer view? Is there such a conception of emotion available to us?

There is another view of the psychology of emotion, one that owes more to Aristotle than James (1884), which has received some attention lately. In this view the emotions are connected to cognition, connected to desires and plans, and connected to what people care about and value. In this view, as we have argued elsewhere (Sabini and Silver, 1982, Silver, Sabini, and Parrott, forthcoming), the sources of emotion are abstract. The cause of anger, for example, is not frustration, as one school of psychology had it (Dollard et al., 1939), but the perception of transgression – an abstract concept (see also Averil, 1978). If we look for the cause of envy, we find the perception or judgment that one has been diminished by the accomplishments of another (Sabini and Silver, 1982, chap. 2). If we look for the source of embarrassment, we find it in the subtleties of the assumptions about the self that we give and give off in social interaction. From this conception of emotion, reason is central.

Similarly, the class of behaviors we call angry is abstract; that is to say, angry responses have nothing in common except their being designed to extract revenge for the transgression suffered (or the transgression the angry person believes he or she suffered). Envious responses too have nothing in common but their aim – restoring self-esteem by lowering the envied. So in this conception, emotional responses are neither blind nor brute.

Still, even though emotions may be connected to assessments and values, they have a defect that leads a Kantian to evict them from moral judgment: They are passive, unwilled. What place can we find for aspects of experience that appear to be integral parts of self but are not willed? If we leave psychology and see the problems the emotions made for Kantian theory on its own grounds, we will have some clues about the place of emotions.

Limitations of the Kantian view

One difficulty with a Kantian view of our moral judgments is that we do give weight to the emotions a person experiences in deciding his or her worth. We do think, for example, that someone who does good works and who does them in a generous spirit is a better person than someone who feels no compassion or sympathy for concrete human suffering, but who does equally good works out of a sense of duty. We prefer our neighbors, friends, and children to have the right emotions. This is not to say that someone with a heart of gold who lets evil loose in the world is a hero, or that there is not something admirable about someone who does good despite misanthropic feelings; rather, it is to claim that all other things being equal, we prefer hearts of gold to hearts of coal. Yet this intuition, that part of what we include in deciding the worth of a person is the state of that person's emotions, conflicts with other intuitions, intuitions that the Kantian view captures.

A central notion of our moral lives is responsibility, and responsibility presupposes choice; emotion is unchosen (but see Adams, 1985, for a view of sin without responsibility). We see emotions, desires, passions, impulses as beyond the will, without control. It is unfair to blame people for what they cannot control. To be sure, we sometimes are responsible for controlling *the expression* of these mental states, but we are not typically seen as responsible for having them in the first place. So the problem is to reconcile our intuitions about the centrality of responsibility to morality with our using people's emotions and desires in our judgments of the worth of their characters. (See Nagel, 1979, for a discussion of this in his essay, "Moral Luck.") Indeed, such aspects of our selves as desires and emotions are so important that Stocker (1976) argues that insofar as a person leads the life a Kantian prescribes, she or he must forgo certain basic human goods – friendship, love, a sense of community. And are these not aspects of the moral life? Although we do not agree with Stocker's strong claim (see Sabini and Silver, 1986), the weaker claim that Kantian theory founded on responsibility slights the good life seems clear enough.

As any Kantian would argue, part of what it is to be the sort of creature worthy of the *respect* we owe each other is to be the sort of creature capable of following rules, of attaching oneself to abstract principles. But part of what it is to be a creature worthy of *sympathy* (Sabini and Silver, 1985) involves a caring that is necessarily beyond the will. We have argued that what it is about pain, emotion, and the transgression of a person's values that is demanding of sympathy is their being beyond the will of the creatures experiencing them; were we able to turn these off at will, they would not demand our sympathy. Thus, we see at least one connection between the passive and the moral. Since any life deemed good would include vulnerability to these states, we see what it is about the moral life that presupposes elements of passivity. This vulnerability makes us proper objects of sympathy and caring.

Perhaps, as Kant has argued, sympathy, like all emotions, is amoral. If this is so, we are indeed victims of a 'moral schizophrenia,' as Stocker (1976) claims; that is, we may be stuck with a necessary disjunction between our feelings and our moral judgments. This may just be a sad fact about the human condition, but before diagnosing schizophrenia, we should look more closely at some roles the emotions play in judgments of character.

Moral judgments and emotions

There are several ways of understanding our judging people, in part, on the basis of the emotions they feel, as well as on the acts they perform. One way is to argue that people have responsibility for their emotions after all. Several philosophers have taken this approach; Solomon (1973) and Sartre (1948), for example, have argued that experiencing an emotion involves choice. But this path is blocked by conceptual connections between emotion and passivity. As Peters (1972) suggests, 'emotion,' as opposed to 'motive' calls attention to the passive, unbidden, disruptive aspect of a passion. Still, there is a way to assign responsibility for emotion, one introduced by Aristotle in the Nichomachean ethics.

An Aristotelian view

Aristotle does not claim that experiencing the passions is a matter of choice at the moment, but he does argue that the passions can be trained. Specifically, he argues that the practice of moderation in action acts back on the passions to produce a balance, or harmony, of the passions themselves. Thus for Aristotle, though we may not be able to change our emotions at the moment, we were once able to become a different person, one who would have different emotions. Aristotle's suggestion is correct in some cases, but far from a general solution.

In some cases, it is reasonable to assess responsibility for becoming a certain sort of person. We know, for example, that it is easier not to use heroin in the first place than to control the consequences of being addicted. Moreover, this is common knowledge. So we have cause to believe that people know the risk they take in starting to use heroin. Also, we know that in some cases, at least, the original exposure was not under the influence of a strong emotion, drug, intimidation, and so on. All these features ground our blaming people for being addicted. If these features are missing, we do not blame them; for example, we do not blame (or blame less) a person who becomes addicted to opiates because he or she was given morphine for the relief of intractable pain. Similarly, to ground claims that people are responsible for their emotions, we must show:

1. that people know, or should know, that their failures to control their passions will result in their becoming the sort of person who will later be unable to control that emotion;
2. that people have, and know they have, techniques to accomplish this – Aristotle's claim that moderation begets moderation is empirical and in need of empirical support; and
3. that people were not (blamelessly) in an uncontrollable emotional state when they failed to do that which would have led to more properly formed emotions (this must be shown to avoid regress).

These are not low hurdles; but we do believe that some people at some moments have been responsible for their emotions – although perhaps this responsibility is iatrogenic, limited to those who have studied Aristotle's theory.

We have argued that people may sometimes be responsible for their emotions, and it is true that responsibility is a ground for judging character; but we judge people's characters on the basis of their emotions even when the requirements of responsibility are not met. We must still find a way to make sense of our judging people on the basis of their emotional lives without blaming them for their unwilled emotions.

Character: aesthetics and morality

The task is delicate: We must find grounds to separate judgments based on will from judgments based on emotion and yet show how both are similar enough to be sensible as judgments of character. Not all types of judgments will do. Pragmatic judgments would not. Consider: In calling someone rich, a good contact, or a dangerous person to cross, we are not making a judgment of character. Unlike moral judgments, these are contingently desirable, good relative to certain goals. We may want our friends to be rich because of what it does to satisfy our taste for aged wines, fresh lobster, and luxurious ways to get from one place to another; but we would want our friends to be *charitable* even if, by virtue of the lottery, we had no use for their largess. Pragmatic judgments of someone's worth to us are dependent on us, on our interests; but moral judgments are not. This is one reason that judgments of character are about the person, rather than about our relation to the person. But moral judgments are not the only judgments of a person; there are also aesthetic judgments. We like the generous spirit not because she gives more than the duty-bound but rich misanthrope, nor because she has willed her generosity – that question rarely comes up – but because a generous spirit is beautiful, the sort of thing that is a pleasure to behold, and misanthropy is ugly. Even if we were convinced that the misanthrope wanted to experience love but could not, and it was not his fault, we would still find him ugly though we would not blame him and might even pity him for being hopelessly disfigured. We blame, reproach, and punish someone who has committed a moral delict; we withdraw from, feel revulsion toward, someone with an ugly soul. We shun the misanthrope and embrace the bighearted not because we blame the misanthrope for becoming such, but simply for being such. In this way judgments of character based on the emotions a person feels, the impulses she or he displays, are like aesthetic judgments.[1] And to judge a person beautiful is just as detached from our interests and

[1] This view is adumbrated in Aristotle's. Though he struggles in the *Nichomachean Ethics* to convince us that his doctrine of the mean is contingent, in the sense of being dependent on the fact that the mean of passions leads to other good, and that though we should think of the mean as a mean we shouldn't think of it as an arithmetic mean,

particularities as is to judge him or her righteous. Thus in aesthetics we can find grounds to judge a person good or bad on the basis of impulses and emotions; these grounds do not include responsibility, but they are objective, what anyone should see, impartial, independent of the judge's interests.

Insofar as we accept that our judgments of character have two distinct sources, one grounded in responsibility and the other independent of responsibility, then we can give value to emotions – other people's as well as our own. If we do so we will be able to understand the place of the romantic virtues, such as integrity, sincerity, and spontaneity, in deciding on or judging a life. These concepts all involve, or at least in some cases involve, not freely chosen action, but the fit between that action and the emotions felt. We think that it is, after all, the urge to give a place to these romantic virtues in a conception of the good life and good character that has led to the recent attacks on traditional morality from Adams (1985), Blum (1980), Kekes (1981), Stocker (1976), and Williams (1981), among others. We think it a mistake, however, to propose either that people are always responsible for their emotions, or for the fit between their emotions and their actions, as some have done, or that people should be blamed for that which they cannot control, as others have argued. It is enough to say that we do in fact judge people on more than their moral worth, and that aesthetics does and should play an important role in deciding on the life we want to lead and the people we want to become. (The question of the possibility of trading moral for aesthetic virtues remains.)[2]

Summary: The psychology of emotions and aesthetics

We have argued that one conception of the emotions – as brutal, painlike – made them fit for the ignoble role Kant assigns them. We then argued that the psychological treatment of the emotions derived

he might well have a more powerful position were he to argue that his principle of the mean is good in itself and if he abandoned labeling his notion 'the mean' (with its claim to precision denied by the qualification that it should not be taken arithmetically) and replaced it with the notion of harmony, which has obvious links to aesthetics.

[2] We have argued that judgments of character are twofold: aesthetic and moral. This division allows us to preserve our intuition that morality implies choice. On the other hand, one might take the Aristotelian tack that morality involves the good life. We then could say that all principled judgments of character are moral although some are grounded in aesthetic concepts and others in the concepts of choice and responsibility. This would allow us to call sincerity or generosity of spirit 'moral' in accord with some of our intuition. We conjecture that the first alternative will better embody the intuitions involved in making judgments of character, but this is work to be done.

from James also fit them to that role. However, we argued, this psychological treatment of the emotions is untenable. Instead, we suggest that the emotions must be seen as involving what a person thinks and wants, and in that way they are a part, an important part, of the self. Nonetheless, they are passive, beyond the will, so they cannot have a place in Kantian morality. But they can have a part in judgments of the self. Specifically, we argue that the emotions a person feels affects our judgment of that person, and that this is not unreasonable on our part, since what the person feels reveals something important about him or her. Further, we argue that these judgments are aesthetic. Moral judgments against a person lead us to blame, and even punish; aesthetic judgments against a person do not justify such treatment, but they do justify avoiding the person, warning friends against the person, and hoping our children do not turn out like him or her. Both moral and aesthetic judgments tarnish (or elevate) a character in a way that pragmatic judgments do not. Both moral and aesthetic judgments are objective, beyond the particularities of the situation of the person making them.

References

Adams, R. M. (1985). Involuntary sins. *Philosophical Review*, XCIV, 295–303.

Averil, J. R. (1979). Anger. In H. Howe & R. Dienstbier (Eds.), *Nebraska Symposium on Motivation*. Lincoln, Nebraska: University of Nebraska Press.

Blum, L. (1980). *Friendship, altruism, and morality*. London: Routledge and Kegan Paul.

Dollard, J., Doob, L., Miller, N., Mowrer, O., & Sears, R. (1939). *Frustration and aggression*. New Haven: Yale University Press.

Ellsworth, P. E., & Tourangeau, R. (1981). On our failure to disconfirm what nobody ever said. *Journal of Personality and Social Psychology*, 40, 363–9.

Frankenhaeuser, M. (1975). Experimental approaches to the study of catecholamines and emotion. In L. Levi (Ed.), *Emotions: Their parameters and measurement*. New York: Raven Press.

Izard, C. E. (1981). Differential emotions theory and the facial feedback hypothesis of emotion activation: Comments on Tourangeau and Ellsworth's "The roles of facial response in the experience of emotion." *Journal of Personality and Social Psychology*, 40, 350–4.

James, W. (1884/1968). What is an emotion? Reprinted in M. Arnold (Ed.), *The nature of emotion*. London: Penguin.

Kekes, H. N. (1981). Morality and impartiality. *American Philosophical Quarterly*, 1981, 295–303.

Maranon, G. (1924). Contribution à étude de l'action emotive de l'adrenaline. *Revue Française Endocrinol.*, 2, 301–25.

Nagel, T. (1979). *Mortal questions*. Cambridge: Cambridge University Press.

Peters, R. S. (1972). The education of the emotions. In R. F. Drearden, P. H. Hirst, and R. S. Peters (Eds.), *Education and the development of reason.* London: Routledge and Kegan Paul.

Plutchik, R. (1962). *The emotions: Facts, theories, and a new model.* New York: Random House.

Sabini, J., & Silver, M. (1982). *Moralities of everyday life.* New York: Oxford University Press.

    (1985). On the captivity of the will: Sympathy, caring and a moral sense of the human. *Journal for the Theory of Social Behaviour,* 23–37.

    (1986). Loyalty as good and duty: A critique of Stocker. (Under editorial review.)

Sartre, J.-P. (1948). *The emotions: Outline of a theory.* New York: Philosophical Library.

Schachter, S., & Singer, J. (1962). Cognitive, social, and physiological determinants of emotional state. *Psychological Review,* 69, 379–99.

Silver, M., Sabini, J., & Parrott, W. G. Embarrassment: A dramaturgic account. *Journal for the Theory of Social Behaviors,* in press.

Solomon, R. (1973). Emotion and choice. *The Review of Metaphysics,* XVII.

Stocker, M. (1976). The schizophrenia of modern ethical theories. *Journal of Philosophy,* 73, 453–66.

Tomkins, S. S. (1962). *Affect, imagery, and consciousness.* Vol. 1. New York: Springer.

    (1981). The role of facial response in the experience of emotion: A reply to Tourangeau and Ellsworth. *Journal of Personality and Social Psychology,* 40, 355–7.

Tourangeau, R., & Ellsworth, P. C. (1979). The role of facial response in the experience of emotion. *Journal of Personality and Social Psychology,* 37, 1519–31.

Williams, B. (1981). *Moral luck.* Cambridge: Cambridge University Press.

Zajonc, R. B. (1980). Feeling and thinking: Preferences need no inferences. *American Psychologist,* 35, 151–75.

    (1985). Emotions and facial efference: A theory reclaimed. *Science,* 5 April, 15.

Part II

Responsibility and culpability

8

The moral worth of retribution

MICHAEL S. MOORE

Retributivism and the possible modes of its justification

Since I will in this chapter seek to justify the retributive theory of punishment, I will first say what such a theory is. *Retributivism* is the view that punishment is justified by the moral culpability of those who receive it. A retributivist punishes because, and only because, the offender deserves it. Retributivism thus stands in stark contrast to utilitarian views that justify punishment of past offenses by the greater good of preventing future offenses. It also contrasts sharply with rehabilitative views, according to which punishment is justified by the reforming good it does the criminal.

Less clearly, retributivism also differs from a variety of views that are often paraded as retributivist, but that in fact are not. Such views are typically put forward by people who cannot understand how anyone could think that moral desert by itself could justify punishment. Such persons scramble about for other goods that punishment achieves and label these, quite misleadingly, "retributivism." The leading confusions seem to me to be seven in number.

1. First, retributivism is sometimes identified with a particular measure of punishment such as *lex talionis*, an eye for an eye (e.g., Wilson and Herrnstein, 1985, p. 496), or with a kind of punishment such as

Robert Kingsley Professor of Law, University of Southern California Law Center; Professor of Law, University of California, Berkeley. This paper was given at a colloquium of the Program of Jurisprudence and Social Policy, University of California, Berkeley; as one of my "Crime and Justice: Legal and Philosophical Perspectives" lectures, sponsored by the Philosophy Department, University of South Carolina, Columbia; at a faculty workshop of the School of Law, New York University; at a meeting of the Saturday Discussion Group of Southern California Legal and Political philosophers; and at a USC Law Center Faculty Workshop. My thanks to the many participants at these readings whose comments made the paper better. I am also indebted to Elizabeth Arthur [whose most recent novel, *Bad Guys* (Knopf, 1986) touches on the concerns of this chapter], Robert Cooter, Mortimer and Sanford Kadish, Herbert Morris, Stephen Morse, Philippe Nonet, Ferdinand Schoeman, Robin West, and the anonymous reviewer for the Cambridge University Press, for their thoughtful, separate critiques.

the death penalty. Yet retributivism answers a question prior to the questions to which these could be answers. True enough, retributivists at some point have to answer the "how much" and "what type" questions for specific offenses, and they are committed to the principle that punishment should be graded in proportion to desert; but they are not committed to any particular penalty scheme nor to any particular penalty as being deserved. Separate argument is needed to answer these "how much" and "what type" questions, *after* one has described why one is punishing at all. It is quite possible to be a retributivist and to be against both the death penalty and *lex talionis,* the idea that crimes should be punished by like acts being done to the criminal.

2. Contrary to Anthony Quinton (1954) and others (see Hart, 1968), retributivism is *not* "the view that only the guilty are to be punished." A retributivist will subscribe to such a view, but that is not what is distinctive about retributivism. The distinctive aspect of retributivism is that the moral desert of an offender is a *sufficient* reason to punish him or her; the principle Quinton advocates make such moral desert only a *necessary* condition of punishment. Other reasons – typically, crime prevention reasons – must be added to moral desert, in this view, for punishment to be justified. Retributivism has no room for such additional reasons. That future crime might also be prevented by punishment is a happy surplus for a retributivist, but no part of the justification for punishing.

3. Retributivism is not the view that punishment of offenders satisfies the desires for vengeance of their victims. The harm that is punishment can be justified by the good it does psychologically to the victims of crime, whose suffering is thought to have a special claim on the structuring of the criminal justice system (see Honderich, 1969, p. 30). To me, this is not retributivism. A retributivist can justify punishment as deserved even if the criminal's victims are indifferent (or even opposed) to punishing the one who hurt them. Indeed, a retributivist should urge punishment on all offenders who deserve it, even if *no* victims wanted it.

4. Relatedly, retributivism is not the view that the preferences of all citizens (not just crime victims) should be satisfied. A preference utilitarian might well believe, as did Sir James Fitzjames Stephen (1967 at p. 152), that punishment should be exacted "for the sake of gratifying the feeling of hatred – call it revenge, resentment, or what you will – which the contemplation of such [criminal] conduct excites in healthily constituted minds . . . ," or that "the feeling of hatred and the desire of vengeance . . . are important elements of human nature

which ought . . . to be satisfied in a regular public and legal manner." Yet a retributivist need not believe such things, but only that morally culpable persons should be punished, irrespective of what other citizens feel, desire, or prefer.

5. Relatedly, retributivism is not the view that punishment is justified because without it vengeful citizens would take the law into their own hands. Usually it is those who are hostile to retributivism, such as Justice Marshall (1976), who link it to this indefensible idea. Punishment for a retributivist is not justified by the need to prevent private violence, which is an essentially utilitarian justification. Even in the most well-mannered state, those criminals who deserve punishment should get it, according to retributivism.

6. Nor is retributivism to be confused with denunciatory theories of punishment (Feinberg, 1971). In this latter view punishment is justified because punishment is the vehicle through which society can express its condemnation of the criminal's behavior. This is a utilitarian theory, not a retributive one, for punishment is in this view to be justified by the good consequences it achieves – either the psychological satisfactions denunciation achieves, or the prevention of private violence, or the prevention of future crimes through the education benefits of such denunciation. A retributivist justifies punishment by none of these supposed good consequences of punishing.

7. Finally, retributivism should not be confused with a theory of formal justice (the treating of like cases alike). Retributivism is not, as McCloskey (1965) has urged, "a particular application of a general principle of justice, namely, that equals should be treated equally and unequals unequally." True, a retributivist who also subscribes to the principle of formal justice is committed to punishing equally those persons who are equally deserving. However, the principle of formal justice says nothing about punishing anybody for anything; such a principle only dictates that, *if* we punish anyone, we must do so equally. Why we should punish anyone is the question retributivism purports to answer, a question not answered by the distinct principle of formal justice.

Retributivism is a very straightforward theory of punishment: We are justified in punishing because and only because offenders deserve it. Moral culpability ("desert")[1] is in such a view both a sufficient as

---

[1] "Moral culpability" as I am here using the phrase does not presuppose that the act done is morally bad, only that it is legally prohibited. An actor is culpable in this conception when, in doing an action violating some criminal prohibition, he or she satisfies those conditions of fair fault ascription. On this, see Moore (1985b), pp. 14–15. Usually, of course, most serious crimes are also serious moral breaches.

well as a necessary condition of liability to punitive sanctions. Such justification gives society more than merely a right to punish culpable offenders. It does this, making it not unfair to punish them, but retributivism justifies more than this. For a retributivist, the moral culpability of an offender also gives society the *duty* to punish. Retributivism, in other words, is truly a theory of justice such that, if it is true, we have an obligation to set up institutions so that retribution is achieved.

Retributivism, so construed, joins corrective justice theories of torts, natural right theories of property, and promissory theories of contract as deontological alternatives to utilitarian justifications; in each case, the institutions of punishment, tort compensation, property, and contract are justified by the rightness or fairness of the institution in question, not by the good consequences such institution may generate. Further, for each of these theories, moral desert plays the crucial justificatory role: Tort sanctions are justified whenever the plaintiff does not deserve to suffer the harm uncompensated and the defendant by his or her conduct has created an unjust situation that merits corrective action; property rights are justified whenever one party, by his or her labor, first possession, or intrinsic ownership of his or her own body, has come by such actions or status morally to deserve such entitlements; and contractual liability is justified by the fairness of imposing it on one who deserves it (because of his or her voluntary undertaking, but subsequent and unexcused breach).

Once the deontological nature of retributivism is fully appreciated, it is often concluded that such a view cannot be justified. You either believe punishment to be inherently right, or you do not, and that is all there is to be said about it. As Hugo Bedau (1978) once put it:

Either he [the retributivist] appeals to something else – some good end—that is accomplished by the practice of punishment, in which case he is open to the criticism that he has a nonretributivist, consequentialist justification for the practice of punishment. Or his justification does not appeal to something else, in which case it is open to the criticism that it is circular and futile.

Such a restricted view of the justifications open to a retributivist leads theorists in one of two directions: Either they hang on to retributivism, urging that it is to be justified "logically" (i.e., nonmorally) as inherent in the ideas of punishment (Quinton, 1954) or of law (Fingarette, 1977); or they give up retributivism as an inherently unjustifiable view (Benn and Peters, 1959). In either case, retributivism is unfairly treated, since the first alternative trivializes it and the second eliminates it.

Bedau's dilemma is surely overstated. Retributivism is no worse off in the modes of its possible justification than any other deontological theory. In the first place, one might become (like Bedau himself, apparently) a kind of "reluctant retributivist." A reluctant retributivist is someone who is somewhat repelled by retributivism but who nonetheless believes: (1) that there should be punishment; (2) that the only theories of punishment possible are utilitarian, rehabilitative, retributive, or some mixture of these; and (3) that there are decisive objections to utilitarian and rehabilitative theories of punishment, as well as to any mixed theory that uses either of these views in any combination. Such a person, as I have argued elsewhere (Moore, 1982b; also Moore, 1984, chap. 6), becomes, however reluctantly, a retributivist by default.

In the second place, positive arguments can be given for retributivism that do not appeal to some good consequences of punishing. It simply is not true that "appeals to authority apart, we can justify rules and institutions only by showing that they yield advantages" or that "to justify is to provide reasons in terms of something else accepted as valuable" (Benn and Peters, 1959, pp. 175–6). Coherence theories of justification in ethics allow two nonconsequentialist possibilities here:

1. We might justify a principle such as retributivism by showing how it follows from some yet more general principle of justice that we think to be true.
2. Alternatively, we can justify a moral principle by showing that it best accounts for those of our more particular judgments that we also believe to be true.

In a perfectly coherent moral system, the retributive principle would be justified in both these ways, by being part of the best theory of our moral sentiments, considered as a whole.

The first of these deontological argument strategies is made familiar to us by arguments such as that of Herbert Morris (1976), who urges that retributivism follows from some general ideas about reciprocal advantage in social relations. Without assessing the merits of these proposals one way or another, I wish to pursue the other strategy. I examine the more particular judgments that seem to be best accounted for in terms of a principle of punishment for just deserts.

These more particular judgments are quite familiar. I suspect that almost everyone at least has a tendency – one that he may correct as soon as he detects it himself, but at least a tendency – to judge culpable wrongdoers as deserving of punishment. Consider some examples

Mike Royko has used to get the blood to the eyes of readers of his newspaper column:

> The small crowd that gathered outside the prison to protest the execution of Steven Judy softly sang "We Shall Overcome". . . .
>
> But it didn't seem quite the same hearing it sung out of concern for someone who, on finding a woman with a flat tire, raped and murdered her and drowned her three small children, then said that he hadn't been "losing any sleep" over his crimes. . . .
>
> I remember the grocer's wife. She was a plump, happy woman who enjoyed the long workday she shared with her husband in their ma-and-pa store. One evening, two young men came in and showed guns, and the grocer gave them everything in the cash register.
>
> For no reason, almost as an afterthought, one of the men shot the grocer in the face. The woman stood only a few feet from her husband when he was turned into a dead, bloody mess.
>
> She was about 50 when it happened. In a few years her mind was almost gone, and she looked 80. They might as well have killed her too.
>
> Then there was the woman I got to know after her daughter was killed by a wolfpack gang during a motoring trip. The mother called me occasionally, but nothing that I said could ease her torment. It ended when she took her own life.
>
> A couple of years ago I spent a long evening with the husband, sister and parents of a fine young woman who had been forced into the trunk of a car in a hospital parking lot. The degenerate who kidnapped her kept her in the trunk, like an ant in a jar, until he got tired of the game. Then he killed her.
>
> [Reprinted by permission: Tribune Media Services]

Most people react to such atrocities with an intuitive judgment that punishment (at least of some kind and to some degree) is warranted. Many will quickly add, however, that what accounts for their intuitive judgment is the need for deterrence, or the need to incapacitate such a dangerous person, or the need to reform the person. My own view is that these addenda are just "bad reasons for what we believe on instinct anyway," to paraphrase Bradley's general view of justification in ethics.

To see whether this is so, construct a thought experiment of the kind Kant (1965, p. 102) originated. Imagine that these same crimes are being done, but that there is no utilitarian or rehabilitative reason to punish. The murderer has truly found Christ, for example, so that he or she does not need to be reformed; he or she is not dangerous for the same reason; and the crime can go undetected so that general deterrence does not demand punishment (alternatively, we can pretend to punish and pay the person the money the punishment would have cost us to keep his or her mouth shut, which will also serve the ends of general deterrence). In such a situation, should the criminal still be punished? My hypothesis is that most of us still feel some inclination, no matter how tentative, to punish. That is the particular judgment I wish to examine. (For those persons – saints or moral lepers, we shall see which – who do not have even a tentative inclination to punish, I argue that the reason for affirming such inclinations are also reasons to feel such inclinations.)

The case against retributive judgments

The puzzle I put about particular retributive judgments is this: Why are these particular judgments so suspect – "primitive," "barbarous," "a throwback" – when other judgments in terms of moral desert are accorded places of honor in widely accepted moral arguments? Very generally, there seem to me to be five explanations (and supposed justifications) for this discriminatory treatment of retributive judgments about deserved punishment.

1. First and foremost there is the popularly accepted belief that punishment for its own sake does no good. "By punishing the offender you cannot undo the crime," might be the slogan for this point of view. I mention this view only to put it aside, for it is but a reiteration of the consequentialist idea that only further good consequences achieved by punishment could possibly justify the practice. Unnoticed by those who hold this position is that they abandon such consequentialism when it comes to other areas of morals. It is a sufficient justification not to scapegoat innocent individuals, that they do not deserve to be punished; the injustice of punishing those who do not deserve it seems to stand perfectly well by itself as a justification of our practices, without need for further good consequences we might achieve. Why do not we similarly say that the injustice of the guilty going unpunished can equally stand by itself as a justification for punishment, without need of a showing of further good consequences? It simply is not the case that justification always requires the showing of further good consequences.

Those who oppose retributivism often protest at this point that punishment is a clear harm to the one punished, and the intentional causing of this harm requires some good thereby achieved to justify it; whereas *not* punishing the innocent is not a harm and thus does not stand in need of justification by good consequences. Yet this response simply begs the question against retributivism. Retributivism purports to be a theory of justice, and as such claims that punishing the guilty achieves something good – namely, justice – and that therefore reference to any other good consequences is simply beside the point. One cannot defeat the central retributivist claim – that justice is achieved by punishing the guilty – simply by assuming that it is false.

The question-begging character of this response can be seen by imagining a like response in areas of tort, property, or contract law. Forcing another to pay tort or contract damages, or to forgo use and possession of some thing, is a clear harm that corrective justice theories of tort, promissory theories of contract, or natural right theories of property are willing to impose on defendants. Suppose no one gains anything of economic significance by certain classes of such impositions – as, for example, in cases where the plaintiff has died without heirs after his cause of action accrued. "It does no good to force the defendant to pay," interposed as an objection to corrective justice theories of tort, promissory theories of contract, or natural right theories of property simply denies what these theories assert: that something good *is* achieved by imposing liability in such cases – namely, that justice is done.

This "harm requires justification" objection thus leaves untouched the question of whether the rendering of justice cannot in all such cases be the good that justifies the harm all such theories impose on defendants. I accordingly put aside this initial objection to retributivism, relying as it does either on an unjustifiable discrimination between retributivism and other deontological theories, or upon a blunderbuss assault on deontological theories as such.

2. A second and very popular suspicion about retributive judgments is that they presuppose an indefensible objectivism about morals. Sometimes this objection is put metaphysically: There is no such thing as desert or culpability (J. Mackie, 1982). More often the point is put as a more cautious epistemological modesty: "Even if there is such a thing as desert, we can never know who is deserving." For religious people, this last variation usually contrasts us to God, who alone can know what people truly deserve. As Beccaria (1964, pp. 17–18) put it centuries ago:

[W]hat insect will dare take the place of divine justice . . . ? The gravity of sin depends upon the inscrutable wickedness of the heart. No finite being can know it without revelation. How then can it furnish a standard for the punishment of crimes?

We might call this the "don't play God" objection.

One way to deal with this objection is to show that moral judgments generally (and judgments about culpability particularly) are both objectively true and knowable by persons. Showing both is a complicated business, and since I have attempted such a showing elsewhere

(Moore, 1982a), let me try a different tack. A striking feature of the "don't play God" objection is how inconsistently it is applied. Let us revert to our use of desert as a limiting condition on punishment: We certainly seem confident both that it is true and that we can know that it is true, that we should not punish the morally innocent because they do not deserve it. Neither metaphysical skepticism nor epistemological modesty gets in our way when we use lack of moral desert as a reason not to punish. Why should it be different when we use presence of desert as a reason to punish? If we can know when someone does *not* deserve punishment, musn't we know when someone *does* deserve punishment? Consider the illogic in the following passages from Karl Menninger (1968):

> The very word *justice* irritates scientists. No surgeon expects to be asked if an operation for cancer is just or not. No doctor will be reproached on the grounds that the dose of penicillin he has prescribed is less or more than *justice* would stipulate. (p. 17)

> It does not advance a solution to use the word *justice*. It is a subjective emotional word. . . . The concept is so vague, so distorted in its applications, so hypocritical, and usually so irrelevant that it offers no help in the solution of the crime problem which it exists to combat but results in its exact opposite – injustice, injustice to everybody. (pp. 10–11)

Apparently Dr. Karl knows injustice when he sees it, even if justice is a useless concept.

Analogously, consider our reliance on moral desert when we allocate initial property entitlements. We think that the person who works hard to produce a novel deserves the right to determine when and under what conditions the novel will be copied for others to read. The novelist's labor gives him or her the moral right. How can we know this – how can it be true – if desert can be judged only by those with Godlike omniscience, or worse, does not even exist? Such skepticism about just deserts would throw out a great deal that we will not throw out. To me, this shows that no one really believes that moral desert does not exist or that we could not know it if it did. Something else makes us suspect our retributive judgments than supposed moral skepticism or epistemological modesty.

3. One particular form of moral skepticism merits separate attention in this context: This is the skepticism that asserts that no one is really responsible for anything because everything we do is caused by factors over which we have no control, and therefore none of us is really guilty or deserving of punishment. "Tout comprendre c'est tout pardonner," as the folk wisdom has it.

The main problem with this bit of folk wisdom is that it is false. To understand all (the causes of behavior) is not to forgive all. To match proverb for proverb: "Everybody has a story," as many convicts well know, realizing that such stories hardly excuse (Morse, 1984, p. 1499).

To do more than match proverbs against this objection to retributivism requires an extended excursion into compatibilist moral psychology. Having done that recently (Moore, 1985a), I will not recapitulate the argument defending the view that most people are responsible for what they do irrespective of the truth of determinism. In any case, if retributivism is to be rejected on hard determinist grounds, all justice theories in property, contract, and torts would have to be rejected as well, since no one could act in a way (viz., freely) so as to deserve anything.

4. A fourth popular suspicion about using moral desert as a justification to punish takes the opposite tack from the last objection. Here the thought is not that *none* of us are guilty, but rather that *all* of us are guilty – so that if we each got what we truly deserved, we would all be punished. How, then, can such a ubiquitous human condition be used to single out some but not all for punishment? Christ, of course, is the most famous purveyor of this argument when he dissuades the Pharisees from stoning an adulteress with an explicit appeal to their own guilt: "He that is without sin among you, let him first cast a stone at her" (John 8:3–11).

If we take this literally (I will give it a more charitable interpretation later), this is pretty clumsy moral philosophy. It is true that all of us are guilty of some immoralities, probably on a daily basis. Yet for most people reading this essay, the immoralities in question are things like manipulating others unfairly; not caring deeply enough about another's suffering; not being charitable for the limitations of others; convenient lies; and so forth (Shklar, 1984). Few of us have raped and murdered a woman, drowned her three small children, and felt no remorse about it afterward, to revert to one of Royko's examples. It is simply false – and obviously so – to equate guilt at the subtle immoralities of personal relationships with the gross violations of persons that violent crime represents. We do not all deserve the punishment of a murderer for the simple and sufficient reason that we are not all murderers, or anything like murderers in culpability.

One can of course quote more scripture here – "He that lusts after a woman has already committed adultery with her" – but that also is to miss some obvious and basic moral distinctions. Freud is surely to be preferred to scripture here, when he urged that we must give credit where credit is due: If our conscience is such that we do not allow ourselves to act on our admittedly wicked fantasies, that makes us a better person than one who not only dreams of such atrocities, but brings them about (see Moore, 1980, p. 1629, n. 198; compare Fingarette, 1955; Morris, 1976, p. 124).

The short of it is that desert is not such an ubiquitous feature of human personality that it cannot be a marker of punishment. To think otherwise is to gloss over obvious moral distinctions, a glossing that to me is so obviously wrong that it can only be a cover for a judgment made on other grounds.

5. It is often said that retributive judgments are "irrational." They are irrational, it is said, because they are based on "emotion rather than reason." Such irrational emotion cannot be the basis for justifying a legal institution such as punishment. Legal institutions can be justified only by reason, not by yielding to irrational emotions, whether ours or others'. Henry Weihofen (1956, pp. 130–1) once stated this objection forthrightly:

It is not only criminals who are motivated by irrational and emotional impulsions. The same is true also of lawyers and judges, butchers and bakers. And it is especially true on such a subject as punishment of criminals. This is a matter on which we are all inclined to have deep feelings. When a reprehensible crime is committed, strong emotional reactions take place in all of us. Some people will be impelled to go out at once and work off their tensions in a lynching orgy. Even the calmest, most law-abiding of us is likely to be deeply stirred. . . . It is one of the marks of a civilized culture that it has devised legal procedures that minimize the impact of emotional reactions and strive for calm and rational disposition. But lawyers, judges and jurors are still human, and objective, rational inquiry is made difficult by the very irrationality of the human mind itself. . . . Consciously we want to be rational. We prefer to think of ourselves as governed by reason rather than as creatures swept by irrational emotions. . . .

[Excerpt from *The Urge to Punish* by Henry Weihofen. Copyright © 1956 by Henry Weihofen. Reprinted by permission of Farrar, Straus and Giroux, Inc.]

This objection, as stated, proves far too much for its own good. Think for a moment about the intimate connection between our emotions and morality, a matter we explore later in this chapter. Although Kantian beings who could know morality without relying upon their emotions are perhaps conceivable – just barely – that surely is not us. We need our emotions to know about the injustice of racial discrimination, the unfairness of depriving another of a favorite possession, the immorality of punishing the innocent. Our emotions are our main heuristic guide to finding out what is morally right.

We do both of them and morality a strong disservice when we accept the old shibboleth that emotions are opposed to rationality. There is, as I have argued elsewhere (Moore, 1982a, 1984; see also de

Sousa, 1980; Scruton, 1980), a rationality of the emotions that can make them trustworthy guides to moral insight. Emotions are rational when they are intelligibly proportionate in their intensity to their objects, when they are not inherently conflicted, when they are coherently orderable, and instantiate over time an intelligible character. We also judge when emotions are appropriate to their objects; that is, when they are *correct.*

The upshot is that unless one severs any connection of our legal institutions to morals, one cannot condemn an institution because it is based on "emotion." Some emotions generate moral insights our legal system could hardly do without, such as the insight that it is outrageously unfair to punish an innocent person. Imagine condemning the legal ban on punishing the innocent because it is based on emotion and not on reason.

To be sure, there is also a sense of rationality opposed to emotionality (Moore, 1984, pp. 107–8). This is the sense in which we view rationality as reason and will and see these faculties as "unhinged" by powerful emotional storms. It is this sense of emotionality we use when we partially excuse a killer because the act was the product of extreme passion, not cool rationality. It is also this sense of rationality versus emotionality that is sometimes played upon by those making this objection to retributivism. The picture is one in which the retributivist emotions unhinge our reason by their power.

Karen Horney's assumption that vindictiveness is always neurotic (and thus always undesirable) is based upon this kind of characterization:

Often there is no more holding back a person driven toward revenge than an alcoholic determined to go on a binge. Any reasoning meets with cold disdain. Logic no longer prevails. Whether or not the situation is appropriate does not matter. It overrides prudence. Consequences for himself and others are brushed aside. He is as inaccessible as anybody who is in the grip of a blind passion. (Horney, 1948, p. 5)

There is more than a little truth to this conception of the emotional base of retributivism. Literature is rich in faithful depictions of otherwise rational and moral people being unhinged by an urge to punish another for a wrong. Susan Jacoby (1984) recounts the tale of Michael Kohlhaas, written into a novel in 1806 by Heinrich von Kleist. Kohlhaas is depicted as a benevolent man, a horse dealer, friendly, kind, loyal to those around him, but one whose life is altered by the dominating passion of revenge. Kohlhaas's animals are maltreated by his neighbor – a man of higher social position – and Kohlhaas, in his unbending quest to make the offending squire pay, "eventually destroys his business and his marriage (his wife is killed by the enemies he has made); burns down the squire's house; murders innocent inhabitants of the castle; and incites a revolt that lays waste to much of the surrounding countryside" (pp. 51–2).

This is pathological and is fairly described as reason being overcome by a domineering, obsessive emotion. Yet it is surely not the case that the retributive urge always operates like this. Pathological cases can be found for any emotions, including benevolent ones. We should not judge the moral worth of an emotion by cases where it dominates reason, unless we are willing to say that such an emotion typically leads to such pathology; and the retributive intuition described here does not. One can have the intuition that the guilty deserve punishment, and one can have emotional outrage when they do not get it, without having one's reason dominated by an emotional storm. We may feel morally outraged at some guilty criminal going unpunished, but that need be no more unhinging of our reason than our outrage at the innocent being punished. In both cases, intense emotions may generate firm moral convictions; in each case, the emotions can get out of hand and dominate reason – but that is no reason to discount the moral judgments such emotions support when they do *not* get out of hand.

Despite the foregoing, I think that the most serious objection to retributivism as a theory of punishment lies in the emotional base of retributive judgments. As thus far construed, the objection is, as we have seen, ill-fated. If stated as an objection to there being an emotional base at all to judgments about deserved punishment, the objection is far too broad to be acceptable. All moral judgments would lose to such a charge if it were well founded. If stated as an objection to the unhinging quality of retributive emotions, the objection is psychologically implausible. Any emotion in pathological cases can unhinge reason, and there is nothing about retributive emotions that make it at all plausible that they always unhinge our reason when we experience them. The objection thus needs a third construction, which is this: The emotions that give rise to retributive judgments are always pathological – not in their intensity or their ability to unhinge our reason, but in their very nature. Some emotions, such as racial prejudice, have no moral worth even if typically experienced in a not very intense way. The true objection here is that the retributive urge is one such emotion.

In discussing this version of the objection to the emotional base of retributivism, I shall by and large rely on Nietzsche, who to my mind remains one of the most penetrating psychologists of the unsavory side of our emotional life. He is also one of the few thinkers to have delved deeply into the psychology of revenge. There is surprisingly little written on revenge in modern psychiatry, in large part because psychiatrists regard revenge "like sex before Freud . . . , condemned as immature and undesirable and thus unworthy of serious scientific investigation" (Harvey Lomas, quoted in Jacoby, 1984, p. 169).

"Mistrust," Nietzsche's Zarathustra advises us, "all in whom the impulse to punish is powerful" (*Zarathustra*, p. 212). Nietzsche clearly believes that the retributive emotions can get in the way of that celebration of life that makes us better − I would say virtuous − human beings. As he said in *The Gay Science:* "I do not want to wage war against what is ugly. I do not want to accuse; I do not even want to accuse those who accuse. *Looking away* shall be my only negation" (p. 223). And as he repeated later: "Let us not become darker ourselves on their [criminals'] account, like all those who punish others and feel dissatisfied. Let us sooner step aside. Let us look away" (p. 254).

What is the awful vision from which we should avert our gaze? If Nietzsche is right, truly a witch's brew: resentment, fear, anger, cowardice, hostility, aggression, cruelty, sadism, envy, jealousy, guilt, self-loathing, hypocrisy and self-deception − those "reactive affects" that Nietzsche sometimes lumped under the French term *ressentiment* (*Genealogy*, p. 74). All this, Nietzsche believed, lies behind our judgments of retributive justice.

Consider first resentment. One of Nietzsche's deepest insights into moral genealogy (Danto, 1965) is how much the retributive urge is based on resentment. As Max Scheler (1961, p. 46), once explained Nietzsche's insight here: "Revenge . . . , based as it is upon an experience of impotence, is always primarily a matter of those who are 'weak' in some respect." If we feel physically, psychologically, or politically weak, we will feel threatened by those we perceive to be stronger, such as those willing and able to use physical violence. Moreover, if we are actually or vicariously injured by such stronger persons, our weakness may prevent us from venting in the most direct way the anger such violation generates. Rather than either venting such anger directly through our own action (of retaliation), or at least feeling able to do so but choosing to refrain, our real or perceived helplessness transforms the anger into the brooding resentment of those who lack power. Such resentment, Nietzsche rightly thinks, can poison the soul, with its unstable equilibrium of repressed anger and repressing fear. A resentful person is burdened with an emotional conflict that is both ugly and harmful. It is better for us, because of this, to "look away" rather than to brood about revenge.

Our weakness and its accompanying emotions of fear and resentment can also make our retributive inclination seem cowardly, herdlike, and weak. As Nietzsche observed at one point: "'Punishment'... is simply a copy ... of the normal attitude toward a hated, disarmed, prostrated enemy, who has lost not only every right and protection, but all hope of quarter as well ..." (*Genealogy*, pp. 72–3). Yet unlike the victor in a fight who has won and who can afford to be merciful to a vanquished foe, those who wish to punish may feel that this is their first opportunity to get back, an opportunity they cannot afford to pass up. When Christ talks about throwing stones, it is not because we are all equally guilty that we should not throw the stones; rather, there is something cowardly in a group of persons throwing stones at one who is now helpless. Such cowardice can be exhibited by the need of such persons for group reinforcement (which is why avengers may refuse to throw the *first* stone – it would set one apart from the group). It is no accident that the retributive urge calls up images of mobs, groups who together finally find the strength to strike back at an only now helpless foe. Our fear and our resentment of criminals can make us look small and cowardly in our retaliation in a way that immediate retaliation by one without fear or resentment does not.

Our fear of criminals need not always be due to our sense of their power to hurt; sometimes we may feel such fears just because they are different. For some people, there is a link between fear of strangers and fear of criminals, a link partly reflected by the extraordinary group reinforcement they receive when their retributive urges are shared. Such a link is also reflected in the we–they attitude many adopt about criminals, an attitude suggesting that criminals are fundamentally different and outside the group about whom we need be concerned. This is the criminal as outlaw, an attitude that, although neither causing nor caused by prejudice and bigotries of various kinds, nonetheless invites such other fears of differences to get expressed in retributive judgments.

Even when we do not feel weak and threatened by criminals, we may find other emotions underlying our retributive judgments that are not very pretty. Surely one of the uglier spectacles of our times are the parties by fraternity boys outside the gates of prisons when an execution is taking place. What makes such spectacles so ugly is the cruelty and sadistic pleasure at the suffering of others that they express. Such people feel entitled to let go of the normal constraints on expressing such unsavory emotions because the legitimacy of retribution licenses it. It is all right to enjoy the suffering of criminals, because it is deserved suffering. Deserved punishment, as Nietzsche perceived, can be "a warrant for and title to cruelty" (*Genealogy*, p. 65). It can give us "the pleasure of being allowed to vent [our] power freely upon one who is powerless, the voluptuous pleasure of doing evil for the pleasure of doing it, the enjoyment of violation" (p. 65). Our retributive judgments, in such a case, look like a rationalization of, and excuse for, venting emotions we would be better off without.

There are admittedly other avenues in this society for people to vent sadistic enjoyment of another's suffering. One that comes to mind are such films as *The Texas Chain Saw Massacre*. Reported audience reaction to a scene depicting a helpless female about to be dismembered by a chainsaw included cries of "Cut the bitch." The unrestrained sadism in such reactions is a deep sickness of the soul. To the extent that our inclinations to punish are based on a like emotion, it too, as Menninger says (1968, p. 201), lines us "up with the Marquis de Sade, who believed in pleasure, especially the pleasure derived from making someone else feel displeasure."

There is also envy and jealousy sometimes to be found lying at the emotional base of our retributive inclinations (*Zarathustra*, p. 213). We seem to have some admiration for criminals, an admiration reflected in the attention we give them in the media and the arts. We may admire their strength and courage; criminals, as Herbert Morris (1976, p. 132) aptly describes it, may manifest "what we too often do not, power and daring, a willingness to risk oneself for the satisfaction of strong desires." Thackery had the same insight, writing *Vanity Fair* in large part to show us how much more we admire strength (Becky) than we do more conventional moral virtues (Amelia). Moreover, within the breasts of most of us beat some criminal desires. Not only may we admire the strength of will criminals may exhibit, but we may also be excited by the desires they allow themselves to satisfy. We thus may suffer a double dose of envy, both of the desires acted on and the strength that is exhibited in acting on them. Such envy and jealousy fuels the retributive urge, because punishment will tear down the object of such feelings.

Guilt has an interesting relationship to envy here. If criminals sometimes do what we might like to do but restrain ourselves from doing by our guilt, crime may excite a particularly virulent kind of envy. We may be envious not only of the power and the satisfaction of desires represented by criminal behavior, but even more of the freedom from guilt we may attribute to the criminal. Our own guilt in such a case may be challenged by apparent examples of such guiltless freedom to act on forbidden desires; if so, our defense is to transform the envy into the desire to destroy that which so challenges our own precarious balance between good and evil.

Guilt can give rise to our retributive judgments about others without the "good offices" of the emotions of envy and jealousy. Such retributivist judgments may simply project our own guilt onto the criminal and by doing so, lessen our guilt feelings because we are better than he. Henry Weihofen (1956, p. 138) aptly describes this Freudian insight about retribution:

> No one is more ferocious in demanding that the murderer or the rapist "pay" for his crime than the man who has felt strong impulses in the same direction. No one is more bitter in condemning the "loose" woman than the "good" women who have on occasion guiltily enjoyed some purple dreams themselves. It is never he who is without sin who casts the first stone.
>
> Along with the stone, we cast our own sins onto the criminal. In this way we relieve our own sense of guilt without actually having to suffer the punishment – a convenient and even pleasant device for it not only relieves us of sin, but makes us feel actually virtuous.

The retributive urge often seems to be accompanied by the additional nonvirtues of self-deception and hypocrisy. Few people like to think of themselves as weak and resentful, fearful, cowardly, cruel and sadistic, envious, jealous, and guilt-ridden. Accordingly, if they possess such emotions and traits when they make retributive judgments, they have every reason to deceive themselves about it. Such self-deception Nietzsche thought to be "the masterpiece of these black magicians, who make whiteness, milk, and innocence of every blackness . . ." (*Genealogy*, p. 47; see also Horney, 1948, p. 4). "These cellar rodents full of vengefulness and hatred" have reconceived their black emotions into an abstract virtue:

> "We good men – *we are the just*" – what they desire they call, not retaliation, but "the triumph of *justice*"; what they hate is not their enemy, no! They hate "injustice," they hate "godlessness"; what they believe in and hope for is not the hope of revenge . . . but the victory of God, of the *just* God, over the godless. . . . (*Genealogy*, p. 48)

Self-deception and hypocrisy themselves are vices, and to the extent that our retributive judgments encourage them – because we cannot affirm the emotional base of such judgments – we would be better without them.

To this basically Nietzschean indictment of the emotions on which retributive judgments seem to be based, we may add the insight of some feminists that the urge to retaliate is an instance of a male and macho stereotype that is itself no virtue. As Susan Jacoby (1984, chap. 6) points out, there are actually two not entirely consistent stereotypes that operate here. One is that revenge is a male prerogative because it is the manly thing to do. The other is that women are the greatest avengers because (harking back to Nietzsche) their physical and political weakness demands subtler, more repressed, and thus more intense modes of retaliation. Such views are compliments neither to men nor to women. Such stereotypes, like racial prejudice and other differences mentioned earlier, do not cause our retributive judgments so much as they find in such judgments a vehicle for their expression.

Finally, consider the kind of "scoring mentality" that accompanies retributive judgments. As Scheler (1961, p. 46) noted: "It is of the essence of revenge that it always contains the *consciousness* of 'tit for tat,' so that it is never a mere emotional reaction." Nietzsche too scorned the "shopkeeper's scales and the desire to balance guilt and punishment" (*Dawn,* p. 86) as a part of the retributive urge. Retributivism requires a kind of keeping track of another's moral ledger that seems distasteful. Retributive judgments seem legalistic, a standing on one's rights or a satisfaction with "doing one's duty" that psychologically crowds out more virtuous modes of relating to others. "Bother justice," E. M. Forster has his protagonist exclaim in *Howard's End.* Margaret later goes on to say that she will have "none of this absurd screaming about justice. . . . Nor am I concerned with duty. I'm concerned with the character of various people whom we know, and how, things being as they are, things may be made a little better" (p. 228). Aristotle (Book VII) understood the same point in his familiar thought that "between friends there is no need of justice." Relate to others in a way that does not concern itself with giving them their just deserts, positive or negative. Those who keep track of favors owed, debts due, or punishments deserved cut themselves off from modes of relating to others that can be both more virtuous (because supererogatory) and also more rewarding than demanding rights or acting on duties.

There is no question, I think, that insofar as the retributive urge is based on such emotions as these, or causes us to instantiate traits such as self-deception, the urge is bad for us. It makes us less well formed, less virtuous human beings to experience such emotions – or, more accurately, to be the sort of person who has such emotions. This insight about what are and what are not virtuous emotions to have persuades many people that they ought not to make retributive judgments. For it is natural to feel that such judgments are contaminated by their black emotional sources. Defense lawyers have long recognized our tendency to withdraw or soften our retributive demands once we see the emotional base for them. Consider Clarence Darrow's appeals to Judge Caverly's virtue in Darrow's famous closing argument in the Loeb and Leopold sentencing hearing:

I have heard in the last six weeks nothing but the cry for blood. I have heard from the office of the State's Attorney only ugly hate. I have heard precedents quoted which would be a disgrace to a savage race.

. . .

[Y]our Honor stands between the future and past. I know the future is with me. . . . I am pleading for life, understanding, charity, kindness, and the infinite mercy that considers all. I am pleading that we overcome cruelty with kindness and hatred with love. . . . I am pleading for a time when hatred and cruelty will not control the hearts of men. When we can learn by reason and judgment and understanding and faith that . . . mercy is the highest attribute of man. . . . If I can succeed . . . I have done something to help human understanding, to temper justice with mercy, to overcome hate with love. I was reading last night of the aspiration of the old Persian poet, Omar Khayyam. It appealed to me as the highest that I can vision. I wish it was in my heart, and I wish it was in the hearts of all. "So I be written in the Book of love, I do not care that Book above, erase my name or write it as you will, so I be written in the Book of Love." (Hicks, 1925, pp. 995, 1084)

Persuasive words. For who does not want to be written in the Book of Love? Who wants to be written in the books of hate, cruelty, cowardice, envy, resentment, and the like? Judge Caverly certainly did not, and decided against a death sentence for Loeb or Leopold.

Yet the more one looks at this argument, the more questionable it becomes. What does the virtue of the holder of a judgment have to do with the truth (or lack of it) of that judgment? Why should we think that Judge Caverly's damaging his virtue by deciding against Loeb and Leopold – increasing his virtue if he decides the other way – has anything to do with the truth of the judgment "Loeb and Leopold deserve to die"? How can a judge expect to reach sound moral conclusions about Loeb and Leopold by focusing on which decision will most enhance *his* (the judge's) virtue? This seems to be a form of ad hominem argument, and a rather selfish version to boot, given its narcissistic preoccupation with one's own virtue.

The most persuasive case against retributivism is thus in danger of complete collapse. The charge is this: Even if it makes us morally worse to make retributive judgments – because of the emotions that give rise to such judgments – that lack of virtue on our part is simply irrelevant to the assessment of whether retributive judgments are true. To assess this issue requires that we look in greater detail at the connections between our emotions and our moral judgments, which I propose to do next.

Morality and the emotions

The charge laid at the end of the last section is a form of the "genetic fallacy" objection. Such an objection urges that it is fallacious to infer the falsity of a proposition from some truths (no matter how unsavory) about the genesis of people's belief in that proposition. A common example is to infer the falsity of our moral beliefs from the fact that they are caused by an education that could easily have been otherwise (see Moore, 1982a, pp. 1097–101). The ad hominem argument presented in the last section is like this, because it infers the falsity of retributivism from the unnice emotional origins of people's belief in retributivism.

To respond adequately to this genetic fallacy objection, the anti-retributivist must establish that the emotional base of a moral judgment is relevant to that judgment's truth. If we leave ethics for a moment, one can see that sometimes it is no fallacy to infer the falsity of a judgment from the truth of some explanation of why people come to such judgment. Suppose the proposition in question was: "Sticks become bent when immersed in water, straight again when removed." Suppose the common explanation for why people believe this proposition to be true is in terms of their perceptual experience with sticks partly immersed in water – namely, they look bent to them. If we have grounds to believe that these perceptual experiences as a class are unreliable – an "illusion" – then it is no fallacy to infer the falsity of the proposition from an explanation of people's beliefs showing such beliefs to be the product of an illusion. Knowing what we do about the unreliability of perceptual experience when light is refracted in mediums of different density, we are entitled to disbelieve those who rely on such experiences in coming to their beliefs about sticks in liquid.

The antiretributivist would make a similar construction of the Nietzschean case against retributivism, likening Nietzsche's explanation of people's beliefs in retributivism (as due to the emotions of *ressentiment*) to an explanation of a perceptual belief in terms of a known illusion or hallucination. Whether there can be such a thing as a moral hallucination or illusion, and if so, whether the emotions of *ressentiment* should be seen as such hallucinating experiences, depends upon an affirmative answer to two questions:

1. Are any emotions epistemically relevant to the truth of moral judgments?

2. If so, is it the virtuous nature of an emotion that tells us whether it has epistemic import?

I shall consider these questions in order.

With respect to the first question, we should distinguish four different views on how the emotions are relevant either to the discovery or to the justification of moral judgments.

1. One is suggested by Kant's famous remarks in the *Groundwork* (1964, pp. 65–7) to the effect that moral worth is found in actions motivated only by reverance for the moral law, not in actions motivated by the inclinations, no matter how benevolent or virtuous. Such a view would make the emotions that generate a moral belief irrelevant to the truth of that belief. Good emotions could as easily generate false beliefs as true ones, and bad emotions could as easily generate true beliefs as false ones. The truth of a moral proposition would be governed solely by reasoning from the categorical imperative or other supreme principle of morality itself discoverable by reason alone, not from any emotional experience.

In this view there is no analogy between the relation of the emotions and moral truth, on the one hand, and the relation of perceptual experiences and scientific truth, on the other. Accordingly, a Kantian about this should find the genetic fallacy objection conclusive when applied to Nietzsche; the lack of virtue of the emotions that generate retributivism has nothing to do with the truth of retributivism because the emotions generally have no epistemic import for the truth of moral judgments. In this view the emotions are relevant neither to justifying a moral judgment as true nor to discovering it to be true.

2. An opposite conclusion about the force of the genetic fallacy objection in this context should be drawn by those who think that the emotions have everything to do with moral truth. This second view about the connection of the emotions to moral truth is the view of the conventionalist (or relativist) about morals. Lord Devlin's writings (1971) on the morality of homosexual behavior provide a convenient example. According to Devlin, homosexual behavior is immoral (and may be legally prohibited) whenever enough people feel deeply enough that it is bad. "It is not nearly enough," Devlin reminds us, "to say that a majority dislike a practice, there must be a real feeling of reprobation. . . . No society can do without intolerance, indignation, and disgust; they are the forces behind the moral law . . ." (p. 40).

In this view, the emotions of a people constitute moral truth. If most people feel deeply enough that a practice is immoral, then it is

immoral, in this conventionalist view. This means that if the emotional base for some moral belief is undermined, then necessarily the
belief cannot be true. If Nietzsche, for example, can show that the
emotions that generate retributivist beliefs are contaminated, then
necessarily retributivism is not morally right.

How could Devlin admit the possibility of this kind of undermining
of the emotional base of retributivism, given the total absence of
reason checking emotion in his conventionalist view of morals? For
someone like Devlin, after all, morals just *are* feelings shared by a
majority. Yet such majority feelings can be changed if that majority
can be emotionally repelled by a subset of its own emotions. And if
enough people are repelled enough by the Nietzschean case against
ressentiment, then the retributive urge must be excluded from those
conventions of shared feelings that constitute morality.

This conventionalist view about morality results in there being no
genetic fallacy objection to be interposed against Nietzsche. To attack
the emotional base of retributivism would be to attack retributivism
itself.

Yet such a strong epistemic connection of the emotions to moral
truth cannot be sustained. That a large percentage of Americans,
perhaps a majority, have feelings of disgust, fear, and hatred of gays
does not end a moral inquiry into the truth or falsity of the proposition that gays may be discriminated against, in housing, employment,
or elsewhere. A person seeking to arrive at the truth about just treatment for minorities cannot accept his or her own emotional reactions
as settling the issue (nor, more obviously, can the person accept the
emotional reactions of others). Each must judge for himself or herself
whether those emotions are harbingers of moral insight or whether
they are the "hallucinations" of the emotional life that must be dis-
carded in our search for the truth. The same, of course, is true for
our sense perceptions vis-à-vis scientific truths. Sticks may look bent
when partly immersed in water, but that does not mean that they
really are bent. Our sense perception is not veridical, and there is no
reason to suppose that our emotions are any better guarantors of
knowledge.

3. This analogy of the emotions to sensory perception suggests a
third way of thinking of the epistemic connection of the emotions to
morality, a conception that is also, unfortunately, misleading. This is
the route of intuitionism. An intuitionist, as I am here using the word,
believes that the emotions stand to moral judgment in a relation exactly analogous to the relation between perceptual experience and
scientific judgment. For an intuitionist, the analogy is only an analogy,

however, for such a person sees morals and science as distinct realms of knowledge, each with their own distinct experiential base. Such an intuitionist will usually be a metaphysical dualist, believing that such distinct modes of knowing must imply that there are distinct modes of being. (An example of this is how introspectionism goes hand in hand with dualism in the philosophy of mind.)

In any case, the intuitionist will regard emotions as crucial to morals, for they are the data from which moral theory is constructed. Without the emotions generating intuitions, there could be no moral insight, for this kind of intuitionist. An intuitionist is not committed to the emotions being veridical; indeed, to maintain the parallel to sensory perception, the intuitionist should say that the felt justice of punishing for its own sake is *good evidence* that it is just to punish for its own sake, but allow that the inference could be mistaken.

4. I must confess there is much in the intuitionist's account that I find tempting. Still, the dead ends of dualistic metaphysics and the lumpy epistemology of discrete cognitive realms is sufficient reason to avoid intuitionism and nonnaturalism in ethics, as it is to avoid introspectionism and dualism in psychology (Moore, 1985, 1987). We can avoid this metaphysical and epistemological lumpiness by thinking of the emotions as heuristic guides to moral insight, but not as the experience out of which moral theory is constructed. In this view, moral knowledge does not rest on its own unique experiential base, the emotions. Such a view could even concede the empiricist idea that all knowledge (moral knowledge included) rests on sensory experience and the inferences drawable from it.

Consider a judgment that another is morally culpable for some harm. An intuitionist would view culpability as a special kind of property not observable by the senses (a "nonnatural" property), and known only by that special faculty of intuition provided by our emotional life. I think, on the contrary, that culpability is not a property in some special realm. True, we cannot see it but must infer its existence from other properties, such as voluntariness of action, accountability, intention, causation, lack of excuse or justification. But then we cannot see those properties either. We infer the existence of an intention in another from behavioral clues; we do not see causal relations, but infer their existence as well. Culpability is no less a natural property of persons than is intentionality, voluntariness, and so on; none are visible properties, all must be inferred from other evidence. Yet these facts do not demand a special mode of existence, and a special mode of knowing, for any of such properties (see my response to Mackie's well-known "queerness" objection in Moore, 1982a).

If we think of (moral) properties such as culpability in this way, then the emotions are not strictly necessary for there to be moral knowledge. We can imagine a being who could make correct inferences about culpability, as about other things such as intentionality, even if he or she were devoid of any relevant emotional life. True, the being would not *feel* about, for example, justice as we feel about it; yet he or she could know injustice, in the sense of being able to pick it out, as well as we.

The emotions are thus heuristic guides for us, an extra source of insight into moral truths beyond the knowledge we can gain from sensory and inferential capacities alone. One might think of them as I would think of conscious experience vis-à-vis knowledge of mind: My conscious experience of deciding to get a haircut is one way I can come to know that I intend to get a haircut; yet I or others can come to know that I intend to get a haircut in a variety of other ways, including perhaps someday by physiological measurements. My introspective, "privileged access" is only a heuristic guide to learning about my sensations, intentions, and so on that others do not possess. It is not essential to an intention that I be conscious of it, any more than it is essential to the injustice of an institution that I or others feel negatively toward it. The usual judgments I make about my intentions may be judgments reached by reflection on my conscious deliberative processes, just as my usual judgments about justice may be reached via some strong feelings; but the usual route to knowledge – of minds or morals – is not to be confused with what mental states or moral qualities *are*.

The upshot of this is that our emotions are important but not essential in our reaching moral truths. Contra Kant, there is an epistemic connection between our emotions and morality, but it is neither of the strong connections that conventionalism or intuitionism would posit. In the present context, the payoff of seeing this latter point lies in seeing when we may find some emotions wanting as epistemic indicators of moral truth. It is possible, in this last view, for there to be emotions that are "moral hallucinations," and it is therefore open to a Nietzschean to claim that our retributive inclinations are of this kind.

We come, then, to the second question – is the virtue of possessing an emotion relevant to that emotion's epistemic import? We should begin by being clear about the two different ways in which the emotions may be connected to morality before we inquire into the relation between them. We have hitherto been discussing what I would call the epistemic connection of the emotions to morality, distinguishing strong views of this connection (like Devlin's) from weaker views, such as my own or Kant's. Yet there is another possible way in which morality is related to our emotional life. This is where the emotions are themselves the objects of moral judgment. I call this the substantive connection of morality to the emotions.

The substantive connection can be grasped by reflecting on the judgments we make when we are not concerned with ascribing legal liability. The part of morality that is incorporated into our criminal law is by and large the morality of will and reason, by virtue of which we make the crudest of responsibility ascriptions. Voluntariness of action, accountability, intentionality, causation, justification, and excuse are the primary categories in terms of which we judge someone as morally culpable and thus legally punishable (Moore, 1984, chap. 2). Compare the less legalistic moral judgments we make in daily life: We often think of ourselves or others as more or less virtuous, depending on what emotions we feel on what occasions (Lyons, 1980; Dent, 1984). We make judgments, in other words, not just about the wrong actions a bad person wills, but also about the evil emotions a bad person feels. As Bernard Williams (1973, p. 207) has noted, there is a morality

. . . about what a man ought or ought not to feel in certain circumstances, or, more broadly, about the ways in which various emotions may be considered as distinctive, mean or hateful, while others appear as creative, generous, admirable, or – merely – such as one would hope for from a decent human being. Considerations like these certainly play a large part in moral thought, except perhaps in that of the most restricted and legalistic kind. . . .

Consider a person who feels little or no compassion for others less fortunate. This person's behavior need not be that of a scrooge – he may do all the morally acceptable things, such as donate to charities, help blind persons across the street, not inflict needless suffering, and so on. Yet he does such things out of a priggish concern for propriety, including the propriety he attains by having a good opinion of himself. He does not feel any compassion for the objects of his charity; indeed, he regards them as inferior beings who exist for him mainly to be the objects of his virtue. Such a person is morally inferior to – less virtuous than – another whose actions may be no better but whose emotional life includes compassion (Blum, 1980).

Contrast this collection of the emotions and morality with the epistemic connection. Staying with the example of compassion: We may take our feelings of compassion for some disadvantaged persons to be the harbingers of a moral insight about what that group deserves. Suppose you travel to India and find the poverty of many Indians to be distressing. You might take that feeling of compassion to be the originator of a moral insight about the nature of distributive justice – namely, that the geographic limits you had previously observed in applying some ideal of distributive justice seem arbitrary, a matter of political expediency at best. In such a case, the emotional experience of compassion may generate a firm moral conviction that distributive justice knows no political boundaries or geographical limits, but extends to all persons.

The epistemic connection of the emotions to morality is quite different from the substantive connection. With the latter, we judge the emotions as virtuous or not; the emotions in such a case are the object of moral evaluation. With the former, we are not seeking to judge the moral worth of an emotion as a virtue; rather, we seek to learn from such emotions the correct moral judgments to make about some other institution, practice, act, or agent.

Having distinguished the two connections of morality to the emotions, it remains to inquire whether there is not some relation between them. One wishing to use Nietzsche's kind of insights to attack retributivism, and yet escape the genetic fallacy objection, must assert that there is some such relation. The idea is that we use our own virtue in possessing an emotion as the touchstone of whether that emotion is "hallucinatory" or not: If the possession of an emotion makes us more virtuous, then that emotion is a good heuristic for coming to moral judgments that are true; if the possession of an emotion makes us less virtuous, then that emotion is a good heuristic for coming to moral judgments that are false. This possibility, of course, would complete the antiretributivist's answer to the genetic fallacy charge. For then the vice of possessing the emotions of *ressentiment* gives us good reason to suppose that the moral judgments to which those emotions give rise – namely, retributive judgments – are false.

This is possible, but what reason do we have to think that such a connection – between the judge's virtue, and the truth of the judgment he or she is making – holds? Counterexamples certainly spring to mind; consider two of them.

1. As Herbert Morris has examined in Chapter 9 of this volume, there is such a thing as nonmoral guilt. Think, for example, of the guilt one might feel at having made a tragic choice: There were only two options, neither happy ones, and one chose to do the lesser evil. Using Philippa Foot's much-discussed example: A railroad switchman can only turn a moving trolley car onto one line or another, but he cannot stop it; he chooses to turn the car onto the line where only one

trapped workman will be killed; on the other line, five workmen were trapped and would have been killed had the trolley car gone their way. The switchman is not morally culpable in directing the trolley on the line where only one workman would be killed. The alternative being even worse, the switchman was justified in doing what he did. Still the switchman should feel regret, remorse, and even guilt at killing the one workman. The switchman who experiences such emotions is a more virtuous person than one who has a "don't cry over what can't be helped" attitude toward the whole affair.

If both moral judgments are right – the switchman is not culpable (guilty), but his feeling guilty is virtuous – then we cannot say that the emotions that make us virtuous are necessarily the emotions that are good heuristic guides to moral truth. For if the latter were true, this switchman's (virtuous) feeling guilty should mean that the associated judgment, "I am guilty," is true; but it is not.

2. Just as some emotions are virtuous even though their associated judgments are not true, so some emotions that are not virtuous to possess may nonetheless spawn judgments that are true. Think of the institution of private property and its Lockean justifications in terms of the exercised liberty of one who mixes her labor with a thing. I think that the Lockean judgment, "she deserves the property right because she created the thing in the first place," to be true when applied to a novelist seeking copyright protections for a novel. Yet I also think that the emotions that are my heuristic guide to that judgment are suspect, at the least, in their enhancement of my virtue.

For are not the emotions that call to mind Lockean intuitions about deserved property entitlements essentially selfish emotions that make us worse for possessing them? (See E. M. Forster, 1936, pp. 22–6; Becker, 1977, p. 96.) We are entitled, from what we have done, to exclude others from the enjoyment of the products of our labor. My intuition is that this is true, but I am not proud of the selfish emotions that generate this intuition. They seem to consist too much of pride and self-congratulation to be virtues. To me at least, the nonvirtuous nature of the emotional base of Lockean property theories does not make me doubt their truth; it would be unfair to deprive another of the products of his or her labor, however much it would be better if we (and the other) did not beat our chests so much about our own accomplishments.

These examples are perhaps controversial, but I doubt that the point they illustrate is. The virtue (or lack of it) in the possession of our emotion is not an infallible guide to the epistemic import such as emotion may possess.

Is the first even a *fallible* guide to the second? A defender of retributivism might well think not. Such a person might compare the situation in science: What is the relevance, he or she might ask, of
the virtue of a perceptual experience (say one induced by drugs) to
the epistemic import of such an experience? What possible reason is
there to think that the moral worth of a visual experience will cor-
relate with its epistemic import? Tripping on LSD and looking at
pornography may be equally lacking in virtue, but only one of them is
likely to produce untrue beliefs about, for example, anatomical features of human beings.

Yet what if we substituted an example where the virtue in question
is not so obviously removed from the truth of any scientific judgments? Suppose we focused on what might be called the "virtues
of a scientist," traits such as analytical capacity, creativity, curiosity,
being careful, and ambition. It is not nearly so implausible to think
that beliefs produced through the exercise of these traits are more
likely true, and that those produced by the analytically dull, the
plodding, the mechanical, the careless or the lazy are more likely
false.

Similarly, in ethics we should recognize that the virtue of (or vice) of
an emotion may often, but not always, be taken as an indication of the
truth (or falsity) of the judgment to which it leads. Indeed, would it
not be remarkable to think that one could arrive at the judgments
about science or morals only through emotions or traits that made
one morally odious? Although not contradictory, it would surely be
an oddly cohering morality that valued, say, equal treatment and also
extolled the virtue of those prejudiced attitudes that typically produce
discriminating judgments. We value moral and scientific truth too
highly to think that there could be any virtues so counterproductive to
the attainment of truth.

In any case, what other criterion could there be for the epistemic
reliability of the emotions? If such reliability had nothing to do with
the virtue of such emotions, what would be our test? Rawls (1971, p.
48) suggests that we look to those "conditions favorable for deliberation and judgment in general" when we seek to isolate those "considered judgments" that in reflective equilibrium justify his two principles of justice. Which conditions are these?

[W]e can discard those judgments made with hesitation, or in which we have
little confidence. Similarly, those given when we are upset or frightened, or
when we stand to gain one way or the other can be left aside. All these
judgments are likely to be erroneous or to be influenced by an excessive
attention to our own interests. (p. 47; see also Copp, 1984)

Yet this test is too dispassionate, too judicial. Rawls's test for *judgments* that have epistemic import cannot be turned into a test for *emotions* because Rawls, like Kant, pretty much ignores the emotional base of moral judgment.

If we look in this way for a purely cognitive test for when emotions are epistemically reliable, my suspicion is that we will always end up slighting the role of the emotions in generating moral insight. We will do this because a purely cognitive test will inevitably seek to derive a criterion of epistemic warrant that is independent of any theory generated from the emotions themselves. It is like attempting to set up a criterion of epistemic warrant for perceptual experiences without using any theory derived from such experiences. Yet surely in science we do not expect to have to come up with some prescientific test for the epistemic import of sensory experience *before* we meld those experiences into a scientific theory. Rather, we rely on the body of scientific theory itself to justify exclusions of experience from the data. It is because we know what we do about optics that leads us to discount the illusion that a stick partly immersed in water looks bent; it is because we know what we do about drugs, mental disease, sensory deprivation, and the like, that we discount hallucinatory perceptual experiences. In science we quite literally explain such experiences away by using the very theories of which such experiences are part of the data. We are entitled to make the parallel move in ethics, so that our substantive moral theories − not some pale, preliminary, judicial, nonmoral litmus test − give us the criteria for weeding out emotions with misleading epistemic import. Those substantive theories of what justice is, for example, make it very unlikely that prejudice could be a virtue, or that compassion could not.

The upshot of all of this is that the genetic fallacy objection with which we began this section is inconclusive when interposed by the retributivist against the Nietzchean analysis of the retributive urge. If Nietzsche is right in asserting that our retributive beliefs are always motivated by the emotions of *ressentiment,* and right that the possession of those emotions makes us less virtuous, then we have grounds to reject retributivism as a philosophy of punishment. True, such a Nietzschean argument could not be a knockdown winner − from what has been said, it is possible that the nonvirtuous emotions of *ressentiment* nonetheless generate true moral judgments about what wrongdoers deserve. Yet this would have to be established by justifying the retributive principle in some way other than by showing it to be the best expression of our more particular judgments about criminals. Without such independent justification of retributivism, Nietzsche gives us reason to believe the retributive principle to be false when he shows us how lacking in virtue are the emotions that generate retributive judgments. For without such an independent justification, here as elsewhere we are entitled to rely on the connection that generally (but not inevitably) holds between the virtue in possessing an emotion and the truth of the judgment that that emotion generates.

The correctness of retributive judgments

As previewed in the first part of this chapter, there are two justificatory routes a coherentist might use in justifying retributivism. First, because of the Nietzschean attack on the retributive urge, a retributivist might abandon the justificatory route that begins with our particular judgments about punishment in individual cases, and instead focus on how retributivism is justified because of its coherence with other, more general moral beliefs we are prepared to accept. He or she might show how there is an odd lacunae in our moral judgments about desert if the retributive principle is not accepted. That is, when passing out rewards, the desert of those whose labor produced them is (for Lockeans) both a necessary and a sufficient condition for allocating a property entitlement in them. The presence of such desert justifies giving the reward to them; the absence of such desert justifies withholding it from them. Similarly, when passing out legal duties to pay for harms caused, the culpability of he or she who caused the harm and the lack of culpability of he or she who suffers the harm, is (in standard corrective justice theories) both necessary and sufficient to justify tort liability. It is only with punishment that we have an asymmetry; namely (as even most nonretributivists will assert), that desert is a necessary condition of punishment, but not sufficient by itself to justify punishment.

Such an asymmetry does not by itself render a deontologist's social theory incoherent if he or she rejects retributivism (although it might if one isolated a general principle of just deserts common to corrective justice, property allocations, and retributive justice). My only point here is that if there were such incoherence without retributivism, the latter would be justified even if the retributive urge is unworthy of us. Nothing in the Nietzschean case against retributivism could prevent this. Still, since my approach is to justify retributivism by using our more particular judgments about punishment, I need to take seriously the Nietzschean case against those judgments.

The problem with the Nietzschean case against retributivism does not lie, as we have seen, in its presupposition that generally there is a strong connection between virtuous emotions and true moral judgments, vices and false moral judgments. The real problem for the Nietzschean critic is to show that retributive judgments are *inevitably* motivated by the black emotions of *ressentiment*. For if the critic cannot show this, then much of the contamination of those particular judgments is lifted. It is lifted because the retributive judgment would then not arise out of the kind of moral hallucination nonvirtuous emotions typically represent; rather, the retributive judgment would be only the vehicle for the expression of the emotions of *ressentiment* – dangerous for that reason, but not lacking in epistemic import for that reason.

Consider an analogy in meta ethics. The position I have defended elsewhere (Moore, 1982a), moral realism, is an admittedly dangerous view about which to proselytize. It is dangerous because many people use moral realism as a vehicle to express intolerance and contempt for autonomy. Many people may even accept moral realism because it seems to them to have this potential for intolerant imperialism against the differing moral beliefs of others. Yet these psychological facts, to my mind, constitute no argument against the truth of moral realism. They do not because I am able to separate moral realism from intolerance: logically I see that a moral realist can defend tolerance, pluralism, and autonomy as much (more?) as anyone, and psychologically I do not see any inevitability in my moral realist views being motivated by intolerance. Making these separations, the fact that many people use moral realism to express their intolerance – or even are motivated to moral realist beliefs by their intolerance – loses any epistemic sting. It makes me cautious about holding forth about moral realism with intolerant audiences, but it does not give me reason to be cautious about the truth of moral realism.

As much seems to me to be true about retributivism. I shall make the argument in three steps: First, that the inevitability of linking *ressentiment* emotions to retributive judgments is weakened when one notes, as Nietzsche himself did, that *anti*retributive judgments are also often motivated by some of those same nonvirtuous emotions; second, that in our own individual cases we can imagine being motivated to make retributive judgments by the virtuous emotions of guilt and fellow feeling; and third, that because punishment is a social institution, unlike private vengeance, it can help us to control the emotions retributive punishment expresses by controlling the aspects of punishment that all too easily allow it to express *ressentiment*.

1. A paraphrase of Zarathustra, of which Nietzsche no doubt would have approved, would be that we should beware all those in whom the

urge to punish is either actually, or claimed to be, nonexistent. As Nietzsche does tell us:

if you are cursed, I do not like it that you want to bless. Rather, join a little in the cursing. And if you have been done a great wrong, then quickly add five little ones: a gruesome sight is a person single-mindedly obsessed by a wrong.... A wrong shared is half right.... A little revenge is more human than no revenge. (*Zarathustra*, p. 180)

Everyone gets angry when their bodily integrity or other important interests are violated by another. If they care about other human beings, they are vicariously injured when someone close to them – or distant, depending on the reach of their empathy – is wronged. It is human to feel such anger at wrongful violation, and Nietzsche's thought is that not to express the anger in some retaliation is a recipe for *ressentiment* itself.

One might of course think that retaliation is a second best solution; better not to feel the anger at all so that the choice of expressing it in action, or of repressing it into the subtle revenge of pity, is not necessary (see Horney, 1948, p. 3). Leaving aside whether such willing away of anger is possible, is it desirable? While it has a saintly ring to it to turn the other cheek so long as it is one's own cheek that has just been slapped, is it virtuous to feel nothing stronger than sympathy for the suffering of others at the hands of wrongdoers? Where is that compassionate concern for others that is outraged because another person could have so unnecessarily caused such suffering?

Karen Horney concluded that "[t]he vindictive person thus is ego-centric . . . because he has more or less severed his emotional relations to other human beings" (1948, p. 12). Yet isn't this even more often true of one who feels anger only when he himself suffers at the hands of a wrongdoer, not when others suffer? An egocentric lack of compassion for others may explain the antiretributivist, forgiving attitude as easily as it may explain the desire for vengeance.

Sometimes the compassion for victims is not absent, but gets transferred to the person who is now about to suffer; namely, the wrongdoer. Such a transfer of compassion is not justified by the relative merits of the two classes of persons, unless we are to think that there is some reason to prefer wrongdoers to victims as the appropriate objects of compassion. "Out of sight, out of mind" is the reason that suggests itself, but this psychological tendency can hardly justify forgetting those who have suffered at the hands of others. My own view is that such a transfer of concern from victim to criminal occurs in large part because of our unwillingness to face our own revulsion at what was done (Gaylin, 1983, p. 123). It allows us to look away from the horror that another person was willing to cause.

We almost cannot bear the sight. We invent for the wrongdoers a set of excusing conditions that we would not tolerate for a moment in ourselves. When they transgress, virtuous people know how ill it lies to "excuse" themselves by pointing to their own childhood or past, their lack of parental love, their need for esteem, and other causes (Moore, 1985a). Virtuous people do not use the childish "something made me do it" because they know that that denies their essential freedom in bringing about some harm. They know that they did it, chose to do it, caused though that choice surely was by factors themselves unchosen. Yet we cannot stand to apply to criminals the same standard of responsibility that we apply to ourselves because we cannot stand to acknowledge that there is such a thing as evil in the world – and, worst of all, that it is not "inhuman" but a part of creatures not so different from ourselves. Lack of anger at criminals, if it does not represent simple indifference to the sufferings of others, may represent our self-deception about the potential for evil in humanity.

Such lack of anger may also represent the same fear of criminals that can motivate retributive judgments. Nietzsche:

There is a point in the history of society when it becomes so pathologically soft and tender that among other things it sides even with those who harm it, criminals, and does this quite seriously and honestly. Punishing somehow seems unfair to it, and it is certain that imagining "punishment" and "being supposed to punish" hurts it, arouses fear in it. "It is not enough to render him *undangerous?* Why still punish? Punishing itself is terrible." With this question, herd morality, the morality of timidity, draws its ultimate consequence. . . . The imperative of herd timidity: "We want that some day there should be *nothing anymore to be afraid of!*" (*Beyond Good and Evil*, p. 114)

By repressing anger at wrongful violation, we may be attempting to deny that we live in a society in which there really are fearful and awful people.

Yet again, our transfer of fellow-feeling from victim to criminal, and its accompanying elimination of anger, may represent something other than indifference or inability to face evil or our own fears. It may represent a narcissism that is itself no virtue. A criminal, after all, represents an opportunity to exercise (and display, a separate point) one's virtue. The virtue in question is compassion for someone now threatened with harm. Yet such egoistic compassion becomes something other than compassion. It becomes just what Nietzsche said it becomes, the elevation of self by pity. Remarkably, one can lose compassionate concern for another by the self-conscious egoistic caricature of compassion we distinguish as pity. In pity we do not care about the other any more for his own sake, but only insofar as he allows *us* to become, in our own and others' eyes, better. We should beware, to adopt yet another paraphrase of Nietzsche, this one by Philippa Foot (1973, p. 168), all those who find others best when they find them most in need. We should beware of them because such people lack precisely the ability to feel that compassion whose outward form they ape.

2. Resentment, indifference to others, self-deception, fear, cowardice, and pity are not virtues. They do not perhaps add up to the witches' brew of a full batch of the *ressentiment* emotions, but to the extent they motivate antiretributive judgments, they make such judgments suspect. If one accepts, as Nietzsche did, that both retributive and antiretributive judgments are often motivated by, or at least expressions of, nonvirtuous emotions, where does that leave us? It should leave us asking whether we cannot make our judgments about punishment in such a way that they are not motivated by either set of unworthy emotions.

When we make a retributive judgment – such as that Stephen Judy deserved the death penalty for his rape-murder of a young mother and his murder of her three children – we need not be motivated by the *ressentiment* emotions. Nor is the alternative some abstract, Kantian concern for justice, derived by reason alone and unsullied by any strong emotional origin. Our concern for retributive justice might be motivated by very deep emotions that are nonetheless of a wholly virtuous nature. These are the feelings of guilt we would have if we did the kinds of acts that fill the criminal appellate reports of any state.

The psychiatrist Willard Gaylin interviewed a number of people closely connected to the brutal hammering death of Bonnie Garland by her jilted boyfriend, Richard Herrin. He asked a number of those in a Christian order that had been particularly forgiving of Richard whether they could imagine themselves performing such an act under any set of circumstances. Their answer was uniformly "Yes." All of us can at least find it conceivable that there might be circumstances under which we could perform an act like Herrin's – not exactly the same, perhaps, but something pretty horrible. All of us do share this much of our common nature with the worst of criminals. (For those with a greater we–they attitude toward criminals, the thought experiment that follows must be run with a somewhat less horrible act than Richard's.)

Then ask yourself: What would you feel like if it was you who had intentionally smashed open the skull of a 23-year-old woman with a claw hammer while she was asleep, a woman whose fatal defect was a desire to free herself from your too clinging embrace? My own response, I hope, would be that I would feel guilty unto death. I couldn't imagine any suffering that could be imposed upon me that would be unfair because it exceeded what I deserved.

Is that virtuous? Such deep feelings of guilt seem to me to be the only tolerable response of a moral being. "Virtue" is perhaps an odd word in the context of extreme culpability, but such guilt seems, at the least, very appropriate. One ought to feel so guilty one wants to die. Such sickness unto death is to my mind more virtuous than the non-guilty state to which Richard Herrin brought himself, with some help from Christian counseling about the need for self-forgiveness. After three years in prison on an eight- to twenty-five-year sentence for "heat of passion" manslaughter, Richard thought he had suffered quite enough for the killing of Bonnie:

HERRIN: I feel the sentence was excessive.

GAYLIN: Let's talk about that a little.

HERRIN: Well, I feel that way now and after the first years. The judge had gone overboard. . . .
Considering all the factors that I feel the judge should have considered: prior history of arrest, my personality background, my capacity for a productive life in society – you know, those kinds of things – I don't think he took those into consideration. He looked at the crime itself and responded to a lot of public pressure or maybe his own personal feelings, I don't know. I'm not going to accuse him of anything, but I was given the maximum sentence. This being my first arrest and considering the circumstances, I don't think I should have been given eight to twenty-five years.

GAYLIN: What do you think would have been a fair sentence?

HERRIN: Well, after a year or two in prison, I felt that was enough. . . .

GAYLIN: How would you answer the kind of person who says, for Bonnie, it's her whole life; for you it's eight years. What's eight years compared to the more years she might have had?

HERRIN: I can't deny that it's grossly unfair to Bonnie but there's nothing I can do about it. . . .
She's gone – I can't bring her back. I would rather that she had survived as a complete person, but she didn't. I'm not, again . . . I'm not saying that I shouldn't have been punished, but the punishment I feel is excessive. I feel I have five more years to go, and I feel that's just too much. There's no . . . I don't see any purpose in it. It's sad what happened, but it's even sadder to waste another life. I feel I'm being wasted in here.

GAYLIN: But what about the people who say, Look, if you got two years, then someone who robs should get only two days. You know, the idea of commensurate punishment. If it is a very serious crime it has to be a very serious punishment. Are you saying two years of prison is a very serious punishment considering what you did?

HERRIN: For me, yes.

[From W. Gaylin, *The Killing of Bonnie Garland*, pp. 325–7. Copyright © 1982 by Pip Enterprises, Inc. Reprinted by permission of Simon & Schuster, Inc.]

Compared to such shallow, easily obtained self-absolution for a horrible violation of another, a deep sense of guilt looks very virtuous indeed.

To be sure, there is an entire tradition that regards guilt as a useless passion (see Kaufmann, 1973). For one thing, it is always backward-looking rather than allowing one to get on with life. For another, it betrays an indecision that Nietzsche among others found unattractive: "The bite of conscience is indecent," Nietzsche thought (*Twilight*, p. 467), because it betrays the earlier decision about which one feels guilty. Yet Nietzsche and his followers are simply wrong here. Guilt feelings are often a virtue precisely because they do look to the past. As Herbert Morris (1976, p. 108) has argued, morality itself – including the morality of good character – has to take the past seriously. The alternative, of not crying over spilt milk (or blood), is truly indecent. A moral being *feels* guilty when he or she *is* guilty of past wrongs.

The virtue of feeling guilty is not raised so that punishment can be justified by its capacity to induce guilt. That is a possible retributive theory of punishment – a kind of moral rehabilitative theory – but it is not mine (see Morris, 1981). Rather, the virtue of our own imagined guilt is relevant because of the general connection between the virtue of an emotion and its epistemic import. We should trust what our imagined guilt feelings tell us; for acts like those of Richard Herrin, that if we did them we would be so guilty that some extraordinarily severe punishment would be deserved. We should trust the judgments such imagined guilt feelings spawn because nonneurotic guilt, unlike *ressentiment*, comes with good epistemic credentials.

Next, we need to be clear just what judgments it is that our guilt feelings validate in this way. First and foremost, to *feel* guilty causes the judgment that we *are* guilty, in the sense that we are morally culpable. Second, such guilt feelings typically engender the judgment that we deserve punishment. I mean this not only in the weak sense of desert – that it would not be unfair to be punished – but also and more important in the strong sense that we *ought* to be punished.

One might think that this second judgment of desert (in either its weak or its strong sense) is uncalled for by our feelings of guilt, that the judgment to which our guilt feelings lead is the judgment that we ought to repair as best we can the damage we have done. Such a view would justify corrective justice theories of punishment, but not retributive theories. Yet I think that this puts too nice a face on our guilt feelings. They do not generate only a judgment that we ought to make amends in this compensatory way. Rather – and this is what troubles many critics of guilt as an emotion – to feel guilty is to judge that we must suffer. We can see this plainly if we imagine ourselves having made provisions for Bonnie's family, comforting them in any way possible, and then feeling that our debt for killing her has been paid. It is so clear that such corrective actions do *not* satisfy guilt that to feel that they do is not to have felt guilty to begin with.

Our feelings of guilt thus generate a judgment that we deserve the suffering that is punishment. If the feelings of guilt are virtuous to possess, we have reason to believe that this last judgment is correct, generated as it is by emotions whose epistemic import is not in question.

Last, we should ask whether there is any reason not to make the same judgment about Richard Herrin's actual deserts as we are willing to make about our own hypothetical deserts. If we experinece any reluctance to transfer the guilt and desert *we* would possess, had we done what Richard Herrin did, to Herrin himself, we should examine that reluctance carefully. Doesn't it come from feeling more of a person than Richard? We are probably not persons who grew up in the barrio of East Los Angeles, or who found Yale an alien and disorienting culture. In any case, we certainly have never been subject to the exact same stresses and motivations as Richard Herrin. Therefore, it may be tempting to withhold from Richard the benefit each of us gives himself or herself: the benefit of being the subjective seat of a will that, although caused, is nonetheless capable of both choice and responsibility (Moore, 1985a).

Such discrimination is a temptation to be resisted, because it is no virtue. It is elitist and condescending toward others not to grant them the same responsibility and desert you grant to yourself. Admittedly, there are excuses the benefit of which others as well as yourself may avail themselves. Yet that is not the distinction invoked here. Herrin had no excuse the rest of us could not come up with in terms of various causes for our choices. To refuse to grant him the same responsibility and desert as you would grant yourself is thus an instance of what Sartre called bad faith, the treating of a free, subjective will as an object (see also Strawson, 1968). It is a refusal to admit that the rest of humanity shares with us that which makes us most distinctively human, our capacity to will and reason – and thus to be and do evil.

Far from evincing fellow feeling and the allowing of others to participate in our moral life, it excludes them as less than persons.

Rather than succumbing to this elitism masquerading as egalitari-
anism, we should ask ourselves what Herrin deserves by asking what
we would deserve had we done such an act. In answering this question
we should listen to our guilt feelings, feelings whose epistemic import
is not in question in the same way as are those of *ressentiment*. Such
guilt feelings should tell us that to do an act like Herrin's is to forfeit
forever any lighthearted idea of going on as before. One should feel
so awful that the idea of again leading a life unchanged from before,
with the same goals and hopes and happiness, should appear re-
voltingly incomprehensible.[2]

3. It is admittedly not an easy task to separate the emotions one
feels, and then in addition, discriminate which of them is the cause of
one's retributive judgments. We can no more choose which emotion it
will be that causes our judgments or actions than we can choose the
reason for which we act. We can choose whether to act or not and
whether to judge one way or another, but we cannot make it be true
that some particular reason or emotion caused our action or our
judgment. We must look inward as best we can to detect, but not to
will, which emotions bring about our judgments; and here there is
plenty of room for error and self-deception.

When we move from our judgments about the justice of retribution
in the abstract, however, to the justice of a social institution that exists
to exact retribution, perhaps we can gain some greater clarity. For if

---

[2] One may have noticed that the thought experiment just concluded has six steps to it.
It is perhaps helpful to separate them explicitly: (1) The psychological presupposition
that it is possible to engage in the thought experiment at all – that we can imagine we
could do an act like Richard Herrin's. (2) The psychological question of what we would
feel if we did such an action – guilty and deserving of punishment. (3) The moral
question of the virtue of that feeling – that guilt is a virtuous emotion to feel when we
have done such a wrongful act. (4) The psychological question of what judgments are
typically caused by the emotions of guilt – the judgments that we are guilty (culpable)
and that we deserve to be punished. (5) The moral question of the correctness of the
first person judgment that we deserve to be punished – as an inference drawn from the
virtue of the emotion of guilt that spawns such a judgment. (6) The moral question of
the correctness of the third person judgment that Richard Herrin deserves to be
punished – as an inference drawn from the fact that we would deserve to be punished
if we had done the act that Herrin did. One might believe that the thought experiment
requires a seventh step – namely, that the state ought to punish those who deserve it.
And in terms of a complete justification of a retributive theory of punishment, this last
step is a necessary one. My aim throughout this paper has been more limited: to
validate particular judgments, such as that Stephen Judy deserved the death penalty.
The thought experiment is designed to get us only this far, leaving for further argument (hinted at in the text that closes this section) that the state has the right and the
duty to set up institutions which give persons their just deserts.

we recognize the dangers retributive punishment presents for the expression of resentment, sadism, and so on, we have every reason to design our punishment institutions to minimize the opportunity for such feelings to be expressed. There is no contradiction in attempting to make a retributive punishment system humane; doing so allows penitentiaries to be faithful to their names – places for penance, not excuses for sadism, prejudice, hatred, and the like.

Even the old biblical injunction – "Vengeance is mine, saith the Lord" – has something of this insight behind it. Retributive punishment is dangerous for individual persons to carry out, dangerous to their virtue and, because of that, unclear in its justification. But implicit in the biblical injunction is a promise that retribution will be exacted. For those like myself who are not theists, that cleansing function must be performed by the state, not God. If the state can perform such a function, it removes from retributive punishment, not the guilt, as Nietzsche (*Genealogy*, p. 95) and Sartre (1955) have it, but the *ressentiment*.

References

Beccaria, *On Crimes and Punishments* (J. Grigson, trans.), in A. Manzoni (ed.), *The Column of Infamy* (Oxford: Oxford University Press, 1964).

L. Becker, *Property Rights* (London: Routledge and Kegan Paul, 1977).

H. Bedau, "Retribution and the Theory of Punishment," *Journal of Philosophy*, Vol. 75 (1978): 601–20.

S. I. Benn and R. S. Peters, *Social Principles and the Democratic State* (London: Allen and Unwin, 1959).

L. Blum, "Compassion," in A. Rorty (ed.), *Explaining Emotions* (Berkeley and Los Angeles: University of California Press, 1980).

C. Calhoun, "Cognitive Emotions?" in C. Calhoun and R. Soloman (eds.), *What Is an Emotion?* (Oxford: Oxford University Press, 1984).

D. Copp, "Considered Judgments and Moral Justification: Conservatism in Moral Theory," in D. Copp and D. Zimmerman (eds.), *Morality, Reason and Truth* (Totowa, NJ: Rowman and Allenheld, 1984).

A. Danto, *Nietzsche as Philosopher* (New York: Macmillan, 1965).

M. Dent, *The Moral Psychology of the Virtues* (Cambridge: Cambridge University Press, 1984).

P. Devlin, "Morals and the Criminal Law," in R. Wasserstrom (ed.), *Morality and the Law* (Belmont, CA: Wadsworth, 1971).

J. Feinberg, "The Expressive Function of Punishment," in his *Doing and Deserving* (Princeton, NJ: Princeton University Press, 1971).

H. Fingarette, "Punishment and Suffering," *Proc. Amer. Phil. Assoc.*, Vol. 50 (1977): 499–525.

"Psychoanalytic Perspectives on Moral Guilt and Responsibility: A Re-evaluation," *Philos. and Phenomenological Research,* Vol. 16 (1955): 18–36.

P. Foot, "Nietzsche: The Revaluation of Values," in R. Solomon (ed.), *Nietzsche: A Collection of Critical Essays* (Garden City, NY: Doubleday Anchor Books, 1973).

E. M. Forster, *Howard's End* (New York: Knopf, 1921).

"My Woods," in his *Abinger Harvest* (New York: Harcourt, Brace and World, 1936).

W. Gaylin, *The Killing of Bonnie Garland* (New York: Penguin Books, 1983).

H. L. A. Hart, *Punishment and Responsibility* (Oxford: Oxford University Press, 1968).

C. E. Hicks (ed.), *Famous American Jury Speeches* (St. Paul, MN: West Publishing, 1925).

T. Honderich, *Punishment: The Supposed Justifications* (London: Hutchinson, 1969).

K. Horney, "The Value of Vindictiveness," *Amer. Journal of Psychoanalysis,* Vol. 8 (1948): 3–12.

S. Jacoby, *Wild Justice: The Evolution of Revenge* (New York: Harper and Row, 1984).

I. Kant, *Groundwork of the Metaphysics of Morals* (Paton trans.) (New York: Harper, 1964).

The Metaphysical Elements of Justice (J. Ladd trans.) (Indianapolis: Bobbs-Merrill, 1965).

W. Kaufmann, *Without Guilt and Justice* (New York: Dell, 1973).

W. Lyons, *Emotion* (Cambridge: Cambridge University Press, 1980).

H. J. McCloskey, "A Non-Utilitarian Approach to Punishment," *Inquiry,* Vol. 8 (1965): 249–63.

J. Mackie, "Morality and the Retributive Emotions," *Criminal Justice Ethics,* Vol. 1 (1982): 3–10.

T. Marshall, concurring in *Gregg* v. *Georgia,* 428 U.S. 153 (1976).

K. Menninger, *The Crime of Punishment* (New York: Viking Press, 1968).

M. Moore, "Responsibility and the Unconscious," *Southern California Law Review,* Vol. 53 (1980): 1563–675.

"Moral Reality," *Wisconsin Law Review,* Vol. [1982]: 1061–1156 (1982a).

"Closet Retributivism," *USC Cites,* Vol. [Spring–Summer 1982]: 9–16 (1982b).

Law and Psychiatry: Rethinking the Relationship (Cambridge: Cambridge University Press, 1984).

"Causation and the Excuses," *California Law Review,* Vol. 73 (1985a): 201–59.

"The Moral and Metaphysical Sources of the Criminal Law," in J. R. Pennock and J. Chapman (eds.), *Nomos XXVII: Criminal Justice* (New York: New York University Press, 1985b).

"Mind, Brain, and Unconscious," in C. Wright and P. Clark (eds.), *Mind, Psychoanalysis, and Science* (Oxford: Blackwell, 1987).

H. Morris, *On Guilt and Innocence* (Berkeley and Los Angeles: University of California Press, 1976).

"Nonmoral Guilt," this volume, Chapter 9.

"A Paternalistic Theory of Punishment," *Amer. Phil. Quarterly*, Vol. 18 (1981): 263–71.

S. Morse, "Justice, Mercy, and Craziness," *Stanford Law Review*, Vol. 36 (1984): 1485–1515.

F. Nietzsche, *Beyond Good and Evil* (Kaufmann, trans.) (New York: Vintage, 1966).

Thus Spoke Zarathustra, in W. Kaufmann (ed.), *The Portable Nietzsche* (New York: Viking, 1954).

The Dawn, in W. Kaufmann (ed.), *The Portable Nietzsche* (New York: Viking, 1954).

The Gay Science (Kaufmann, trans.) (New York: Vintage, 1974).

On the Genealogy of Morals (Kaufmann, trans.) (New York: Vintage, 1969).

Twilight of the Idols, in W. Kaufmann (ed.), *The Portable Nietzsche* (New York: Viking, 1954).

A. Quinton, "On Punishment," *Analysis*, Vol. 14 (1954): 1933–42.

J. Rawls, *A Theory of Justice* (Cambridge, MA: Harvard University Press, 1971).

Mike Royko, "Nothing Gained by Killing a Killer? Oh Yes, There Is," *Los Angeles Times*, March 13, 1981, Sec. II, p. 7.

J.-P. Sartre, *The Flies*, in *No Exit and Three Other Plays* (New York: Vintage, 1955).

M. Scheler, *Ressentiment* (Holdheim trans.) (New York: Free Press, 1961).

R. Scruton, "Emotion, Practical Knowledge, and Common Culture," in A. Rorty (ed.), *Explaining Emotions* (Berkeley and Los Angeles: University of California Press, 1980).

J. Shklar, *Ordinary Vices* (Cambridge, MA: Harvard University Press, 1984).

R. de Sousa, "The Rationality of the Emotions," in A. Rorty (ed.), *Explaining Emotions* (Berkeley and Los Angeles: University of California Press, 1980).

Sir James Stephen, *Liberty, Equality, Fraternity* (Cambridge: Cambridge University Press, 1967).

P. F. Strawson, "Freedom and Resentment," in his *Studies in the Philosophy of Thought and Action* (Oxford: Oxford University Press, 1968).

H. Weihofen, *The Urge to Punish* (New York: Farrar, Straus and Cudahy, 1956).

B. Williams, "Morality and the Emotions," in his *Problems of Self* (Cambridge: Cambridge University Press, 1973).

J. Wilson and R. Herrnstein, *Crime and Human Nature* (New York: Simon and Schuster, 1985).

9

Nonmoral guilt

HERBERT MORRIS

Most of us share the belief that we sometimes are and sometimes are not guilty. To deny it would seem to flout common sense. But, of course, philosophers have done precisely this. They have offered arguments to demonstrate the radical view that none of us is, or indeed ever could be, guilty – arguments, for example, that cast doubt upon our ever possessing free choice or our having an identity that extends over time. Were we to take seriously such views, the appropriateness, even rationality, of our ever feeling guilty would also be thrown into doubt, for this feeling generally arises because of a belief in one's guilt.

A shared assumption appears to underlie the opposing views of common sense and these philosophers. Guilt requires "culpable responsibility for wrongdoing." Thus, if one lacked free choice or if one acted under a reasonable mistake of fact or if another, not oneself, were responsible for wrongdoing, one would not be guilty. Common sense proceeds on the assumption the requirement is sometimes satisfied; the philosophers dispute it.

From the fact that we defeat attributions of guilt by citing absence of culpability, it is easy to conclude that the criteria for guilt, summarized by the phrase "culpable responsibility for wrongdoing," impose constraints (I call them "moral constraints") on the concept's application. Failure to satisfy these constraints implies absence of moral guilt, which is then assumed to be the only genuine guilt (apart from a formal concept of guilt such as we find in law). On this view, which I take to be commonly held, one's feeling guilty, despite one's not being guilty, would be inappropriate.[1] Such a view provides a hegemony over the whole sphere of guilt for moral guilt alone.

My principal aim here is to challenge this view. I believe it provides

---

[1] Joel Feinberg puts it quite succinctly: "Guilt consists in the intentional transgression of prohibition, a violation of a specific taboo, boundary, or legal code, by a definite voluntary act" (citing H. K. Lynd, *On Shame and the Search for Identity*). In Feinberg, *Doing and Deserving* (1970), p. 231. Princeton, NJ: Princeton University Press.

a distorted picture of guilt's role in our lives. My starting place for inquiry is our emotional life, components of which seem to me devalued by this conception of what constitutes "genuine guilt."

My attention has been drawn to three types of case, each of which must be regarded as puzzling if one subscribes to the view that guilt is moral guilt and moral guilt alone. First, individuals report experiencing guilt, at least occasionally, over certain states of mind alone, even those states over which they appear to have no control. I have wondered what sense might be made of such experiences, and I have wondered, too, whether one's feeling might be appropriate though it arises in circumstances where, because there is no "voluntary act," one is not "culpably responsible for wrongdoing." I have considered, with respect to these states, whether we might perhaps even be guilty, but not in a sense subscribed to by philosophers. I have next been concerned with the now familiar, though no less perplexing because of that, phenomena of "survivor" and associated kinds of guilt. Here, as in the former case, individuals with no culpable involvement report feeling guilty. Still more strangely, they may claim they are guilty. I wondered what sense could be made of this and whether they might be correct. Finally, individuals report feeling guilty in circumstances where not they but others have acted wrongly and where they have no culpable relationship to the wrongdoing; they too, despite apparent moral innocence, seem prepared to say not just that they feel guilty, but that they are guilty. Here too I have wondered whether the feelings might be appropriate and whether they might correspond to a state of guilt that is not conventionally moral.

These phenomena would all seem, at least on the face of it, to conflict with the common view that moral guilt and it alone is the touchstone for genuine guilt and appropriate guilt feelings – even allowing for some disagreement, as there is bound to be, over what constitutes moral guilt. Individuals would either be misdescribing their feelings (it's shame, for example, not guilt) or reflecting some conceptual confusion (regret, for example, is what they should be feeling) or, while truly feeling guilty, mistaking the true cause of their feeling (displacement is at work). As for the possibility that they are guilty, not just feeling it, this is a gross conceptual confusion, for one cannot be guilty if one is not morally guilty.

My response to these cases has been quite different. First, I am skeptical about any claim of widespread misuse of terms for emotional states, and I am generally disposed to accept first-person reports as accurate. More important, my reaction to such reports is that they may be entirely appropriate. Finally, I am also skeptical about the "hegemony" of moral guilt over the whole sphere of guilt. I believe that, if individuals sincerely believe themselves guilty, good reasons exist for accepting the belief. Problems arise only because of our longing for a neater conceptual world than we in fact possess. In these cases, then, feeling guilty is often not merely explainable, but has a justification as well.

My intent is not, of course, to proselytize for more guilt. Some people surely feel too much of it, and some people might well do with a bit more. Whether we experience too little or too much guilt, whether such inquiries in the abstract make sense at all, do not interest me here. I would, however, be greatly concerned if the views I present promoted a tendency to put everyone, as it were, in the same boat, the morally guilty and the nonmorally guilty. Moral categories serve us well, and I would like to believe that my position does not promote their devaluation. Just as we draw distinctions among the morally guilty, some incurring by their conduct more, some less, guilt, so we should continue to view moral guilt as importantly different from any nonmoral kind we may come upon. Finally, in each case I describe of nonmoral guilt, nonmoral because one is not "culpably responsible for wrongdoing," I believe the guilt incurred by the person derives from what may fairly be described as a fundamental moral posture toward the world.

This study divides into five sections. I first address the issue of appropriateness, setting out prevalent conceptions of when feeling guilty is or is not appropriate, and because it is frequently invoked in those situations of concern to me, I also offer an analysis of "neurotic guilt." I then turn to the criteria that have guided my own judgments of appropriateness. In the second section, because I place such weight on a contrast between moral and nonmoral guilt, I offer brief analyses of a commonly accepted philosophical conception of moral guilt and the nature of its associated feelings. In the final sections I turn to three kinds of anomalous cases: guilt for states of mind alone, guilt over unjust enrichment, and guilt over the actions of others.

Appropriateness

The common view I find wanting links appropriateness in a tight way to moral guilt. One appropriately feels guilty when one is guilty; one's response is inappropriate if one is aware of being guilty but does not feel it. Further, responses are inappropriate if disproportionate – being overcome with intense guilt for something minor or feeling a twinge for something rather significant or experiencing guilt too briefly or too persistently.

Whether one feels guilty appropriately or inappropriately, one's state would presumably have an accompanying explanation. Freud subscribes to this plausible view in a well-known passage from *Totem and Taboo:*

An obsessional neurotic may be weighed down by a sense of guilt that would be appropriate in a mass-murderer, while in fact, from his childhood onwards, he has behaved to his fellow-men as the most considerate and scrupulous member of society. Nevertheless, his sense of guilt has a justification: it is founded on the intense and frequent death-wishes against his fellows which are unconsciously at work in him. It has a justification if what we take into account are unconscious thoughts and not intentional deeds. Thus the omnipotence of thoughts, the overvaluation of mental processes as compared with reality, is seen to have unrestricted play in the emotional life of neurotic patients and everything that derives from it.[2]

Freud is here describing what we sometimes label "neurotic guilt." The concept is rich and complex, and a full grasp of its meaning would require familiarity with those cases in the psychological literature from which it evolved. This is my understanding of what these cases reveal. First, neurotic guilt requires that one feel guilty. If one is unaware of feeling guilty, as one might be when the feeling is entirely unconscious, there is no neurotic guilt. Second, the guilt that one acknowledges experiencing is inappropriate, given the beliefs one cites to support the feeling. This may be so for any number of reasons. The acknowledged belief may be irrational, as when one continues to claim fault and responsibility when on the evidence presented none was present; or it is inappropriate because, given the person's acknowledged belief, there is either no ground for guilt, as, say, when one accepts that one was not at fault, "I know I'm not to blame but I still can't help feeling guilty"; or when the intensity of the reaction is greater than warranted by one's beliefs about the seriousness of the guilt, "I know it was trivial but it's killing me." Third, however, one also holds either acknowledged beliefs, as is commonly so with death wishes for one's parents, or if acknowledged, there is no acceptance that these beliefs account for one's feeling, as when one says, "Oh, yes, I did that, but it never affected me at all." The causative, though unacknowledged beliefs, provide what Freud labels a "justification" for the feeling. There is implied, then, in neurotic guilt the idea of

[2] *Standard Edition* (1913), 13:87.

displaced feelings, feelings that are linked by the person experiencing them to an object other than the object in fact causing the feeling. The concept, then, of neurotic guilt implies both ignorance of the real object of one's feelings and a mistake in one's citation of what accounts for the feeling, its intensity, or its duration. Neurotic guilt is a species of self-deception and as such requires obliqueness. It is here that the idea of unconscious thought processes has its particular appeal, for we cannot comprehend how we should simultaneously have in mind what is in fact so, tell ourselves a deliberate lie, be duped, and have our feelings respond accordingly. Neurotic guilt also implies not just ignorance and self-deception, but a motivated ignorance and a motivated false attribution. One's acknowledged guilt adheres to an object with less painful associations than the avoided object. Defense operates. Finally, however, neurotic guilt is more than merely displaced guilt, serving defensive ends, for it is guilt experienced by a neurotic. As such, it is marked by typical neurotic features. There is a longing to experience guilt; it is an absorbing project, and the search for guilt, the dwelling upon it, and ruminating about it, are central themes in the neurotic's life. They are attached to inappropriate objects and, compelled by circumstances to relinquish some particular object, they quickly seize upon a substitute so that their hunger can be satisfied. It follows from all this that, while we may be able to determine displacement by attending to a quite limited segment of a person's life, in order to ascertain the presence of neurotic guilt, we should have to cast our net wider, and seek evidence of neurosis as well.

I need now to say something more about my own use of the concept "appropriate feelings." First, I do not, by labeling feelings "appropriate," imply that all persons similarly situated would be obligated to have the feeling. Nor, of course, do I imply that the person is, or is on the way to becoming, something of a moral monster if the feeling is not present. Were a person invulnerable to feeling guilty in moral situations, we should be pulled in these directions or toward judgments of psychopathy, but such responses seem out of place when an individual does not experience guilt in nonmoral situations.

The first factor I rely upon is common acceptance of the reported feeling without a corresponding widespread inclination to seek for some explanation other than that offered by the person having the feeling. If we are disposed to think the feeling natural, the object cited as occasioning it an acceptable one, and if there is no strong pull to view the feeling as displaced, there is good reason to regard it as appropriate. Any inappropriateness would then derive not from having the feeling, but from its undue persistence or intensity.

A second consideration I rely upon is existence of widespread respect for attitudes underlying the feeling. Thus, if individuals experience guilt in nonmoral situations as an inevitable by-product of what we regard not necessarily as an obligatory but nevertheless as a perfectly acceptable, even perhaps admirable stance toward the world, I have thought this reason to regard the feeling as appropriate. Views of moral reality differ, and when this difference manifests itself in differences in emotional experiences, we are justified, I believe, in according the feeling a respectful response.

Moral guilt and guilt feelings

I want briefly in this section to examine several issues concerning moral guilt and guilt feelings. This should throw into bold relief the apparently anomalous nature of the nonmoral cases. I say something, then, about the conditions for being morally guilt, the nature of the state one is in when these conditions obtain, and the nature of the attendant feelings.

The concept "culpable responsibility for wrongdoing," intrinsic to the thesis I reject, is open to different interpretations. This is my understanding of it. There must be a *doing;* it must be a *conscious* doing; it must be a *free* doing; there must be *wrong*doing; there must be a *moral* wrongdoing; it must be by a *person;* it must be by a *moral person;* this person must be *responsible* for the wrongdoing; the guilty person must be the *self-same* person as the one responsible for the wrongdoing; the person must be *at fault* with respect to wrongdoing. Each of these conditions requires careful elucidation, but I am going to assume they capture those conditions whose existence is presupposed by a person's being morally guilty of wrongdoing. Once these conditions are satisfied, a person is in the state of being guilty. What does that imply?

First, moral requirements establish a moral order of things in which some actions are and some actions are not to be performed and where violation constitutes wrongdoing. When one conducts oneself in compliance with the limits embodied in that order, one is joined together with others; one is part of a moral community; one is part of a larger whole. The first important implication of one's being guilty, then, is one at least temporary separation from this community. Second, a guilty act disrupts the moral order, causing what is viewed as an imbalance that requires righting. Next, the guilty individual, because he or she has damaged that which individuals highly value, is an appropriate object of indignation and resentment. The guilty person has also usurped a privilege not provided by the rules. Principles have been subordinated to one's personal judgment or one's own interest. There is implied, then, an absence of appropriate deference. Being a guilty person also implies one's being obligated to restore damaged relationships, to make amends and offer reparation for actual damage done. One's effective reestablishing of what has been damaged and one's reconciliation with the moral community seem also to require emotional reactions, attitudes, and conduct, such as guilt, contrition, repentance, and confession, that reflect recognition of one's proper relationship to moral norms, including an attitude of appropriate deference and humility.

What, then, is it to feel guilt? A person who feels guilty has certain beliefs and feelings and is disposed to feel and act in certain characteristic ways. More specifically, a person who is feeling guilt will be feeling bad because of a unique set of beliefs that allow us to define the feeling. First, one realizes that something one values has been damaged, and this thought alone causes some pain. Second, just as there is a special satisfaction attached to thinking of oneself as the creator of what is valuable, so a special dissatisfaction derives from the realization that one has oneself damaged or destroyed what one values. Third, in feeling guilty one reproaches oneself in a manner that corresponds to the reproach one would have visited upon another had they been the responsible party. Fourth, part of one's feeling bad is accounted for by one's feeling apart and separated from those to whom one was attached. Finally, feeling guilty, we feel weighted down not just by these distressing feelings, but by a feelings of obligation as well – to confess, to make amends, to repair, and to restore. When all is said, then, the state of the person feeling guilt implies a division within the person, a separation from others and a need to put things right and together with oneself and others.

Let us now turn our attention to nonmoral guilt.

Guilt for states of mind alone

When contrasting thought and deed, we may have in mind any number of different mental states. I limit my own discussion to one of these: the wish that evil befall another.

Imagine someone who, feeling intense anger, wishes that another be struck dead. People commonly, particularly when the person is someone close to them, feel guilty over such wishes. Let us quickly survey some of the responses we can anticipate to questions about the appropriateness of such feelings and whether they might have, as some are sure to claim, a moral basis.

In the analysis I offered in the above section, guilt requires a deed. The most questionable of the cited criteria for moral guilt, I have listed it principally because moral philosophers have appeared to subscribe to it.[3] Just as some philosophers would question the moral status of a command that imposed a duty to perform what is impossible, so they would be troubled by the moral status of any command that addressed itself to thought alone, carrying as it would the implication that a failure to comply constituted wrongdoing for which one could be morally guilty. Moral guilt may be seen as incurred by damage to a relationship, damage that puts one in debt to another, that gives rise to familiar reparative and restorative obligations, a status that makes understandable asking for and gaining forgiveness. But if one has yet to act, how, it may be wondered, can there be damage? Moral wrongs that occasion guilt seem to require intrusion into the sphere of rights of others. Until there is such intrusion, we are immunized from moral condemnation. Morality allows, then, for a sphere of privacy where one's wishes and fantasies are matters of concern only to the person having them. It may be claimed, to be sure, that a person who wishes evil for another and who derives satisfaction from the fantasies intrinsic to such wishes may not be as admirable a person as one free of such propensities. But this assessment does not imply any moral guilt. Such guilt is incurred only when a specific moral wrong has been committed for which one is responsible.

Another compelling, more serious, objection to moral guilt for wishes is certain to be raised. Wishing evil for another often derives from the natural emotion of anger. While some few individuals might achieve liberation from such disruptive feelings, most cannot. But morality concerns the humanly attainable, and failures here might be thought to be immune from moral censure. Morality does not require the extraordinary. Wishes, then, that are the result of natural emotions should not be viewed as incurring moral guilt.

The moral situation is, in actuality, far less clear than this picture would suggest. Christian morality focuses precisely on conditions of heart and mind – the inner life of the human being. This view is also reflected in the formula that law, as contrasted with morality, takes

---

[3] See Feinberg, op. cit.

external conduct for its concern. Reserved for morality, then, is the internal sphere – whatever that might be.[4] Neither the maxim "Law is concerned with external, morality with internal conduct," nor the often quoted biblical sayings of Jesus, such as that concerning lust, make clear whether wishes alone, without any accompanying conduct, and despite an inability to control their onset, are a basis for guilt.

Another response of interest comes from Freud. In *Civilization and Its Discontents* he observes[5] that feeling guilt is initially experienced as anxiety, an anxiety that certain conduct one wishes to engage in will meet with the loss of the parent's love or with punishment. In this early stage of our development there is, as yet, no internalization, no superego and therefore no disposition to punish oneself; there is merely a fear of discovery and imagined loss and punishment. It is only when internalization has occurred that one can, for Freud, properly speak of a conscience and a sense of guilt. He writes:

At this point . . . the fear of being found out comes to an end; the distinction, moreover, between doing something bad and wishing to do it disappears entirely, since nothing can be hidden from the super-ego, not even thoughts.[6]

. . . Bad intentions are equated with bad actions, and hence come a sense of guilt and a need for punishment.[7]

With a superego in place, aware as it is of one's wishes, it then responds; that is, one responds to oneself, as one imagines one's parents would respond to one, not discriminating between wishes or intentions and deeds, and one feels guilty. One has internalized the anxiety, and to quiet it one attacks oneself as one imagines one's parents would attack one. It is not, of course, Freud's intention in these passages to address issues of moral guilt or the appropriateness of the feeling. Nor does he raise the question, "Why should the child attribute to the parent a lack of discrimination between wish and deed?" He believes, however, that he has made understandable one's experiencing guilt over wishes and intentions.

It will be recalled, however, that in *Totem and Taboo* another view surfaced about guilt in connection with wishes. It may provide an answer to the question why the child imagines that the parents will fail to discriminate between wishes and deeds. In that work Freud claimed that guilt felt over unconscious wishes had a justification. This was

[4] For the meaning behind this formula and what truth there may be in it, see Morris, "Punishment for Thoughts," in *On Guilt and Innocence* (1976). Berkeley: University of California Press.
[5] *Standard Edition* (1930), 21:123ff.
[6] Ibid., p. 125.
[7] Ibid., p. 128.

so because an unconscious belief in omnipotence of thought erases the distinction between wish and deed. Freud appears to have subscribed to the view that one can only be guilty if one believes one is perpetrating some harm.

Professor Herbert Fingarette, in his essay "Real Guilt and Neurotic Guilt,"[8] influenced by these views, adopts a position incompatible with our first response to whether wishes could occasion moral guilt. He writes:

> Moral guilt accrues by virtue of our wishes, not merely our acts. Of course legal guilt depends primarily upon our acts, though we should note that even here the assessment of motives plays a role. But the question of moral guilt does not wait for acts; it is in profound degree a question of what one harbors in one's heart. This is the gist of Freud's basic concept of "psychic reality." In the psychic economy, the wish is omnipotent. To wish is, psychologically, to have done. Hence a person suffers guilt for his wishes, even his unconscious ones.[9]

I find this passage puzzling. Let us leave aside what truth there may be in the claim that one is morally guilty by virtue of one's wishes alone. What is troubling is that the argument offered in its defense does not appear to support it. Moral guilt would accrue not by virtue of a wish alone, but, of course, given reliance on a conception of omnipotent thinking, because a wish is regarded by its possessor as equivalent to a deed. And so moral guilt would rest not upon a wish alone, but upon the fact that a person believes, unconsciously to be sure, that in wishing one is doing. This would be as little like guilt over wishes as the guilt that would be incurred by a believer in voodoo who supposed that another's death would be brought about by sticking pins in a doll. Such a person is guilty because of a belief that what is being done will lead to death, not because of merely sticking pins in a doll.

Further, the case of unconscious wishes and beliefs is, of course, strikingly different from a morally guilty practitioner of voodoo. Such a person is aware of the belief that is held – namely, that one can bring about death in a certain way – while for Freud and Professor Fingarette, by definition one is either an infant – that is, a morally innocent agent – or one is an adult who is unaware of the unconscious magical belief. Normally, however, if I am unaware that by doing X I shall bring about Y, even if it is the case that I wish for Y, it is not the case that I am morally guilty in bringing about Y by doing X. It would

---

[8] *On Responsibility* (1967), pp. 82–94. New York: Basic Books.
[9] Ibid., p. 89.

appear to be a consequence of Professor Fingarette's reliance on Freud's views of psychic reality that infants and one's unconscious were the subjects of moral guilt. But this will not do.

So far, then, no persuasive argument has been presented that merely to wish for evil for another is a basis for moral guilt, and a number of reasons have been offered why such wishes do not provide such a basis. Freud's explanations for why one might feel guilty over wishes might make one's having the feeling understandable, though not necessarily appropriate, and such a feeling would not be grounded upon a true belief in one's moral guilt. We need, I think, a new start.

Someone says, "I feel guilty whenever I think of killing her," or "I am bothered by my conscience whenever I think of being unfaithful." The confession may surprise us, but not the feelings reported in it. We might even be tempted to say, "Well, I should hope you're feeling guilty!" What might explain such feelings?

Two somewhat different types of mental operation often appear to play a role in such cases, each of which naturally results in one's feeling guilty even though one has as yet to do anything. First, when one recollects something wrong that one has done, one may find oneself again, or perhaps for the first time, feeling guilty. A causal relation then exists between one's recollection and one's feelings. This does not surprise us at all. Likewise, sometimes when we think of acting in a certain way, in circumstances where we have not as yet done so, we may find ourselves feeling guilty, a state that would have been induced in us by imagining ourselves acting in a certain way — say, killing someone.

A second and somewhat different explanation for feeling guilty with regard to wishes is this: To wish for another's death is both to imagine the other's death and to experience gratification as a consequence of what we imagine. Now one could, of course, as a consequence of one's imagined act, also imagine oneself feeling guilty; but a constitutive aspect of imagined feeling is one's actually feeling as one imagines oneself feeling, sometimes in an attenuated way, to be sure. There is indeed something omnipotent, something magical in the phenomena of wishes, for fantasied gratification is integral to their nature and fantasied gratification produces actual gratification. Gourmands frequently exploit this truth by imagining feasts, thereby inducing states similar to those they would be experiencing were they in fact to feast. Thus, imagined wrongful action and imagined guilt over such action can lead one to feel guilty.

In the first case I have described above there is a causal relation between wishing and one's feeling guilty; in the latter case it is constitutive of imagining one's feeling guilty that one feels that way.

What can we now say about the appropriateness of these feelings? If we ask about either of the situations I have described, "Is the person guilty of anything?", the answer might seem to be "As yet, nothing." Of course it would be strange to describe the feelings in these situations as inappropriate, for we often value their existence and may urge individuals to engage in imaginative exercises ("Just think of how you will feel!") in the hope the feeling will be aroused and the individual induced to forbear from wrongful conduct. These cases alone establish that it would be wrong to insist upon actual moral guilt as a condition for the appropriateness of one's feeling guilty.

The more interesting question is this: Might one be guilty and not just be feeling guilty because of one's wishes? Put another way, might the feelings have not just an explanation, but a justification? I believe so. Recall the nature of wishing. To wish is to imagine a situation that incorporates gratification as a constituent element; in wishing one experiences the gratification one imagines. It also, and now more to the point, constitutes a reality, a reality that may be viewed as damaging to valued relationships with others. Here then is still another interpretation of the phrase "omnipotence of thought," as applied to wishes, for wishes and experienced gratification, say at the death of a loved one, might itself be viewed as injurious to or destructive of a valued relationship. Mental states "alone," then, hardly captures this conception of mental states as constitutive of relationships. Individuals may believe that, entirely apart from their free choice with respect to these matters, their condition fails to meet standards they have set for themselves and that they thereby incur guilt. Their feelings would then correspond to a belief in their guilt. If a person chooses to adopt such a regulative principle, such a demanding moral posture, something others might view as supererogatory from a moral point of view, it nevertheless, so I believe, is a position that should not be ruled out as irrational or conceptually odd. It may gain our admiration.

Still other possibilities of guilt and guilt feeling exist where, as yet, there is no wrongful action. Imagine a person who wishes to kill another and who is convinced that should circumstances prove favorable, an intention to kill will be formed and an attempt made. It all depends on such matters as overcoming fear, adequate assurance that escape is possible, and perhaps some confidence that one will not be tormented by guilt. Should these matters be favorably resolved, one will act; otherwise one will not. Alternatively, suppose a person is convinced that had something fortuitous not occurred, one's wishes would have been converted into deeds and one would have killed. "I was enraged, and I would certainly have strangled him had I not suddenly noticed that he had a birthmark on his forehead just like my little sister. God must have been looking over me."

Now we can imagine a person in the above situation identifying with those who kill. The person might then feel, as a consequence of identification with someone who has actually killed, some guilt. Imaginative activity would be linked to identification, and causally or otherwise, linked to the imaginative activity might be some guilty feelings. This provides an explanation for one's feeling guilty and, as such, is similar to that offered for the feelings we may have when we imagine ourselves performing some wrongful deed. And, as with those other explanations for feeling guilty, nothing about the feeling seems inappropriate – particularly, again, because it may serve to inhibit wrongful conduct.

However, it may also be the case that one's feeling guilty in such circumstances derives from one's judgment that one is guilty. The fact that blood appears sometimes on one person's hands rather than another's, and that this may be fortuitous, no doubt played its role in leading Jesus to cut through the reality of what people did and did not do, probe more deeply, and discount differences between people that had before been treated as of great moral significance. In this view one's differences from another are less important than one's similarities. With such a disposition, derived from a moral posture toward the world, one may come to believe that one is in fact guilty. Such a guilt derives, then, not from having done something wrong, but from some conception of the moral solidarity of human beings. The basis for the guilt is not a deed, but one's sharing a common humanity. Where that is one's belief, one's feeling guilty has not just a psychological explanation but a justification, for it is grounded on what many would regard as a well-founded judgment of guilt.

Guilt over unjust enrichment

Consider these situations:

> A flood causes the death of all in a large family but one individual who survives through pure chance.
> A life-preserving machine is detached from one person and at-

tached to another who has in no way participated in the action; the former person dies and the latter survives.

There are two siblings, one of whom is born healthy and intelligent, the other sickly and retarded.

There are two brothers, equally deserving of their father's generosity; the father capriciously leaves all his wealth to one son and disinherits the other.

Of two individuals, one merits praise for a job well done while the other does not, but praise is bestowed equally upon both.

A person receives reward and praise for saving another's life, but it is undeserved, the result of mistaken identity.

It is not, I believe, uncommon for individuals to report feeling guilty in these situations. Certain important themes appear to recur. First, those reporting such feelings view themselves as similarly situated with others in some morally relevant respect. Second, they believe themselves no more entitled than another to possess the good they do. One either possesses something of value which one deserves no more than another or one possesses something of equal value with another which one deserves less than the other, or one has been given a benefit which one does not deserve in a situation in which such bestowal is normally regulated by principles of entitlement or desert. In these cases individuals have either no right to possess something of value or they have no more right to possess it than others who do not or, if they may be said to possess the right, as say in the proceeds of a lottery, it is recognized that only chance, not their merit or desert, accounts for their good and another's ill fortune. So while no blame attaches to them, what they possess cannot be justified by appeals to justice or fairness. It is for this reason alone, and not of course because of some unjust conduct, that I label these cases ones of "unjust enrichment."

Finally, and of great importance, in most instances identificatory ties exist between the more and less fortunate. The stronger these ties, the more intense one's feeling of guilt. And so these feelings commonly arise in familial contexts or where a group has been designated by some common characteristic for persecution or where one's particular life situation, say a serious illness, disposes one toward identification with others similarly situated.

What sense can we make of these situations?

We may, of course, wish to deny the accuracy of the report of one's feelings. This impulse should be checked. The telltale signs of guilt are too evident for the feeling itself to be questioned. There is frequent foregoing good that life might offer, a disposition to get rid of what one claims one has no right to possess, even going so far as to punish oneself, certainly often attempting some form of reparation, and of course, simply reporting that one feels guilty. More credible than doubt over the feeling's existence is doubt felt over its appropriateness, even its rationality.

Confronted by a friend's revelation of such feelings, we can imagine thinking, even saying:

> I do not doubt the genuineness of your feelings, but you ought not to feel as you do, for you are not to blame for such things. You have behaved throughout as one would expect a decent and reasonable person to behave. You should not add to the burden of your loss the burden of an unjustified guilt.

These words may strike a responsive chord; but our compassionate response does not address fully, and it is probably good that it does not, the inappropriateness we may think present. At the same time as we attempt to talk sense to the person, we may be wondering where the real difficulty lies. The person's feelings may have any number of different, overlapping explanations. Sometimes, it is something straightforwardly wrong that one has done and then hidden from oneself. What appeared, given the initial description, as pure chance was in fact influenced by the person's conduct. Or one might simply have wished that it be another and not oneself who suffered or that it be oneself and not another who benefited, and one feels guilty over preferring oneself. Operative, too, may be the unconscious belief that one's good fortune has been obtained at the expense of another so that one feels responsible for that other's misfortune. It's possible that one's wish has associated with it the unconscious belief that one effectuated a situation that, prospectively or retrospectively, one wished for. Finally, we can surmise that guilt, because it allows for our feeling we have played some responsible role in the world, might serve to allay feelings of anxiety occasioned by the sense of utter helplessness people experience in some of these situations.[10]

All this has some plausibility and in any particular case might serve adequately to explain one's feeling guilty; but I find unconvincing explanations solely in terms of displacement or purely defensive functions. My own immediate impulse upon learning that someone feels guilty in these situations has been to think their reaction quite "natural," entirely to be expected given the facts, rather than as inappropri-

---

[10] See, on the topic of guilt as a defense against anxiety, W. R. D. Fairbairn (1943),"The Repression and the Return of the Bad Objects," in Fairbairn (1952), *Psychoanalytic Studies of the Personality*. London: Routledge and Kegan Paul.

ate or a sign of some neurosis. Consequently, I believe we should look further than depth psychology for a completely satisfactory explanation.

Karl Jaspers, in his book *The Question of German Guilt*,[11] raises the possibility that the feelings we have been considering may have a basis in one's being guilty. He writes:

> Morality is always influenced by mundane purposes. I may be morally bound to risk my life, if a realization is at stake; but there is no moral obligation to sacrifice one's life in the sure knowledge that nothing will have been gained. Morally we have a duty to dare, not a duty to choose certain doom. Morally, in either case, we rather have the contrary duty, not to do what cannot serve the mundane purpose but to save ourselves for realizations in the world.
>
> But there is within us a guilt consciousness which springs from another source. Metaphysical guilt is the lack of absolute solidarity with the human being as such – an indelible claim beyond morally meaningful duty. This solidarity is violated by my presence at a wrong or a crime. It is not enough that I cautiously risk my life to prevent it; if it happens, and if I was there, and if I survive where the other is killed, I know from a voice within myself: I am guilty of still being alive.
>
> . . . Thousands of Germans sought, or at least found death in battling the regime, most of them anonymously. We survivors did not seek it. We did not go into the streets when our Jewish friends were led away; we did not scream until we too were destroyed. We preferred to stay alive, on the feeble, if logical, ground that our death could not have helped anyone. We are guilty of being alive. We know before God which deeply humiliates us. What happened to us in these twelve years is like a transmutation of our being.[12]

Jaspers's point in this moving passage is open, I believe, to at least two interpretations. A distinction is drawn between the demands of morality and some higher demand, one beyond "morally meaningful duty." A moral duty might require that we dare, but only if something were possibly to be gained by doing so. A failure to act in these circumstances would occasion, for Jaspers, moral guilt. But just what is metaphysical guilt? Is it brought about – to consider just one possibility – by the mere fact of one's survival when one happens to be present at some wrong or crime from which others have suffered and not escaped? This seems suggested by the words, "if I survive where the other is killed . . . I am guilty of still being alive." Is it rather that the guilt arises from not fulfilling the metaphysical requirement to act in accord with the principle of human solidarity, even if one's action would be futile in preventing evil and certain to bring about death?

11 Jaspers (1961). New York: Capricorn Books.
12 Ibid., pp. 71–2.

While some of Jaspers's language suggests that it is the mere fact of survival that occasions guilt, I believe the more plausible reading would have guilt incurred by a failure to act. In the first interpretation guilt would be unavoidable; in the other, it is avoidable through sacrificial but futile action. Jaspers in this passage, then, does not respond to the issue directly relevant to guilt over mere survival. His words do, however, suggest a quite reasonable basis for one's feeling guilty and being guilty.

The feelings may have their source in one's belief that one's more fortunate situation has created an obligation to rectify fortuitous imbalances or injustices. In this interpretation, one is feeling guilty because of obligations yet to be met.

Duties and obligations can, of course, arise because of the existence of circumstances over which one has no control. Goods known by one to be stolen must be returned even though the possessor was without fault in acquiring them. It has also, of course, been claimed that more is required of those who have more. This may seem particularly true when what one possesses is not attributable to one's merit. Certainly, the guilt felt by someone who retains an undeserved reward is not perplexing to us. And no doubt some of the guilt felt in other cases I have described arises from failure to fulfill what one views as one's obligations. But does this suggestion, added to the others, exhaust the possibilities? I think not.

Imagine someone who experiences guilt over being a survivor saying the following:

It has been difficult for me to accept that I preferred my friend's death to my own when one of us had to die. I even think that my feeling guilty is partly explained by that preference and certain odd, unconscious, beliefs I had about my responsibility for his death. I also realize that I feel some guilt over not doing all that I reasonably could to show my gratitude for my good fortune. But when all those bases are covered, I still seem to feel guilty just over the fact that I profited from something I see as unfair, that I should have been miraculously saved and not my friend.

These remarks suggest an interesting possibility. A person might be guilty just because of benefiting from a distribution that cannot be defended as fair or just or deserved. One's guilt would derive from being in an unjust position with regard to those with whom one identified. It would be this guilt that gives rise to impulses to redress imbalances. One's obligations would follow from one's guilt, not one's guilt from unfulfilled obligations. Guilt would be based, as it were, on mere possession, not on remaining in possession or otherwise failing to fulfill obligations. If there is such a guilt, it would contrast sharply with moral guilt. It would be a guilt independent of any choice to do wrong and, as such, a blameless guilt. One's true guilt would correspond to one's acknowledged guilt.

Feeling guilty, then, would both mark one's attachment to principles of fairness and justice and manifest one's solidarity with others. While nonmoral, it would derive from a moral posture toward others. One's feelings would track the scope of one's identificatory ties with the less fortunate, those before whom one feels guilty. Some individuals appear capable of a rather limited range of such ties, others of encompassing the whole of humankind and perhaps even the animal kingdom as well.

I believe we understand, and even occasionally greatly admire, individuals who feel as I have described. Their moral posture, revealed in their emotional response, is no less commendable than that adopted by others. In fact, in reflecting upon such cases we may be more troubled by persons who do not experience at least a twinge of guilt and an accompanying desire to rectify morally indefensible imbalances. The absence of these feelings may signal insensitivity, a lack of humility, a failure to grasp emotionally how much of the good one possesses cannot be tallied on the credit side of our personal moral ledger sheet. We may not ask of ourselves or of others that guilt be felt in these situations. But should we and others so feel, there need be nothing untoward about it, and any pathology in emotional responses would derive not from feeling guilty, but from an abnormal intensity or persistence of such feelings.

Vicarious guilt[13]

Consider the following. You are an American who has occasion to visit Hiroshima shortly after the end of World War II and you report feeling guilty over what has taken place, even though you have not personally participated in the decision to drop the bomb and even though you were horrified by it. Or consider a German youth of today who reflects upon events during the Nazi period, events that took place before his birth. Imagine that the youth reports feeling guilty over what was done by the Nazis.

Again, as with the former group of cases, doubt might arise, at least initially, over the fit between the feeling and the language used to

[13] See Feinberg, "Collective Responsibility," op. cit., pp. 222–51, and Morris, "Shared Guilt," op. cit., pp. 111–38.

describe it. We may be pulled to thinking that such persons confuse and hence misdescribe their feelings, taking either mortification or anxiety or shame for guilt. In particular, people commonly treat interchangeably the terms "shame" and "guilt"; and if one is in fact feeling shame over what others do, such phenomena seems common and not especially perplexing. Shame, unlike guilt, does not imply individual responsibility. It seems natural that just as one might take pride occasionally in one's American identity, so one might occasionally feel shame because of it. People always have and probably always will, despite commitment to a conception of individual responsibility, think of themselves as worth more or worth less because of what others with whom they identify have done, whether it be a member of their family or sex or race or team.

Although we do sometimes misdescribe our feelings, this explanation does not, I believe, dispose of all cases in which people report feeling guilty over the actions of others. As with cases of unjust enrichment, persons who report feeling guilty reveal guilt's characteristic signs, principally reparative dispositions, dispositions we clearly associate with guilt, but not with shame. Further, their thinking tends to focus less on their worth as persons than on the wrongful deeds that have been performed by those with whom they identify. Their feeling disposes them to confess rather than to hide or flee. Although some, then, may misdescribe their feelings, many, I believe, do not. If they do feel guilty, what might explain it?

Frequently, individuals, while not responsible for wrongdoing, knowingly benefit from it. Few would doubt that one who knowingly receives and utilizes stolen goods is guilty and, should they feel guilty, their feeling would match appropriately their state. But if, for example, a present-day American youth feels guilty over the internment of Japanese-Americans during World War II, the feeling need not, I believe, have its source in some judgment that one has benefited in some way from that internment.

Still another possible explanation connects with a line of argument presented to justify guilt with regard to thought alone. One may believe that only accidental differences exist between oneself and those who have perpetrated wrongs, that chance has placed another rather than oneself in a causal role, and that, consequently, what in one's parents led to their acting wrongfully is equally in oneself. I have no doubt that this may play some role in explaining the guilt experienced by some individuals over what their parents or fellow nationals have done. But this still does not appear to provide an entirely satisfactory explanation for these cases. It is not evident that those who feel guilty are in the grip of a thought such as, "there but for the grace of God go I." One may be thinking of oneself as guilty without judging oneself in this way, think of oneself as guilty just because one is an American or a German. An identification with others, then, may be operative that is not limited to particular aims or dispositions that have led to evil.

If we are attacked, we commonly feel anger toward our attackers. If we ourselves deliberately injure what we care for, we may also understandably reproach ourselves, identifying in so doing a present self with a past self. All of this is straightforwardly understandable because individuals generally possess a sense of self-identity, an identity that extends over time. I suggested earlier that imagined activity in which we identify with some future self might also result in our feeling guilty in the present.

Suppose now that it is another real person with whom we identify – a twin, say, or a parent. If that person is attacked by another, identification implies that the feelings aroused in us are, of course, much the same as if we were ourselves attacked. One's identification with another implies, for example, that we suffer when they do, just as we are pleased when they are. We imagine their feelings, thereby "entering into" them. We have the feelings we imagine them to be having as contrasted with our merely responding in an appropriate way, say with sympathy, to the feelings we imagine them to be having.

Now let us consider what might be felt when an individual with whom we identify engages in wrongdoing. Of course, we retain our own identity at the same time as we identify with the wrongdoer. Consequently, we can suppose we should experience some chagrin, some mortification, some anxiety, at finding ourselves caught up in evil because another has chosen it. But these are essentially "sympathetic," responsive emotions, rather than identificatory ones; they respond to the other's state and do not, as identification implies, enter into it. Identification would have us imagine what our own reactions would be were we the wrongdoer. It does not require that in imagining how another would feel we imagine a state that corresponds to how those with whom we identify do or did in fact feel. They may not, of course, have been feeling guilty; but the process of identification, once operative, carries a psychological momentum so that, in identifying with the person engaged in wrongdoing, one imagines how one would oneself feel, not how the other with whom one identifies actually feels. Ironically, then, one may find oneself feeling responsively guilty – namely, feeling guilty over the fact that those with whom one identifies did not feel guilty when they should have. One takes responsibility for their emotional deficiencies.

Such feelings, derived from identification with others, can of course be carried to pathological extremes. This would be so if one literally believed that when another killed, one had oneself killed. Such delusion is possible. But surely the feelings connected with identificatory processes are often perfectly normal, and it is their total absence that may occasion concern. I believe we understand and may admire a child's assuming special obligations to make amends and reparations for harm done by his or her parents. Such action reveals an unwillingness to abandon one's identity in circumstances where strong inducement exists to reject it. The question, "What does all this have to do with me? I didn't do anything," based upon familiar moral criteria for guilt, may for some strike a frivolous note. For their inclination is to say, "Well, because you are an American and Americans have, after all, the responsibility for the evil that was done." Individuals may assume a responsibility to be what they see themselves as being. Because they have defined themselves in a manner that reveals identification with others, the actions of those others are granted a power over them, determining their feelings and their obligations. Individuals may in these circumstances believe themselves guilty.

We may have great difficulty finding a philosophically satisfying account of personal identity. It is, however, a principal assumption underlying one's ever being guilty. We assume such identity; we take responsibility for what we have done and view ourselves, the guilty person, as the self-same person responsible for wrongdoing. Now, if we accept the legitimacy of identificatory ties moving not just to ourselves when we acted in the past – our not having changed in any relevant way – can we not also find it acceptable that individuals establish those identificatory ties with others and that they may do this without irrationality? We might not ourselves make such commitments; but others reveal through their emotional responses that they have. Some even reveal, as much religious thought makes evident, a scope of identification that embraces the human race. I do not myself presently see that such a position is open to challenge. Again, as with guilt over thought alone and guilt over unjust enrichment, a fundamental moral posture toward the world both underlies and justifies a guilt that diverges from the philosopher's predominant conception of moral guilt.

10

Provocation and culpability

ANDREW VON HIRSCH AND NILS JAREBORG

A perpetrator of a crime deserves reduced punishment, we commonly think, when the conduct has been provoked. Why so? An inquiry into provocation might shed light on the theory of culpability – and particularly, on the seldom considered question of *extent* of culpability.

I

Provocation typically involves situations where the defendant feels wronged by the victim – and responds in anger with the crime with which he or she is charged. The defendant is not warding off any immediate danger, however. Whatever harm was inflicted through the victim's misconduct has already occurred, and may not have involved any physical threat to the defendant.

It cannot be said, in such a situation, that the defendant's conduct is justified.[1] Self-defense against a criminal assault is justified, in that the injury inflicted on the aggressor is deemed the right[2] (or at least a permissible)[3] outcome: Where the actor must be injured if he does

This essay is based on a faculty seminar held at the Law Faculty at Uppsala University, in May 1985. The authors wish to thank the participants, particularly Alvar Nelson, Barry Feld, Ulf Göranson, Lena Holmqvist, and Lennart Åqvist for their contributions to the discussion. The authors are grateful also to Michael Moore, Ferdinand Schoeman, Richard Singer, and P. O. Träskman for their helpful comments on the manuscript.

[1] On justification and excuse generally, see J. L. Austin, "A Plea for Excuses," *Proceedings of the Aristotelian Society* 57 (1957): 1, reprinted in J. L. Austin, *Philosophical Papers* (Oxford: Oxford University Press, 1961), chap. 6; H. L. A. Hart, *Punishment and Responsibility* (Oxford: Oxford University Press, 1968), chaps. 1 and 2; Eric D'Arcy, *Human Acts* (Oxford: Oxford University Press, 1963), chap. 2; Jerome Hall, *Principles of the Criminal Law*, 2nd ed. (Indianapolis: Bobbs-Merrill, 1960), 232–7.

[2] On justification as involving situations where the outcome is right in the circumstances, see George Fletcher, *Rethinking Criminal Law* (Boston: Little, Brown, 1978), 759, 769–73.

[3] On justification as involving situations where the outcome is permissible but not necessarily desirable in the circumstances, see Joshua Dressler, "New Thoughts About the Concept of Justification in the Criminal Law: A Critique of Fletcher's Thinking and Rethinking," *UCLA Law Review* 32 (1984): 61.

not hurt his assailant, the law deems it preferable that the assailant suffer.[4] The provoked defendant, however, is not acting in self-defense, but only retaliating in anger after the provoking event. The actor might have exercised restraint without suffering further injury from the provoker.

If self-defense is not involved, could it be argued that the victim "had it coming" – that the act is justified or partially justified as a response the victim deserves? Surely not. Although the victim might deserve punishment, the actor lacks authority to inflict it. Penalizing malefactors is not a legitimate role for an individual; it is a state function, to be undertaken with appropriate due process safeguards.[5]

If not justifiable, can the conduct be *excused*? Conduct is excused in certain situations where – although the outcome is not deemed desirable – the actor should be exempted from blame for acting as she or he did.[6] Textbook examples are situations of duress and necessity, where the defendant injures an innocent victim, in order to avert a threat to his own life or safety from another source, human or natural.[7] But the provoked actor faces no immediate threat from any such source if he refrains from retaliating. He also is claiming extenuation only, not complete exoneration. Theories of excuse in the substantive criminal law could thus be applicable only by analogy – to suggest why provocation constitutes a *partial* excuse, warranting reduction of punishment.

In common law, provocation was treated as an extenuating circumstance in cases of homicide. There, it reduced the degree of homicide from murder to manslaughter.[8] The common-law doctrine stressed two elements. First, the act had to be done in hot anger, shortly after the victim's provoking behavior, when the person had virtually lost his

---

[4] *Model Penal Code* §3.04; *German Penal Code* (Strafgesetzbuch) §32; *Swedish Penal Code* (Brottsbalken) §24:1.

[5] The reasons for not giving individuals the right to inflict purportedly deserved punishment should be familiar enough. They include the lack of sufficient safeguards that the supposed wrongdoer obtain a fair determination of guilt, or punishment commensurate with the gravity of the offense. Private retribution would, in our judgment, offend against basic ideas of a *Rechtstaat*.

[6] On excuse as involving situations where the outcome is undesirable but the actor should be exempted from blame, see Fletcher, *Rethinking*, 577–9.

[7] Where the threat comes from another actor, the defense is duress. *Model Penal Code* §2.09 and, in somewhat different fashion, *German Penal Code* §35 and *Swedish Penal Code* §23:5. When the threat comes from natural circumstances, the defense is necessity. For the present legal status of the necessity defense, see text accompanying notes 18–20.

[8] Richard G. Singer, "The Resurgence of Mens Rea: I – Provocation, Emotional Distress and the Model Penal Code," *Boston College Law Review* 27 (1986): 243; Paul H. Robinson, *Criminal Law Defenses* (St. Paul, MN: West, 1984), vol. 1, 480–1, 484–7; see also *German Penal Code* §213.

capacity for self-control. If the actor waited and had an opportunity to cool off, he would no longer qualify. Second, the victim's misbehavior had to be of such an aggravated nature as would cause a "reasonable person" to lose control.[9] There was a manifest tension between the first of these requirements, stressing the actor's subjective state, and the second, referring to what a hypothetical reasonable person would do. Many of the oddities of the case law on provocation reflect this tension.[10] The common law doctrine's rationale, however, received little critical examination.

Outside of homicide, provocation was merely a factor for the court to consider when imposing sentence. No legal doctrine was thought necessary, since the choice of sentence was a matter for judicial discretion. It was not even clear how much that choice should depend on the actor's culpability: According to traditional rehabilitation doctrine, the sentence was supposed to depend instead on the offender's treatability and likelihood of returning to crime.[11]

Now, however, sentencing theory is giving more emphasis to the offender's deserts – to the degree of gravity of his criminal acts.[12] This increases the importance of issues of culpability. There also is movement toward regulating sentencing discretion and making factors of extenuation and exacerbation explicit. New sentencing guidelines, such as Minnesota's and Washington's, list provocation as a mitigating factor justifying a sentence below the normally recommended levels.[13] Once provocation is given an explicit role in deciding the sentence, it becomes important to decide how that notion should be interpreted.

Should we carry over, from homicide law, the restrictive doctrines concerning hot anger and the reasonable person? To decide, we need to examine the conceptual basis for provocation. That examination, in turn, requires us to begin on more familiar ground: with the con-

[9] Singer, "The Resurgence of Mens Rea"; J. W. Cecil Turner, *Russell on Crime,* 12th ed. (London: Stevens, 1984), 517–53; Glanville Williams, *Textbook of Criminal Law,* 2nd ed. (London: Stevens, 1983), chap. 24.
[10] These oddities are well documented in Singer, op. cit.
[11] Andrew von Hirsch, *Past or Future Crimes: Dangerousness and Deservedness in the Sentencing of Criminals* (New Brunswick, NJ: Rutgers University Press, 1985), chap. 1.
[12] Ibid., chaps. 3–7.
[13] The Minnesota guidelines list as a mitigating factor that "the victim was an aggressor in the incident." *Minnesota Sentencing Guildelines and Commentary* §II.D.2.a(1); the Washington guidelines make it a mitigating factor that "to a significant degree, the victim was an . . . aggressor, or provoker of the incident." *Rev. Code of Washington* §9.94A.120. For a description and analysis of the Minnesota and Washington guidelines, see Andrew von Hirsch, Kay A. Knapp, and Michael Tonry, *The Sentencing Commission and Its Guidelines* (Boston: Northeastern University Press, 1987), chaps. 2, 5, and 8.

cept of culpability as it applies to excuses. If we understand why certain conduct should be excused completely, we may better comprehend why other conduct warrants extenuation.

II

One notion of culpability concerns the defendant's capacity to conform. A person is not culpable to the extent that his or her ability to exercise self-control was impaired when engaging in the conduct.[14] The theory has its simplest application in the requirement of a voluntary act: Injuring someone during a convulsion is not criminal,[15] because no volition whatever is involved. It also undergirds some excuses, such as that of insanity. The person is not culpable when his mental condition deprived him of a minimal capacity for choice.[16]

Does this conception exhaust the idea of culpability? It has sometimes been treated as though it does: There has been a tendency to assimilate excuses to questions of the volitional character of the actor's behavior.[17] We see this occurring with the defense of necessity. Necessity addresses situations where, through disastrous natural circumstances, the actor must kill or injure an innocent person to forestall imminent death or injury to himself. The paradigm case is the castaway who kills and eats his companion in the lifeboat, in order to save himself from starving. The English common law rejected this defense in a celebrated case decided a century ago,[18] but some American jurisdictions are beginning to allow it and recognize its status as an excuse.[19] The German penal code has long recognized excusing necessity.[20]

An often-heard explanation of the necessity excuse emphasizes the actor's having no other option.[21] Since death was the only alternative,

---

[14] See Hart, *Punishment and Responsibility*, chaps. 2 and 6; Gary Dubin, "Mens Rea Reconsidered: A Plea for a Due Process Concept of Criminal Responsibility," *Stanford Law Review* 18 (1966): 322; Nils Jareborg, "The Two faces of Culpa," *Revue Internationale de Droit Pénale* 50 (1979): 307, 325–40.

[15] *Model Penal Code* §2.01(2)(a).

[16] See, e.g., *Model Penal Code* §4.01. The insanity defense also has a well-known cognitive branch that exonerates the defendant when his mental condition deprives him of the capacity to understand the act's character or wrongfulness. Ibid.

[17] See Fletcher, *Rethinking*, 802–7.

[18] *Regina* v. *Dudley and Stephens*, 14 Q.B.D. 273 (1884). See also A. W. Brian Simpson, *Cannibalism and the Common Law* (Chicago: University of Chicago Press, 1984).

[19] *People* v. *Lovercamp*, 43 Cal. App. 3d 823, 118 Cal. Rptr. 110 (1974). See also Herbert Fingarette, "Victimization: A Legalist Analysis of Coercion, Deception, Undue Influence, and Excusable Prison Escape," *Washington & Lee Law Review* 42 (1985): 65.

[20] *German Penal Code* §35.

[21] See, e.g., George Fletcher, "Rights and Excuses," *Criminal Justice Ethics* 3 (1984): 17, 23.

how could he or she have refrained? The extremity of the circumstances – his fear of extinction, and weakened, hunger-induced mental condition – makes it unrealistic to attribute any real choice to the actor. But how convincing is this explanation? The threat of imminent death does not necessarily deprive an actor of the capacity to decide. People can (and sometimes do) *choose* to die when continuing to live entails consequences they cannot accept. The castaway *could* prefer his own death to killing someone else, and some high-minded persons might so act. Lack of food and water may affect someone's judgment, but – as one of us has elaborated elsewhere[22] – it does not necessarily do so enough so to negate the actor's control over his acts.

If we turn to provocation, how useful is the idea of diminished volition? Some commentators, including H. L. A. Hart,[23] invoke it – and it does seem reflected in the common law's requirement that the act be done in hot anger. An act done in the heat of the moment, arguably, is less than fully volitional. True, the actor had *some* choice, which is why the conduct is not fully excused. His ability to exercise self-control is diminished, however, by the immediacy of the affront and the lack of time to regain composure. When I lash out in fury, I am not quite myself, and may be less culpable. If I wait, brood, and *then* strike, how can I assert the act is not fully my choice?

What is troublesome about the volition theory, however, is that it focuses entirely on the defendant's emotional state. As long as the circumstances have so enraged him as to becloud his capacity for choice, just why he became enraged would hardly matter. Yet provocation, as ordinarily understood, seems to involve misconduct on the part of the victim to which the defendant *properly* could take offense. The reasons for the actor's choice should count, not merely the capacity to choose.

III

If we wish to seek reasons for action, why not those related to self-preservation?[24] An actor is not culpable, arguably, if he or she acted

---

[22] For discussion of why necessity cannot be explained in terms of impaired volition, see Andrew von Hirsch, "Review Essay: Lifeboat Law," *Criminal Justice Ethics* 4 (1985): 88, 92–3.

[23] Thus Hart asserts: "In cases . . . exemplified in 'provocation' and 'diminished responsibility,' if we punish at all we punish *less*, on the footing that, although the accused's capacity for self-control was not absent its exercise was a matter of abnormal difficulty." Hart, *Punishment and Responsibility*, 153.

[24] Self-preservation is also an element of the justification of self-defense, but not the sole element. The crucial added component – that which makes it a justification – is the idea of it being preferable that the assailant instead of the victim should suffer the harm. See text accompanying note 4, *supra*.

to preserve certain vital interests. Notice that we no longer are speaking of the actor's control over the act. Even if the actor is quite capable of choice and deliberately commits the act, he still is not culpable if he acts to safeguard sufficiently important interests of his own.

This theory explains some excuses better – notably, that of necessity. Why should the castaway be excused? Because he acts to preserve the most vital interest, his life. Why is one not to blame for preferring one's own life? Because someone is not to blame for failing to be a saint. Insisting on law-abiding behavior when its consequence is the actor's own death would be demanding extraordinary qualities of altruism.[25]

To understand this rationale, one must distinguish between sufficient reason for an act's being right or permissible, all things considered, and good reason for acting, given the actor's situation. In situations of necessity, the actor's need for self-preservation is *not* a sufficient reason for killing the victim, all things considered, because the innocent victim's life has as much value as the actor's. That is why the act should not be considered justified.[26] Self-preservation is nevertheless a good reason for the actor's conduct – because he has only his own life to lead and must act as he did to continue it. We wish to withhold blame from the actor because we recognize the importance, from the actor's perspective, of continuing his life. We speak of not demanding saintliness from the actor, because saintliness consists precisely in a heroic willingness to sacrifice one's own vital interests to higher purposes. While admiring such willingness, we feel we scarcely can blame someone for not having it.[27]

Can this theory explain provocation? Not so easily, since it is not obvious how the person is defending any vital interests. The provoking victim's misconduct, as we noted at the outset, has *already* occurred; it is not a case protecting oneself against injury.

It might be argued, however, that the provoked actor – while not acting to preserve his or her life as is the person in the lifeboat – is trying to protect a secondary, social interest. When the actor is wrong-

---

[25] See von Hirsch, "Review Essay: Lifeboat Law," 92–3.

[26] Ibid., 90–1.

[27] In accounting for such excuses, German scholars have developed a principle of *Zumutbarkeit*, or *Vorwerfbarkeit:* that blame should be withheld in circumstances where demanding compliance cannot fairly be expected. See Hans-Heinrich Jescheck, *Lehrbuch des Strafrechts: Allgemeiner Teil,* 3rd ed. (Berlin: Duncker and Humblot, 1978), 394–5, 408–10. The difficulty with this principle is the elastic character of the concept of fair expectation: It does not illuminate *what* it is that may or may not fairly be expected, or *why* so. It is preferable to devise more specific explanations – such as that of self-preservation – that do not contain such question-begging qualifiers as fairness or excessiveness.

ed and does not respond, he is *shamed*. The shame does not pass when the provoking act is completed, but continues to the present: If the actor fails to act and lets the provoker get away with the conduct, the actor is diminished in his own eyes and in those of others. One needn't assert that it is *desirable* for the defendant to reclaim his standing in this fashion, since one is not asserting the conduct to be justified. Nor need one claim that the interest in one's standing is as important as the interest in physical self-preservation, since one is not claiming the conduct to be excused completely. However, the interest in not being shamed surely might have *some* significance in a person's life. As long as it has, does the person not deserve reduced blame if he or she offends to safeguard that interest?

The argument has plausibility in certain special situations – oddly, not very attractive ones. Consider the classic "affair of honor." *A*, the actor, lives in a place having mores comparable to those of Sicily a few decades ago. He discovers, and it becomes publicly known, that his eventual victim, *V*, is having an illicit romance with his wife. If he does not retaliate, he becomes an object of scorn in the community. He strikes back at *V* to preserve his own good name.[28]

One might well object to the social convention to which *A* is deferring, the convention about cuckolded husbands' "honor." This convention is manifestly sexist and also reflects warped moral priorities, in that it treats marital fidelity as having more importance than human life or safety. *A*, however, would have an answer. He does not need to defend the code of marital honor, because he is not claiming his action to be justified. Adulterers might deserve to have nothing befall them. What he is asserting, instead, is in the nature of a partial excuse. It is a fact in his community – whether desirable or not – that cuckolds are publicly scorned if they take no action; the risk to his good name stems simply from that fact. The *only* way he could prevent himself from being publicly treated with contempt is to act as he did. To deny his extenuation because one thinks the community has no business shunning complacent husbands is akin to denying the necessity excuse because one thinks the typhoon had no business sinking the defendant's ship and making him and his victim castaways.

---

[28] An actual case of this nature comes to mind. The defendant, an immigrant worker in a papermill a half-century ago, was – while drunk and semiunconscious – sodomized by a fellow worker. The perpetrator of the act of sodomy informed the defendant's friends, who taunted the defendant as effeminate. After receiving this abuse for some days, the defendant killed the person who thus had shamed him. *State* v. *Gounagias,* 153 Pac. 9 (Washington S. Ct. 1915).

We leave it to readers to consider whether one should accept our hypothetical Sicilian gentleman's claim to extenuation – and suspect their judgment will not be unanimous. We point out, however, how special this situation is, in that the actor faces a *real* threat to an objective, definable interest in reputation. He will actually be shunned if he does not retaliate.

The theory thus cannot explain ordinary situations of provocation. There, the actor commits the crime simply because he or she is outraged by the victim's conduct. Neither reputation nor any other definable, present interest is at stake. While the betrayed husband or wife may be very angry, in a typical Swedish or American neighborhood he or she will not be ostracized for failing to act. Unlike the case of the man in the lifeboat, it cannot be argued that refraining from the crime will make the actor's position worse. The claim of extenuation comes not from currently threatened interests, but from the defendant's sense of grievance.

This complicates matters. When explaining necessity and duress, we could focus on the defendant's reasons for the action, as our theory of self-preservation did. The person's psychic state need not be considered in deciding whether or not to excuse.

With provocation, however, psychology is unavoidable. The central feature of provocation situations is the actor's sense of outrage at the victim's conduct. Psychology, however, has not had a happy history in the criminal law. Psychological issues have tended to be couched in reductionist terms that treat feelings, motives, and reasons interchangeably. To account for provocation, we have to be more careful.

IV

We require, therefore, a third account. To provide it, let us state – and then explain – what we call the principle of resentment. The principle offers extenuation (though not complete exoneration) when *the actor acts in anger at the victim, and has good reason for being angry in virtue of some wrong or impropriety suffered at this victim's hands.* As this statement should make clear, having been angered by the victim is not enough. All sorts of things V does might exasperate A, and some things V does may infuriate A so much as to make it hard for him to exercise self-control. It is normally up to the actor, nevertheless, to restrain his temper. What is crucial to A's claim of extenuation is his having had *good reason* for his anger, stemming from some misdeed committed by the victim against him or someone close to him. Let us emphasize, however: It is only A's *anger* that is warranted, not the deed that results from it. The criminal act, we should recall, is not justified, but only, perhaps, less culpable because of the nature of the sentiment involved.

The sentiment is a familiar one in everyday discourse: outrage or, as it once aptly was called, *resentment*. When someone else gets something that I want for myself, I may be angery, but I have no justification for my anger. If my competitor has lied or cheated, however, I now have a valid reason: I *resent*. In the former case of mere anger, I should do my best to control my feelings. In the latter case, I am entitled not only to feel displeasure, but to manifest it to the cheater in an appropriate fashion. The distinction between anger and resentment has been explored by a few philosophers: Joseph Butler in his "Sermon on Resentment" written two centuries ago,[29] P. F. Strawson in his 1962 essay, "Freedom and Resentment,"[30] and Jeffrie Murphy in a useful recent treatment.[31]

The displeasure that is occasioned by wrongdoing is commonly termed *indignation* when strangers are the victims. One can be indignant about all sorts of misdeeds in this troubled world: from repression in Chile or South Africa to neglect of the poor at home. The sentiment is termed *resentment*, however, when that wrongdoing is directed against oneself or someone to whom one is close.[32] One resents being swindled. (Lately, the word has been corrupted to signify any long-harbored animus, as in "He resents his brother's success"; but we adhere to the word's original, moral significance.)[33]

When one is wronged, Murphy points out,[34] anger may be the *appropriate* response. If I cannot resent serious wrongs done to me, I may have a deficient sense of my own worth and assign too little value to my own rights. The logic of resentment is that it is not only occa-

[29] Joseph Butler, *Fifteen Sermons* (1726), sermon 8.
[30] P. F. Strawson, "Freedom and Resentment," *Proceedings of the British Academy*, vol. XLVIII (1962), reprinted in P. F. Strawson, *Freedom and Resentment and Other Essays* (London: Methuen, 1974), chap. 1.
[31] Jeffrie G. Murphy, "Forgiveness and Resentment," in *Midwest Studies in Philosophy, VII: Social and Political Philosophy*, ed. P. A. Finch, T. E. Uhling, Jr., and H. K. Wetterstein (Minneapolis: University of Minnesota Press, 1982), 503–16.
[32] Resentment differs from desire for vengeance, in that the latter may not involve any moral judgment at all. The wish to avenge may be triggered by an accidental injury. The object of the vengeance may not be the original wrongdoer, but someone connected with him, such as a member of his family. In clan feuds, if the original perpetrator died, one took vengeance on his child or relative, although they had nothing to do with the triggering incident.
[33] The *Oxford English Dictionary* defines resentment as "a strong feeling of ill-will or anger against the author or authors of a wrong or affront." *Oxford English Dictionary* (Oxford: Oxford University Press, 1933), vol. 8, 510.
[34] Murphy, "Forgiveness and Resentment."

sioned but warranted by the behavior of the person at whom it is directed.

Although more could be said about the sentiment of resentment, our question is narrower: the connection between resentment and partial excuse in the criminal law. We need to explain why acting out of resentment makes a person less blameworthy, and hence entitled to extenuation.

Does resentment make it particularly difficult to control one's actions? Sometimes, it might – but that cannot be the explanation. Any strong ill feeling can impel its possessor toward action against the person who occasions it. The strength of the feeling cannot be extenuating in itself, however, since the criminal law aims precisely at helping us control intense emotions of hatred, rage, and the like. To understand why resentment may be extenuating, we need to look not at the intensity of the feeling, but at the interaction between that feeling and the moral inhibitions which are supposed to control it.

When one is angry, one's moral sense should serve only as, so to speak, a bridle to the passions. Its proper role is to keep the anger in check and prevent it from spilling over into action. Ordinarily, there is nothing equivocal about that restraining role. If the self-restraint fails, then one's moral inhibitions have not functioned as they should, and that hardly makes one any less to blame.

In situations of resentment, however, the role of the moral sense is more equivocal: It becomes the spur as well as the bridle to the passions. Having been wronged, one is *properly* angry. Far from having a purely suppressing role, one's sense of right and wrong is part of what prompts and gives legitimacy to the anger. Not only is the feeling legitimate, but so are various forms of acting the feeling out: displaying outrage and taking a variety of steps against the instigator. It is only *certain* forms of acting out that are wrong and that one's moral sense should inhibit. Conscience thus has a divided role, of encouraging animus against the instigator, prompting one to take certain actions against him, and yet restraining one from making other kinds of responses. This divided role complicates self-restraint in fallible human beings, and our sympathy for the provoked person – our sense of the appropriateness of extenuation – stems therefrom.

The difficulty, it should be noticed, is not purely cognitive. The distinction between permissible and impermissible responses to wrongdoing may be apparent enough: I may remonstrate with the colleague who wrongs me, complain to other colleagues, possibly even invoke departmental or university action; but I may not assault him or burn his latest manuscript. Where the problem lies is in the translation of such knowledge into action. When one is very angry, it takes a strong effort of moral self-restraint to desist. When one's moral sense helps generate the anger as well as being supposed to hold it back, however, then mustering the appropriate self-restraint at just the right stopping point is more complicated. There stands my awful colleague before me, laughing off the remonstrance I think myself entitled to make, telling me he is proud of his affront to me, and telling me the university and my other colleagues will ignore my protests. A part of my sense of right tells me I should do *something*, while another part may tell me I may not go too far. If I do go too far then I am surely to blame, but the degree of blame that is appropriate is less than that for an unprovoked assault. Blame is reduced because the actor was moved to transgress in part because of, rather than despite, his sense of right and wrong.

This should also explain why there should be *good* reason for the actor's sense of injury or affront. When the actor has taken affront without just cause, then his sense of values is merely deficient, and he has no particular claim to our sympathy. Provocation becomes a persuasive claim when the actor's animus testifies to the soundness, not to the deficiency, of his moral judgment. It is where an actor both *should* feel angry and yet must try to control that justifiable anger that he or she becomes less to blame for overstepping the bounds.

V

With this much theory in place, we now can examine traditional provocation doctrine. Should "hot anger" (i.e., action immediately after the provoking event) be required? Should the "reasonableness" test be retained?

Consider the following case. *A* sits on his lawn, watching his child play with a ball. The ball rolls onto the street and, before *A* can stop him, the child rushes out to retrieve it. He is struck and severely injured by a car, driven by *V*, that is proceeding slowly down the street. In rage and despair, *A* seizes the lawn chair he is sitting on and strikes *V* with it. He is charged with and convicted for assault, and now urges a mitigated punishment.

A has certainly acted in hot anger. However, he has no just reason for being enraged at *V*, since the injury was manifestly not *V*'s fault. If mitigation is sought, its basis would have to be our first theory, about capacity to conform. The shock, it would have to be argued, was so great as temporarily to diminish *A*'s capacity for self-control. One could not utilize our theory concerning resentment, because *A* does not have *good* reason for outrage at *V*'s conduct.

When the conformity principle is thus the grounds for claiming mitigation, the common law's requirement of acting in hot anger would make sense. The claim to impairment of volition is most plausible in the proximate aftermath of the event, when the actor's inhibitions and reflective capacities have not had the chance to reassert themselves. True, *A* could become still angrier with lapse of time, as he broods over his child's injuries; but lapse of time should also allow his powers of self-control opportunity to recuperate. If he waits a day and then assaults *V*, he may be angrier than ever, but it becomes progressively less plausible to assert to act was less than fully his choice. On the other hand, the "reasonable person" test seems inappropriate in this situation. When someone is made so upset that his volition is impaired, the basis for mitigation is not the rationality of his choices, but the choices not being fully the person's own. (The ultimate case of lost volition involves the excuse of insanity, and that scarcely could be a matter of the "reasonableness" of the behavior!)

Let us, however, alter the facts of the case. *V* is a neighbor who has often before harassed *A*'s child. The injury occurred because, while *A* was temporarily in the house, *V* goaded the child into playing "bumper tag" with him in his car, and the injury was occasioned by the grossest negligence, if not actual spite. Suppose *A* commits the assault on *V* after some hours of reflection.

This is now a case of acting in outrage. The injury to the child is *V*'s fault, and *A* has good reason for his anger at *V*. The basis for mitigation would be different: our principle of resentment.

Here, the "hot anger" requirement of common law ceases to make sense. Since the claim no longer is that the person had his capacity for choice impaired, the momentary shock of the event is immaterial. What now matters is *A*'s being angry for good reasons – and the sense of grievance may grow. The anger is not just a momentary emotional turbulence, and involves as much cognition as feeling; it may last, reinforced by the sense of having been aggrieved.

What of the other common-law requirement, that a "reasonable person" would react similarly? Here, the requirement is not totally misplaced. It serves as a proxy – although a clumsy and imprecise one – for something that *is* essential to the resentment principle: namely, that the actor should have good reason for his anger.[35]

---

[35] A somewhat better formulation is the requirement of "adequate" provocation, set forth in some statutes [e.g., *Maine Statutes*, tit. 17-A, §203(1) (B)]. This requirement, however, is often merely put in as an addition or elaboration of the "reasonableness" standard, as is true in Maine (§203(2)(B)).

What, then, should the standard for provocation be? We propose that the common law requirements be replaced by two separate tests, reflecting the two conceptions of impaired volition and resentment, respectively.[36] Let us take each in turn.

The first test is based on diminished volition. Its criterion would be that the actor had become so infuriated[37] as temporarily to suffer partial loss of the capacity for choice. The scope of this claim might vary with the jurisdiction's general rules on diminished capacity, but our preference would be to keep the standard narrow, to cover only the clearest cases of impairment of the will.[38]

If this first test is not met, one would proceed to a second test, based on the principle of resentment. This would be true provocation in the ordinary sense of that term. The criterion would be that the actor acted in anger after having been wronged by the victim. The victim's wrongdoing would supply the grounds for anger that the principle requires; and that, in turn, would eliminate the need to speculate on how the hypothetical "reasonable person" might have responded. There also would, for reasons just discussed, be no requirement that the actor must act immediately after the provoking conduct. It is not enough, however, to show merely that the actor *felt* aggrieved by the victim's conduct, or that others of his background might feel similarly. To establish a case for provocation under the resentment principle, one must show that the actor's sense of grievance was in some fashion warranted.

How should we determine whether the actor has been sufficiently wronged to satisfy the resentment principle? The most straightforward cases are those where the victim's acts constituted criminal behavior of a significant nature. Instances would include our just-cited

---

[36] This possibility, of two *separate* grounds for mitigation – one based on diminished volition and the other on justified anger – is suggested in Andrew Ashworth, *Sentencing and Penal Policy* (London: Weidenfeld and Nicholson, 1983), 168.

[37] There should, arguably, be a similar doctrine of diminished volition based on fear instead of anger. That might reduce the punishment for acts done in panic during an emergency, even where the act cannot be excused on grounds of necessity. The *Model Penal Code* provides that murder is reduced to manslaughter if the act was committed "under the influence of extreme . . . emotional distress for which there is reasonable explanation. . . ." *Model Penal Code* §210.3(1)(b); Robinson, *Criminal Law Defenses* vol. 1, 488–91. This distress could include fear as well as anger – and the doctrine might be extended beyond homicide.

[38] We wish to restrict this claim because it deals, ex hypothesi, with situations of unwarranted anger. The normally plausible situations of provocation – where the actor has been wronged by the victim – will have been dealt with through our principle of resentment. What remains are only cases where the actor has not been wronged but reacts nevertheless (for whatever reason) with such extreme emotions as to impair his capacity for choice. Here, in our judgment, extenuation should be granted only when a strong case of impairment has been made.

case of the victim's injuring the actor or his dependents through gross negligence or malice; cases of battered wives who eventually assault their spouses in circumstances not justifiable as self-defense; and cases of retaliation against the theft or destruction of valued property. Here, the reprehensibleness of the victim's behavior is manifest, and so is the actor's reason for outrage.

The next class of cases comprise those where the victim behaved toward the actor in a manner that is not criminal, but nevertheless infringes commonly recognized standards of decent behavior. Where civil law recognizes the wrongfulness of such conduct (for example, by providing a tort remedy), the answer may be straightforward enough. The difficulty arises when the conduct is reprehensible but not illegal at all – as are various personal calumnies and betrayals. Here, the victim's actions may still be plainly wrong by any common-sense assessment, but fashioning a standard of wrongdoing for the courts' guidance will be no easy matter. Whether and to what extent to recognize legal but wrongful conduct would depend, therefore, on our confidence in sentencing courts' ability to distinguish it from innocuous behavior on the victim's part.[39]

What about conduct that is not harmful, but merely insulting? The answer depends upon whether, in a plural society, insults should be regarded as substantial grievances. Our own inclination would be ordinarily to deny insult this status, but the matter may warrant further discussion.

What if the victim was apparently at fault, but not actually so? Suppose V, when he injured A's child, seemed to be driving negligently, but (unknown to A) had actually suffered an epileptic or psychotic episode. A's claim to extenuation should still be sustained. The resentment principle is concerned with the actor's having rational grounds for his anger, not with the victim's actual deserts.[40]

[39] The courts may more readily be able to make such judgments in countries such as Sweden, having considerable social cohesion and consensus on limits of permissible behavior, than in countries with deeper social tensions and normative disagreements, such as the United States.

[40] A final issue concerns victim wrongdoing directed at someone other than the actor. The principle of resentment, as we have described it, concerns *personal* resentment, where the actor has suffered in some fashion from the victim's wrongdoing. This includes injuries or affronts to persons close to the actor – since the actor has an interest in the welfare of such persons. Where the wronged individual is someone having no particular connection to the actor, however, the principle would not apply. The actor might still be indignant – but the notion of justified personal resentment no longer holds. Having in no fashion been injured by the victim, the actor has no good reason for responding with such anger that the normal moral restraints are understandably compromised. The actor cannot claim the principle of resentment when he "punishes" someone for wrongdoing directed at third persons.

The law of provocation has suffered from the lack of a coherent theoretical basis. We hope our suggested principle of resentment will furnish such a basis. It is only that idea we have sketched; we have not provided, nor intended to provide, the doctrinal particulars. Once the theory is established, however, courts and commentators should be able to fill in those specifics.

We also hope that our discussion of provocation makes it clear that culpability is a much more complex notion than legal writers have traditionally assumed. It is not enough to consider questions of volition and self-control: The reasons for the actor's conduct are equally important. Those reasons, moreover, cannot be boiled down to concerns about defending specific interests; the actor's feelings, and their moral basis, are likewise important.

11

Responsibility and the limits of evil
Variations on a Strawsonian theme

GARY WATSON

> Responsibility is . . . one aspect of the identity of character and conduct.
> We are responsible for our conduct because that conduct is ourselves
> objectified in actions.
> — John Dewey, "Outlines of a Critical Theory of Ethics"

> There is nothing regrettable about finding oneself, in the last analysis, left
> with something which one cannot choose to accept or reject. What one is
> left with is probably just oneself, a core without which there could be no
> choice belonging to the person at all. Some unchosen restrictions on
> choice are among the conditions of its possibility.
> — Thomas Nagel, *The Possibility of Altruism*

> Our practices do not merely exploit our natures, they express them.
> — Peter Strawson, "Freedom and Resentment"

Introduction

Regarding people as responsible agents is evidently not just a matter
of belief. So regarding them means something in practice. It is shown
in an embrace or a thank you, in an act of reprisal or obscene gesture,
in a feeling of resentment or sense of obligation, in an apology or
demand for an apology. To regard people as responsible agents is to
be ready to treat them in certain ways.

In "Freedom and Resentment,"[1] Peter Strawson is concerned to
describe these forms of treatment and their presuppositions. As his
title suggests, Strawon's focus is on such attitudes and responses as
gratitude and resentment, indignation, approbation, guilt, shame,
(some kinds of) pride, hurt feeling, (asking and giving) forgiveness,
and (some kinds of) love. All traditional theories of moral responsibility acknowledge connections between these attitudes and holding one
another responsible. What is original to Strawson is the way in which

To Sally Haslanger and Brian Skyrms, I am grateful for discussing bits and pieces of
this material with me; to Ferdinand Schoeman, for comments on an earlier draft.

[1] *Proceedings of the British Academy,* 1962, reprinted in *Free Will,* edited by Gary Watson,
Oxford University Press, 1982, pp. 59–80. Hereafter, page references in the text will
be to the latter edition.

they are linked. Whereas traditional views have taken these attitudes to be secondary to seeing others as responsible, to be practical corollaries or emotional side effects of some independently comprehensible belief in responsibility, Strawon's radical claim is that these "reactive attitudes" (as he calls them) are *constitutive* of moral responsibility; to regard oneself or another as responsible just is the proneness to react to them in these kinds of ways under certain conditions. There is no more basic belief which provides the justification or rationale for these reactions. The practice does not rest on a theory at all, but rather on certain needs and aversions that are basic to our conception of being human. The idea that there is or needs to be such an independent basis is where traditional views, in Strawson's opinion, have gone badly astray.

For a long time, I have found Strawson's approach salutary and appealing. Here my aim is not to defend it as superior to its alternatives, but to do something more preliminary. A comparative assessment is not possible without a better grasp of what Strawson's theory (or a Strawsonian theory)[2] *is*. As Strawson presents it, the theory is incomplete in important respects. I will investigate whether and how the incompleteness can be remedied in Strawsonian ways. In the end, I find that certain features of our practice of holding responsible are rather resistant to such remedies, and that the practice is less philosophically innocent than Strawson supposes. I hope that the issues uncovered by this investigation will be of sufficient importance to interest even those who are not as initially sympathetic to Strawson's approach as I am.[3]

Strawson's theory

Strawson presents the rivals to his view as responses to a prima facie problem posed by determinism. One rival – consequentialism – holds that blaming and praising judgments and acts are to be understood, and justified, as forms of social regulation. Apart from the question of its extensional adequacy, consequentialism seems to many to leave out something vital to our practice. By emphasizing their instrumental efficacy, it distorts the fact that our responses are typically personal reactions to the individuals in question that we sometimes think of as

[2] My interpretation of Strawson's essay will be in many places very conjectural; and I will sometimes signal this fact by speaking of a "Strawsonian" theory.
[3] I have learned much from the penetrating exploration of Strawson's essay by Jonathan Bennett: "Accountability," in *Philosophical Subjects*, edited by Zak van Straaten, Oxford: Clarendon Press, 1980, pp. 14–47.

eminently appropriate reactions quite aside from concern for effects. Rightly "recoiling" from the consequentialist picture, some philosophers have supposed that responsibility requires a libertarian foundation, that to bring the "vital thing" back in, we must embrace a certain metaphysics of human agency. This is the other rival.

What these otherwise very different views share is the assumption that our reactive attitudes commit us to the truth of some independently apprehensible proposition which gives the content of the belief in responsibility; and so either the search is on for the formulation of this proposition, or we must rest content with an intuition of its content. For the social-regulation theorist, this is a proposition about the standard effects of having and expressing reactive attitudes. For the libertarian, it is a proposition concerning metaphysical freedom. Since the truth of the former is consistent with the thesis of determinism, the consequentialist is a compatibilist; since the truth of the latter is shown or seen not to be, the libertarian is an incompatibilist.

In Strawson's view, there is no such independent notion of responsibility that explains the propriety of the reactive attitudes. The explanatory priority is the other way around: It is not that we hold people responsible because they *are* responsible; rather, the idea (*our* idea) that we are responsible is to be understood by the practice, which itself is not a matter of holding some propositions to be true, but of expressing our concerns and demands about our treatment of one another. These stances and responses are expressions of certain rudimentary needs and aversions: "It matters to us whether the actions of other people . . . reflect attitudes toward us of good will, affection, or esteem on the one hand or contempt, indifference, or malevolence on the other." Accordingly, the reactive attitudes are "natural human reactions to the good or ill will or indifference of others toward us [or toward those we care about] as displayed in *their* attitudes and actions" (p. 67). Taken together, they express "the demand for the manifestation of a reasonable degree of good will or regard, on the part of others, not simply towards oneself, but towards all those on whose behalf moral indignation may be felt . . ." (p. 71).

Hence, Strawson accuses rival conceptions of "overintellectualizing" our practices. In their emphasis on social regulation, consequentialists lose sight of sentiments these practices directly express, without which the notion of moral responsibility cannot be understood. Libertarians see the gaping hole in the consequentialist account, but rather than acknowledging that "it is just these attitudes themselves which fill the gap" (p. 79), they seek to ground these attitudes in a metaphysical intuition – "a pitiful intellectualist trinket for a philosopher to wear as a charm against the recognition of his own humanity" (p. 79). Holding responsible is as natural and primitive in human life as friendship and animosity, sympathy and antipathy. It rests on needs and concerns that are not so much to be justified as acknowledged.

Excusing and exempting

To say that holding responsible is to be explained by the range of reactive attitudes, rather than by a commitment to some independently comprehensible proposition about responsibility, is not to deny that these reactions depend on a context of belief and perceptions in particular contexts. They are not mere effusions of feeling, unaffected by facts. In one way, Strawson is anxious to insist that these attitudes have no "rationale," that they neither require nor permit a "rational justification" of some general sort. Nevertheless, Strawson has a good deal to say about the particular perceptions that elicit and inhibit them. Reactive attitudes do have internal criteria, since they are reactions to the moral qualities exemplified by an individual's attitudes and conduct.[4]

Thus, reactive attitudes depend upon an interpretation of conduct. If you are resentful when jostled in a crowd, you will see the other's behavior as rude, contemptuous, disrespectful, self-preoccupied, or heedless: in short, as manifesting attitudes contrary to the basic demand for reasonable regard. Your resentment might be inhibited if you are too tired, or busy, or fearful, or simply inured to life in the big city. These are causal inhibitors. In contrast, you might think the other was pushed, didn't realize, didn't mean to. . . . These thoughts would provide reasons for the inhibition of resentment. What makes them reasons is, roughly, that they cancel or qualify the appearance of noncompliance with the basic demand.[5]

In this way, Strawson offers a plausible account of many of the

---

[4] Reactive attitudes thus permit a threefold classification. Personal reactive attitudes regarding others' treatment of one (resentment, gratitude, etc.); vicarious analogues of these, regarding others' treatment of others (indignation and approbation); self-reactive attitudes regarding one's own treatment of others (and oneself?) (guilt, shame, moral self-esteem, feeling obligated). Many of the reactive attitudes reflect the basic demand (on oneself and others, for oneself and others), whereas others (for example, gratitude) directly express the basic concern.

Contrary to some of Strawson's discussion, responsibility does not concern only other-regarding attitudes. You can hold yourself responsible for failing to live up to an ideal that has no particular bearing on the interests or feelings of others. It may be said that others cannot *blame* you for this failure; but that would be a moral claim.

[5] Below, this remark is qualified significantly.

"pleas" that in practice inhibit or modify negative reactive attitudes. One type of plea is exemplified by the aforementioned reasons for inhibited sentiments. This type of plea corresponds to standardly acknowledged *excusing* conditions. It works by denying the appearance that the other failed to fulfill the basic demand; when a valid excuse obtains, the internal criteria of the negative reactive attitudes are not satisfied. Of course, justification does this as well, but in a different way. "He realized what he was doing, but it was an emergency." In general, an excuse shows that *one* was not to blame, whereas a justification shows that one was not to *blame*.

Strawson distinguishes a second type of plea. These correspond roughly to standard *exempting* conditions. They show that the agent, temporarily or permanently, globally or locally, is appropriately exempted from the basic demand in the first place. Strawson's examples are being psychotic, being a child, being under great strain, being hypnotized, being a sociopath ("moral idiot"), and being "unfortunate in formative circumstances." His general characterization of pleas of type 2 is that they present the other either as acting uncharacteristically due to extraordinary circumstances, or as psychologically abnormal or morally undeveloped in such a way as to be incapacitated in some or all respects for "ordinary adult interpersonal relationships."

In sum, type-2 pleas bear upon the question of whether the agent is an appropriate "object of that kind of demand for goodwill or regard which is reflected in ordinary reactive attitudes" (p. 65). If so, he or she is seen as a responsible agent, as a potential term in moral relationships, as a member (albeit, perhaps, in less than good standing) of the moral community. Assuming the absence of such exemptions, type-1 pleas bear upon the question of whether the basic demand has been met. These inhibit negative reactive attitudes because they give evidence that their internal criteria are not satisfied. In contrast, type-2 pleas inhibit reactive attitudes because they inhibit the demand those attitudes express (p. 73).

When reactive attitudes are suspended on type-2 grounds, we tend to take what Strawson calls an "objective view." We see individuals not as ones to be resented or esteemed but as ones to be controlled, managed, manipulated, trained. . . . The objective view does not preclude all emotions: "It may include repulsion and fear, it may include pity or even love," though not reciprocal adult love. We have the capacity to adopt an objective view toward capable agents as well; for certain kinds of therapeutic relationship, or simply to relieve the "strains of involvement," we sometimes call upon this resource.

As we have seen, one of Strawson's concerns is to deny the relevance of any theoretical issue about determinism to moral responsibility. In effect, incompatibilists insist that the truth of determinism would require us to take the objective attitude universally. But in Strawson's view, when we adopt the objective attitude, it is never a result of a theoretical conviction in determinism, but either because one of the exempting pleas is accepted, or for external reasons – fatigue, for example, or relief from the strain of involvement. No coherent thesis of determinism entails that one or more of the pleas is always valid, that disrespect is never meant, or that we are all abnormal or undeveloped in the relevant ways. Holding responsible is an expression of the basic concern and the basic demand, whose "legitimacy" requires neither metaphysical freedom nor efficacy. The practice does not involve a commitment to anything with which determinism could conflict, or which considerations of utility could challenge.

Blaming and finding fault

This is the basic view as Strawson presents it. For convenience, we may call it the expressive theory of responsibility. With certain caveats,[6] the expressive theory may be called a nonconsequentialist form of compatibilism; but it is not the only such form. It can be clarified by contrasting it with another.

Consider the following common view of blame and praise: To blame someone morally for something is to attribute it to a moral fault, or "shortcoming," or defect of character, or vice,[7] and similarly for praise. Responsibility could be construed in terms of the propriety conditions of such judgments: that is, judgments to the effect that an action or attitude manifests a virtue or vice.[8]

As I understand the Strawsonian theory, such judgments are only

---

[6] The term "compatibilism" denotes the view that determinism is compatible with responsibility. Hence it may presuppose that determinism is an intelligible thesis. Since Strawson seems skeptical about this presupposition, he might refuse this appellation.
[7] See Robert Nozick, *Philosophical Explanations* (Harvard University Press, 1981, p. 224).
[8] Such a view is hinted at by James Wallace: "Answers to [the question of when an action is fully characteristic of an excellence or a vice] are fundamental for an account of the conditions for the appropriateness of praise, blame, reward and punishment and for an account of the derivative notion of responsibility" (*Virtues and Vices*, Cornell University Press, p. 43). This also seems to be R. Milo's view in *Immorality* (Princeton University Press, 1984). I don't say that such a view is necessarily incompatibilist – it could be insisted that conduct fully exemplifies a virtue or a vice only if determinism is false (this is clearly the Abélardian view, discussed below) – but it is clear how a compatibilist version would go.

part of the story. They indicate what reactive attitudes are reactions *to* (namely, to the quality of the other's moral self as exemplified in action and attitude), but they are not themselves such reactions. Merely to cite such judgments is to leave out something integral to the practice of holding responsible and to the concept of moral responsibility (of being one to whom it is appropriate to respond in certain ways). It is as though in blaming we were mainly moral clerks, recording moral faults, for whatever purposes (the Last Assizes?).[9] In a Strawsonian view, blaming is not merely a fault-finding appraisal – which could be made from a detached and austerely "objective" standpoint – but a range of responses to the agent on the basis of such appraisals.[10] These nonpropositional responses are constitutive of the practice of holding responsible.

I will have something to say later about the nature of these responses. Clearly they make up a wide spectrum. Negative reactive attitudes range from bombing Tripoli to thinking poorly of a person. But even those at the more covert and less retributive end of the spectrum involve more than attributions of defects or shortcomings of moral character. Thinking poorly (less well) of a person is a way of regarding him or her in view of those faults. It has subtle implications for one's way of treating and interacting with the other. (Where the other is dead or otherwise out of reach, these implications will be only hypothetical or potential.) It is the sort of attitude that is forsworn by forgiveness, which itself presupposes the attribution of (former) fault.

Some critical questions

I turn now to certain hard questions for the expressive theory. It accounts nicely for "excusing conditions," pleas of type 1; but exactly – or even roughly – what is its account of type-2 pleas? The "participant" reactive attitudes are said to be "natural human reactions to the good or ill-will or indifference of others as displayed in their attitudes and actions" (p. 67); but this characterization must be incomplete, for some agents who display such attitudes are nevertheless exempted. A

---

[9] Consider Jonathan Glover's remark: "Involved in our present practice of blame is a kind of moral accounting, where a person's actions are recorded in an informal balance sheet, with the object of assessing his moral worth." (*Responsibility*, Routledge and Kegan Paul, 1970, p. 44.)

[10] "Blaming is a type of response to faults in oneself or in others," Robert Adams, "Involuntary Sin," *Philosophical Review*, January 1985, p. 21. Adams does not tell us what kind of response it is. Since he thinks that thinking poorly of someone *is* a form of unspoken blame (ibid.), he must think that thinking poorly of is more than noting a moral fault. I think this is correct.

child can be malicious, a psychotic can be hostile, a sociopath indifferent, a person under great strain can be rude, a woman or man "unfortunate in formative circumstances" can be cruel. Evidently reactive attitudes are sensitive not only to the quality of others' wills, but depend as well upon a background of beliefs about the objects of those attitudes. What are those beliefs, and can they be accommodated without appealing to the rival accounts of responsibility that Strawson sets out to avoid?

Strawson says that type-2 pleas inhibit reactive attitudes not by providing an interpretation which shows that the other does not display the pertinent attitudes, but by "inhibiting" the basic demand. It would seem that many of the exemption conditions involve *explanations* of why the individuals display qualities to which the reactive attitudes are otherwise sensitive. So on the face of it, the reactive attitudes are also affected by these explanations. Strawson's essay does not provide an account of how this works or what kinds of explanations exempt.

The problem is not just that the theory is incomplete, but that what might be necessary to complete it will undermine the theory. Strawsonian rivals will rush to fill the gap with their own notions. So it will be said that what makes some of these explanations exempting is that they are deterministic; or it will be said that these conditions are exempting because they indicate conditions in which making the basic demand is inefficacious. To the extent that some such account seems necessary, our enterprise is doomed.

In the following sections, I investigate a Strawsonian alternative. Following Strawson's idea that type-2 pleas inhibit reactive attitudes *by* inhibiting the basic demand, I propose to construe the exempting conditions as indications of the constraints on intelligible moral demand or, put another way, of the constraints on moral address.

I shall not attempt anything like a comprehensive treatment of the type-2 pleas mentioned by Strawson. I discuss, first and rather briefly, the cases of being a child and being under great strain. I then turn to a more extended discussion of "being unfortunate in formative circumstances," for this looks to be entirely beyond the resources of the expressive theory.

Demanding and understanding

As Strawson is fully aware, being a child is not simply exempting. Children "are potentially and increasingly capable both of holding, and being objects of, the full range of human and moral attitudes, but are not yet fully capable of either" (p. 75). Children are gradually becoming responsible agents; but in virtue of what are they potentially and increasingly these things? A plausible partial answer to this question is "moral understanding." They do not yet (fully) grasp the moral concepts in such a way that they can (fully) engage in moral communication, and so be unqualified members of the moral community.

The relevance of moral understanding to the expressive theory is this: The negative reactive attitudes express a *moral* demand, a demand for reasonable regard. Now a very young child does not even have a clear sense of the reality of others; but even with this cognitive capacity, children may lack an understanding of the effects of their behavior on others. Even when they understand what it is to hurt another physically, they may lack a sense of what it is to hurt another's feelings, or of the various subtle ways in which that may be done; and even when these things are more or less mastered, they may lack the notion of *reasonable* regard, or of justification. The basic demand is, once more, a moral demand, a demand for reasonable regard, a demand addressed to a moral agent, to one who is capable of understanding the demand. Since the negative reactive attitudes involve this demand, they are not (as fully) appropriately directed to those who do not fully grasp the terms of the demand.

To be intelligible, demanding requires understanding on the part of the object of the demand. The reactive attitudes are incipiently forms of communication, which make sense only on the assumption that the other can comprehend the message.

No doubt common views about the moral capacities of children are open to challenge, and the appeal to the notion of understanding itself raises important issues.[11] However, what is important here is whether these views can be understood by the Strawsonian theory, and it seems the ordinary view that reactive attitudes make less sense in the case of children is intelligible in Strawsonian terms; this exemption condition reflects constraints arising from the notion of moral demand.

---

[11] Do *we adults* fully comprehend the notions of justification and reasonable regard? Does understanding presuppose a disputable cognitive view of morality? Certainly conceptions of children are subject to cultural variation. William Blackstone discusses the case of an 8-year old boy who was tried for setting fire to some barns. Because he was found to exhibit "malice, revenge, and cunning, he was found guilty, condemned and hanged accordingly." (In *Commentaries on the Laws of England (1765–7)*, as quoted by Jennifer Radden, *Madness and Reason*, George Allen and Unwin, 1985, p. 136.)

It is doubtful that diminished moral understanding is the only relevant factor here. Surely various capacities of concentration and "volitional" control are relevant as well. I do not know how the expressive theory could take these into account.

In a certain sense, blaming and praising those with diminished moral understanding loses its "point." This way of putting it smacks of consequentialism, but our discussion suggests a different construction. The reactive attitudes are incipient forms of communication, not in the sense that resentment et al. are usually communicated; very often, in fact, they are not. Rather, the most appropriate and direct expression of resentment is to address the other with a complaint and a demand. Being a child exempts, when it does, not because expressing resentment has no desirable effects; in fact, it often does. Rather the reactive attitudes lose their point as forms of moral address.[12]

Not being oneself

Let's consider whether this kind of explanation can be extended to another of Strawson's type-2 pleas: "being under great strain." Strawson includes this plea in a subgroup of exemptions that include "he wasn't himself" and "he was acting under posthypnotic suggestion." His statement of the rationale in the case of stress is somewhat cryptic:

We shall not feel resentment against the man he is for the action done by the man he is not; or at least we shall feel less. We normally have to deal with him under normal stresses; so we shall not feel towards him, when he acts under abnormal stresses, as we should have felt towards him had he acted as he did under normal stresses. (pp. 65–6)

I take it that what leads Strawson to group these cases together is that in each case the agent, due to special circumstances, acts *uncharacteristically*.

When you learn that someone who has treated you extremely rudely has been under great strain lately, has lost a job, say, or is going through a divorce, you may reinterpret the behavior in such a way that your erstwhile resentment or hurt feelings are inhibited and now seem inappropriate. How does this reinterpretation work? Notice, again, that unlike type-1 pleas, the new interpretation does not con-

---

[12] Reactive attitudes are even more clearly pointless in the case of a radically disintegrated personality, one that has no coherent moral self to be addressed. The case of the sociopath is much more complicated, but arguably something similar may be said here. Those who deal with sociopaths often lose the sense that such characters have a moral self at all; despite appearances, there is "no one home."

For case studies and psychiatric commentary, see Hervey Cleckley, *The Mask of Sanity*, C. V. Mosby, 1941. For philosophical discussion, see Herbert Fingarette, *On Responsibility*, Chap. 2; Vinit Haksar, "The Responsibility of Psychopaths," *The Philosophical Quarterly*, Vol. 15 (1965); M. S. Pritchard, "Responsibility, Understanding, and Psychopathology," *The Monist*, Vol. 58 (1974); Antony Duff, "Psychopathy and Moral Understanding," *American Philosophical Quarterly*, Vol. 14 (1977); and Jeffrie Murphy, "Moral Death: A Kantian Essay on Psychopathy," *Ethics*, Vol. 82 (1972).

tradict the *judgment* that the person treated you rudely; rather, it provides an explanation of the rudeness.

What Strawson says about this case seems plausible. What seems to affect your reactive attitudes is the thought that she's not herself, that the behavior does not reflect or fully reflect the person's moral "personality." The following remark indicates the same phenomena: "He was drunk when he said that; I wouldn't hold it against him." (There is room here for disagreement about the bounds of the moral self. Some parts of folk wisdom have it that one's "true self" is revealed when drunk. To my knowledge, this has never been claimed about stress.) Again, what is the Strawsonian rationale?

Perhaps this type of case can also be understood in terms of the conditions of intelligible moral address. Insofar as resentment is a form of reproach addressed to an agent, such an attitude loses much of its point here – not, as before, because the other does not fully understand the reproach, but because *he* or *she* (the true self) repudiates such conduct as well. Unlike the case in which the agent acts rudely in the absence of "strain," here the target of your resentment is not one who "really" endorses the behavior you are opposing. You see the behavior as not issuing from that person's moral self, and yet it is the person, qua moral self, that your resentment would address.

The point can be put more generally in this way: Insofar as the negative reactive attitudes express demands (or in some cases appeals) addressed to another moral self, they are conceptually conditioned in various ways. One condition is that, to be fully a moral self, the other must possess sufficient (for what?) moral understanding; another is that the conduct in question be seen as reflecting the moral self. Insofar as the person is subject to great stress, his or her conduct and attitudes fail to meet this latter condition.

I am unsure to what extent these remarks accord with Strawson's own views. They are in any case exceedingly sketchy, and raise problems I am unable to take up here. For one thing, the notion of moral address seems essentially interpersonal, and so would be unavailing in the self-reflexive case. We have negative reactive attitudes toward and make moral demands upon ourselves. To determine whether this is a fatal asymmetry, we would have to investigate the reflexive cases in detail. For another thing, the notion of moral self is certainly not altogether transparent. Why are our responses under stress not reflections of our moral selves – namely, reflections of the moral self under stress? Clearly then, the explanation requires development.

It will be recalled, however, that I am not trying to determine whether a Strawsonian account of the exemption conditions is the *best* account, but to indicate what such an account might be. It will be enough for my purposes here if we can be satisfied that a Strawsonian theory has the resources to provide *some* explanation.

To recapitulate, then, the thesis is this: First, type-2 pleas indicate in different ways limiting conditions on moral address. These are relevant to reactive attitudes because those attitudes are incipiently forms of moral address. This thesis makes sense of Strawson's remark that pleas of this type inhibit reactive attitudes by inhibiting moral demand. Second, given that those conditions are satisfied, type-1 pleas indicate that the basic demand has not been flouted, contrary to appearances (though here again, we must distinguish excuse from justification).

On this account, the practice of holding responsible does indeed seem metaphysically modest, in that it involves no commitments to which issues about determinism are relevant. In a subsequent section I will consider some more bothersome features of our practice; but first I want to call attention to some general issues raised by the account given so far.

Evil and the limits of moral community

To understand certain exempting and extenuating considerations, I have appealed to the notion of the conditions in which it makes sense morally to address another. I suggested that in different ways these conditions are not (fully) satisfied by the child and the person under severe stress. In the case of children, it seemed plausible to speak of a lack of understanding. What is involved in such understanding is a complex question. Obviously we do not want to make *compliance* with the basic demand a condition of moral understanding. (After all, for the most part, children *do* "comply," but without full understanding.) For the negative reactive attitudes come into play only when the basic demand has been flouted or rejected; and flouting and rejecting, strictly speaking, require understanding.

These remarks raise a very general issue about the limits of responsibility and the limits of evil. It is tempting to think that understanding requires a shared framework of values. At any rate, some of Strawson's remarks hint at such a requirement on moral address. He writes that the reactive attitudes essentially involve regarding the other as "a morally responsible agent, as a term of moral relationships, as a member of the moral community" (p. 73). This last phrase suggests shared ends, at some level, or a shared framework for practical reasoning. Thus, comembers of the moral community are potential interlocutors. In his discussion of Strawson's essay, Lawrence Stern suggests this point:

. . . when one morally disapproves of another person, it is normal to believe that he is susceptible to the appeal of the principles from the standpoint of which one disapproves. He either shares these principles or can come to share them.[13]

Does morally addressing another make sense unless we suppose that the other can see some reason to take us seriously, to acknowledge our claims? Can we be in a moral community with those who reject the basic terms of moral community? Are the enemies of moral community themselves members? If we suppose that moral address requires moral community, then some forms of evil will be exempting conditions. If holding responsible requires the intelligibility of moral address, and if a condition of such address is that the other be seen as a potential moral interlocutor, then the paradox results that extreme evil disqualifies one for blame.

Consider the case of Robert Harris.

On the south tier of Death Row, in a section called "Peckerwood Flats" where the white inmates are housed, there will be a small celebration the day Robert Alton Harris dies.

A group of inmates on the row have pledged several dollars for candy, cookies and soda. At the moment they estimate that Harris has been executed, they will eat, drink and toast to his passing.

"The guy's a misery, a total scumbag; we're going to party when he goes," said Richard (Chic) Mroczko, who lived in the cell next to Harris on San Quentin Prison's Death Row for more than a year. "He doesn't care about life, he doesn't care about others, he doesn't care about himself.

"We're not a bunch of Boy Scouts around here, and you might think we're pretty cold-blooded about the whole thing. But then, you just don't know the dude."

San Diego County Assistant Dist. Atty. Richard Huffman, who prosecuted Harris, said, "If a person like Harris can't be executed under California law and federal procedure, then we should be honest and say we're incapable of handling capital punishment."

State Deputy Atty. Gen. Michael D. Wellington asked the court during an appeal hearing for Harris, "If this isn't the kind of defendant that justifies the death penalty, is there ever going to be one?"

What crime did Robert Harris commit to be considered the archetypal candidate for the death penalty? And what kind of man provokes such enmity that even those on Death Row . . . call for his execution?

On July 5, 1978, John Mayeski and Michael Baker had just driven through

---

[13] "Freedom, Blame, and Moral Community," *Journal of Philosophy*, February 14, 1974, p. 78.

[a] fast-food restaurant and were sitting in the parking lot eating lunch. Mayeski and Baker . . . lived on the same street and were best friends. They were on their way to a nearby lake for a day of fishing.

At the other end of the parking lot, Robert Harris, 25, and his brother Daniel, 18, were trying to hotwire a [car] when they spotted the two boys. The Harris brothers were planning to rob a bank that afternoon and did not want to use their own car. When Robert Harris could not start the car, he pointed to the [car] where the 16-year-olds were eating and said to Daniel, "We'll take this one."

He pointed a . . . Luger at Mayeski, crawled into the back seat, and told him to drive east. . . .

Daniel Harris followed in the Harrises' car. When they reached a canyon area . . ., Robert Harris told the youths he was going to use their car in a bank robbery and assured them that they would not be hurt. Robert Harris yelled to Daniel to get the .22 caliber rifle out of the back seat of their car.

"When I caught up," Daniel said in a recent interview, Robert was telling them about the bank robbery we were going to do. He was telling them that he would leave them some money in the car and all, for us using it. Both of them said that they would wait on top of this little hill until we were gone, and then walk into town and report the car stolen. Robert Harris agreed.

"Michael turned and went through some bushes. John said, 'Good luck,' and turned to leave."

As the two boys walked away, Harris slowly raised the Luger and shot Mayeski in the back, Daniel said. Mayeski yelled: "Oh, God," and slumped to the ground. Harris chased Baker down a hill into a little valley and shot him four times.

Mayeski was still alive when Harris climbed back up the hill, Daniel said. Harris walked over to the boy, knelt down, put the Luger to his head and fired.

"God, everything started to spin," Daniel said. "It was like slow motion. I saw the gun, and then his head exploded like a balloon, . . . I just started running and running. . . . But I heard Robert and turned around.

"He was swinging the rifle and pistol in the air and laughing. God, that laugh made blood and bone freeze in me."

Harris drove [the] car to a friend's house where he and Daniel were staying. Harris walked into the house, carrying the weapons and the bag [containing] the remainder of the slain youths' lunch. Then, about 15 minutes after he had killed the two 16-year-old boys, Harris took the food out of the bag . . . and began eating a hamburger. He offered his brother an apple turnover, and Daniel became nauseated and ran to the bathroom.

"Robert laughed at me," Daniel said. "He said I was weak; he called me a sissy and said I didn't have the stomach for it."

Harris was in an almost lighthearted mood. He smiled and told Daniel that it would be amusing if the two of them were to pose as police officers and inform the parents that their sons were killed. Then, for the first time, he turned serious. He thought that somebody might have heard the shots and that police could be searching for the bodies. He told Daniel that they should begin cruising the street near the bodies, and possibly kill some police in the area.

[Later, as they prepared to rob the bank,] Harris pulled out the Luger, noticed blood stains and remnants of flesh on the barrel as a result of the point-blank shot, and said, "I really blew that guy's brains out." And then, again, he started laughing.

. . . Harris was given the death penalty. He has refused all requests for interviews since the conviction.

"He just doesn't see the point of talking," said a sister, . . . who has visited him three times since he has been on Death Row. "He told me he had his chance, he took the road to hell and there's nothing more to say."

. . . Few of Harris' friends or family were surprised that he ended up on Death Row. He had spent seven of the previous 10 years behind bars. Harris, who has an eighth-grade education, was convicted of car theft at 15 and was sentenced to a federal youth center. After being released, he was arrested twice for torturing animals and was convicted of manslaughter for beating a neighbor to death after a dispute.

Barbara Harris, another sister, talked to her brother at a family picnic on July 4, 1978. He had been out of prison less than six months, and his sister had not seen him in several years.

. . . Barbara Harris noticed his eyes, and she began to shudder. . . . "I thought, 'My God, what have they done to him?' He smiled, but his eyes were so cold, totally flat. It was like looking at a rattlesnake or a cobra ready to strike. They were hooded eyes, with nothing but meanness in them.

"He had the eyes of a killer. I told a friend that I knew someone else would die by his hand."

The next day, Robert Harris killed the two youths. Those familiar with the case were as mystified as they were outraged by Harris' actions. Most found it incomprehensible that a man could be so devoid of compassion and conscience that he could kill two youths, laugh about their deaths and then casually eat their hamburgers. . . .

. . . Harris is a dangerous man on the streets and a dangerous man behind bars, said Mroczko, who spent more than a year in the cell next to Harris'. . . .

"You don't want to deal with him out there," said Mroczko, . . . "We don't want to deal with him in here."

During his first year on the row, Mroczko said, Harris was involved in several fights on the yard and was caught trying to supply a prisoner in an adjacent yard with a knife. During one fight, Harris was stabbed and the other prisoner was shot by a guard. He grated on people's nerves and one night he kept the whole cell block awake by banging his shoe on a steel water basin and laughing hysterically.

An encounter with Harris always resulted in a confrontation. If an inmate had cigarettes, or something else Harris wanted, and he did not think "you could hold your mud," Mroczko said, he would try to take them.

Harris was a man who just did not know "when to be cool," he said. He was

an obnoxious presence in the yard and in his cell, and his behavior precipi-
tated unwanted attention from the guards. . . .

He acted like a man who did not care about anything. His cell was filthy,
Mroczko said, and clothes, trash, tobacco and magazines were scattered on
the floor. He wore the same clothes every day and had little interest in
showers. Harris spent his days watching television in his cell, occasionally
reading a Western novel.[14]

On the face of it, Harris is an "archetypal candidate" for blame. We
respond to his heartlessness and viciousness with moral outrage and
loathing. Yet if reactive attitudes were implicitly "invitations to dialogue" (as Stern puts it), then Harris would be an inappropriate
object of such attitudes. For he is hardly a potential moral interlocutor, "susceptible to the appeal of the principles from the standpoint
of which one disapproves." In this instance, an invitation to dialogue
would be met with icy silence (he has "nothing more to say") or murderous contempt.

However, not all communication is dialogue. Harris refuses dialogue, and this refusal is meant to make a point. It is in effect a
repudiation of the moral community; he thereby declares himself a
moral outlaw. Unlike the small child, or in a different way the psycho-
path, he exhibits an inversion of moral concern, not a lack of understanding. His ears are not deaf, but his heart is frozen. This characteristic, which makes him utterly unsuitable as a moral interlocutor,
intensifies rather than inhibits the reactive attitudes. Harris's form of
evil *consists* in part in being beyond the boundaries of moral community. Hence, if we are to appeal to the constraints on moral address to
explain certain type-2 pleas, we must not include among these constraints comembership in the moral community or the significant possibility of dialogue – unless, that is, evil is to be its own exemption. At
these outer limits, out reactive attitudes can be nothing more (or less)
than a denunciation forlorn of the hope of an adequate reply.

The roots of evil

I said that Harris is an archetypal candidate for blame – so, at least,
we react to him. Does it matter to our reactions how he came to be so?
Strawson thinks so, for, among type-2 pleas, he includes "being un-

[14] From Miles Corwin, "Icy Killer's Life Steeped in Violence," *Los Angeles Times,* May 16,
1982. Copyright, 1982, *Los Angeles Times.* Reprinted by permission. For the length of this
and the next quotation, I ask for the reader's patience. It is very important here to work
with realistic and detailed examples.

fortunate in formative circumstances." We must now investigate the relevance of such historical considerations to the reactive attitudes. As it happens, the case of Robert Harris is again a vivid illustration.

[During the interview] Barbara Harris put her palms over her eyes and said softly, "I saw every grain of sweetness, pity and goodness in him destroyed. . . . It was a long and ugly journey before he reached that point."

Robert Harris' 29 years . . . have been dominated by incessant cruelty and profound suffering that he has both experienced and provoked. Violence presaged his birth, and a violent act is expected to end his life.

Harris was born Jan. 15, 1953, several hours after his mother was kicked in the stomach. She was 6½ months pregnant and her husband, an insanely jealous man, . . . came home drunk and accused her of infidelity. He claimed that the child was not his, threw her down and kicked her. She began hemorrhaging, and he took her to the hospital.

Robert was born that night. His heartbeat stopped at one point . . . but labor was induced and he was saved. Because of the premature birth, he was a tiny baby; he was kept alive in an incubator and spent months at the hospital.

His father was an alcoholic who was twice convicted of sexually molesting his daughters. He frequently beat his children . . . and often caused serious injury. Their mother also became an alcoholic and was arrested several times, once for bank robbery.

All of the children had monstrous childhoods. But even in the Harris family, . . . the abuse Robert was subjected to was unusual.

Before their mother died last year, Barbara Harris said, she talked incessantly about Robert's early years. She felt guilty that she was never able to love him; she felt partly responsible that he ended up on Death Row.

When Robert's father visited his wife in the hospital and saw his son for the first time, . . . the first thing he said was, "Who is the father of that bastard?" When his mother picked him up from the hospital . . . she said it was like taking a stranger's baby home.

The pain and permanent injury Robert's mother suffered as a result of the birth, . . . and the constant abuse she was subjected to by her husband, turned her against her son. Money was tight, she was overworked and he was her fifth child in just a few years. She began to blame all of her problems on Robert, and she grew to hate the child.

"I remember one time we were in the car and Mother was in the back seat with Robbie in her arms. He was crying and my father threw a glass bottle at him, but it hit my mother in the face. The glass shattered and Robbie started screaming. I'll never forget it," she said. . . .

"Her face was all pink, from the mixture of blood and milk. She ended up blaming Robbie for all the hurt, all the things like that. She felt helpless and he was someone to vent her anger on."

. . . Harris had a learning disability and a speech problem, but there was no money for therapy. When he was at school he felt stupid and classmates teased him, his sister said, and when he was at home he was abused.

"He was the most beautiful of all my mother's children; he was an angel," she said. "He would just break your heart. He wanted love so bad he would beg for any kind of physical contact.

"He'd come up to my mother and just try to rub his little hands on her leg or her arm. He just never got touched at all. She'd just push him away or kick him. One time she bloodied his nose when he was trying to get close to her."

Barbara Harris put her head in her hands and cried softly. "One killer out of nine kids. . . . The sad thing is he was the most sensitive of all of us. When he was 10 and we all saw 'Bambi,' he cried and cried when Bambi's mother was shot. Everything was pretty to him as a child; he loved animals. But all that changed; it all changed so much."

. . . All nine children are psychologically crippled as a result of their father, she said, but most have been able to lead useful lives. But Robert was too young, and the abuse lasted too long, she said, for him ever to have had a chance to recover.

[At age 14] Harris was sentenced to a federal youth detention center [for car theft]. He was one of the youngest inmates there, Barbara Harris said, and he grew up "hard and fast."

. . . Harris was raped several times, his sister said, and he slashed his wrists twice in suicide attempts. He spent more than four years behind bars as a result of an escape, an attempted escape and a parole violation.

The centers were "gladiator schools," Barbara Harris said, and Harris learned to fight and be mean. By the time he was released from federal prison at 19, all his problems were accentuated. Everyone in the family knew that he needed psychiatric help.

The child who had cried at the movies when Bambi's mother dies had evolved into a man who was arrested several times for abusing animals. He killed cats and dogs, Daniel said, and laughed while torturing them with mop handles, darts and pellet guns. Once he stabbed a prize pig more than 1,000 times.

"The only way he could vent his feelings was to break or kill something," Barbara Harris said. "He took out all the frustrations of his life on animals. He had no feeling for life, no sense of remorse. He reached the point where there wasn't that much left of him."

. . . Harris' family is ambivalent about his death sentence. [Another sister said that] if she did not know her brother's past so intimately, she would support his execution without hesitation. Barbara has a 16-year-old son; she often imagines the horror of the slain boys' parents.

"If anyone killed my son, I'd try my damnedest, no matter what it took, to have my child revenged," Barbara Harris said. "I know how those parents must suffer every day.

"But Robbie in the gas chamber. . . ." She broke off in mid-sentence and stared out a window. "Well, I still remember the little boy who used to beg for love, for just one pat or word of kindness. . . . No I can't say I want my brother to die."

. . . Since Harris has been on Death Row, he has made no demands of time

or money on his family. Harris has made only one request; he wants a digni-
fied and serene ceremony after he dies – a ceremony in marked contrast to
his life.

He has asked his oldest brother to take his ashes, to drive to the Sierra, hike
to a secluded spot and scatter his remains in the trees.[15]

No doubt this history gives pause to the reactive attitudes. Why does it
do so? "No wonder Harris is as he is!" we think. What is the relevance
of this thought?

Note, to begin with, that the story in no way undermines the judgments that he is brutal, vicious, heartless, mean.[16] Rather, it provides
a kind of explanation for his being so. Can the expressive theory
explain why the reactive attitudes should be sensitive to such an
explanation?

Strawson's general rubric for type-2 pleas (or the subgroup in
which this plea is classified) is "being incapacitated for ordinary interpersonal relationships." Does Harris have some independently identifiable incapacity for which his biography provides evidence? Apparently, he *is* incapacitated for such relationships – for example, for
friendship, for sympathy, for being affected by moral considerations.
To be homicidally hateful and callous in Harris's way is to lack moral
concern, and to lack moral concern is to be incapacitated for moral
community. However, to exempt Harris on these grounds is problematic. For then everyone who is evil in Harris's way will be exempt,
independently of facts about their background. But we had ample
evidence about *this* incapacity before we learned of his childhood
misfortunes, and that did not affect the reactive attitudes. Those misfortunes affect our responses in a special and nonevidential way. The
question is why this should be so.

This would seem to be a hard question for compatibilist views generally. What matters is whether, in one version, the practice of holding responsible can be efficacious as a means of social regulation, or
whether, using the expressive theory, the conditions of moral address
are met. These questions would seem to be settled by how individuals
are, not by how they came to be. Facts about background would be, at
most, evidence that some other plea is satisfied. In themselves, they
would not seem to matter.

A plea of this kind is, on the other hand, grist for the incom-

---

[15] Miles Corwin, op. cit. Copyright, 1982, *Los Angeles Times.* Reprinted by permission.
[16] Although, significantly, when his past is in focus, we are less inclined to use certain
reactive epithets, such as "scumbag." This term is used to express an attitude about the
appropriate treatment of the individual (that he is to be thrown in the garbage, flushed
down the toilet, etc.). Some other reactive terms are "jerk," "creep," "son of a bitch."

patibilists' mill. For they will insist on an essential historical dimension to the concept of responsibility. Harris's history reveals him to be an inevitable product of his formative circumstances. And seeing him as a product is inconsistent with seeing him as a responsible agent. If his cruel attitudes and conduct are the inevitable result of his circumstances, then he is not responsible for them, unless he was responsible for those circumstances. It is this principle that gives the historical dimension of responsibility and of course entails the incompatibility of determinism and responsibility.

In this instance, however, an incompatibilist diagnosis seems doubtful. In the first place, our response to the case is not the simple suspension of reactive attitudes that this diagnosis would lead one to expect, but ambivalence. In the second place, the force of the example does not depend on a belief in the *inevitability* of the upshot. Nothing in the story supports such a belief. The thought is not "It had to be!" but, again, "No wonder!"

Sympathy and antipathy

How and why, then, does this larger view of Harris's life in fact affect us? It is too simple to say that it leads us to suspend our reactive attitudes. Our response is too complicated and conflicted for that. What appears to happen is that we are unable to command an overall view of his life that permits the reactive attitudes to be sustained without ambivalence. That is because the biography forces us to see him as a *victim,* and so seeing him does not sit well with the reactive attitudes that are so strongly elicited by Harris's character and conduct. Seeing him as a victim does not totally dispel those attitudes. Rather, in light of the "whole" story, conflicting responses are evoked. The sympathy toward the boy he was is at odds with outrage toward the man he is. These responses conflict not in the way that fear dispels anger, but in the way that sympathy is opposed to antipathy. In fact, each of these responses is appropriate, but taken together they do not enable us to respond overall in a coherent way.

Harris both satisfies and violates the criteria of victimhood. His childhood abuse was a misfortune inflicted upon him against his will. But at the same time (and this is part of his very misfortune) he unambivalently endorses suffering, death, and destruction, and that is what (one form of) evil is. With this in focus, we see him as a victimizer and respond to him accordingly. The ambivalence results from the fact that an overall view simultaneously demands and precludes regarding him as a victim.

What we have here is not exactly a clash between what Thomas Nagel has called the objective and subjective standpoints.[17] It is not that from the more comprehensive viewpoint that reveals Harris as a victim, his responsibility is indiscernible. Rather, the clash occurs within a single point of view that reveals Harris as evil (and hence calling for enmity and moral opposition) and as one who is a victim (calling for sympathy and understanding). Harris's misfortune is such that scarcely a vestige remains of his earlier sensibilities. Hence, unless one knew Harris as a child or keeps his earlier self vividly in mind, sympathy can scarcely find a purchase.

Moral luck and moral equality

However, what is arresting about the Harris case is not just the clash between sympathy and antipathy. The case is troubling in a more personal way. The fact that Harris's cruelty is an intelligible response to his circumstances gives a foothold not only for sympathy, but for the thought that if *I* had been subjected to such circumstances, I might well have become as vile. What is unsettling is the thought that one's moral self is such a fragile thing. One tends to think of one's moral sensibilities as going deeper than that (though it is not clear what this means). This thought induces not only an ontological shudder, but a sense of equality with the other: I too am a potential sinner.[18]

This point is merely the obverse of the point about sympathy. Whereas the point about sympathy focuses on our empathetic response to the other, the thought about moral luck turns one's gaze inward. It makes one feel less in a position to cast blame. The fact that my potential for evil has not been nearly so fully actualized is, for all I know, something for which I cannot take credit. The awareness that, in this respect, the others are or may be like oneself clashes with the distancing effect of enmity.

Admittedly, it is hard to know what to do with this conclusion. Equality of moral potential does not, of course, mean that Harris is not actually a vile man; on the contrary, it means that in similar circumstances I would have become vile as well. Since he is an evil man, we cannot and should not treat him as we would a rabid dog.

---

[17] In *The View from Nowhere*, Oxford University Press, 1985.

[18] In "Determinism and Moral Perspectives," *Philosophy and Phenomenological Research*, September 1960, Elizabeth Beardsley calls attention to the perspective evoked by such cases as Harris, though she links this perspective too closely, in my opinion, to the notion of determinism.

The awareness of moral luck, however, taints one's own view of one's moral self as an achievement, and infuses one's reactive attitudes with a sense of irony. Only those who have survived circumstances such as those that ravaged Harris are in a good position to know what they would have done. We lucky ones can only wonder. As a product of reflection, this attitude is, of course, easily lost when the knife is at one's own throat.

Determinism and ignorance

Nothing in the foregoing reflections is necessarily inconsistent with the expressive theory. The ways in which reactive attitudes are affected by sympathy and moral luck are intelligible without appealing to any of the conceptions of responsibility that Strawson eschews. Nevertheless, our attitudes remain puzzling in a number of respects.

Earlier we questioned an incompatibilist diagnosis of our example on the grounds that the historical explanation need not be construed as deterministic. Horrid backgrounds do not inevitably give rise to horrid people. Some manage somehow to survive a similar magnitude of misfortune, if not unscathed, at least as minimally decent human beings. Conversely, people are sometimes malicious despite a benign upbringing. What do we suppose makes the difference?

Strictly speaking, no one who is vicious in *just* the way we have interpreted Harris to be could fail to have had an abusive childhood. For our interpretation of who Harris is depends upon his biography, upon our interpretation of his life. Harris's cruelty is a response to the shattering abuse he suffered during the process of socialization. The objects of his hatred were not just the boys he so exultantly murdered, but the "moral order" that mauled and rejected him. (It is significant that Harris wanted to go out and kill some cops after the murder; he wanted not just to reject authority, but to confront it.) He defies the demand for human consideration because he has been denied this consideration himself. The mistreatment he received becomes a ground as well as a cause of the mistreatment he gives. It becomes part of the content of his "project."

Thus, someone who had a supportive and loving environment as a child, but who was devoted to dominating others, who killed for enjoyment, would not be vicious in the way Harris is, since he or she could not be seen as striking back at "society"; but such a person could be just *as* vicious. In common parlance, we sometimes call such people "bad apples," a phrase that marks a blank in our understanding. In contrast to Harris, whose malice is motivated, the conduct of "bad apples" seems inexplicable. So far, we cannot see them as victims, and there is no application for thoughts about sympathy and moral luck.

However, do we not suppose that *something* must have gone wrong in the developmental histories of these individuals, if not in their socialization, then "in them" – in their genes or brains? (Suppose a certain kind of tumor is such that its onset at an early age is known to be strongly correlated with the development of a malicious character. This supposition is no doubt bad science fiction; that a complex and articulated psychological structure could be caused by gross brain defect seems antecedently implausible.) Whatever "nonenvironmental" factors make the difference, will they not play the same role as Harris's bad upbringing – that is, will they not have victimized these individuals so that thoughts about sympathy and moral luck come into play? Or can evil be the object of unequivocal reactive attitudes only when it is inexplicable?

If determinism is true, then evil is a joint product of nature and nurture. If so, the difference between any evil person and oneself would seem to be a matter of moral luck. For determinism seems to entail that if one had been subjected to the internal and external conditions of some evil person, then one would have been evil as well. If that is so, then the reflections about moral luck seem to entail that the acceptance of determinism should affect our reactive attitudes in the same way as they are affected in Harris's case. In the account we have suggested, then, determinism seems to be relevant to reactive attitudes after all.

Actually, this conclusion does not follow without special metaphysical assumptions. For the counterfactuals that underlie thoughts about moral luck must be constrained by the conditions of personal identity. It may be that no one who had been exposed to just the internal and external conditions of some given individual could have been me. To make sense of a counterfactual of the form, "If i had been in C, then i would have become a person of type t," C must be supposed to be compatible with i's existence as an individual (i must exist in the possible world in which C obtains). For example, it is widely held that genetic origin is essential to an individual's identity. In that case, the counterfactual, "If I had had Harris's genetic origin and his upbringing, then I would have been as evil as he," will not make sense. Now it might be that Harris's genetic origins are among the determinants of his moral development. Thus, even if this is a deterministic world, there may be no true counterfactual that would support the thought that the difference between Harris and me is a matter of moral luck. There is room for the thought that there is something "in me" by virtue of which I would not have become a vicious person in Harris's circumstances. And if that factor were among my essential properties, so to speak, then that difference between Harris and me would not be a matter of moral luck on my part, but a matter of who we essentially were. That would not, of course, mean that I was essentially good or Harris essentially evil, but that I would not have been corrupted by the same circumstances as those that defeated Harris. To be sure, to suppose that this difference is in itself to my moral credit would be odd. To congratulate me on these grounds would be to congratulate me on being myself. Nevertheless, this difference still might explain what is to my credit, such moral virtues as I may possess. This will seem paradoxical only if we suppose that whatever is a ground of my moral credit must itself be to my credit. But I see no compelling reason to suppose this.

Historical responsibility

Libertarians believe that evil is the product neither of nature nor of nurture, but of free will. Do we understand what this might mean?

It is noteworthy that libertarians will be able to agree with much of what we have said about moral luck. Harris's history affects us because it makes us wonder how *we* would have responded, and thus shakes our confidence that we would have avoided a pernicious path in those circumstances. But this effect is perfectly compatible with Harris's responsibility for how he did respond, just us we would have been responsible for how we would have responded. The biography affects us not because it is deterministic, libertarians can say, but because it shakes our confidence that we would have exercised that freedom rightly in more dire straits. We are not, of course, responsible for our formative circumstances – and in this respect we are morally lucky and Harris is unlucky – but those circumstances do not determine our responses to them. It is the individual's own response that distinguishes those who become evil from those who do not.

This idea is nicely captured by Peter Abélard: "Nothing mars the soul except what is of its own nature, namely consent."[19] The idea is that one cannot simply be caused to be morally bad by the environment. So either Harris's soul is not (morally) marred, or he has been a

[19] From "Intention and Sin," reprinted in Herbert Morris (ed.), *Freedom and Responsibility* (Stanford University Press), p. 169.

willing accomplice to the malformation of the self. His evil means that
he has consented to what he has become – namely, one who consents
to cruelty. Thus, Abélardians try to fill the statistical cracks with the
will. The development of the moral self, they will say, is mediated by
consent.

We should be struck here by the a priori character of libertarian
convictions. How is Harris's consent to be construed, and why *must* it
have occurred? What evidence is there that it occurred? Why couldn't
Harris just have become that way? What is the difference between his
having acquiesced to what he became and his simply having become
that way? The libertarian faces the following difficulty: If there is no
such difference, then the view is vacuous, for consent was supposed to
explain his becoming that way. If there is a difference, what evidence
is there that it obtains in a particular case? Isn't there room for considerable doubt about this, and shouldn't libertarians, or we, insofar as
we are libertarians, be very doubtful about Harris's responsibility –
and indeed, on the Abélardian thesis, even about whether Harris is an
evil man, whether his soul is morally marred? (Notice that the tumor
case is a priori impossible on that thesis, unless we think of the tumor
somehow as merely presenting an occasion for consent – as inclining
without necessitating.) One suspects that the libertarian confidence in
their attributions of historical responsibility is rooted in a picture
according to which the fact that Harris became that way *proves* that he
consented. Then, of course, the appeal to consent is explanatorily
vacuous.

Epistemology apart, the attempt to trace the evil self to consent at
an earlier stage is faced with familiar difficulties. If we suppose (fan-
cifully) that Harris, earlier on, with full knowledge and deliberation,
launched himself on his iniquitous career,[20] we would be merely
postponing the inquiry, for the will which could fully and deliberately
consent to such a career would have to have its roots in a self which is
already morally marred – a self, therefore, which cannot itself be seen
simply as a product of consent. Are we instead to suppose that at some
earlier stage Harris slipped heedlessly or recklessly into patterns of
thought and action which he ought to have known would eventuate in
an evil character? (This seems to have been Aristotle's view in *Nicomachean Ethics*, Book III.5.) In that case, we would be tracing his
present ways to the much less egregious faults of negligence.[21]

---

[20] If such a thing ever occurred, it must have occurred at a stage when Harris clearly
would have fallen under the exemption condition of "being a child."
[21] Adams makes this point; op. cit.

Responsibility for the self

Strawson and others often charge libertarians with a metaphysically dubious conception of the self. The foregoing reflections indicate a basis for this charge. Libertarianism combines the Abélardian view about consent (or something like it) with the principle (or something like it) that to be responsible for anything, one must be responsible for (some of) what produces it. If we think of agents as consenting to this or that *because* they are (or have?) selves of a certain character, then it looks as though they are responsible for so consenting only if they are responsible for the self in which that consent is rooted. To establish this in each case, we have to trace the character of the self to earlier acts of consent. This enterprise seems hopeless, since the trace continues interminably or leads to a self to which the individual did not consent. The libertarian seems committed, then, to bearing the unbearable burden of showing how we can be responsible for ourselves. This burden can seem bearable only in a view of the self as an entity that mysteriously both transcends and intervenes in the "causal nexus," because it is both product and author of its actions and attitudes.

Must libertarians try to bear this burden? Perhaps the idea that they must rests upon a view of the self to which libertarians need not be committed. Perhaps the trouble arises in the first place from viewing the self as a thing standing in causal relation to acts of consent. The libertarian might say that to talk about the (moral) self is not to talk about an entity which necessitates specific acts of consent, but to talk about the sorts of things to which an individual tends to consent. To speak of Harris's moral self is not to explain his conduct, but to indicate the way he is morally. What we are responsible for are the particular things we consent to. We need not consider whether we are responsible for the genesis of the entity whose characteristics necessitate those acts of consent, for there is no such entity. In a way, of course, one is derivatively responsible for one's self, since one's moral self is constituted by the character of what one consents to, and one is responsible for what one consents to.[22]

The historical dimension of the concept of responsibility results from the principle that one is not responsible for one's conduct if that is necessitated by causes for which one is not responsible. This leads to

---

[22] It is noteworthy that Harris himself seems to accept responsibility for his life: "He told me he had his chance, he took the road to hell and there's nothing more to say." (From the end of the first extract from the Corwin article.)

a problematic requirement that one be responsible for one's self only
if one thinks of the self as an entity that causes one's (its) actions and
willings. Libertarians can reject this view. What they must affirm is
that we are responsible for what we consent to, that consent is not
necessitated by causes internal or external to the agent, and that if it
were, we could not properly hold the individual responsible for what
he or she consents to. These claims are far from self-evident. But they
hardly amount to a "panicky metaphysics" (p. 80).[23]

In the end, however, I do not think that libertarianism can be so
readily domesticated. The idea that one is responsible for and only
for what one consents to is not of course distinctive of libertarianism;
that idea has no historical implications. What is distinctive is the further requirement that consent be undetermined. I do not think the
idea that consent is undetermined is in itself particularly problematic.
The trouble begins only when we ask why this is *required*. The ground
of this requirement is the intuition that unless consent were undetermined, we would not truly be *originators* of our deeds. We would be
merely products, and not, as it were, producers. It is this intuition to
which the libertarian finds it so difficult to give content. "Being an
originator" does not mean just "consenting to," for that is already
covered by the first thesis. Nor is this notion captured simply by
adding the requirement of indeterminism; that is a merely negative
condition. Attempts to specify the condition in positive terms either
cite something that could obtain in a deterministic world, or something obscurely transcendent.

I suspect, then, that any metaphysically innocuous version of libertarianism must leave its incompatibilist component unmotivated.

Ignorance and skepticism

I have been exploring some ways in which the expressive theory
might explain the relevance of certain historical considerations.
Whatever the best explanation may be, the remarkable fact is that we
are, for the most part, quite ignorant of these considerations. Why
does our ignorance not give us more pause? If, for whatever reason,
reactive attitudes are sensitive to historical considerations, as Strawson
acknowledges, and we are largely ignorant of these matters, then it
would seem that most of our reactive attitudes are hasty, perhaps

---

[23] For an attempt at libertarianism without metaphysics, see David Wiggins, "Towards
a Credible Form of Libertarianism," in T. Honderich (ed.), *Essays on Freedom of Action*,
Routledge and Kegan Paul, 1973.

even benighted, as skeptics have long maintained. In this respect, our ordinary practices are not as unproblematic as Strawson supposes.

It might be thought that these suspicions about reactive attitudes have no bearing on responsibility, but with the expressive theory, that cannot be easily maintained. As we normally think of the matter, not all considerations that affect reactive attitudes are strictly relevant to responsibility. For example, if one shares a moral fault with another, one may feel it inappropriate to blame the other. Here the point is not that the other is not responsible or blameworthy, but that it is not *one's* business to blame. One should tend to one's own faults first.[24] Thoughts about moral luck seem to be continuous with this ordinary phenomenon. The thought is not that the other is not blameworthy, but that one may be no better, and that indignation on one's part would be self-righteous and indulgent. By calling our attention to our general ignorance of historical considerations, the skepticism we have just been considering is merely an extension of these reflections.

With an expressive theory, however, it is not clear that a general skepticism about the propriety of the reactive attitudes can be separated from skepticism about responsibility. For the latter concept *is* the concept of the conditions in which it is appropriate to respond to one another in reactive ways. In a Strawsonian view, there is no room for a wedge between the practices that evince the reactive attitudes and the belief in responsibility. In a particular case, one may believe another to be responsible without actually responding to him or her in reactive ways (due to strains of commitment and so on), because one may regard the other as blameworthy, as an appropriate object of the reactive attitudes by others in the moral community. But if one thinks that *none* of us mortals is in a position to blame, then it is doubtful that any sense can be given to the belief that the other is nonetheless blameworthy. One can still attribute cowardice, thoughtlessness, cruelty, and so on, to others; but as we have seen, these judgments are not sufficient in a Strawsonian view to characterize the practice of holding responsible. We might try to appeal to the reactive attitudes of a select group of actual or hypothetical judges (here is another job for God to do),[25] but then the connection to reactive attitudes becomes so tenuous or hypothetical that the attitudes lose the central role they are given in "Freedom and Resentment," and the

---

[24] Montaigne would not agree: "To censure my own faults in some other person seems to me no more incongruous than to censure, as I often do, another's in myself. They must be denounced everywhere, and be allowed no place of sanctuary." ("On the Education of Children," in *Essays*, Penguin Classics, 1971, p. 51.)

[25] Just as Berkeley tried to save the thesis that material objects consist in ideas.

expressive theory loses its distinctive character. It then collapses into the view discussed in the section called "Blaming and finding fault."

Objectivity and isolation

It remains unclear to what extent our ordinary practices involve dubious beliefs about ourselves and our histories. To acknowledge the relevance of historical considerations is, on any account, to acknowledge a potential source of skepticism about those practices; moreover, in a Strawsonian account (though not in a libertarian account), such skepticism cannot be readily separated from skepticism about responsibility itself. In this respect, Strawson is inordinately optimistic about our common ways.

However, these practices are vulnerable to a different kind of suspicion. This suspicion is related to Strawson's conception of the place of "retributive" sentiments in those practices, and to his claim that that practice, so conceived, is not something that is optional and open to radical criticism, but rather is part of the "framework" of our conception of human society. One could agree that the expressive theory best gives the basis and content of the practice of holding responsible and still maintain that abandoning this practice is not only conceivable but desirable, for what it expresses is itself destructive of human community. I conclude with some comments on this further issue.

Consider some remarks by Albert Einstein:

> I do not at all believe in human freedom in the philosophical sense. Everybody acts not only under external compulsion but also in accordance with inner necessity. Schopenhauer's saying, "A man can do what he wants, but not want what he wants," has been a very real inspiration to me since my youth; it has been a continual consolation in the face of life's hardships, my own and others', and an unfailing well-spring of tolerance. This realization mercifully mitigates the easily paralysing sense of responsibility and prevents us from taking ourselves and other people all too seriously; it is conducive to a view of life which, in particular, gives humor its due.[26]

Significantly, in the same place Einstein speaks of himself as a "lone traveler," with a "pronounced lack of need for direct contact with other human beings and human communities," who has

> never belonged to my country, my home, my friends, or even my immediate family, with my whole heart; in the face of all these ties, I have never lost a sense of distance and a need for solitude – feelings which increase with the years.

[26] Albert Einstein, *Ideas and Opinions*, Crown Publishers, 1982, pp. 8–9.

The point that interests me here is not that these remarks confute Strawson's claim that reactive attitudes are never in practice affected by an acceptance of determinism, but that they corroborate his central claim about the alternative to the reactive, participant stance. The "distance" of which Einstein speaks is just an aspect of the "detachment" Strawson thinks characterizes the objective stance. At its extremes, it takes the form of human isolation. What is absent from Einstein's outlook is something that, I suspect, Strawson cherishes: the attachment or commitment to the personal, as it might be called.[27]

Whatever its grounds, Einstein's outlook is not without its appeal. Perhaps part of its appeal can be attributed to a fear of the personal, but it is also appealing precisely on account of its repudiation of the retributive sentiments. In another place, Einstein salutes the person "to whom aggressiveness and resentment are alien."[28] Can such an ideal of the person be pursued only at the cost of the attachment to the personal? Must we choose between isolation and animosity?

Some of Strawson's remarks imply that we must:

Indignation, disapprobation, like resentment, tend to inhibit or at least to limit our goodwill towards the object of these attitudes, tend to promote at least partial and temporary withdrawal of goodwill. . . . (These are not contingent connections.) But these attitudes . . . are precisely the correlates of the moral demand in the case where the demand is felt to be disregarded. The making of the demand *is* the proneness to such attitudes. . . . The holding of them does not . . . involve . . . viewing their object other than as a member of the moral community. The partial withdrawal of goodwill which these attitudes entail, the modification they entail of the general demand that another should if possible be spared suffering, is . . . the consequence of *continuing* to view him as a member of the moral community: only as one who has offended against its demands. So the preparedness to acquiesce in that infliction of suffering on the offender which is an essential part of punishment is all of a piece with this whole range of attitudes. . . . (p. 77) [From *Proceedings of the British Academy*, Vol. 48 (1962), pp. 1–25. Reprinted by permission of the British Academy.]

This passage is troubling. Some have aspired to rid themselves of the readiness to limit goodwill and to acquiesce in the suffering of

27 To what extent Einstein lived up to this outlook, I am not prepared to say. Some other writings suggest a different view: "External compulsion can . . . reduce but never cancel the responsibility of the individual. In the Nuremberg trials, this idea was considered to be self-evident. . . . Institutions are in a moral sense impotent unless they are supported by the sense of responsibility of living individuals. An effort to arouse and strengthen this sense of responsibility of the individual is an important service to mankind" (op. cit., p. 27). Is Einstein taking a consequentialist stance here?
28 Ibid.

others not in order to relieve the strains of involvement, nor out of a conviction in determinism, but out of a certain ideal of human relationships, which they see as poisoned by the retributive sentiments. It is an ideal of human fellowship or love which embodies values that are arguably as historically important to our civilization as the notion of moral responsibility itself. The question here is not whether this aspiration is finally commendable, but whether it is compatible with holding one another morally responsible. The passage implies that it is not.

If holding one another responsible involves making the moral demand, and if the making of the demand *is* the proneness to such attitudes, and if such attitudes involve retributive sentiments and hence[29] a limitation of goodwill, then skepticism about retribution is skepticism about responsibility, and holding one another responsible is at odds with one historically important ideal of love.

Many who have this ideal, such as Gandhi or King,[30] do not seem to adopt an objective attitude in Strawson's sense. Unlike Einstein's, their lives do not seem characterized by human isolation: They are often intensely involved in the "fray" of interpersonal relations. Nor does it seem plausible to suppose that they do not hold themselves and others morally responsible: They *stand up* for themselves and others against their oppressors; they *confront* their oppressors with the fact of their misconduct, *urging* and even *demanding* consideration for themselves and others; but they manage, or come much closer than others to managing, to do such things without vindictiveness or malice.

Hence, Strawson's claims about the interpenetration of responsibility and the retributive sentiments must not be confused with the expressive theory itself. As these lives suggest, the retributive sentiments can in principle be stripped away from holding responsible and the demands and appeals in which this consists. What is left are various forms of reaction and appeal to others as moral agents. The boundaries of moral responsibility are the boundaries of intelligible moral address. To regard another as morally responsible is to react to him or her as a moral self.[31]

---

[29] Rather than attempting to separate retribution from responsibility, one might try to harmonize retribution and goodwill. This possibility seems to me worth exploring.

[30] For these examples, and the discussion in this section, I am indebted to Stern (op. cit.).

[31] We have, of course, seen reasons why these boundaries require further delineation.

12

Statistical norms and moral attributions

FERDINAND SCHOEMAN

Moral philosophers since the time of Aristotle have grappled with the appropriateness of attributing fault to an agent for behavior caused by something external to the agent. Even in the Garden of Eden, Adam and Eve each try to shift blame from themselves for eating some of the forbidden fruit by pointing to external influences. Evident in our institution of blame is our practice of sorting out factors attributable to the agent and factors attributable to extraneous causes. Apparently we identify behavior that stems from character – or at least from a will not overborne by distorting influences – as the most appropriate object of moral judgment, since this most clearly reflects the moral self. The extent of a person's contribution to an act has always been a central parameter of moral evaluation.[1] The traditional challenge has been to differentiate behavior attributable to an agent and behavior not so attributable when everything about an agent is itself causally attributable to outside factors.

Over the past thirty years, a branch of psychology called *attribution theory* has sought a means of differentiating what is attributable to the environment and what to the individual. Although its principal objective is to articulate causes of human behavior, because of the apparent relevance of the causal origin of behavior to moral attributions, some advocates of the theory allege the theory to be pregnant with significant moral implications – implications that would upset some normal judgmental practices. In this view, to the extent that we can find causes outside the individual for certain behavior, to that extent we

The author would like to thank Claudia Mills, Michael Moore, Michael Stocker, Kent Greenawalt, Alison Wylie, Herbert Morris, Jonathan Adler, John Sabini, Michael Costa, John Fischer, Hugh Wilder, and Davis Baird for creative comments on earlier versions of this paper, and Thomas Cafferty for helpful suggestions of what to read in the psychological literature. A version of this chapter has been presented at the University of Alabama at Birmingham Philosophy Colloquium, and at the Eastern Division Meetings of the APA, 1986.
[1] David Daube, "Error and ignorance as excuses in ancient law," in his book *Ancient Jewish law* (Leiden: Brill, 1981).

must reduce our estimate of the individual's own causal contribution to the act. Ross and Anderson characterize the failure to judge in light of this perspective as "the fundamental attribution error."[2]

[T]he *fundamental attribution error* is the tendency for attributers to underestimate the impact of situational factors and to overestimate the role of dispositional factors in controlling behavior. As "intuitive" psychologists, we seem too often to be nativists, or proponents of individual differences, and too seldom S–R behaviorists. We too readily infer broad personal dispositions and expect consistency in behavior or outcomes across widely disparate situations and contexts. We jump to hasty conclusions upon witnessing the behavior of our peers, overlooking the impact of relevant environmental forces and constraints.

The issue I wish to consider is whether insight in apportioning causal responsibility for actions properly affects our moral evaluations of behavior and agents. The idea would be that the more we see behavior as stemming from causes external to the agent, the less the behavior can be causally attributed to him or her; and the less the agent's causal contribution, the less his or her moral contribution. The level of moral accountability is alleged to be a function of the level of causal contribution and to vary directly with it. I find this use of causal insight both appealing and wrong. In what follows, I critically explore the seductive character of this picture. Though I will challenge the attributionist arguments, I do find latent in the attributionist perspective, and will explore, an important moral position that philosophers have not adequately addressed.

The attributionist perspective has considerable potential for understanding both large-scale social evil and cultural relativism. It can be argued, for instance, that anti-Semitism was so widespread among the Germans in the late 1930s that individual anti-Semites in that context were less responsible for their attitudes than are anti-Semites in less racist societies. Analogous remarks can be made about tolerance for racism generally or sexism or slavery in various contexts. Attribution theory has the appeal that it explains why we would judge a present-day racist differently than we would a racist of an earlier generation, where the racism is accountable by enculturation or particularly confusing, fearful, trying, and morally chaotic circumstances.

The critic might retort that it is one thing to explain behavior and

---

[2] "Shortcomings in the attribution process: On the origins and maintenance of erroneous social assessments," in *Judgment under uncertainty: Heuristics and biases,* ed. Daniel Kahneman, Paul Slovic, and Amos Tversky (New York: Cambridge University Press, 1982), p. 135.

quite another to excuse it. Discovering causes is useful and important for both scientific and social purposes, but this has little to do with assessing a given person's moral *capacities*. It might very well be enlightening to find that we have a tendency seriously to underestimate the situational influences on individuals in explaining their behavior. To the extent that we believe the environment contributed more, the individual's contribution must be seen as diminished. This relates to causal histories. Still, the case has yet to be made for extracting any general moral relevance from such a causal discovery. To cast the issue in traditional compatibilist terms, it is only insofar as these newly appreciated causal factors are seen as *disabling* rational judgment or as placing unfair burdens upon agents that they can be seen as morally charged. Merely to show that the offending behavior is causally attributable to the environment does nothing by itself to excuse that behavior. After all, maybe everything is attributable to the environment.

To help make the discussion more concrete, I introduce a practical problem to which attribution theory would seem to be morally relevant (section I), then offer some background on attribution theory (section II), and next evaluate the moral claims attribution theorists have made or might make for their theories (section III). In the final section (section IV), I offer a comparison of the meaning of psychological theories in the cognitive and the moral domains. My objective is to assess whether anything new and challenging for our traditional conception of responsibility is injected into the controversy by attribution theory. I conclude, after much searching, that there is.

I. A sample problem

In this section I introduce a practical problem attribution theorists think can be analyzed in terms of their framework. In discussing this problem and making some preliminary remarks about the theory, I mention a few methodological issues that attribution theorists must take to heart.

Everyone is familiar with the experiment Stanley Milgram conducted on obedience to authority.[3] Experimental subjects were assigned the role of asking questions to a person and administering, they believed, increasingly strong shocks when the person answered the questions incorrectly. Under some testing conditions, two-thirds of those participating continued with the full battery of shocks, even

---

[3] Stanley Milgram, *Obedience to authority* (New York: Harper & Row, 1974).

though they believed the respondent was being seriously hurt by the shocks and wanted to stop the experiment. Indeed, they were told by the respondent that he had a heart condition and that the shocks could kill him. Nearly all of those who finished the battery of shocks felt great anxiety with what they were doing, but when they indicated that they wanted to quit, they were told by the experimenter that they had to continue, that it was in the interest of science that they continue, and finally that the experimenter would take full responsibility if something terrible happened to the person being shocked.

Nearly everyone questioned about the experimental setup, without being told the results, judged that he or she would quit the experiment at the first signs of protest by the person being shocked, and expected everyone else to act likewise. People thought the compliance rate would be very near zero.

An attribution theorist looking at the high compliance rate in the Milgram experiment would say that in any given case, greater causal responsibility than is generally assumed must be attributed to the background environment and much less to the experimental subject. Interestingly, even if everyone participating had quit early in the experiment, the uniformity of response still would have provided the attribution theorist with evidence that the response is attributable largely to the environment and only marginally to the individual personalities. Only a robust diversity of responses in a constant setting would have suggested that the individual personalities loom large in accounting for the observed outcome. Rather than concluding from Milgram's study something about people in general who confront certain conditions, the attribution theorist seems committed to drawing conclusions about the effectiveness of the environment in occasioning a given response in most people subjected to it. What we learn is that individuals as such contribute little to the outcome; the evidence is that we need to know little about specific individuals to predict their responses in this environment.

It will be noted that this way of dividing up what belongs to the individual and what to the environment is unusual and does not track our nontechnical ways of apportioning causal credit. There is no problem with such nonstandard divisions so long as they are not confused with the standard, or substituted for them without argument; but it is important to focus for a moment on this difference. Behavior common to nearly all people would in the attribution theorist's account be credited to the environment, rather than to a common nature. Since we normally think that part of what a person is includes what he or she shares with others of the species or community, we might wonder why the attribution theorist deals this aspect of self to the outside world.

To the extent that the outside world is reflected in a person biologically or socially, the outer–inner dichotomy is misleading. A person's tendency to get hungry on a given schedule or to think about things in a scientific way is no less his or hers just because others share it. Nor are such tendencies less the person's than those idiosyncratic to him or her. We do not need to know about these common factors in the agent specifically to be able to predict how the agent will behave, whereas we do need to know the idiosyncratic factors. However, its usefulness in making predictions is not the only basis for regarding some factor as an integral part of a person. Behavior that stems from widely shared aspects of a person would normally be seen as attributable to the person, and not just, or primarily, to the environment. There is a reason for this. We regard people as responsible for what they are, even when much or most of what they are they share with others. We won't want to give up this perspective without good reason.

Let us now tentatively explore the kind of moral relevance the compliance rate information suggests. I begin by assuming that I am an experimental subject, and like most, I horrify myself by completing the battery of shocks. My first response is to regard myself as morally indistinguishable from a murderer, saved only by the duplicity of the experimenter from being an actual murderer. Then I find out that I am one of a substantial majority who responded this way. Might I find any consolation in the latter discovery?

One thing I find out by learning of the test results is that I am not worse than most people. I am not a statistical monster. Comforting as this may be, it does not yet show anything mitigating about what I did. It is the next step in the attribution theorist's account that suggests just this. First of all, it is observed that in light of the general response, the environment must be thought largely causally responsible for the particular reactions, and that individuals contributed much less than would normally be assumed. (Remember, the *expected* compliance rate was close to zero.) To the extent that I contributed less to an outcome than would normally be supposed, to that extent I deserve less blame or credit than would normally be assessed. This comes out more clearly if we compare the actual test outcome with a possible alternative. Suppose that nearly all subjects in Milgram's experiment refused to comply, but that I was among the compliant. In this case, very little of my response is attributable to the environment and almost all is attributable to me. This suggests it is morally worse to comply in a context where others refuse than to comply in a context where others also comply. The fact of others complying under similar conditions indicates less personal contribution to the outcome, and this diminished contribution lessens the credit or blame attributable to the agent.

What must be kept in mind is that our situation is characterized by a radical disparity between how people actually respond and what people anticipate they and others would do. Is this difference in actual and predicted outcomes morally relevant in assessing individual blame? Our reactions to compliers, even to ourselves if we happen to be among the compliers, is that they have done something that almost no one else would have done, suggesting that something about *them in particular* is salient in bringing about the worrisome result. So in this context one would tend to judge the individual harshly. In discovering that most respond in the same way, we find that there is less that is salient about the individual compliers in accounting for the outcome, and more about the environment. The question is whether this new information is mitigating, and if so, for what specific reasons? Is it true that the more we see environmental factors as accounting for a given outcome the less credit or blame we assign to individual agents? We will come back to these questions.

II. Attribution theory

In this section I lay out the framework and alleged moral import of attribution theory. Attribution theory stems in part from efforts at achieving a critical understanding of the role of personality in human behavior. Normally and naïvely we think there is a personality that possesses and inhabits an individual and that characterizes or causes consistent patterns of behavior throughout a wide variety of contexts. We presume that knowing what a person is like in one context allows us to predict what the person is like in other contexts. We think we can make these extrapolations because we assume that the personality is operative and revealed in most contexts; once we get a glimmer of this, we will know what principle is functioning in all the contexts the individual may encounter. Personality assessment studies have been concerned with the extent to which characteristics seem uniform through a wide variety of contexts. To the extent that they do not, the notion of a personality is called into question.

Those who deny the predictive role of personality claim to have discovered that behavior in one context is not a good predictor of behavior in diverse contexts and that fundamentally there is no *pat-*

tern of behavior that is context-independent. What turns out to be a better predictor, according to these researchers, is knowing the base rates of how people in general act under a particular circumstance. So if you see me behave in a particular way in context A and want to know how I am likely to behave in context Z, knowing how people in general behave in Z is a better predictor of *my* behavior in Z than is knowing how I behaved in A and assuming that my personality, which gave rise to my A-relevant behavior, will also govern my Z-relevant behavior.

Those who debunk personality theory offer an account of why we inevitably attribute personalities to people, even though nothing performs the role personalities are assigned in the public estimation. According to this account:

1. We are very hasty in making generalizations about the inner workings or causal properties of people and objects, and confidently base predictions on what is revealed in very limited encounters.
2. We typically are not disappointed in our causal hypotheses because we tend to confront people in a relatively narrow range of contexts.
3. Even if we do happen upon counterexamples, we either do not notice or discount them or explain them away because we are hesitant to modify our picture once formed. Once possessed of a little evidence, we close off inquiry about the person.[4]

The thrust of attribution theory was to assign to the environment and away from the individual much of what we regard as the underlying causal basis of behavior. What is the connection between skepticism about personalities on the one hand, and this new sort of causal division on the other? The answer must be that the connection is tenuous. Whether there are personalities in the traditional sense has to do with how much intrapersonal consistency there is between contexts encountered. Whether we should attribute causal responsibility to the individual or to the environment has to do with what the base rates turn out to be. In theory, these can vary independently. People could act consistently in a wide variety of contexts and share their ways of being consistent. People could act consistently in a wide variety of contexts and not share their ways with others. Individuals could

---

[4] This perspective is forcefully worked out in Walter Mischel's classic *Personality and assessment* (New York: Wiley, 1968).

exhibit little consistency through contexts and still act as others do in those contexts. Finally, there could be little consistency throughout contexts and little pattern in how subjects in general respond. Whether there are things like personalities that function as we naïvely think and whether there are patterns of response discoverable among different agents are two entirely separate questions.[5]

We have good reasons for being skeptical about efforts at causal apportionment, particularly when this is based on an analysis of variation.[6] For instance, suppose that an environmental change in one direction leads to less variance in response, but that a change in the other direction leads to more. If one had tested only in the direction leading to less variation, one would have attributed more to the environment, whereas testing across the spectrum of environmental changes indicates that the environmental factors balance out in portraying an overall picture of environmental contribution. Despite these reservations, for purposes of this discussion I will accept the attribution theorist's position on causal apportionment. It is a daring theory because it takes something central to our ways of looking at ourselves and tells us that this is based on an error in attribution of causal roles. What moral difference will this discovery make?

As a start to answering this, we review some of the discussions attribution theorists have offered to connect causal and moral assessment. We begin with Fritz Heider's influential book, *The Psychology of Interpersonal Relations*.[7] Besides being an attribution theorist, Heider is a careful observer of evaluation practices.

Heider finds it crucial first to distinguish personal and impersonal causality, where the critical factor is intention.

... intention is the central factor in personal causality, that it is the intention of a person that brings order into the wide variety of possible action sequences by coordinating them to a final outcome. Therefore, if we are convinced that *o* did *x* intentionally we generally link the *x* more intimately with the person than if we think that *o* did *x* unintentionally. By the same token, if we account for an act by a person's stupidity or clumsiness, that is by ability factors, we tend to hold him less responsible than if we take the act as an indication of his motives. Thus it is that the question of premeditation is

[5] See John Sabini and Maury Silver, "Dispositional vs. situational interpretations of Milgram's obedience experiments: The fundamental attributional error," *Journal of the Theory of Social Behavior* 13, 1983: 147–54.

[6] R. C. Lewontin, "The analysis of variance and the analysis of causes," *American Journal of Human Genetics* 26, 1974: 400–11. I am indebted to Davis Baird for bringing this article to my attention.

[7] Fritz Heider, *The psychology of interpersonal relations*, reprint ed. (Hillsdale, NJ: Lawrence Erlbaum Associates, Inc., 1983).

important in the decisions regarding guilt. . . . People are held responsible for their intentions and exertions but not so strictly for their abilities. (p. 112)

Earlier, Heider indicates what he means by "intention." First, he identifies acting intentionally with acting purposively: "True personal causality is restricted to instances where p tries to cause x, where x is his goal," even if the individual is not aware of his goal (p. 100). Unintended consequences are sometimes still attributable to an agent, but in an attenuated form. Heider differentiates acts intended as means and acts intended as ends. After all, what you want as a means is less tied to you than what you want as an ultimate end.

Heider thus treats the various factors of what a person does as differentially attributable to him and these factors themselves as differentially identifiable with the agent. He distinguishes abilities from desires and each of these from level of motivation. Heider claims that an act intended is, typically, more closely identified with the individual than an act that resulted from a disability or incompetence. Intentions are salient in explaining behavior, since they are not part of the steady background of abilities.

Heider identifies four developmental stages of attribution. The most primitive stage consists in attributing much to an individual that he (or she) cannot control at all, just so long as there is some connection between the person and the event at issue. For example, what my family or my country does is attributable to me. Second comes the stage of attributing to an individual anything to which he is causally connected. The penultimate stage consists in attributing to an individual only what he intends. The final stage consists in seeing what an individual intends as only in part attributable to him, and apportioning much of this to environmental factors:

Finally there is the stage at which even p's own motives are not entirely ascribed to him but are seen as having their source in the environment. We may say about an action of p's "It is not his fault that be behaves like that. He has been provoked." We mean by this that anybody would have felt and acted as he did under the circumstances. The causal lines leading to the final outcome are still guided by p, and therefore the act fits into the structure of personal causality, but since the source of the motive is felt to be the coercion of the environment and not p himself, responsibility for the act is at least shared by the environment. . . . (p. 114)

Two points are worth noting about this passage. First, there is the strong suggestion that the pattern of how people in general would behave in the same situation represents the norm by which we can judge any particular case. I reassure myself morally by behaving the way others, similarly situated, would behave. Second, Heider correctly observes that *some* factors that cause behavior, even intentional behavior, may attenuate attributions of responsibility. However, he slides from this to a far more radical claim: When environmental factors can be shown to cause intentional behavior, moral responsibility must be shared between the individual and the environment. He generalizes from the case of provocation in a way that may not at all bear the moral burden he places on the analysis. Consider this example. Suppose I offer to pay college students several hundred dollars to speed on the highway. Now we have shifted the source of the motive to the environment, and we can reasonably predict that nearly everyone propositioned will speed. Is the agent less morally accountable for speeding under these circumstances than under others where the motivation is not supplied by the environment, like speeding for the thrill of it? Factors that mitigate work in more subtle ways than this. Many environmental factors can generate higher than normal base rates and introduce new causal stories without qualifying as an excuse. Attribution theorists may be insufficiently sensitive to this.

[A]s we have seen in the naïve analysis of action, the change x is not always attributed to the person. Sometimes it is attributed to luck, for example, or at least partly to such environmental factors as task difficulty. *Personal responsibility then varies with the relative attribution of environmental factors to the action outcome;* in general, the more they are felt to influence the action, the less the person is held responsible. One may consider the different forms in which the concept of responsibility has been used as successive stages in which attribution to the person decreases and attribution to the environment increases. (p. 112)

It will be recognized that the issue of responsibility includes the problem of attribution of action. That is, it is important which of the several conditions of action – the intentions of the person, personal power factors or environmental forces – is to be given primary weight for the action outcome. Once such attribution has been decided upon, the evaluation of responsibility is possible. (p. 114)

We might expect bipolar attribution to represent a more sophisticated approach to understanding than attribution to one or the other pole, for after all, the former requires taking into account of more than one pattern of condition-effect interaction. This is one reason why in everyday life we burden the environment or subject with the whole responsibility for the effect in question, only to recognize the contribution of both upon more careful examination. Kurt Lewin has proposed the general formulation that behavior is a function of the person and the environment. This may appear to be a truism, yet it must be held to the fore as a constant reminder lest the tendency to unipolar attribution lead to the neglect of one or the other factors. (p. 154)

Attribution theorists, beginning with Heider, offer an explanation for why environmental factors are systematically excluded in lay efforts at understanding human behavior – the relative salience of the person acting against a social background that stays relàtively fixed.

Behavior . . . has such salient properties it tends to engulf the total field rather than be confined to its proper position as a local stimulus whose interpretation requires the additional data of a surrounding field. (p. 18)

First we are told that responsibility can be assessed only after causal factors are analyzed and then that every action integrates both environmental and personal factors. What would seem to follow from this is that attributions of responsibility to people should be attenuated to the extent that environmental factors contribute to the behavior in question. In holding people accountable in general, we have a tendency to simplify by treating the issue of causal attribution as having one of only two possible outcomes: Either the agent is fully causally and morally responsible, or the environment is fully causally responsible and the agent is insulated from any moral attribution.

Harold Kelley wrote important papers on causal and moral attribution that elaborate competing and interacting factors like those just mentioned. One principle Kelley introduces is labeled "the augmentation principle." Basically, this principle indicates that the greater the obstacles, costs, and inhibitions an agent overcomes in performing a given action, the greater the causal role and the moral attribution assigned to the agent.

When there are known to be constraints, costs, sacrifices, or risks involved in taking an action, the action once taken is attributed more to the actor than it would be otherwise.

[footnote] Behavior of low social desirability is attributed more to the person than is behavior of high social desirability. The former usually implies an action contrary to social norms, that is, a behavior enacted despite inhibitory external causes.[8]

It is assumed that people are equipped with strong inhibitions against harmful behavior; thus harmful actions are probably the result of

[8] Harold Kelley, "The process of causal attribution," *American Psychologist* 28, 1973: 114.

especially powerful and profound inclinations that haunt the agent's character. However, if the agent transgresses a norm for the sake of preventing loss to himself, he or she is judged more compassionately than if the transgression is aimed at securing some gain.[9]

This perspective does account for many of our judgmental practices. For instance, when people say such things as "boys will be boys," they mean that if a boy misbehaves, that does not indicate as serious a flaw in the child as if it had been a girl who engaged in the same act type. The behavior might be attributed to male immaturity, and hence more to disabilities than to bad intentions. For this reason, it does not count very much against a boy to misbehave. Recall Heider's remark that it is the intention behind the act that is most closely identified with the agent, and consequently intentions serve as the primary basis for moral evaluation. Since a male's immaturity may be salient in our picture of the child's behavior, the intention will not have to be as strong to result in action, because what it had to overcome was less significant a factor in the case of boys than in the case of girls.

If we return to the Milgram experiment and observe the kind of statements attribution theorists make about it, we get an argument for the immediate relevance of statistical norms to enlightened moral attributions. According to this position, the failure of most subjects to exercise moral judgment effectively in a given context points out something about our environment. The discovery of this environmental impact makes the transgression less attributable to the agent than the same behavior in a context where almost everyone refrained from giving shocks to the limit. Consequently, these environmental factors ought to temper our condemnation of those who fare poorly on such trials. Our tendency to judge subjects in this experiment harshly is based on our preconceived, but incorrect, belief that almost no one in this situation would risk administering life-threatening shocks. Our judgment stems from our beliefs about how the average person would respond to the situation, rather than from the truth about this. Once we appreciate the full extent of the environmental influences, we will attribute less fault to the compliant subjects.

This is the orthodox attitude of attribution theorists, though their acknowledgment of it as such is not always explicit. Generally sticking to the cognitive and predictive realm, they point out that subjects told about the Milgram experiment and asked to assess the *character* of a

---

[9] Harold Kelley, "Attribution in social interaction," in E. E. Jones et al., eds., *Attribution: Perceiving the causes of behavior* (Morristown, NJ: General Learning Press, 1971), p. 19.

complier rate them lower than normal on personal moral qualities like dependency and warmth, and higher than normal on factors like aggressiveness. The idea is clearly implied that *these Milgram subjects cannot be flawed or as bad as naïve subjects are prone to judge them.* The reason for the misguided moral assessment stems from a *faulty attribution of behavior to character, rather than to environment.* Connected with this is the common failure to see oneself and those like one as able to respond the way the Milgram subjects characteristically did. Some passages from Nisbett and Ross's classic *Human inference: Strategies and shortcomings of social judgment*[10] can be used to substantiate this assessment of the field.

Perhaps the most direct evidence of the layperson's tendency to underestimate the role of situational factors in controlling behavior is Bierbrauer's (1973) investigation of lay impressions of the forces operating in the classic Milgram (1963) obedience study. In Bierbrauer's study, observers were exposed to a vebatim reenactment of one subject's obedience to the point of delivering the maximum shock to the supposed victim, and then were asked to predict how other subjects would behave. Bierbrauer's observers consistently and dramatically underestimated the degree to which subjects generally would yield to the situational forces that they had viewed at first hand. . . . In other words, they assumed that *the obedience of the particular subject whom they had "observed" reflected his distinguishing personal dispositions rather than the potency of the situational pressures and constraints* that acted upon *all* subjects. (pp. 121–2; emphasis added)

In a remarkable demonstration of the failure of consensus information to affect causal attribution, Miller, Gillen, Schenker, and Radlove (1973) showed that consensus information about the behavior of subjects in Milgram's (1963) obedience study had little effect on judgment about a particular subject who delivered the highest possible amount of shock to a confederate. All subjects in Miller's and colleagues' experiment were told about Milgram's procedures, including that his subject sample was a cross-section of the community in which the study was conducted. Some subjects also were shown the results, notably that 65 percent of the subjects delivered the maximum possible shock. All subjects were then told about two people who had delivered the maximum shock and were asked to rate these people on a number of trait scales, including warmth, likableness, dependency, aggressiveness, and attractiveness. The consensus information had an effect on only one of eleven such trait ratings. That is, the knowledge that giving the maximum shock was actually the modal response did not reduce subjects' tendency to make strong negative dispositional inferences about a particular person who showed that response. (p. 131)

---

[10] Richard Nisbett and Lee Ross, *Human inference: Strategies and shortcomings of social judgment* (Englewood Cliffs, NJ: Prentice-Hall, 1980).

Here, Nisbett and Ross explicitly criticize the subjects of Miller's study for not altering their morally loaded personality evaluations of Milgram subjects after learning of the high base rate for compliance. To be oblivious to the mitigating effects of general compliance is just another striking instance of the fundamental attribution error. Miller and his co-authors specifically found the following:

High-shock persons were rated significantly more dependent, weak, cold, unintelligent, maladjusted, conforming, unlikable, aggressive, unattractive, and follower-type than low-shock persons.[11]

They conclude that given the high base rate of compliance in Milgram's original experiment, *one cannot point to morally defective aspects of personality to account for the problem,* but must place the weight on environmental factors instead.

The implications for perceiving harmful obedience to be the result of defective personality when available behavioral evidence does not support such a position are significant. . . . (p. 128)

The idea here, again explicit, is that the introduction of environmental factors to account for behavior diminishes the agent's level of moral accountability. The evidence that the behavior is attributable to the environment is the high base rate for compliance in the experiment. So it would seem as if we are following a moral inference pattern of this sort:

The more atypical an act type is in a given context, the more the individual performing the act is accountable for it.

The more common an act type is in a given context, the less the individual performing the act is accountable for the act and the more the environment is accountable.

Note that this is a moral rather than an empirical claim, because the very point of the writing of attribution theorists about accountability is to distinguish what people are prone to do – discount the environment when assessing culpability – and what they should do. Attribution theorists credit themselves with introducing an enlightened view on the measure of accountability. This is a position that deserves attention.

It is worth mentioning one final methodological observation that relates to the attribution theorist's practice of classifying causes as belonging either to the environment or to the character of an agent.

---

[11] Miller, Gollen, Schenker, and Radlove, "Perceptions of obedience to authority," *Proceedings, 81st Annual Convention, American Psychological Association,* 1973: 127.

Even if it is true that the environment competes with character or personality as an explanatory variable, it does not thereby compete with the will or intention of the agent. Even in the face of an environmental explanation, each of our acts could still be the product of our wills, for which we may be held fully responsible on any theory of responsibility that turns on choice and will.[12]

III. Critical discussion

In this section I critically examine the moral implications some psychologists have drawn from the fundamental attribution error. I travel down numerous, circuitous paths in pursuit of an array of possible rationales for the position. This section is divided into two subsections: In subsection A, the paths that do not seem ultimately adequate are considered; in subsection B, the more auspicious paths are followed.

A. *The inauspicious paths*

Attribution theory in general reveals a pragmatic and predictive conception of causal analysis. Something is treated as a causal factor insofar as it offers a basis for reliable predictions of behavior. An effect is not attributed to an individual if information about him or her does not alter our judgment of the probability of that person engaging in the behavior in question, when compared with the probability that would be assigned on the basis of general base rates.

Also, finding out about a person that he or she does what most people do in a given context offers very little information about *him* or *her*, because that is what would have been predicted anyway just on the basis of base rates. Only statistically unusual behavior is treated as having any information value about a given agent.[13] Earlier I voiced some concern about using analysis of variance as a criterion of causal contribution. At this juncture one can also mention the problem of assuming that what is predictively useful is causally informative. Again, I intend to keep the focus of the paper on the moral implications of attribution theory and avoid the issue of the methodological adequacy of the theory itself.

This scheme of interpreting what it is to be a causal factor, whatever its value in predicting behavior, would seem to be poorly suited to

---

[12] I am indebted to Michael Moore for bringing this point to my attention.
[13] See Edward Jones and Keith Davis, "From acts to dispositions: The attribution process in person perception," in Leonard Berkowitz, ed., *Advances in experimental social psychology*, Vol. 2 (New York: Academic Press, 1965).

ordinary talk about what is attributable to an individual. Even if 98 percent of a population pays its taxes, we would tend to think it to a person's credit if he pays. If he does so out of a sense of fairness, this would tend to count still more to his credit, even if that was the basis for nearly everyone's compliance.

The approach we have seen attribution theorists take is not inevitable. An alternative approach involves treating these environmental factors as of problematical moral significance. In this second, critical approach, one could follow the compatibilist line and say that environmental causal factors are mitigating only when they literally undermine an agent's capacity to act rationally or when they make the personal costs of moral compliance excessive. According to the *Model Penal Code,* section 2.09, a person has a defense for an illegal act he is charged with if he acted as a result of a threat of force "which a person of reasonable firmness in his situation would have been unable to resist." However, the fact that there are environmental causes is not what is critical in attenuating culpability; rather it is the diminished level of rational abilities or the moral costs. Since behavior for which an individual *can* be held responsible is just as much subject to causal explanation as behavior that is excusable, causation drops out as a factor in differentiating these two classes of acts. Philosophers, and social theorists in general, have yet to come up with a general account of what kinds of interferences with an individual undermine moral accountability. For instance, if someone programs me to be just like you and you are a paradigm responsible, autonomous agent, does it follow that I am also responsible and autonomous? Could the answer to this be "Yes" if before I was programmed, I expended every effort to be unlike you? These and other problems, like the relevance of propaganda and socialization, are largely unaddressed in philosophical treatments of responsibility.[14] Yet acknowledging the incompleteness of this area of understanding is a far cry from conceding that any kind of environmental influence or cause diminishes agent accountability merely because it is a causal factor.

It makes sense to talk about the environment being more of a cause in case *A* as opposed to case *B* if one is concerned with what kind of action to take to change things. Whenever behavior in a certain con-

---

[14] See Michael Slote, "Understanding free will," in *Journal of Philosophy* 77, 1980: 136–50; Ferdinand Schoeman, "Responsibility and the problem of induced desires," *Philosophical Studies* 34, 1978: 293–301; Patricia Greenspan, "Behavior control and freedom of action," *Philosophical Review* 87, 1978: 25–40; and Daniel Dennett, *Elbow room* (Cambridge, MA: MIT Press, 1984).

text is undesirable and we want to take action to change this pattern, we have several courses open to us. We can try to change the character or motivation of the agents so that they will act differently in similar circumstances; we can try to change the environment so that the troublesome contexts are less likely to arise; or we can attempt to do both. Now, if the vast majority of agents acts the same way in a particular context, this may provide some reason to think it is economical to work on the environment rather than on the individuals. This decision in no way forces us to attenuate our estimation of the individual accountability, for that attitude speaks to a different issue. However, even if the environment is assigned a major causal role, it may be that the environment is not easily alterable in this respect but that individuals are, and this would be a reason to focus on changing the individuals and ignoring the environment. It could even be that though we cannot change agents so that they would act differently in that particular context, holding them accountable would have favorable consequences for their behavior in other contexts, or perhaps failing to hold them accountable would have unfavorable consequences in most other contexts.[15] It is of the utmost importance not to conflate such issues of efficient social policy with assessments of accountability. I will readdress this issue and suggest that there is a moral thesis lurking in the attributionist's approach that has not been adequately confronted. Ultimately, this moral thesis accounts for the continual allure of incompatibilism, even when as a metaphysical position it is repeatedly defeated. Any position vanquished that often must have something to it.

Those who judge Milgram's subjects harshly and are uninfluenced by the base rates for compliance, according to the attribution theorists themselves, treat these subjects as having certain morally significant personality or character defects. It is not clear to me why the attribution theorists want to fault this assessment. The fact that a defect is more widespread than most people assume is not transparently relevant to the issue of whether or not there is such a personality defect. The issue of whether a defect is idiosyncratic, because it stems from a given individual's particular conditions, or widespread, because it stems from the cultural background, is not established as germane to the question of whether any given individual is to be faulted.

15 I am indebted to Michael Costa for basically writing this paragraph for me. For an enlightening account of responsibility that integrates issues such as these with theory, see Joel Feinberg's collection of essays, *Doing and deserving* (Princeton, NJ: Princeton University Press, 1970).

Several considerations might support the attribution theorist's position. One is that the mere fact that most people fail in a given environment suggests that succeeding in that environment is difficult.

If we know that only one person succeeded or only one person failed out of a large number in a certain endeavor, then we shall ascribe success or failure to this person – to his great ability or to his lack of ability. On the other hand, if we know that practically everyone who tries succeeds, we shall attribute the success to the task. The task is then described as being easy. If hardly anyone succeeds it is felt to be difficult.[16]

So in a context where most fail one must (or can plausibly) presume that something makes the task difficult, and given this difficulty, failure reflects less badly on any given individual. How else do we come to know a task is difficult but that there is a high failure rate? In the Milgram experiment we know that nearly all the subjects indicate that they want to quit and are domineered into continuing. The anxiety they experience in administering high-voltage electrical shocks gives us evidence of their vulnerability to forces or factors they were not prepared or equipped to oppose.

The issue of the relationship between difficulty of task and mitigation is worth addressing in some detail. Consider social pressures to adopt values that we know lead people to do self- or other-regarding harms. Statistical norms, it could be suggested, are indicative of social pressures to behave in certain ways – ways that effectively reduce the availability of certain options. In this context, it could be suggested that statistical norms signal social pressures and that social pressures in turn affect the degree of attribution we assign for behavior. For instance, women abused in a marital relationship find it difficult to take action to protect themselves because of omnipresent social messages to the effect that if they are not flourishing in their marriage, it is their own fault, and in any event it is their duty to put up with whatever adversity marriage occasions. We know that many women bear their staggering anguish silently. We do not wish to blame them for their situation or suffering. So we point to causes "outside" of them, like socialization and abject options, to account for their tolerance in a way that does not reflect adversely on them.

The questions we have to deal with now is whether socialization, as revealed in base rates, makes certain decisions hard, and if so whether it should be treated as mitigating for that reason. The notion of a hard or difficult choice is ambiguous; it can mean that something is

---

[16] Fritz Heider, *The psychology of interpersonal relations* (New York: Wiley, 1958), p. 89.

unlikely to be selected for a variety of reasons, or it can mean that the options engender moral conflict. Compare two scenarios:

1. I am socialized to value affluence, and someone offers me a large sum of money if I lie under oath during an upcoming custody dispute or paternity suit. Declining the offer may be difficult for me in the sense that I have a lot to gain by accepting it and therefore I feel strongly tempted to do so. This kind of difficulty does not provide a mitigating circumstance, though it will go a long way toward predicting and explaining complicity rates. In the case of deciding whether to perjure myself for a large sum of money, what we mean by calling the decision hard is that I have a powerful incentive for lying. Unless declining to lie will result in psychic imbalance for me, or unless some other special circumstance can be introduced here, the difficulty of the decision makes no difference to our moral assessment of the agent.[17] (I do feel the attributionist's urge to acknowledge that if someone would be willing to lie for a very small gain, that would be an aggravating factor in our assessment of the agent. I suppose this shows that the agent's character is more flawed than someone who had a higher threshold. Here we want to distinguish having a price and being corrupted by an offer. Being corrupted by an offer suggests *losing a battle* between moral and other considerations in a way that having a price does not.)

2. Now suppose I am offered a bribe to lie, as above, but that what tempts me about the bribe is my need to pay for an operation for my child, who will otherwise die or be left significantly handicapped. Here too we want to say the agent faces a hard decision, but now we mean that the moral picture itself is cloudy — that we have a presumptive case of moral conflict. In contrast with the kind of difficulty first discussed, the difficulty of a decision occasioned by conflicting moral considerations will be mitigating.

The reason that "merely" feeling strongly tempted to do something improper is not an excuse is that we hold people up to a standard of maturity, and expect mature people to deal with a broad range of emotions and levels of desire. (Recall the standard use in the *Model Penal Code* to characterize duress: that which a person of *reasonable* firmness would have been *unable* to resist. How would we test whether a given threat or offer is one a reasonable person would have been able to resist?) That many or most fall short of this standard does little

---

[17] See H. Fingarette, "Victimization: A legalist analysis of coercion, deception, undue influence, and escusable prison escape," *Washington and Lee Law Review* 42, 1985: 65–118; and M. Moore, "Causation and the excuses," *California Law Review* 73, 1985: 1091–149.

to undermine it directly. The picture is different when what compete are not only inclinations and judgment, but also judgment from one moral perspective and judgment from another. Unless one distinguishes between motivational conflict and moral conflict, one will mistakenly think that assessing a person's behavior involves gauging just how tempted a given individual is to err. While this is highly relevant to predicting behavior, it is largely irrelevant to moral attributions.

But how can we tell whether some set of circumstances is overbearing unless we see how people actually respond to it? Of course this is relevant information, but the problem is that various factors, some morally relevant and some irrelevant, show up in the resultant base rates. Disabilities as well as inclinations, and various combinations of these, contribute to and hence become conflated in the outcome. So long as this is true, we must be cautious about drawing mitigating inferences from base rate data.

Applied to a case introduced above, we can say that the failure of a woman to leave a violent domestic environment is not "excused" because is it is thought that the temptations of staying are powerful. It is excused because it is thought to reflect a situation in which a person has no viable options and because staying reflects moral sentiments that are admirable in most contexts. To see that it is not the strength of motivation that counts as mitigating, compare the cases of the woman staying and the man abusing. His motivation to abuse may be as powerful as her motivation to stay. Citing that fact wins the husband no points.

We can try a different approach to the mitigating aspects of base rates that involves making some accommodation to human nature, as revealed in human practices. There is, after all, some descriptive content to our notion of the reasonable person, the person of reasonable firmness. We find from experience what errors people slide easily into, and we think we should be understanding of these. This perspective is at times connected to the issue of whether we can see ourselves performing a certain act. To the extent that we can, we tend to be more sympathetic, more forgiving.

We can be sympathetic and forgiving for two entirely different reasons. One reason is that we appreciate how difficult a situation is to manage, what the pressures are that must be overcome in performing adequately that in effect give one a more complex picture of the moral landscape than one might have been disposed to assume. In this context, being sympathetic does lead to being morally generous to those who fail.

Another reason people have for being morally generous is they can see themselves falling prey to a certain line of behavior, and that this act of identification in itself makes them prone to leniency. After all, many would want to be treated mercifully if they failed in this way. In Shakespeare's *Measure for Measure*, Isabella, pleading for her condemned brother's life, appeals in this way to Angelo, the man who sentenced her brother to death for fornication:

[G]o to your bosom,
Knock there, and ask your heart what it does know
That's like my brother's fault; if it confess
A natural guiltiness such as is his,
Let it not sound a thought upon your tongue
Against my brother's life.

This second basis cannot be thought mitigating in any critical sense. It offers no excuse; it is just an acknowledgment of personal behavioral tendencies, even ones that are widespread. But unless these tendencies really point to factors that make moral compliance itself morally problematic or undermine rational capacities, no basis for mitigation is being offered.

We can directly address the issue of the kind of excuse being proposed here. Excuses normally work by indicating something about the act or agent that makes the bad act less blameworthy than acts of that general sort are. Excuses, like defenses, are central to our conception of justice in that they help the law to maintain one of its primary functions – protecting the innocent from harm or injury. For instance, if I steal a car because I was threatened with being put into a pit full of rats or snakes and I am terrified by such creatures, my theft might be excused. One could not infer from my behavior that I had any disregard of the law or its values. A closer look at the total context of my theft points out something about the quality of my will at the time of my act that we regard as relevant. (Had I been willing to murder a person to avoid the company of these feared creatures, we would not have permitted the defense to count for much; the objective character of our evaluations is also significant.) Other excuses, like provocation, operate by setting a threshold of what we can fairly expect of a person. Does conformity with the norm in and of itself tend to show either that the behavior in question is morally reasonable, on the one hand, or that it is beyond the realm of legitimate expectation for normal mortals, on the other? Since the behavior we are concerned with is not morally reasonable, we have to explore the path of legitimate expectations.

In thinking about legitimate expectations, we must first of all differentiate motivation from ability. To know that almost everyone breaks a given law is not to be tempted to excuse violators if the reason for noncompliance is widespread confidence in not being apprehended. This would suggest that the difficulty is one of motivation, not of diminished abilities. Compliance may be unattractive and only in that regard difficult.

Let us use an example to illustrate that last point. Suppose that most fathers who get divorced fail within a year of the divorce to keep up their child support payments. Attribution theorists would attribute such failure to environmental factors, rather than to personality factors about the given men. It is easy enough to see what is tempting about discontinuing child support. It is also easy to point to socialization factors that explain the efficacy of such temptation. Little of what makes this failure tempting, understandable, and predictable would have any moral weight in excusing nonsupport.

Thus far our critical examination of rationales relating base rates and excuses has not left us with anything very encouraging; but there are still some routes we can explore, and we turn to them now.

B. The auspicious paths

One might challenge my claims about the differential moral relevance of base rates by arguing that it is insufficiently sensititve to issues of cultural and moral relativity. Isn't it, after all, worse to support slavery now than it would have been to do so two hundred years ago? The reason for this cannot be that we have different information now; rather, the reason must lie with the fact that there was a social consensus about the legitimacy of slavery, and in light of this consensus, there was something reasonable about finding the institution legitimate – namely, that the respected social institutions of the period promoted its legitimacy. Admittedly this is an appeal to authority, but such an appeal looms larger in social knowledge than we in general and philosophers in particular are wont to admit.[18]

In the same vein, one must suggest that lack of a fair opportunity to acquaint themselves with right moral norms is morally excusing. To an extent, we offer such an excuse to foreigners who violate our rules as a result of being truly unacquainted with our moral perspective.[19] The *Model Penal Code*, section 2.13, defines the defense of entrapment

---

[18] See John Hardwig, "Epistemic dependence," *Journal of Philosophy* 82, 1985: 335–50.
[19] I am grateful to Michael Moore for this point.

as available to a defendant who violates the law when a public law
enforcement official, or someone cooperating with such an official,
"make[s] knowingly false representations designed to induce the belief that such conduct is not prohibited." There are numerous historical situations where those in authority made deliberate efforts at
keeping moral, social, and political positions from being recognized as
controversial. Would it be fair or reasonable to expect the correct
resolution of an issue when access to information and the terms of the
debate are radically limited?

What settles the question of how much responsibility and initiative
individuals should take to examine basic social presuppositions? Answering this question will require judging the extent to which changes
in social understanding are the result of acquiring new facts or perspectives that some groups had no access to. The standard position is
that knowing that most people *will not* press certain moral questions
on themselves in a given context provides no independent basis for
exonerating any given instance of uncritical attitudes. There would be
an excuse only if there were not a fair opportunity to see problems as
problems. But might not one retort that there is always so much to
examine that one *cannot* effectively scrutinize all that seems fishy, and
because one cannot do this, one cannot be fairly faulted for not succeeding? Furthermore, agents respond to the environment as they
understand it. A lot of factors that are not exactly voluntary color our
appreciation of the relevance of information.[20]

Conceding this hermeneutical factor of cultural relativism, however, does not yet clearly point to the way in which we can deal with the
Milgram experiment failures. The explicit culture of the experimental subjects treated compliance here as heinous and unattractive when
viewed from the outside. People asked about the experiment almost
universally claimed that they personally would not have complied and
that only a tiny fraction of the actual experimental subjects would
comply. Nevertheless, actual compliance was so high that one feels
forced to infer culturally implicit aspects of the situation that put it on
a par with explicit social norms advocating compliance. The point is
that we are inclined to seek some mechanism that corrupts our basic
moral equipment to account for the discovered outcome, rather than
acknowledge that nearly every normal soul harbors such murderous
potential.

As way of sympathetically probing the relevance of high base rates
to excuses, we can explore some nonmoral spheres of judgment. I

---

[20] I am grateful to Alison Wylie for this suggestion.

touch on a variety of situations in which we withhold criticism precisely because we think that environmental factors are less than ideal for encouraging model behavior, even though it can be maintained that people still had a choice.

1. In order that people are offered real options in the political contexts, we think it crucial that there be vigorous public debate. We do not just presume that people should figure things out for themselves, using libraries and approaching experts as they see fit. We appreciate the significance of something being seen as a debatable public issue in which reasoned dissent is an option.
2. Advocates for consumer interests want product labels to display considerable information, even information that extremely conscientious consumers could be expected to know.
3. We concern ourselves with the bad examples that role models set. We know that some people will take this bad behavior as establishing the standard for everyone. Because of the susceptibility of people to these messages, we think that individuals who are role models have some special responsibility not to be a corrupting influence. The very category of role model suggests this influence on ordinary judgment and behavior.
4. Finally, if we think about the professional options for women in the past we concede that for many women, even bright and independent women, the pursuit of a career did not seem for them a real option because of the social attitudes they internalized. These attitudes constituted a barrier as effective as outright discrimination. We do not fault our female ancestors for being less professionally ambitious than are the women of our generation.

The point of these observations is that in numerous realms, we do not take high levels of independent, active, and critical thinking for granted or assume that this level establishes the norm by which we should judge people. In everyday life we appreciate the significance of alternatives seeming "available." We do this despite realizing that if the individuals involved had been more resolute, they would not have fallen below the threshold of what we expect. Why should there be this difference between moral attributions and these other kinds of attribution?

In asking this question, we are asking what concessions we should make to human weaknesses, limitations, and motivational structures.

We have seen that attribution theorists would make more generous concessions than most legal philosophers. Here the disagreement is a moral one. In this context, it is incumbent on moral philosophers as it is on attribution theorists to justify drawing the line where they do. Instead of facing this challenge directly, philosophers and lawyers have been content with showing the confusions involved in treating causal analyses as themselves mitigating. To date, there has been little interest on the part of compatibilists in relating the metaphysics of responsibility to common judgments taken from political and social life.[21] What can be said for the attribution theorists' position is that it treats moral judgments on a par with judgments in other domains and has something like an objective criterion – statistical norms – for assessing what is fair and reasonable to expect of people.

There is another point that can be credited to the attributionist position. This is something that underlies our tendencies to have sympathy and understanding for this perspective. It is the view that when people err, if the error comes from facets of personality that the person is not blameworthy for having, it is not quite right to blame the person for this error. If the person had had a fair opportunity to develop himself or herself, an opportunity that presupposes a nurturing background, an enlightened education, and adequate encouragement for rational and moral habits, only then is it entirely fair to blame people. This of course is too high a standard to impose as a practical condition for accountability. But it does represent an ideal that should press upon us. By bringing out the features of character that though authentic in the individual are nevertheless corruptions caused by background conditions, we are reminded of our moral responsibilities. From this perspective, it is not enough to say that certain conditions are compatible with responsibility and choice, since not everyone who experiences them ends up bad. There is a responsibility to generate a society in which the powerful, humanly distorting conditions are not present.[22] People ought to be given the opportunities that promote responsible attitudes before we can comfortably and confidently attribute their misdeeds to them as moral agents.

An analogy for appreciating this perspective is provided by the standard treatment of police entrapment. We treat police entrapment as a legal defense because we think the government should not be in

[21] I know of only one paper on this connection and that is an unpublished manuscript by Tim Scanlon. See also Susan Wolf, "Asymmetric freedom," *Journal of Philosophy* 68, 1980: 161–85, and "Sanity and the metaphysics of responsibility," in this volume.
[22] John Wideman's book *Brothers and keepers* is a literary representation of this perspective.

the business of encouraging crime, of making crime attractive to a being who would otherwise not have violated the law, or of misleading someone about the illegitimacy of wrongful behavior. Strictly speaking, it is important to recognize here that it is because the encouragement came from an authority that the defense can be raised. If someone other than a state agent, or someone acting at the agent's behest, had pestered a person to engage in criminal activity and the person eventually relented, that person would have no entrapment defense.[23] Many social factors besides police entrapment dispose people to regrettable behavior. Still, the authority of the source of the encouragement weighs in *our* evaluation of the agent.

Following this analogy, one could suggest that we recognize an informal authority – something that functions like authority in public consciousness – in many of the social factors that dispose people to wrongful behavior. Wrongs attributable to such quasi-authoritative environmental influences, it could be argued, should be seen as morally troubling – interfering with attributions. The more we understand how humans develop moral attitudes, the more we should be willing to recognize diverse factors as playing the same role as authoritative sources of envaluation.

Someone may object to this treatment of the reasons police entrapment constitutes a defense. The concern may focus on the observation that the wrongdoer is no less wrong in the case when the encouragement comes from an authority than when it comes from another source. After all, the wrongdoer did not know that the source of encouragement was an officer of the law. In this view, the reason that entrapment counts as a defense is to discipline law enforcement agencies – something extraneous to moral evaluation of offending, entrapped citizens.

Even if this criticism is thought to be sound, it would not show that moral attributions are not vulnerable to defenses related to authoritative encouragement. Although a person is no worse when he or she succumbs to inducements of authorities disguised as ordinary citizens, we think that when an agent, including the state, has fallen below a certain level of rectitude, that agent has lost any standing to criticize. Analogously, if quasi-authoritative social forces have significantly contributed to wrongdoing by themselves falling below a moral threshold, then these authoritative forces lack the standing to blame others for misdeeds attributable to this failing. Certain threshold social conditions must obtain for the moral apparatus to become en-

---

[23] See Gerald Dworkin, "The serpent beguiled me and I did eat: Entrapment and the creation of crime," *Law and Philosophy* 4, 1985: 17–40.

gaged. This involves matters of degree; appreciating the extent to which a society encourages corrupt attitudes is an important factor in moral assessment. What is at issue here is not just a matter of efficiency, but also one of fairness.

There are significant problems with the approach being offered here. For one, we might think that one aspect of moral evaluation of a person rests on what he or she looks up to as an authority. There is no position so obnoxious that one cannot find someone with considerable credibility who has espoused it. Although I am sympathetic with this concern, I am also convinced that most determinations of moral legitimacy cannot be arrived at by a process of rational, critical evaluation. The basis of this conviction is developed here.

These perspectives underlie our attraction to excuse-relevant causal theories like attribution theory. If the cause is understood to come from an authority, formally or informally recognized, something corrupting in the environment can be said to relieve some of the moral pressure otherwise attributable to the individual. Seen in this light, causal theories do more than tell us what we should do *if* we desire to bring about certain results; they counsel us to strive for a certain kind of environment as well.

IV. Concluding perspective

An issue similar to the one discussed throughout this chapter has bubbled in a different philosophical caldron. In the area of cognitive judgments and logical inferences, discoveries about the discrepancies between widespread dispositions and mathematical notions of what a correct inference would suggest has led to several responses. The most radical response, one defended by L. Jonathan Cohen, has been to argue that the common dispositions are necessarily correct and that it is the logic that must be reevaluated.[24] A second approach has been to write off most people as logical incompetents. A third, a more ambitious and constructive approach, one pioneered by Kahneman and Tversky,[25] has been to seek out heuristics or patterns of judgment that streamline judgmental processes and work out well for the

[24] In addition to this claim, Cohen argues that a non-Pascalian probability tracks ordinary judgments better than mathematical probability does and is furthermore found to be the (unacknowledged) standard in both scientific confirmation and judicial settings. Cohen develops these points in his books, *The probable and the provable* (Oxford: Oxford University Press, 1977) and *The implications of induction* (London: Methuen, 1970), and in numerous articles.

[25] See the papers collected in *Judgment under uncertainty: Heuristics and biases*, ed. Kahneman, Slovic, and Tversky, and the review of the literature in Nisbett and Ross, *Human inference*.

majority of cases, but may mislead in unusual cases. This third approach presupposes that there is an independent standard for judging right and wrong. It stands as an ultimate arbiter, but is cumbersome or impossible for everyday use with ordinary tasks. Recent studies of the limits of computability suggest that many rational tasks would be beyond our limits if we were restricted to mechanical procedures.[26]

In the case of moral assessments including attributions, one might surmise that something analogous to the third strategy mentioned is operable here too. This approach involves assuming that there is some critical standpoint by which we can make moral assessments of behavior and agents in addition to various moral heuristics that are helpful for the common run of situations. For instance, it might be suggested that a largely reliable guide for correct behavior is doing what people in authority tell one to do or following the example set by most others. These heuristics can lead to troublesome results, but for the most part they represent a reliable guide to action and judgment. We can see how following them is part of moral life, just as following inferential heuristics is part of cognitive life. Both are indispensable for ordinary functioning. Indeed, if basic structures for understanding and acting were not shared in this way, it is improbable that we could have social structures at all. We have to begin somewhere uncritically in order to arrive at a perspective from which we can eventually make assessments. To the extent that people are unfamiliar with the breakdown cases, they may not feel entitled to make an independent judgment – indeed, they may not be aware of the need to refer to the more critical perspective they are capable of exercising. We have to recognize that however rational we attempt to be, recognizing a perspective as critical of, and superior to, our own is often a function of how we frame the point. Special conditions must be met before we are positioned to see something as a serious challenge.

Though we have to be prepared to recognize that morality is more than a matter of heuristics, at times we may be practically limited to heuristics because the complexity of a particular determination would require more resources than we are in a position to expend. (It would be a disaster to act on the basis of a philosophical position that seemed well reasoned if that position counseled radical disregard for ordinary standards.) The right answer may be inaccessible to us except by lucky coincidence between our heuristics and truth. As in other domains of

---

[26] See Christopher Cherniak, "Computational complexity and the universal acceptance of logic," *Journal of Philosophy* 91, 1984: 739–58.

life, in morals we require the support of heuristics we know are not completely trustworthy. In morals, as in science and other complex activities, we may need to rely on authorities, consensus, role models, and other unreliable strategies to a far greater extent than moral philosophers have been in the habit of recognizing.

I have argued that attribution theory itself is only problematically relevant to moral attribution and to an understanding of excusing conditions. The suggestions and explicit claims made by orthodox attribution theorists for what occasions bona fide moral reevaluation of presumptively guilty behavior is itself morally naïve. However, as I tried suggesting, there may be something to their perspective after all.

13

Guilt, punishment, and desert

RICHARD BURGH

That the culpable offender deserves to suffer the pain of legal punishment is an intuition shared by most; what is not shared is its justificatory basis. Utilitarians, appealing to the fact that in every other instance the deliberate infliction of suffering is wrong, except where necessary to promote a greater good, object to retributive justifications on the grounds that they are nothing more than veiled rationalizations for revenge.[1] They argue that the justification of punishment must involve an appeal to its beneficial consequences. Though attractive, philosophers have come to see utilitarianism as inadequate. Not only does it fail to capture the intuition that the guilty *deserve* punishment, but without making reference to right relevant properties of persons, it appears to violate the Kantian injunction that persons are *never* to be treated as merely a means to the well-being of others. Most writers on punishment have noticed this. However, unwilling to abandon the utilitarian intuition that the moral justification of punishment must include the promotion of a socially worthwhile

I am grateful to Professors Robert Good, Carol Nicholson, and Ferdinand Schoeman for their helpful comments on previous drafts of this paper.

[1] I here restrict "retributivism" to those justifications in which the consequences of punishment are deemed irrelevant to the justification of punishment. In this view the justification of punishment must solely look back to the crime. That someone has committed a crime is the only acceptable reason for punishing that person. The only acceptable reason for punishing that person in a given manner and degree is that the punishment is equal to the crime, and whoever commits a crime must be punished in accordance with his or her desert. See Edmund Pincoff, *The Rationale of Legal Punishment* (New York, 1966), pp. 3–4.

Benn and Peters, *The Principle of Political Thought* (New York, 1959), p. 204, argue that to appeal to retributivism is to give up the very attempt at justification. In *Furman* v. *Georgia*, 408 US 238 (1972), retributive punishment was characterized in terms of "naked vengeance." Ewing, *The Morality of Punishment* (Montclair, 1970), p. 14, though not a utilitarian, argued that retributive punishment is incapable of being brought into rational connection with other ethical beliefs. Honderich, *Punishment: The Supposed Justifications* (London, 1976), p. 143, also not a utilitarian, thought it unthinkable that anyone would defend the traditional retributive theory in which we are obliged rather than permitted to punish offenders because they deserve it. See also Sidgwick, *Methods of Ethics* (New York, 1966), p. 81.

end, they have endeavored to justify punishment by qualifying the utilitarian account with considerations of desert. Initially this was argued for on the conceptual ground that the restriction of punishment to the deserving is part of the very definition of punishment.[2] However, it was soon seen that an appeal to definition leaves unanswered the moral question which initially generated the problem – why, on utilitarian grounds, is it *morally* permissible to punish the culpable offender? Following H. L. A. Hart, philosophers responded to this with the suggestion that any morally tolerable account of punishment must see it as a compromise between conflicting moral principles. The principle of utility justifies the general practice of punishment, while the principle of desert justifies the allocation of punishment.[3] However, the success of this combined theory ultimately depends on solving two problems. First, the qualified principle of desert must be justified by an appeal to principles of justice. That is to say, since we ordinarily think it wrong to cause people to suffer for the benefit of others, it is incumbent upon us to show why we are permitted to do this to the culpable offender in the form of punishment.

Second, in order to render punishment compatible with justice, it is not enough that we restrict punishment to the deserving; we must in addition restrict the degree of punishment to the degree that is deserved. We do not think of the offender as deserving unlimited punishment; rather, we think of him or her as deserving a degree of punishment proportional to the gravity of the offense committed. The problem is that when it comes to determining the degree to which the offender should be punished, the principle of utility may conflict with the principle of desert. That is to say, in order to achieve the particular utilitarian aim, the offender may have to be punished

---

[2] See, for example, A. M. Quinton, "On Punishment," *The Philosophy of Punishment,* ed. Acton (Great Britain, 1969), who argues that retributivism is essentially a conceptual thesis concerning the definition of punishment, while utilitarianism is a moral thesis concerning the justification of punishment. Mabbot, "Punishment," *The Philosophy of Punishment,* at times seems to make this same point. J. Rawls, "Two Concepts of Rules," *Theories of Ethics,* ed. P. Foot (Oxford, 1967), argues for a similar thesis in terms of the distinction between justifying a practice and justifying an act that falls under that practice.

Fingarette, "Punishment and Suffering," *Proceedings and Addresses of the American Philosophical Association,* 50, 6 (August 1977): 499–525, argues that retributivism is a conceptual thesis on the grounds that it is the essence of the law, as an instrument of power, that those who violate the law be made to suffer. However, rather than justifying punishment, Fingarette thinks that his view allows us to see clearly why retributive punishment is an evil.

[3] H. L. A. Hart, "Prolegomena to the Principles of Punishment," in *Punishment and Responsibility* (New York, 1968); the rudiments of Hart's thesis can be found in Ewing, op. cit., Raphael, *Moral Judgement* (London, 1955), and Ross, *The Right and the Good* (New York, 1965).

to a degree that exceeds what he or she deserves. In such a situation, we are left with the following dilemma. If we restrict punishment to what is deserved, then, on utilitarian grounds, we act wrongly, since the punishment is wasted. If, on the other hand, we impose a degree of punishment that will achieve our utilitarian aim, then we act wrongly, since the offender is treated unjustly.[4]

In an attempt to derive penal desert from a nonretributive conception of justice, philosophers have typically appealed to either principles of distributive justice or those of corrective justice. Those following the lead of Hart saw penal desert as an instance of distributive justice, where the concern is with the distribution of benefits and burdens within a context of competing claims for both the acquisition of the benefits and the avoidance of the burdens. Justice consists in realizing a distribution that renders a fair share to each. In this view the problem of punishment can be stated as follows: Given that all persons have the right not to be burdened for the benefit of others, how do we distribute the burdens of punishment on terms which are fair? The answer: By restricting punishment to the voluntary offender, we distribute it fairly since everyone is given a fair opportunity to avoid it.[5]

Those of a more Kantian persuasion, following the lead of Herbert Morris, saw penal desert as an instance of corrective justice, where the concern is with rectifying distortions in the distribution of benefits and burdens that arise out of unjust enrichments or unjust losses. The principle requires that such enrichments be annulled and such losses be compensated. In this view the justification of punishment is tied to correcting distortions in the distribution of benefits and burdens caused by crime. The suffering involved in punishment restores the distribution by offsetting the advantage the offender obtained over law-abiding citizens.[6] Though attractive, both strategies are, as I have

---

[4] See Alan Goldman, "The Paradox of Punishment," *Philosophy and Public Affairs*, 9 (1979): 42–58.

[5] H. L. A. Hart, "Changing Conceptions of Responsibility," in *Punishment and Responsibility*, op. cit., pp. 208–9. More recently this justification was adopted by George Fletcher, *Rethinking the Criminal Law* (Boston, 1978), pp. 418–19, 491–5.

[6] Herbert Morris, "Persons and Punishment," *Monist*, 52, 4 (October 1968): 475–501; Jeffrie Murphy, *Retribution, Justice, and Therapy* (Boston, 1979), pp. 77–115 and 223–49. Andrew Von Hirsh relied upon this argument in his book *Doing Justice: The Choice of Punishments* (New York, 1976), pp. 47–8. However, in his recent book, *Past or Future Crimes: Deservedness and Dangerousness in the Sentencing of Criminals* (New Brunswick, NJ, 1985), pp. 57–60, he has come to doubt the force of this argument. Michael Davis, "How to Make Punishment Fit the Crime," *Ethics* 93 (July 1983), argues that the relevant measure of punishment is not the harm to the victim, but the "value of the unfair advantage he [the offender] takes of those who obey the law" (p. 744). Though

argued elsewhere, highly inadequate.[7] They not only fail to justify penal desert, but do not even address the problem of resolving possible conflicts between utility and desert.

Given this quagmire, it is tempting to conclude that perhaps penal desert cannot be reconciled with justice.[8] However, I argue that one can derive the concept of penal desert from a wider ethical principle which steers a course between retributivism and utilitarianism. I derive this concept from the principle of compensation – the person who is responsible for wrongfully harming a party ought to compensate the party for that harm – which in part underlies the law of torts.[9] In order to appeal to this principle, I argue for a version of the traditional legal thesis that crimes, unlike torts, are social harms. Punishment will then be justified on the grounds that it compensates society for this harm. This view, though nonretributive, will capture the backward-looking retributive intuition that the culpable offender should be punished because he or she *deserves* it. It also captures the forward-looking utilitarian intuition that the infliction of suffering for the sake of suffering is the worst type of cruelty, that if punishment is to be justified, it must be in terms of the good results it produces.

I

As a prelude to my discussion, let us briefly consider the principle of compensation – first noting how an appeal to it differs from an appeal to retribution, and second noting how an appeal to it allows us to deal with the issue of imposing on an individual for the benefit of others. Unlike retributive desert in which the target is the offender and its basis is the offense (see note 1), the desert involved in compen-

these theories clearly stress the concept of desert, I view them as nonretributive in that the offender's desert is tied to the forward-looking consequence of reestablishing an equilibrium in the distribution of benefits and burdens.

[7] Richard Burgh, "Do the Guilty Deserve Punishment?" *The Journal of Philosophy*, 79, No. 4 (April 1982): 193–210.

[8] In response to the difficulties of defending penal desert, Von Hirsh, in *Past or Future Crimes* (chaps. 4–5), has concluded that explanations of penal desert in terms of some more inclusive principle of justice are not enlightening. Instead, he thinks that penal desert can rest on the much simpler idea of censure. Though the idea of censure is crucial for understanding punishment, as I argue, it alone cannot justify penal desert (see the second half of section II of the present chapter).

[9] I am not suggesting that all of tort law can be understood in terms of this principle. To see this, one need go no further than the doctrines of strict and absolute liability that are now deeply entrenched in the law of torts. For an excellent discussion of the complexity of tort law, see Jules L. Coleman, "Moral Theories of Torts: Their Scope and Limits," Parts I and II, *Law and Philosophy, 1 and 2* (1982, 1983): 371–90 and 5–36.

sation has two targets as well as two bases. The wrongfully injured party deserves to be made whole again, and the party responsible for the harm deserves to be held liable for making him (or her) whole. Furthermore, the force of this notion of desert can be captured by Hohfeld's notion of a claim right. The party responsible for the wrongful injury deserves to compensate the injured party in the sense that he (or she) has an obligation to do so, and the injured party deserves to be compensated, in the sense that he has a right against the injurer to be compensated. We avoid the problem of retributivism that the imposition of suffering is nothing more than veiled revenge, since in this view the responsible party's desert *includes* the forward-looking aim of satisfying the desert of the injured party. We impose upon the wrongdoer not to make him suffer, but in order to rectify an unjust loss. If this rectification must involve the wrongdoer's suffering, then he deserves to suffer not as an end in itself, but as a means of effecting this rectification. We avoid the problem that plagued utilitarian theory – namely, treating him merely as a means, because he deserves to be held liable for restoring the party harmed. This of course needs further explanation, which we can provide by examining the bases of the desert of each party.

Corrective justice, being concerned with distortions in the distribution of benefits and burdens that arise out of wrongful losses and wrongful enrichments, can best be conceived as the basis for what the wrongfully injured deserves. Questions of compensation arise when a party was made worse off by being wrongfully harmed in the sense of having a right not to be harmed against the party that caused the harm. To compensate the party is to raise the party to the position he or she held prior to the harm. This can mean literally repairing the damage, or in cases where the damage cannot be repaired, it can be understood in terms of giving something to the harmed party such that after receiving it, it leaves the party on the same indifference curve as he or she would have been if there had been no harm. That the party has a right to compensation is captured by corrective justice; it rectifies the distortion in the distribution. Furthermore, since the obligation to compensate must fall on someone, its imposition is itself a requirement of corrective justice. But why should this obligation fall on the party responsible for the harm? Interestingly, here the principle is silent. Since its connection with justice is derived from its role in remedying unjust departures from a prevailing distribution, it would seem that so long as the wrongful gains and losses are annulled, corrective justice would be served. To be sure, if the injurer were to gain from the wrongful injury he or she inflicted, corrective justice would require its annulment as well, and as a matter of efficiency this perhaps could be accomplished by requiring him or her to compensate the victim. The point, however, is that, though corrective justice requires that this matter be decided, it is not a matter decidable by corrective justice.[10]

Given that the obligation to restore the harmed party must be allocated to someone, on whom should it fall? Notice, we only have two alternatives: the one who caused the harm or some third party. (If we grant that corrective justice requires the compensation of the victim, then we can immediately rule out that the victim should absorb the cost.) Our problem is accounting for that aspect of the principle which requires it to fall on the one responsible for the harm. This is a question of distributive justice for which there *appears* to be a straightforward answer. Aristotle told us long ago that justice consists in treating equals equally and unequals unequally. If the one responsible for the harm and innocent third parties were equal regarding the harm, then justice would require distributing the burden equally among them. However, by hypothesis they are not equal: That one of the parties is responsible for the harm marks a relevant difference between them. Distributing the burden on this basis is fair, since we are merely requiring the wrongdoer to rectify a distortion for which he or she was responsible. Since the wrongdoer was responsible for the harm, he or she hardly has a basis to complain for being made to repair the harm.

While this answer may appear plausible, it begs an important question. If our criterion for what constitutes a relevant difference is responsibility for the harm, then of course one of the parties being responsible marks a relevant difference. But why should responsibility for the harm be our criterion of relevance? After all, one could just as easily say that having the ability to absorb the cost of compensation ought to be the criterion of relevance. In this case, having the ability to pay would mark a relevant difference between the parties. What we need, in other words, is a defense of the view that responsibility matters when it comes to assigning the obligation for compensation. Without such a defense, the appeal to responsibility presupposes what must be established.

By way of articulating such a defense, consider what is wrong with using wealth as a criterion of relevance. Let us suppose that A has been wrongfully harmed. Our question is, from whom does A have a

---

[10] For a defense of this, see Coleman, "Moral Theories of Torts: Their Scope and Limits: Part II," *Law and Philosophy*, 2 (1983): 5–36.

right to seek compensation? Who is obligated to pay for the damages? Since this payment involves giving up some portion of one's assets, it follows that A has a right to call on someone to pay only if that person does not have a right to what constitutes the payment. After all, if the person had a right to that portion of his (or her) assets that would compensate A, he could always refuse A on that basis. Thus the basis for liability must involve pointing to some feature of a person that minimally shows that he is not entitled to what A is asking. Imagine two persons, B and C. B owns sufficient assets to compensate A, and C is responsible for harming A. To say that A has a right to seek compensation from one of these persons is to say that one of them has an obligation to give up what is necessary to effect this compensation, which is to say he or she does not have a right to it. Our question thus becomes: Is owning sufficient assets to cover A's compensation a relevant consideration for showing that one does not have a right to those assets? Put this way, the answer must be "No," for to say it is would be tantamount to saying that having a right to assets is a relevant consideration for not having a right to them. After all, to say a person owns the assets is to say he or she has a right to them. Hence, if owning them is a relevant consideration for A's having a right to them, then having a right to assets becomes a relevant consideration for not having a right to them – a conclusion, I take it, which is absurd.[11] Saying this, of course, is compatible with saying that B should compensate A – it may be the charitable thing to do. The point is though charity may require it, it is not required by A's right to compensation.

We are not confronted with these difficulties if the obligation to compensate is assigned to the person responsible for the harm. Furthermore, there is a strong argument for making this assignment. Recall, to say that A has been wrongfully harmed is to say that A had a right not to be harmed in the way that he or she was. To say that A has this right is to say that there is some B such that B has an obligation not to do what will harm A. In the words of H. L. A. Hart, "the idea is that of one individual being given . . . exclusive control . . . over another person's duty so that in the area of conduct covered by that duty the individual who has the right is a small scale sovereign to whom the

---

[11] One may be tempted to see a progressive taxation scheme, in which one's tax rate is determined by one's level of income, as a counterexample to this. However, it need not be viewed this way, for two reasons. First, our obligation to pay taxes can reasonably be construed as payment for goods received from the operation of public institutions, such as roadways, schools, and police.

Second, that one's tax obligation is determined by one's income can be construed as a requirement for desirable social policy – it is easier for the wealthy to absorb the cost – rather than a requirement of anyone's right to the money.

duty is owed."[12] To say this is minimally to say that if *B* wishes to do some *X* which will harm *A*, *B* must request *A* to waive or extinguish the duty and *A* as a condition for this may require a payment from *B*. In this sense the "concept of a right belongs to that branch of morality which is specifically concerned to determine when one person's freedom may be limited by another's."[13] If we grant that this is a branch of morality, that *A* does have this control over *B*, then what are we to say if *B* does *X* to *A* without being relieved of the obligation not to do it? If *A* was in the position to require payment from *B*, as a condition for doing *X*, then if *B* does *X* without paying *A*, would we not have to say that *A* is in the position to require the payment? If *A* were not morally in this position, then it would make little sense to say *A* was in the moral position to require payment in the first place. Thus if we grant that persons do have claim rights, we are committed to granting that they have a right to compensation against those who harm them by invading their right. In this sense, the concept of a claim right entails that the obligation to compensate be allocated to the one who is responsible for the harm.

II

Let us now consider how an appeal to compensation can justify legal punishment. I have already presented the general contour of an answer in terms of viewing punishment as the means by which the offender compensates society for the social harm for which he or she is responsible. Having shown how the principle of compensation incorporates a sense of desert that includes both forward- and backward-looking considerations, I must now show that there is a social harm aspect of crime for which punishment is the appropriate remedy.

But first it will be instructive to consider the customary view for connecting punishment with social harm. Most legal systems distinguish torts from crimes in terms of the nature of the harm calling for redress. In the words of Blackstone, crimes are social harms affecting "the whole community, considered as a community, in its social aggregate capacity . . . they strike at the very being of society, which cannot subsist where actions of this sort are suffered to escape with impunity." In contrast torts, being private harms, are "imma-

[12] Hart, "Bentham on Legal Rights," *Oxford Essays in Jurisprudence*, 2nd series, ed. A. W. B. Simpson (Oxford, 1973), p. 193.
[13] Hart, "Are There Any Natural Rights?" *Human Rights*, ed. A. I. Meldon (Irvine, 1970), p. 66.

terial to the public."[14] Given this characterization, crimes, insofar as they constitute social harms, must be prohibited, and are hence responded to with punishment; while torts, insofar as they are immaterial to the public, may be permitted provided the wrongdoer compensates the victim. Putting it this way is not to suggest that crimes and torts are mutually exclusive, since many crimes are also torts in that they damage some individual. Nor is it to suggest that all crimes are torts, since there are some crimes, such as possession of counterfeit dies, that do not harm individuals, and some torts, such as trespassing upon land that one honestly and reasonably believes to be one's own, that are not crimes. The point is there is a category of conduct that is prohibited by pain of punishment by virtue of the social harm to which it gives rise. This mode of analysis is clearly problematic in that it calls for a criterion which clearly distinguishes harms "that strike at the very heart of society" from harms which are "merely private."[15] However, even assuming such a criterion, a serious problem remains concerning its ability to justify punishment. So long as that aspect of criminal conduct which is prohibited by pain of punishment is conceived to be a social harm, an appeal to social harm will tell us little regarding the moral justification of punishment, for it only shifts the inquiry to the question "Why are we morally justified in punishing those who do what is prohibited?" To speak in terms of the need to eliminate such conduct raises the clash with the Kantian injunction that persons ought not to be treated merely as means.[16]

In what follows I articulate a justification for the tort–crime distinction which will be a version of the thesis that crimes are social harms.

[14] 3 Bl. Comm. 2; 4 Bl. Comm. 5.

[15] Blackstone's failure to articulate such a criterion prompted Austin to reject the public–private distinction on the grounds that in their remote consequences, all supposedly private wrongs affect the entire community and all criminal wrongs affect individuals. Austin, *Lectures on Jurisprudence*, 4th ed. (London, 1873), pp. 416, 517. In the twentieth century Roscoe Pound argued that public and private harms are merely correlatives of one another, labels attaching to different aspects of the same harm. Thus the private harm resulting from the violation of a particular contract can be restated as a public harm involving an attack on the security of transactions. R. Pound, *Jurisprudence, or the Philosophy of Positive Law* (St. Paul, 1959), pp. 23–4, 328–30. See Robert Drane and David J. Neal, "On the Moral Justifications for the Tort/Crime Distinction," *California Law Review*, 68 (1980): 402–3.

[16] A recent attempt to understand the distinction between crimes and torts in terms of the prohibition of social harm is that of Nozick, *Anarchy, State and Utopia* (New York, 1974). Nozick addresses the question "Why not respond to all violations with compensation?" by arguing that there are some violations for which compensation will be inadequate. Private wrongs are those people do not fear when they know they will be compensated fully. In contrast, "public wrongs are those people are fearful of, even though they know they will be compensated fully if and when the wrongs occur" (p. 67). His argument for prohibiting such wrongs by pain of punishment "assumes that merely

However, my characterization of social harm will significantly differ from the customary view in the following way: Rather than focusing on those harms that are made criminal by an appeal to social harm, I focus upon those mental conditions that excuse criminal liability, and attempt to understand why they do not also exclude tort liability.[17] In this sense I will not be concerned with social harm as a criterion for making conduct criminal. Rather, for that range of conduct which is criminal, my concern will be with understanding why the presence of certain mental conditions excuses criminal liability, but not tortious liability. I argue for a sense of social harm that explains this difference. That is to say, I argue for a sense of social harm that results only from the culpable offense. In this sense, the presence of mental conditions, loosely characterized as "mens rea," excuse criminal liability by blocking the generation of this social harm. I then argue that this sense of social harm justifies liability for punishment in the sense that the offender's punishment is the means by which he or she compensates society for this harm.

The fault upon which tort liability rests has been called social fault in that it is based upon the failure to live up to an ideal standard of conduct expected of a good citizen, even if living up to the standard is beyond the knowledge or capacity of the particular defendant. Though the law of torts does concern itself with intent, it does not distinguish between the intended and unintended consequences of an intended act. All that is required is that one did intend the act which had as a consequence, whether intended or not, the invasion of the legitimate interest of another. In this sense liability extends to consequences one did not intend, and could not have reasonably foreseen.[18] The tort of conversion, for example, occurs when a person exercises dominion or control over the movable property of another which is in fact inconsistent with the other's rights. That his or her

to require an attacker to compensate his victim for the effects of the attack would not sufficiently deter attacks so as to leave people unfearful" (p. 69). Nozick thinks his argument is nonutilitarian in that it goes against the assumption that only the effects and consequences of an action are relevant to deciding whether it may be prohibited. His argument focuses on the general fear resulting from its not being prohibited. Though perhaps this is nonutilitarian, his argument for punishing those who do what is prohibited is utilitarian; that is, it deters violations. See Drane, pp. 410–13.

[17] Tort law distinguishes among cases that are governed by fault liability, strict liability, and absolute liability. Cases covered by fault liability require that the defendant was at fault in causing harm to the plaintiff, whereas those covered by strict liability allow the plaintiff to recover even if the defendant was not at fault. In contrast, absolute liability neither requires fault on the part of the defendant nor can it be defeated by a defense of negligence on the part of the plaintiff. In this essay I am concerned only with the conditions for fault liability, since it poses the interesting contrast with criminal liability.

[18] William Prosser, *Law of Torts*, 3rd ed. (St. Paul, 1964), p. 34.

purpose was not to do so is irrelevant.[19] Thus liability may be imposed despite mistake, ignorance, or necessity. It may even be imposed for acts that are the normal and usual thing in the community. In this sense fault, merely marking the distinction between the person who has deviated from the standard and the person who has not, is disconnected from blame and condemnation.[20]

In contrast, criminal liability is based on personal fault in the sense that during a criminal proceeding, where the outward conduct fits the definition of the crime, and responsibility is not strict, the capacity, knowledge, and intentions of the accused is always the first consideration in determining liability. In this sense a person is guilty of theft (as defined by the *Model Penal Code*) if he (or she) takes or exercises unlawful control over the movable property of another with the *purpose* to deprive him (or her) thereof. Liability may be excluded by showing the defendant did not have the capacity to control his behavior due to insanity or infancy. Or even where the person did have this capacity, he may be excused from liability on the grounds that he acted, for example, from necessity, or mistake.

Our question is, why do we value a system that takes mental conditions, loosely characterized by "mens rea," into account for determining criminal liability, but not tort liability? Put differently, why within a criminal proceeding must we, in addition to establishing that the defendant violated the law, also establish culpability, while within a tort proceeding culpability is irrelevant, liability being decided by a finding that the defendant harmed the plaintiff by failing to live up to an ideal standard of conduct? There are many answers to these questions. However, I consider only one, which due to its prominence has been accepted by many.[21] I then suggest an answer that stresses the concept of social harm.

---

[19] This is nicely exemplified by contrasting *Poggi* v. *Scott*, 1914, 167 Cal. 372, 139 P. 815, with *Salt Springs Nat. Bank* v. *Wheeler*, 1872, 48 N.Y. 492. In *Poggi* the defendant, on moving into a building, found barrels of wine in the plaintiff's cellar. Thinking they were abandoned, he sold them for junk. He was held liable for conversion. In *Salt Springs Nat. Bank*, the plaintiff sent three bills of exchange to the defendant, who allowed them to get mixed up with other papers that he then threw into the wastebasket. Though the bills were destroyed, the defendant was not held liable for conversion. Though in both cases the defendant did not intend to dispose of the property of another, the cases differ in that in the first the defendant did intend to dispose of the wine, though under the mistaken belief that it was abandoned, whereas in the second he did not intend to dispose of the bills (Prosser, p. 83).
[20] See Prosser, pp. 506–7.
[21] For an answer that stresses moral guilt as the basis for 'mens rea,' see Jerome Hall, *Principles of Criminal Law* (Indianapolis, 1960), chaps. III–VI. Bentham's utilitarian defense of 'mens rea' can be found in his *Principles of Morals and Legislation*, chap. XIII.

The answer takes the following form: It is said that the importance of mental elements which exclude criminal liability is required by distinct principles of justice which protect the individual against the claims of society. Criminal proceedings investigate the sanity of the accused; what he or she knew, believed, or foresaw; or questions of whether he or she was coerced by threats or driven by passion, because it would be *unfair* to hold criminally liable those who could not have helped violating the law. This argument is then coordinated with the utilitarian argument that it is preferable to live in such a society because, by maximizing the choices of the individual, it ensures that the individual can protect himself or herself against liability.[22]

To be sure, this captures much of what we value in a system of law that requires mens rea for criminal liability. However, there must be more to it than this, because precisely the same argument can be made for including mental conditions as a condition for tort liability. Is it, after all, any less unfair to shift the cost of an injury, in a tort proceeding, to the injurer when he or she could not have helped doing what he or she did? And would it not perhaps be preferable to live in a society where individuals are provided the maximum opportunity to choose whether they will be held tortiously liable, thus ensuring that they can protect themselves against financial ruin?[23] If the entire difference in the basis of tort and criminal liability revolved around issues of fairness and predictability, then the movement of tort law in the direction of objective standards of fault would have to be seen as irrational.

For a thorough critique of both approaches, see Hart, "Legal Responsibility and Excuses," in *Punishment and Responsibility*, pp. 35–44.

[22] This runs through much of the writing of H. L. A. Hart. See, for example, "Prolegomenon to the Principles of Punishment," pp. 22–4; "Legal Responsibility and Excuses," pp. 37 and 46–50; "Punishment and the Elimination of Responsibility," pp. 180–1; and "Changing Conceptions of Responsibility," pp. 201 and 207. All are found in *Punishment and Responsibility* (see note 3).

Fletcher, *Rethinking the Criminal Law*, p. 492, argues that the attribution of wrongdoing to a particular offender always turns on whether it is *fair* to hold that individual accountable for the wrongful act. Von Hirsh, *Past and Future Crimes*, also appears to accept this line of thought, though by stressing the condemnatory element in punishment, he qualifies it with the claim that a case must be made that the prohibited conduct is reprehensible, if the attribution of liability is to be *fair*; p. 56. Hyman Gross, *A Theory of Criminal Justice* (New York, 1979) pp. 74–87, also viewing the criminal law as an institution of blame and condemnation, argues that it is only *fair* to blame an actor for harm that person caused when the harm is subject to his or her control, and this is captured by the culpability requirements of the criminal law.

[23] Our tort system does provide for protection in that an individual can contract with an insurance company to insure against the cost of tort liability. However, this is of no help to an individual who cannot afford the insurance or who happens to be underinsured.

How then do we account for the value we place on a system that
requires mens rea for criminal liability, but not tort liability? The
answer is to be found by stressing the fact, recently emphasized by
such thinkers as Von Hirsh, Fletcher, and Gross, that the criminal
law, unlike tort law, is an institution of blame and condemnation.[24]
Though a tort and a crime may involve equal personal harm, it is only
appropriate to blame or condemn a person for causing that harm if it
can be shown that he or she intended to cause it. It is for this reason
that the criminal law recognizes excuses such as necessity and mistake,
whereas tort law does not. Why is it that blame is restricted to the
culpable wrongdoer? What is so significant about intentional wrongdoing that we condemn and blame the wrongdoer? That is to say,
what is there about intentional wrongdoing that unintentional wrongdoing lacks and that blame and condemnation capture? Interestingly,
apart from appeals to fairness, Von Hirsh, Fletcher, and Gross are
silent with respect to these questions (see note 22). However, we can
go beyond questions of fairness and point to a social harm resulting
from intentional wrongdoing, but not unintentional wrongdoing,
which blame and condemnation can be conceived as capturing. Both
the law of torts and the law of crimes can be understood as protecting
individuals against harm – the law of crimes protects individuals by
prohibiting harmful conduct, while the law of torts protects individuals by requiring that the harmed individual be compensated by
the person who caused that harm. Following Feinberg, let us understand harm in terms of the defeat, setback, or invasion of an interest.[25] In this sense, whether someone is intentionally or unintentionally harmed, the harm for them is the same in the sense that the
invasion of the interest is the same. However, the intentional harm
generates an additional harm in the sense that it constitutes a *repudiation* of the value of the interest invaded. This connection between
intentional wrongdoing and repudiation of values, as well as the characterization of this repudiation as a social harm, needs explanation.
Let us first consider the connection between intentional wrongdoing
and repudiation of values.

Recent work in action theory on the concept of intentional action
can elucidate this connection. Following the work of Arthur Danto
and Bruce Aune, I think we can say that to intentionally do X is to

[24] Von Hirsh, 1985; Fletcher, 1973; Gross, 1979.
[25] We can understand an interest to mean the following: To say that a person has an
interest in x is to say that "he stands to gain or lose depending on the nature or
condition of x." Feinberg, *Harm to Others* (Oxford, 1984), p. 34.

commit oneself to do X.[26] Further, following the work of Michael Robins, I think the notion of commitment must ultimately be understood normatively in the sense that the agent "binds" himself (or herself) to X. Thus, to say that A intentionally did X is to say that at some prior time A bound himself to do X where the force of the bond is understood in terms of the intention giving one a reason to choose the means to do x, as well as a reason to do X in the first place.[27] It is this notion of binding oneself that captures the sense of repudiation. The person who intentionally acts wrongly, by invading the legitimate interest of another, has repudiated the legitimacy or value of the interest by committing or binding himself to the act of wrongdoing. It is by stressing the aspect of repudiation that we can appreciate the importance of intent as a condition for blame and condemnation and hence criminal liability. What we condemn is the commitment to wrongdoing. Thus, for example, the person who takes the property of another, sincerely and reasonably believing that it was abandoned, invades the interests of the owner, but by not committing himself to the act of wrongdoing does not repudiate the value of those interests. We require that he compensate the owner, since he did indeed do harm, though we do not blame or condemn, since the invasion did not constitute a repudiation of what we conceive to be of value. However, why conceive of this repudiation as a social harm and why conceive of punishment as compensation for this harm?

It is a truism that a society is not a mere collection of individuals. Rather, among other things, it is individuals bound together by a normative order, the existence of which depends upon a commitment to interests of common value.[28] Further, for any given society there will be a relative ranking of the value of these interests, some interests, presumably, being so fundamental that without them it would not be worth living in the society. In the sense that society is, in part, constituted by these shared values, it has an interest in the values not being repudiated. Thus a repudiation of these values, constituting an

[26] Arthur Danto, *Analytical Philosophy of Action* (Cambridge, 1973), p. 193. Bruce Aune, *Reason and Action* (Dordrecht, 1977), p. 136.

[27] Michael Robins, *Promising, Intending, and Moral Autonomy* (Cambridge, 1984), pp. 20–44.

[28] Though an analysis of the nature of a normative order is controversial – are they theoretical constructs analyzable in terms of individuals and their actions and relations, or must the analysis always contain social terms – it is not controversial that a commitment to common values is a defining feature of a normative order. See, for example, Karl Popper, *Conjectures and Refutations* (London, 1963), chap. 16, and Maurice Mandelbaum, "Social Facts," ed. Patrick Gardner, *Theories of History* (Glencoe, 1959).

invasion of an interest of society, can be conceived as harming society
– the degree of harm being determined by the relative ranking of the
valued interest. Thus an individual is harmed when his or her interests are invaded. Society is harmed when this invasion constitutes a
repudiation of the value of the interest.

In what sense does punishment compensate society for this harm?
Notice first that the harms for which punishment will be the appropriate remedy will be those attendant upon the invasion of an interest
conceived valuable enough to be the object of criminal legislation.
Recall that the aim of compensation is to make the harmed party
whole again. Since the harm to society is constituted by the repudiation of the value of an interest, it follows that the appropriate compensation must involve a reaffirmation of that value. A necessary
condition for this reaffirmation is a condemnation of its repudiation.
Now it seems plausible to assume that this condemnation must involve
a condemnation of the offender, and punishment, making the offender suffer, is the way of emphatically expressing this condemnation so that there can be no doubt that it is genuine. Insofar as punishment is the device for unequivocally expressing this condemnation, it
compensates society.[29]

III

Justifying punishment in terms of its expressive function is, of course,
not new.[30] What is new is tying this justification to compensation for
social harm. Stressing this linkage enables us to escape the objection

[29] In arguing that the offender deserves to suffer the pain of punishment, I have
claimed that making the offender suffer is the way of condemning the renunciation of
the value of the invaded interest. However, as Benn pointed out long ago, condemnation or denunciation does not imply the deliberate imposition of suffering. We can
after all, as Feinberg noted, easily imagine public rituals which, while dispensing with
the usual media of hard treatment, so emphatically condemn the offender that there
could be no doubt they were genuine. Hence if my justification is to succeed, it will have
to be shown that there are not other equally *effective* vehicles of condemnation that fall
short of making the offender suffer and do not involve the violation of some other
equally important moral injunction. This is clearly an empirical issue, one that cannot
be settled by philosophical analysis. As such, it goes beyond anything I can hope to
show; but surely this is not a fault with my thesis, since virtually all justifications of
punishment presuppose some important empirical claims. Furthermore, I take it that
my empirical assumption is relatively noncontroversial. Imagine, if you will, such rituals
and ask if they would *in fact* work within *our* society. If one does this I think one will find
that, no matter how elaborate the ritual, unless it *imposes* upon the offender, the condemnation will be seen as mere lip service.
[30] In evidence to the Royal Commission on Capital Punishment, Cmd. 8932. Lord
Denning argued that the ultimate justification of punishment is that it is the emphatic

that denunciatory or expressive justifications of punishment confuse the justification of punishment with the immediate aim of any criminal legislation, which clearly is to denounce certain types of conduct.[31] To see why my account does not involve this confusion, we must re-emphasize the distinction between the harm that justifies criminal prohibition and the social harm that arises out of the intentional violation of the criminal prohibition. In arguing that compensation for social harm is a legitimate reason for punishing a person for violating a prohibition, it does not follow that social harm itself justifies a prohibition. In this sense my account does not confuse the justification of punishment with the justification for prohibiting or denouncing conduct. Though escaping this confusion brings, perhaps, a far greater problem which my account does appear to generate.

If the social harm resulting from crime is constituted by the repudiation of the value of the interest protected by the law, and if punishment is justified on the grounds that it compensates society for this harm, then why emphasize the actual commission of the prohibited act as a condition for punishment? After all, the intentional commission of the act is just one way of repudiating the interest. Put differently, suppose that the verbal repudiation of the value of the interest is equivalent to the repudiation attendant upon the intentional invasion of that interest? By hypothesis, the social harm would be the same. Hence, if punishment is ultimately justified on the grounds that it compensates society for this harm, why would it not follow that these acts should be equally punishable? This objection, dealing with the moral limits of the criminal law, raises issues which, for my purpose, need not be settled here. Nevertheless, the following comment will show why my account need not commit us to prohibiting and hence punishing mere verbal repudiations. In my understanding, social harm involves the invasion of the interest society has in not having its constitutive values repudiated. Thus, consider the value placed on the interest in physical integrity. Clearly the value of this interest, in part, justifies the criminal prohibition of assault. The social harm connected with assault involves repudiating the value of

denunciation by the community of a crime. Morris R. Cohen, *Reason and Law* (Glencoe, 1950), p. 50, took a similar tack and argued that punishment is a communal expression of disapproval. Though such expression is a deterrent, the deterrence is secondary, the expression being primary.

This thesis is not to be confused with the *conceptual* thesis that reprobation, rather than justifying punishment, is part of the very definition of punishment. See, for example, Joel Feinberg, "The Expressive Function of Punishment," *Doing and Deserving* (Princeton, 1970), pp. 95–118; and Carritt, *The Theory of Morals* (London, 1928), p. 111.

[31] Hart, "Prolegomenon to the Principles of Punishment," p. 7.

this interest. Now from the fact that we think the prohibition of the invasion of this interest is justified, it does not follow that the prohibition of its verbal repudiation is justified. We may, after all, think it valuable to allow people the freedom verbally to repudiate the value of an interest so long as the repudiation does not involve the invasion of the interest. In such a situation the punishment of the person who verbally repudiated the interest without invading it would not be justified, since the verbal repudiation was not prohibited. However, the punishment of the person who repudiated the interest by intentionally invading it would be justified, since the invasion of the interest was prohibited. My point is we are only justified in punishing a person who violates a legal prohibition and, despite the social harm they cause, we may have good reasons for not prohibiting verbal repudiations. However, given that an act is prohibited, we justify the punishment of the person who intentionally violates the prohibition by an appeal to the resulting social harm. Social harm, in other words, though justifying the punishment of the offender, need not be sufficient for justifying the prohibition that defines the offense. Thus my account does not commit us to punishing persons who repudiate the value of interests without invading those interests.

IV

Let us now see how my account of punishment resolves the difficulties, mentioned in the first part of this chapter, that have plagued other defenses of punishment.

As I noted, retributive justifications have been objected to on the grounds that they are nothing more than veiled rationalizations for revenge, while utilitarian justifications have been objected to on the grounds that they violate a conception of justice that most will refuse to abandon. Accounts that have responded to these difficulties by qualifying the utilitarian account with considerations of desert have failed because they do not adequately defend penal desert or they do not provide the means for resolving potential conflicts between the utilitarian and desert aspects of the theory.

An account of punishment in terms of compensation for social harm avoids the difficulties of both retributivism and utilitarianism. The offender deserves punishment in the sense that anyone responsible for harm deserves to be held liable for rectifying the harm. In this sense the offender's desert, containing both forward- and backward-looking considerations, captures the spirit of both retributivism and utilitarianism while avoiding the difficulties of each. Insofar as the punishment is necessary for achieving the forward-looking aim of compensation, the offender's punishment is socially worthwhile. Insofar as it is he or she who deserves to compensate society, the punishment does not violate the Kantian injunction against treating persons as merely means.

Furthermore, defending punishment by an appeal to compensatory justice preserves the principle that the degree of punishment deserved must be proportional to the gravity of the offense committed. To see this, we must make explicit an ambiguity in the concept of proportional punishment. The claim that punishment ought to be proportional to the gravity of the crime may reflect a comparative or absolute judgment.[32] As a comparative judgment, we are saying that crimes should be punished relative to one another in the following two senses. First, more serious crimes should be punished more severely than less serious crimes. Doing this involves grading penalties in terms of severity and crimes in terms of seriousness so that the severity of the penalty reflects the seriousness of the crime. Second, equally culpable offenders should be punished equally. Though the absolute judgment entails the comparative judgment, it is saying much more. Not only does it require the equal punishment of equally culpable offenders and the ranking of crimes in terms of severity, but it assumes that for any offense there is a punishment that exactly matches its gravity. Now I think it hardly needs arguing that as an absolute judgment the principle of equality is incoherent, in the sense tht establishing such a match requires that we be able to quantify suffering and culpability in commensurable units – a task that is surely impossible. Hence the principle of proportionality, if it is to be understood, must be understood as reflecting a comparative judgment.

Viewed as a comparative judgment, the principle is preserved for the following reason: In my view one crime is more serious than another insofar as it gives rise to a greater social harm; that is, involves a repudiation of a more valued interest. Since this social harm is compensated by condemning the repudiation, it follows that more serious crimes should receive stronger condemnation, reflecting the fact that a more valued interest has been repudiated. Since punishment is the device for expressing this condemnation, we are left with the conclusion that more serious crimes should be punished more severely than less serious ones.

However, a rigid separation between those who deserve punish-

---

[32] For a more extended discussion of this distinction, see Von Hirsh, *Past or Future Crimes*, pp. 38–46. Von Hirsh discusses the distinction in terms of ordinal and cardinal magnitudes of punishment.

ment and those who do not is at times unsatisfactory, because though a convicted criminal may have had the capacity to control his or her behavior, this capacity may have been impaired by a mental state or situation. This is typically the case when a person acts under extreme anger because provoked, or extreme fear because threatened. Such impairment, diminishing the culpability of the offender, is usually seen as a good reason for administering a less severe punishment. Hence, though two offenders may have committed equally serious crimes in the sense of invading the same interest, they may nevertheless be seen as deserving different punishments on the grounds that they are not equally culpable.

This relationship between diminished capacity, diminished culpability, and severity of deserved punishment is readily understood when penal desert is viewed under the model of compensation for social harm. Social harm is a complex notion, being a function of the value of an interest and the degree to which the interest is repudiated. A person who intentionally violates the law, when his (or her) ability to control his action was impaired by the action of some other, has repudiated the value of the interest embodied by the law, though to a lesser degree than if he had not been impaired. In this sense the social harm for which this person is responsible is reduced, thus diminishing his culpability. Since punishment is compensation for social harm, the severity of the punishment he deserves is also decreased.

Now clearly this defense, though preserving comparative proportionality, tells us virtually nothing about how severely we should punish. Before we can do this, we must fix the absolute severity levels for at least some crimes.[33] In claiming that the principle of proportionality is silent, I am not suggesting that all penalty scales are equally acceptable, since there are, presumably, other moral considerations that would limit the degree of punishment we are permitted to impose on anyone.[34] The point is that though other moral considerations may limit the severity of punishment, they do not determine the severity of punishment. The severity is determined by asking what degree of punishment will express a level of condemnation that will reaffirm the validity of the repudiated value. This is admittedly a vague question, leaving the legislature significant freedom to set the absolute severity level where it pleases. However, in setting this level,

---

[33] See Von Hirsh, *Past or Future Crimes*, p. 39.

[34] Though desert is always a relevant reason for a person being treated in a certain way, it is not always a conclusive reason, since other moral reasons might override giving the person what he or she deserves. Clearly an exploration of these considerations is important. However, I do not have the space to do it here.

the typical utilitarian considerations of deterrence and incapacitation are morally excluded from the deliberation, since they cannot be reconciled with the comparative proportionality requirement of deserved punishment. This, of course, does not mean that controlling the aggregate crime rate through deterrence and incapacitation is lost. If punishment deters, it will still deter when it is not imposed for this reason. If the aggregate crime rate can be controlled by incapacitating the offender, it will still have this effect when the offender is not punished for this reason. The point is that in order to justify punishment as well as set the level at which the culpable offender should be punished, we do not have to rely upon these controversial empirical claims, which commit us to acting unjustly.[35]

Though my argument does not depend upon the deterrent effect of punishment, I would nevertheless like to point out one connection between it and the account I have given. Many researchers argue that the mechanism which explains the deterrent effect of punishment is not the simple one of punishment offsetting the gains of crime, but

---

[35] I say controversial for the following reasons. First, the seemingly simple claim that punishment deters is highly complex. Leaving aside the distinction between general and special deterrence and focusing on general deterrence, the following issues must be addressed. The deterrent effect of punishment is a function of the nature of the audiences to which the threat is addressed, as well as the nature of the threatened behavior. Moreover, different kinds of people are drawn to different types of criminal activity. Hence, before the general deterrent effect of specific penalties can be measured, the potential offenders to whom these threatened penalties apply must be identified. After this identification is made, it might turn out that some crimes cannot be deterred. For an excellent discussion of these issues, see Franklin Zimring and Gordon J. Hawkins, *Deterrence* (Chicago, 1973), pp. 92–209. Furthermore, assuming that the deterrent effect of punishment has been shown, it is still highly controversial whether the deterrent effect can be increased by increasing the severity of punishment. There is a vast literature on this point. See, for example, Rusche and Kirchheimer, *Punishment and Social Structure* (New York, 1939), pp. 193–205; Schwartz, "The Effect in Philadelphia's Increased Penalties for Rape and Attempted Rape," *J. Crim. L.C. and P.S.*, 59 (1968), pp. 509–15; Tittle, "Crime Rates and Legal Sanctions," *Social Problems*, 16 (1969), pp. 409–13; Sellin, "Death and Imprisonment as Deterrents to Murder," in Bedeau, ed., *The Death Penalty in America* (Garden City, NY, 1964); and Loftin and McDowall, "The Deterrent Effect of the Florida Felony Firearm Law," *J. of Crim. Law & Criminology*, 75, 1 (1984), pp. 250–9.

Second, though it may appear obvious that incapacitating the offender will reduce the crime rate, since it removes him or her from the population of active criminals, it is not obvious that it reduces the *aggregate* crime rate. Such a reduction assumes, for instance, that the convicted criminal is the high-rate offender, whereas in fact he or she might be the occasional offender, the high-rate offender having learned how to escape detection. It also assumes that the high-rate offender works alone, so that removing him or her eliminates that number of predicted offenses. But the bulk of offenses may be committed in groups, so that arresting one member of the group has little effect on the activities of the whole. For an illuminating discussion of these problems, see Von Hirsh, *Past or Future Crimes*, pp. 115–27.

rather punishment communicating that the threatened behavior is wrong — a communication that ultimately affects the moral attitudes of the individual. If indeed this is the mechanism by which punishment maintains compliance with the law, then an account of punishment in terms of compensation for social harm preserves the deterrent effect. At the legislative level, the severity of punishment is set by judging the value of the interest the law seeks to protect. At the judicial level, the punishment is imposed on the offender to compensate society for the social harm attendant upon the violation. If punishment deters by the communication and reinforcement of values, then this will be preserved. Since we punish the culpable offender on the grounds that he or she deserves to compensate society, we do not treat him or her unjustly.

In conclusion, I would like to point out two qualifications of my defense of punishment. First, the justification I have offered does not commit us to any particular *form* of punishment. Second, my justification is historically and culturally specific. Let me explain. To say the offender deserves punishment in the sense that he or she deserves to compensate society for the social harm for which he or she is responsible is to presuppose at least two facts about society. First, society must see itself as harmed by crime. It is after all conceivable that a society, vis-à-vis its constitutive values, may be so secure that a repudiation of its values is not conceived as a harm. In such a situation, not seeing itself in need of compensation, it would not seek compensation from the offender. Second, even if it were to see itself in need of a compensation, in the sense of a reaffirmation of its values, it is conceivable that it could effect this reaffirmation without punishing the offender (see note 29). Though historically our society is not at this stage, there may come a time when it is. If this were to come to pass, then punishment would not be justified.

Also there is presently in our society a growing demand for capital punishment, a demand which my account may appear to justify. After all, the sanctity of life, being one of our most cherished values, may seem to call for a punishment that involves taking the life of the murderer — this being the only thing that would compensate society for the repudiation of this value. This, however, is a mere appearance for two reasons. First, on the assumption that murder is the gravest of crimes, all that follows from my account is that, given a penalty scale, the most severe penalty should be reserved for it. My account is silent on how severe the severest penalty should be, or what form the punishment should take. Second, even if one could plausibly argue that this penalty should be death, there may be other moral considerations which would count against it. One might, for instance, argue that no punishment that ends a person's life can be rendered compatible with the injunction that one must show respect for the dignity of persons.[36]

An exploration of whether this is so is clearly beyond the scope of this chapter. What I have attempted to do is articulate a theory of punishment, based upon the concept of social harm, which preserves our intuition that the culpable offender deserves to suffer the pain of punishment and our utilitarian intuition that to be justified, the institution must be socially worthwhile. The theory further explains the tort – crime distinction in terms of the value placed on mens rea in determining criminal liability, but not tort liability, as well as the relationship between diminished capacity and diminished culpability. Insofar as my account explains these portions of our common experience, it has, I think, furthered our thinking concerning the justification of punishment.

[36] Jeffrie Murphy, *Retribution, Justice, and Therapy* (Holland, 1979), p. 243, argues, for example, that it is "by no means clear that one can show respect for the dignity of a person as a person if one is willing to interrupt and end his most uniquely human capacities and projects."

14

Intention, foreseeability, and responsibility

GERALD DWORKIN

> If one says that there is a crucial difference between an intending and a
> permitting will where *moral* evil is concerned – as one must – then that
> must mean that the will relates differently to what it intends and what it
> permits. Otherwise the distinction is meaningless and arbitrary.
> – Richard McCormick, *Ambiguity in Moral Choice*

> If it (the consequent event) is pre-conceived, it manifestly adds to the
> goodness or badness of the action. For when someone considers that
> much that is bad can follow from what he does, and does not give it up on
> that account, this shows that his will is the more inordinate.
> – St. Thomas, *Summa Theologica*

This is *not* an essay on the doctrine of double effect; for, among other
reasons, there seems to be no agreement as to what the doctrine is, or
what its role in evaluating acts is supposed to be.[1] However, embedded in any version of that doctrine is a distinction between what one
intends and what one merely foresees, and that distinction is supposed to have *some* bearing on *some* issue concerning right and wrong,
or good and bad, or praise and blame.

This *is* an essay on the distinction between what we intend and what
we merely foresee and on why one might rationally think that such a
distinction is relevant in *some* fashion to issues of responsibility.

1

The impulse to distinguish between intended and foreseen effects
originates in particular cases, although there may be theoretical considerations that bolster such an impulse. I start, therefore, by presenting some cases in which there seems to be such a distinction at work.

My thanks to Robert Young, Shelly Kagan, and the students in my spring 1986 seminar
for useful comments.
[1] Compare the formulations of the doctrine in Nancy Davis, "The Doctrine of Double
Effect: Problems of Interpretation," *Pacific Philosophical Quarterly* 65 (1984), p. 108,

A. In the course of waging a just war, a naval shipping yard is targeted for a bombing attack (with conventional munitions). The naval yard is located at the edge of a heavily populated city. It is known to the planners that a number of civilians will die as a result of the attack.

A'. In the course of waging a just war, it is decided that it is necessary to break the morale of the citizens of the aggressor nation. As part of such a strategy, it is decided to bomb centers of population.

B. In our system of criminal justice, and any other which is both feasible and just, it is inevitable that a certain number of (legally) innocent persons will be convicted of crimes and sentenced to prison.

B'. In order to increase the deterrent effect of penalties for a particularly hard-to-detect crime, the officials of the criminal justice system decide to frame and convict and sentence a certain number of innocent persons.

C. A doctor faced with an elderly patient dying of ovarian cancer prescribes increasing doses of morphine in order to control her pain. He foresees that at some point, the morphine will cause her death.

C'. A doctor faced with an elderly patient dying of ovarian cancer accedes to her wishes to die and injects her with a lethal dose of morphine.

D. Captain Oates, an Arctic explorer, wanting to give his companions a better chance of survival, walked away from camp into a blizzard and certain death.

D'. Another explorer, in a similar situation, too weak to walk away, shoots himself.

E. A government official proposes a policy of freezing Social Security payments at their current level in order to reduce the budget deficit. He foresees that this will result in a reduced life expectancy for a certain number of persons.

E'. A government official proposes to reduce the budget deficit by reducing the number of persons drawing Social Security payments. He sees that a reduction in payments will result in

with that of J. P. Gury as quoted in Joseph M. Boyle, Jr., "Towards Understanding the Principle of Double Effect," *Ethics* 90 (July 1980), p. 528. The former is a doctrine about what action *might* be permissible, the latter about what actions *are* permissible. The latter, but not the former, requires that the act in question be morally good, or at least neutral.

an increased mortality sufficient to secure the reduction in
mind.[2]

In each of these contrasting pairs of cases, the first case is supposed
to present some consequence (a death, a conviction of an innocent
person) that is foreseen but not intended by the persons involved in
making the decision. The second case is supposed to present the same
consequence as intended by the persons involved.

In this essay I consider two issues:

1. Is there such a distinction, and how should it be understood
   or analyzed?
2. What role can such a distinction play in a reasonable system
   of moral responsibility, and what account can we give of the
   basis of such a role?

Having introduced the distinction in the traditional terms used (i.e.,
intended versus merely foreseen), I now intend to drop that terminology. From long experience I have found that discussions of these
issues are inevitably contaminated by the presence of disputes about
when we use, or are justified in using, the word "intend." To avoid
arguing about our ordinary (or legal) usage of the notion of intended
consequences, I will from now on use the more artificial terminology
of *direct* versus *indirect* intention.

                                2

I first want to argue that there is a distinction between consequences
that one directly intends and those one indirectly intends. This distinction can be drawn in two ways (what I shall call objective and
subjective versions), and it is only the second that can be thought
relevant to issues of responsibility.

The objective version of the distinction, which could equally well be
called the causal version, has to do with the ways in which an agent's
goals are actually brought about, with the causal path from a given
event to the goal of the agent.

Consider case A. The death of civilians in the vicinity of the factory
is in one sense a necessary part of the causal chain. It is nomologically
true that if the factory is destroyed, so are the civilians; and indeed
the temporal order may be such that some civilians are struck before

---

[2] This example is due to Michael Coughlan in an unpublished paper, "The Principle of
Double Effect: Operable But Perverse."

the factory is – so that one traditional analysis, which speaks of the indirectly intended effect as occurring after the directly intended effect or at least simultaneously with it, cannot be correct. However, in another sense it is not a necessary part of the causal chain; that is, the effect is not brought about via the death of the civilians. A true explanation of why, say, the war was won would not have to mention the death of the civilians, but would have to mention the destruction of the munitions factory.

There are undoubtedly many complications here. We may have "wild" causal chains whereby the intended means lead to the desired goal but by unforeseen causal routes – as in Dan Bennett's example of firing a gun at someone. It misses, but the noise startles a herd of wild boar, which tramples the intended victim to death. Alternatively, we may have cases of overdetermination, where the same effect is produced (via different causal paths) or alternative ends (equally desired by the agent) are produced.

Further, this "objective" route leads to results that are not compatible with the analysis of various traditional examples used by defenders of the doctrine of double effect. Thus, in the traditional case of the performance of a craniotomy on a fetus in order to save the life of the mother, the causal path is via the skull's being reduced in size, not via the death of the fetus. So the traditional contrast with the hysterectomy of a cancerous womb cannot be made.[3]

Nevertheless, in spite of complications and difficult cases, the distinction itself can be understood and used in practice. The relevant question to ask is this: "In these circumstances, with this end to be achieved, is the end in question brought about through the causal efficacy of this event?" Does the explanation of how the effect is brought about require mention of the event or not?

Now even if this distinction marks *a* difference in the world, it is not a difference that can, or ought, to play a role in assessments of moral responsibility. It is not that no difference in causal structure can play such a role; there are many familiar cases in which causal structure is significant – intervening causal agents as in Hart's discussion on causality and the law; the lapse in time between the action of an agent and the time at which the effect takes place as in a statute of limitations for causing the death of a person; whether an attempt causes its aim or misfires. In some cases the rationale will be the need for some

---

[3] Actually it also cannot be made using the alternative analysis which I introduce as the "subjective" analysis. It turns out that the use of many examples in the medical context involving the death of somebody are very misleading. It is hardly ever the case that death is required as a means to one's ends. One clear exception is mercy killing.

convention to make things definite; in some cases it will be in terms of what it is fair to hold an agent responsible for.

How can the fact that a given morally significant effect occurs in the world as causally producing a certain end, rather than occurring as a by-product of the production of that end, make a difference to the responsibility of the agent? From a consequentialist standpoint what is significant is the value added or subtracted from the world by *all* elements of the causal sequence. A loss is no more or less a loss because it is the causal means to some good end as opposed to being a causal by-product. Of course there might be other, more indirect, connections a consequentialist might use to assign significance to the distinction. For example, it might be that people who act in such a fashion that bad results are directly intended rather than indirectly intended are more disposed to bring such results about; that is, are more dangerous people.[4] However, any such indirect connections are linked with the character and the dispositions of the agent and thus are more reasonably handled under the "subjective" version of the distinction.

As to nonconsequentialist positions, which have been traditionally seen as more supportive of the distinction, they must either take the difference in causal structure as brute or basic (which is always a possible move, but one that should be delayed as long as possible) or give some rationale for why a nonconsequentialist view should care about such a distinction.

With the other (problematic) distinctions for which moral significance has been claimed, such as doing versus allowing, intended versus accidental, initiating a causal sequence versus diverting one that is already in existence, the rationale has been in terms of the connection of such a distinction with the character of the agent, or with what the agent is viewed as *doing*, or with some other connection with moral agency. Again, these are most plausibly linked with how the agent views what she is doing, or how she reasons about what to do, or what she desires. None of these is a matter of just how the world is, but how the agent views the world and therefore the difference in causality, in and of itself, cannot be by itself the sole rationale.

---

[4] In an unpublished paper, written with Charles Fried, we argued that where the probability of the means in question was less than 1, it was necessarily true that the agent would not abandon the plan when he or she discovered that the probability of the means had increased (since this made the final goal more likely to be achieved), whereas an agent who learned that the probability of a causal by-product had increased was not thereby committed to going ahead with the plan. I now think this line of argument has a number of problems.

The other attempt has been to invoke a notion of rights, as in Foot's explanation of why we may not take something from someone on the grounds that it is harmful to that person, but may be allowed not to give it back if he or she loses it. The analogous view, with respect to our distinction, would be that people have the right not to be harmed as causal means to the production of some good, but not the right not to be harmed as causal side effects. I think there is something to this view, but what is right about it is more correctly understood as the right to not be the object of another person's intended harm, as opposed to being the object of indirect harm. So again I believe whatever is plausible about this view is best understood according to the "subjective" version of the distinction.

The relevant analysis of the distinction, what I have been calling the "subjective" version, is in terms of the agent's practical reasoning about what to do, in particular the means–end reasoning about how to achieve some particular goal. Raising the question about whether some particular event is directly or indirectly intended is always relative to a particular *plan* of the agent. The agent has some end E that is desired. E may be desired for its own sake, or it may be itself a means in a more inclusive plan. The agent then engages in reasoning about how to achieve E.[5] A strategy is constructed that involves M as a means to achieving E. M may be an action that the agent can perform, or it may be the result of some action A that the agent can perform. I will assume that the latter is the general form of the schema. The agent also believes that F will occur as a causal by-product of the plan. So, schematically, the plan P looks like this:

$$P: \quad A \rightarrow M \rightarrow E$$
$$\downarrow$$
$$F$$

All the arrows represent causal relations believed by the agent to hold. They represent how the agent conceives the plan. They may not be the way the world actually works. Since we usually raise questions about responsibility ex post when M and F have actually occurred, and since the causal beliefs in question are often fairly trivial, the arrows will usually represent the actual causal paths in the world. This, however, is not essential to the schema.

As indicative of what the agent believes, they can be tested for by

[5] Often the reasoning is not explicit or conscious on the part of the agent. If that is the case, then my analysis involves a reconstruction of the unconscious reasoning of the agent.

questions involving counterfactuals. In particular, assuming rationality, would the agent perform (try to) A if given the information that M (or F) would not occur? Under P, if the agent believed that M would not take place, he or she would abandon P. But if the agent were told that F would not occur, he or she would continue with P.[6]

In case A, for example, the agent's reasoning is, roughly, as follows. In order to win the war I must destroy the enemy's capacity to fight. One (efficient) way of destroying his capacity to fight is by preventing the enemy's weapons from getting ammunition. One way to accomplish that is by destroying the factories that manufacture the ammunition. One way to accomplish that is by dropping bombs on those factories. The destruction of the factories is a causal means by which the agent hopes to achieve the end. It is the variable she manipulates to arrive at the goal. Its failure to occur (the nondestruction of the factory) means that the agent's plan has failed. If the agent were told in advance that the bombs would not destroy the factory, she would, if rational, cancel the orders.[7]

Obviously it is possible to ask different questions with added infor-

---

[6] In a recent article, "Intending as a Means," *Pacific Philosophical Quarterly* 66, 1985, pp. 216–23, Kwong-Loi Shun has presented an ingenious example involving overdetermination.

> A driver of a run-away tram has to choose between letting the tram continue on its course, thereby killing a railroad guard on the right track, and steering it to the left, thereby killing two railroad workers on the left track. The hearts of the two workers can be transplanted after their death to two patients, thereby saving their lives, but the organs of the guard cannot be so used. Knowing these facts, the driver realizes that three of the five lives at stake will be preserved if he steers to the left, while only two will be preserved if he lets the tram continue on its course. Being motivated solely by a desire to maximize the number of lives preserved, he steers to the left, intending to kill the workers as a means to saving the patients. . . . Suppose the driver had believed that, perhaps by some miracle, the workers' deaths would not come about despite his steering to the left. . . . In this counterfactual situation, he would still have believed that he could enable three of the five lives at stake to be preserved (patients die, guard and workers live) by steering to the left. Since there is no change in his expectation about the number of lives preserved and since he is motivated solely by a desire to maximize this number, he would not have been less likely to steer to the left in the counterfactual situation. Still he intends to kill the two workers as a means . . ." (pp. 218–19).

What this example shows is not that there is anything wrong with the analysis but that causation cannot be captured adequately in cases of overdetermination by a counterfactual analysis. It remains true that the agent chooses to turn the trolley onto the left track *because* he envisages saving the lives of the two patients *by* killing the two men on the tracks.

[7] Of course, one can imagine a scenario in which this would not hold. The agent is told the bombs will not destroy the factory, but will kill Hitler who is having lunch in a nearby tavern.

mation that would not give the same results. If the agent were told that M would not occur but that N would be produced by A which would lead to E, and if N did not differ in relevant respects (its moral and other costs, its side effects, etc.), then the agent would go ahead with P. Or again, if the agent were given new information about F, say that F would lead to something the agent also desired, then he or she might go ahead even if M were not to take place. All this shows is that there are always alternative Ps for the agent to consider. This does nothing to undermine the possibility of drawing the distinction between directly and indirectly intended results relative to a given P.

There are some problems with the subjective version of the distinction. For a particularly stupid (or superstitious) agent, the P may have no relation to the actual causal relationships in the world.[8] If an agent believed that it was the loud noise made by bombs that would destroy the morale of the enemy, and that the death of the civilians was merely an unfortunate consequence, then in the subjective version only the noise is directly intended, not the deaths.

There are also complications such as the agent having more than one E which is sought. Consider the story of David and Uriah. David sent Uriah off to battle in the belief that he would be killed, and David could then wed Bathsheba. Suppose David also believed that if Uriah managed to escape death, he would win a major battle against David's enemies. David adopts a plan to kill Uriah, but he would go ahead with his order to send Uriah into battle even if he were informed that Uriah would not die. The counterfactual fails. One would still want to say that having adopted a plan to kill Uriah, and having sent him into battle, Uriah's death, should it occur, was directly intended. Here one must relativize the test to a given goal, E. It has to be understood as preceded by a clause, such as "With respect to achieving E, if. . . ."

This way of drawing the distinction is not original with me. The essential ideas are already in Bentham's illuminating discussion of intention. He draws the distinction in terms of direct versus oblique intentions.

A consequence, when it is intentional may either be directly so, or only obliquely. It may be said to be directly or lineally intentional, when the prospect of producing it constituted one of the links in the chain of causes by which the person was determined to do the act. It may be said to be obliquely or collaterally intentional, when, although the consequence was in contempla-

---

[8] This is an issue raised by theorists in the criminal law about so-called impossible attempts, such as the person who "attempts" to kill another by sticking pins in a voodoo doll.

tion, and appeared likely to ensue in case of the act's being performed, yet the prospect of producing such consequence did not constitute a link in the aforesaid chain.[9]

Having set out the distinction, I now turn to the main task, which is to see whether something can be said in favor of incorporating such a distinction into a theory of moral responsibility.

3

There is a familiar distinction in moral theory between act evaluation and agent evaluation. The former is a theory about the rightness or wrongness of states of affairs brought about by an agent; the latter focuses on the praise or blameworthiness of the agent. The distinction between direct and indirect intention has traditionally been linked (via the doctrine of double effect) with the evaluation of acts. The distinction was supposed to be related to how to decide what to do, to the evaluation of alternative courses of action. Since I am going to be focusing on the significance of the distinction for the responsibility of the agent, it might be thought that I am shifting to agent evaluation and away from act evaluation. Such a characterization would be misleading.

A little thought should make one suspicious of the sharp distinction between act and agent evaluation. It is clear that for one type of consequentialist moral theory, some such distinction has to be drawn. If what is morally important is what *happens*, then we can have people who try and do bad things producing good results and vice versa. For a certain kind of consequentialist it makes sense to blame the agent while applauding the result. Note, however, that for many consequentialists, including I believe all the classical utilitarians, rightness or wrongness of acts was not determined by the *actual* consequences

---

[9] Bentham, *Principles of Morals and Legislation*, p. 202. Bentham's linking of the distinction to the determination of the agent to act is consistent with his view that "strictly speaking, nothing can be said to be good or bad, but either in itself; which is the case only with pain or pleasure: or on account of its effects. . . . A man's intentions then on any occasion may be styled good or bad with reference either to the consequences of the act, or with reference to his motives." However, since Bentham concedes that the goodness or badness of the consequences depends on circumstances that are independent of the agent and his or her will, all that a person can do is "to know them or not to know them; in other words, to be conscious of them, or not conscious. To the title of Consciousness belongs what is to be said of the goodness or badness of a man's intentions, as resulting from the consequences of the act. . . ." This would seem to put Bentham in the camp of the "expected utility" theorists, but there is contrary textual evidence.

of one's actions, but by the *expected* consequences, – that is, the foreseeable consequences.[10] Thus, J. S. Mill:

... it is intention, that is, the foresight of consequences, which constitutes the moral rightness or wrongness of an act.[11]

But for such a consequentialism that evaluates actions rather than results it will be impossible to evaluate the act without evaluating the agent. What the agent *did* will be a function of how the agent thought of what he or she was doing, what the agent was expecting to happen, and this is some of the information that goes into an evaluation of the agent.

Obviously a nonconsequentialist view that focuses on intentions or motives or willings will have even less room for this way of carving things up.[12] For on such a view one cannot speak of good acts done by blameworthy agents; one can only speak of good results brought about by culpable persons.

Let me begin with the uncontroversial. Nobody wishes to make the strong claim that an agent is never responsible for what is indirectly intended. There may be competing and alternative explanations for why we are responsible for what we know will inevitably, or very likely, come about as a result of what we do. However, it is agreed upon by all that the fact that one did not directly intend to bring about a certain result is not a complete excuse or justification. To know that, say, harm will befall another as a result of what one does, and to go ahead with one's plans is, at the least, to be willing to accept such harm, and for that one must be accountable to others. One of the two main categories of excuse that Aristotle uses, that of ignorance, is not available to the agent.

Further, there is no immediate route to the severing of the action from one's character that is present in all denials or weakening of responsibility. If one can truly say, "I did not know harm would eventuate," and if one was not negligent in some way for not having such knowledge, then the links between one's acts and the harm are *only* causal. One did it, but it is not a reliable sign of one's values and character. But once knowledge or belief of consequences is on the scene, so is the possibility of sin. One had a reason for refraining from

[10] Sidgwick seems to have held both views at different times.
[11] Mill's editorial notes to James Mill, *Analysis of the Phenomena of the Human Mind,* 2nd ed. (London: Longmans Green Reader and Dyer, 1869), pp. 401–2, n. 69.
[12] This is only one type of nonconsequentialist view. Various rights-based theories place much less emphasis on intentions, willings, and so on.

acting, and if one nevertheless went ahead, one must be able to account for one's action.

So it is not a matter of responsibility versus lack of responsibility, but rather a different degree of responsibility when one indirectly intends some harm or evil. The weakest claim that has some bite is that (under certain circumstances) one is not as responsible for what one indirectly intends as for what one directly intends.

I want to consider a number of hypotheses that have been put forward in the literature to account for such a difference in degree of responsibility. Since I find none of them completely satisfying, I will end by trying to develop an alternative view of my own.

Fried

It is difficult to extract a clear account from the sections on "Intention and Respect for Persons," but I would suggest that the key elements are in the following remarks:

Intention gives prominence to the central conception of human efficacy, which is efficacy according to purpose; at the same time, intention contrasts to that kind of efficacy the causality of which merely runs through my person or my movements but is not invested with the personal involvement of purpose.[13]

If we use harming another as the means to our end, then we assert that another person may indeed be our means, while if we merely accept the risk that others will be harmed as we pursue our ends, and do not make that harm a part of our projects, then it is still possible to assert that those others are not reduced to the status of means in our system.[14]

The first statement claims that there is a kind of link between what we directly intend and human agency or efficacy which is not present in indirect intention. The second quote claims there is a link between direct intention and using another as a means that is not present in indirect intention. I find it hard to respond to these claims other than by labeling them as what lawyers call "conclusory"; that is, they assert what is to be shown. With regard to the first claim, it is true enough that what I indirectly intend is no part of my purpose in that it is not my ultimate goal or the means to my goal. But to say that what I indirectly intend *merely* runs through my person is misleading, for it suggests that such consequences may be assimilated to what happens

[13] Charles Fried, *Right and Wrong* (Cambridge, MA: Harvard University Press, 1978), p. 27.
[14] Ibid., p. 29.

as a result of what I do. However, we are not faced here with mere causality, but with foresight. It is not just that I produce some harm, but that I produce it knowing that I will produce it.

As to the second claim, again I do not see the intervening links in the argument. It is true that with indirect intention I do not use the person as a means in the literal sense, since harm to him is not a causal means in my plan. But the question remains why do I not use him as a means, in the Kantian sense, when I go ahead with my plans in the face of the fact that he will be harmed by what I do. This move is similar to the one that a positive versus negative rights theorist makes when she claims that when I push somebody into the river (to inherit her money), I am treating her as a means to my ends, but if I fail to save her I am not. In both cases I am prepared to listen to the case for the difference, but I have not heard it yet.

Nagel

For Nagel, there is a special relation between direct intention and evil that does not hold in the case of indirect intention:

> . . . what is it to aim at something, what differentiates it from merely producing the result knowingly. The difference is that action intentionally aimed at a goal is guided by that goal. Whether the goal is an end in itself or only a means, action aimed at it must follow it and be prepared to adjust its pursuit if deflected by altered circumstances – whereas an act that merely produces an effect does not follow it, is not guided by it, even if the effect is foreseen. What does this mean? It means that to aim at evil, even as a means, is to have one's action guided by evil. . . . But the essence of evil is that it should repel us.[15]

This account seems correct as far as it goes. As the analysis of direct intention itself indicates, the agent in practical reasoning has to tailor his or her plan so that the desired causal relations are maintained. There is no room for relief that the bad result does not occur. The harm is the tool that connects the agent to her ends, and there cannot be a greater responsibility when one acts (although our question is whether there can be less). There is a respect, though, in which the explanation is misleading. In stressing being guided by evil, it is tempting to assimilate this to the case in which the agent is guided by evil qua evil; that is, the case of the sadistic torturer. But in Nagel's case (which is that of someone who, needing to accomplish some great good, twists the arm of an innocent bystander), the agent does not

[15] T. Nagel, *The View from Nowhere* (New York: Oxford University Press, 1986), pp. 181–2.

desire the harm qua evil. If the agent could accomplish the good end by offering a large amount of cash, he or she would do that instead.[16]

While phenomenologically accurate, I would like to explore the question of whether a more fundamental account could be given of the significance of the distinction. Is this idea of being guided by evil fundamental, or can we get a little deeper? Some suggestions of Philippa Foot are helpful in this connection.

Foot

In her original thoughts on this topic, Foot argued that all the legitimate justificatory work people used the doctrine of double effect for could be done more satisfactorily by the distinction between positive and negative duties.[17] She now thinks there are cases that cannot be handled without the distinction between direct and indirect intention. While not giving any explanation of the phenomena (other than their necessity for correct moral judgments), she believes that the principle has an interesting extension to how the will of an agent is disposed even if there is no action in question.

For would it not be objectionable if, in a hospital where patients were dying for lack of a transplant, the death of someone in the hospital with several transplantable organs were automatically treated as good news.[18]

The intuitive idea here is that one's attitude toward harm is different depending on whether it is directly or indirectly intended. It is as if one welcomed the harm in the former case, but accepted it in the latter. The notion of welcoming seems too strong for many cases of direct intention, and the idea of acceptance seems to apply to both cases if accepting is equated with going ahead in the face of the knowledge that one will cause harm.

I believe that all these accounts have something right about them. What is needed is a framework in which they can be integrated into a

---

[16] In addition there is a puzzling asymmetry to such cases. For if the essence of evil is that it should repel us, the essence of good ought to be that it attracts us. And why is it not open for the agent to stress that she is guided by the good in question rather than the evil? But perhaps this goes more directly to the question of whether on balance the agent is justified, rather than the question of differential responsibility for direct versus indirect intention (I owe these points to Shelly Kagan).

[17] "The Problem of Abortion and the Doctrine of Double Effect," *Oxford Review*, no. 5, 1967.

[18] "Morality, Action and Outcome," in *Morality and Objectivity*, ed. S. Blackburn (London: Routledge and Kegan Paul, 1985), p. 26.

fuller story; a story about why people like us might have an interest in having such a distinction in our theory of responsibility. My general framework uses an idea present in earlier work of Nagel and Scanlon – namely, the thought that if we act in such a way as to harm others, and we are nevertheless acting legitimately, there must be a justification that we can address to the person who is harmed.

Although the justification is "to" the victim, when one is considering issues of responsibility the argument proceeds by appealing to the potential victim both as victim and as agent; that is, to his or her interest in being free from responsibility under certain conditions. Being responsible is being accountable to others in terms of formal or informal sanctions. It is also being accountable *in foro interno* to the restrictions of conscientious assessment of one's own actions. In the pursuit of our legitimate aims we would prefer not to be bound by the impact of our actions on others. But our being free of responsibility gives the same freedom to similarly situated others, so we must balance the potential loss to our interests that comes from others being free of responsibility against the potential gain that comes from our being free.[19]

To take a clear case, it is obvious why one would not wish to be held responsible for the unintentional and unforeseeable harmful consequences of one's actions. Since acting under these conditions does not manifest any fault of character, since one is always liable to produce such harm whenever one acts, since there is no way of taking into account such harms, it seems more reasonable to let such losses lie where they fall.

In other cases, and negligence is an example, a similar kind of reasoning might not justify barring responsibility totally, but only allow a weakening of the range or intensity of the sanctions.

Diminishing the degree of responsibility for the harms that we indirectly intend gives us a greater scope for acting. We are at least sometimes permitted to act in spite of the costs to others. I want to suggest that a combination of consequentialist and nonconsequentialist considerations can account for the reasonableness of this extended freedom.

Nonconsequentialist considerations suggest a limitation on the freedom from responsibility of the following sort. Agents whose responsibility is limited over a certain range of actions should not be manifesting via those actions a worse character than those on whom greater

---

[19] Of course these gains and losses will vary from person to person and situation to situation. What is required is some judgment about gains versus losses taken over the class of all agents.

responsibility is imposed. If we are freer with respect to our indirectly intended effects than to our directly intended ones, it must not be the case that acts producing the former manifest worse character than those producing the latter.

This requirement is a weak one. It does not demand that the character manifested be better; merely that it not be worse. So, for example, if there is a moral statute of limitations with respect to deaths as a result of our acts, it need not be true that acts which result in deaths for which we are not responsible represent a better set of character traits than acts which cause deaths for which we are responsible; it is only required that they do not represent a worse set.

Such a requirement is a reflection of the significance of what Strawson refers to as the "reactive attitudes" we have to others and their actions. We are concerned not simply with what happens, or even with what people do, but with how our interests are taken into account by others. Our response to the actions of others is not simply a function of what will produce the best outcomes, but of attitudes (partly socially created and partly instinctive) of resentment or gratitude toward the actors' intentions and beliefs about us. As Mill suggested in another context, it matters not simply what we do, but what kind of people we are.

I want to claim that what moral theologians refer to as the "quality of the will" in the case of indirect intending is no worse than the quality of the will in the case of direct intention. All the relevant indicia point in the right direction, and although they may not add up to what McCormick refers to as a "crucial difference between an intending and a permitting will," they satisfy the requirement. It is not more callous or malevolent or cruel or mean to proceed with one's plans in the face of harm caused by one's acts than when the harm is a causal means to one's ends. There is not less room (but more) to be glad that harm did not in fact eventuate. There is not less ability (but more) to alter one's plans so that the end can be achieved at less cost.[20] It is not more obvious (but less) that one is using people as a means to one's ends when their harm is indirectly rather than directly intended. And it is not more clear (but less) that we are failing to show respect for persons in the one case than in the other.

Remember that we are considering cases in which there is some good end to be achieved by our actions. We are considering persons

[20] It is a little-known fact that more than 700,000 leaflets, warning the population to leave the city, were dropped on Hiroshima two days before the dropping of the atomic bomb. One may regard such a measure as very unlikely to have a practical effect and still recognize the moral possibility of such measures.

of good will. It is also the case that the harms in question will usually be less serious than death. What I am claiming is that in acting for the good, in otherwise permissible ways, the imposition of costs is not to be charged against our virtue in the same fashion when the costs are indirectly intended as when they are directly intended.

However, satisfaction of the requirement on the character of the will is only a necessary condition; for unless there is some gain to our interests by restricting responsibility, we stand to lose by the increased harm that is allowed into the world. The gain cannot simply be greater freedom, for since important harms may be at stake, there has to be something significant about the nature or quality of the freedom. I suggest it is the freedom associated with acting for good ends. Since acting for good ends frequently has foreseeable adverse consequences on someone, somewhere, unless our responsibility were restricted, we would be able to so act on many fewer occasions.

Note, however, that since the restriction on directly intending harm retains a greater weight, it serves to increase our responsibility relative to a conception that allows us to act for the greatest good with harms to be considered only as weighed against costs. Therefore the distinction between direct and indirect intention is a compromise. It neither allows us to act simply to maximize the good, nor forbids us from acting for the good when others will be harmed. It claims a point somewhere in the middle. Under certain circumstances it might allow one to act for the good when the costs are the same as long as they are indirectly intended, but not directly. Being this kind of compromise, it is open to attack from either extreme; either from the standpoint of simple maximization or from a more rigorous counting of the indirectly intended harms to others. Depending on what one takes as the baseline, the account may be conceived either as weakening responsibility (where the baseline is do no harm) or as increasing it (where the baseline is do harm as long as the total outcome is favorable). Since I regard any maximizing thesis as an implausible account of *moral* reasoning, I have framed the issue as a weakening of responsibility.

Perhaps the clearest application of this device is to the clarification of various role responsibilities. A role is in part defined by the limits of responsibility it brings with it. As a teacher, I am entitled to ignore the impact of a bad grade on my student's psyche. As a doctor, I am entitled to ignore the fact that if my patient uses all of an available drug, there will be none left for other patients. As a lawyer, I may disregard the fact that if my probably guilty client goes free, other persons may become the victim of future crimes. As a general, I can act to secure a military objective in spite of the fact that I know some noncombatants will be harmed. In these and other cases, to promote certain important interests we restrict the range of consequences for which the agent is held responsible. The distinction enables us to do this on a wholesale rather than retail basis; that is, role by role.

The two parts of the requirement tie together in a plausible fashion for a nonmaximizing ethical theory of which all deontological views are a special subset. For the first requirement says that the costs of promoting good ends must be considered more weighty or significant when those costs are reflected in the character and the will of the agent. It is consistent with a view that says that one must pay special attention to harms even when promoting good ends. It is only if the pursuit of the good does not signify going counter to virtuous character that we may open the door a bit wider to the pursuit of good ends.[21] It is only when this requirement is satisfied that pursuit of good ends can be brought into play.

I have not tried to give any big answer to any big question – that is, to formulate the principle(s) that incorporate the distinction in our practical reasoning. I have tried to give a little answer to a little question – that is, is there any reason to attribute moral significance to the distinction at all? What remains is (almost) everything. One must provide the details of how the distinction interacts with a number of others that have been proposed (doing–allowing, deflecting–starting, harming–not doing good) and thus achieve the only full understanding possible of the distinction itself.

[21] This account bears a certain resemblance to what Scheffler calls "protected-zone prerogatives," which allow an agent to act in ways that further his or her own projects and that do not maximize the good; but in my account the prerogative is to act for good ends, not for the agent's own ends, and I am not committed to any kind of maximizing thesis. I can explain the "good of" the distinction without a view of the total good and its maximization. Cf. Scheffler, *The Rejection of Consequentialism* (New York: Oxford University Press, 1982).

Index of names